T0318462

CSR, Sustainability, and Leadership

With the acceptance of CSR (corporate social responsibility) and sustainability as important business performance indicators, it is now timely to assess the impact that leadership has on the development of these processes. *CSR, Sustainability, and Leadership* seeks to explore the integration of these three elements through an examination of concerns and trends in contemporary organizations. The authors discuss empirical and theoretical studies, which focus on processes and practices that inform the field.

Organizations wish to not only participate in responsible behaviour but also actively lead within their local environments. However, businesses are failing in their execution of CSR because of ineffective leadership. Business leaders are central to an organization's purpose in the world, and this book will inform a robust discussion about social issues which are pressing to scholars, policymakers, not-for-profit organizations, and students.

Gabriel Eweje is Associate Professor and Director of the Sustainability and CSR Research Group at the School of Management, Massey Business School, Massey University, New Zealand.

Ralph J. Bathurst is Senior Lecturer at the School of Management, Massey Business School, Massey University, New Zealand.

Routledge Studies in Leadership Research

CSR, Sustainability, and Leadership

Edited by Gabriel Eweje
and Ralph J. Bathurst

Routledge
Taylor & Francis Group
New York London

First published 2017
by Routledge

711 Third Avenue, New York, NY 10017
2 Park Square, Milton Park, Abingdon, Oxfordshire OX14 4RN

Routledge is an imprint of the Taylor & Francis Group, an informa business

First issued in paperback 2018

Library of Congress Cataloging-in-Publication Data
A catalog record for this book has been requested.

ISBN: 978-1-138-69585-6 (hbk)
ISBN: 978-0-367-02658-5 (pbk)

Typeset in Sabon
by Apex CoVantage, LLC

Contents

Illustrations

Figures

Tables

Contributors

Saleem Ali is Professor and Chair in Sustainable Resource Development at the Sustainable Minerals Institute, University of Queensland, Australia.

Anona Armstrong is Professor of Governance and Head of the Governance Research Program at College of Law and Justice, Victoria University, Australia.

Ralph J. Bathurst is Senior Lecturer at the School of Management, Massey Business School, Massey University, New Zealand.

Dianne Bolton is Associate Professor of Management at Swinburne Business School, Swinburne University of Technology, Australia.

Amali Ediriweera is Graduate Research Student of the Governance Research Program at College of Law and Justice, Victoria University, Australia.

Gabriel Eweje is Associate Professor and Director of the Sustainability and CSR Research Group at the School of Management, Massey Business School, Massey University, New Zealand.

Hadi Farid is Senior Postdoctoral Fellow at the School of Hospitality Tourism & Culinary Arts, Taylor's University, Malaysia.

Patricia Grant is Senior Lecturer at the Department of Management, Faculty of Business and Law, Auckland University of Technology, New Zealand.

Fatemeh Hakimian is Postdoctoral Research Fellow of Management at the Department of Business Strategy and Policy at Faculty of Business and Accountancy, University of Malaya, Malaysia.

Kumudini Heenetigala is Research Fellow of the Governance Research Program at the College of Law and Justice, Victoria University, Australia.

Mirza Sadaqat Huda is PhD Student at the Centre for Social Responsibility in Mining, University of Queensland, Australia.

Loi Teck Hui is Managing Director and Managing Partner at Loi & Mokhtar Consulting Sdn Bhd/Loi & Mokhtar (Chartered Accountants), Malaysia

Mohd Nazari Ismail is Professor at the Department of Business Strategy and Policy at Faculty of Business and Accountancy, University of Malaya, Malaysia.

Dima Jamali is Professor of Management and Kamal Shair Endowed Chair in Leadership at the Olayan School of Business, American University of Beirut, Lebanon.

Terry Landells is Lecturer at Swinburne Business School, Swinburne University of Technology, Australia.

Chitra Desilva Lokuwaduge is Lecturer of Accounting at Victoria University, Australia

Angela Ma is Assistant Professor at the Division of Business and Management, United International College, Beijing Normal University-Hong Kong Baptist University, China.

Peter McGhee is Senior Lecturer at the Department of Management, Faculty of Business and Law, Auckland University of Technology, New Zealand.

Junichi Mizuo is Professor of Business Administration at Surugadai University, Japan.

Nadine Mohanna is Researcher at the Olayan School of Business, American University of Beirut, Lebanon.

Hagop Panossian is Instructor at the Olayan School of Business, American University of Beirut, Lebanon.

Elen Riot is Associate Professor at the University of Reims Champagne-Ardenne, France.

Ralph Tench is Professor of Communications Education at the Leeds Business School, Leeds Beckett University, United Kingdom.

Martina Topić is Lecturer at the Leeds Business School, Leeds Beckett University, United Kingdom.

Minyu Wu is Assistant Professor at the Division of Business and Management, United International College, Beijing Normal University-Hong Kong Baptist University, China.

Acknowledgements

We would like to thank the chapter authors and reviewers for their magnificent contributions to the production of this book. We appreciate you. Without your hard work and commitment, this project would not have come to completion. It has been fantastic to work with you all.

In addition, we are most grateful to Massey University, New Zealand, in particular, the School of Management, for its support of our work on this project and of our work on CSR, sustainability, and leadership.

We offer our thanks to David Varley, the commissioning editor at Routledge, for believing in us and encouraging us to publish this book. Also, we thank Brianna Ascher, the editorial assistant at Routledge, for her patience. She did an outstanding job coordinating this book with us.

And, finally, a special thank you to our families for their unwavering support in this project. Without their love and support, this book would not have been possible. Gabriel would like to thank Darlene, Monique, and Simone, and Ralph thanks Michelle.

Gabriel Eweje and Ralph J. Bathurst

Foreword

Separately, sustainability and leadership have been the subject of much academic and societal scrutiny for over two decades. Yet weaving them together has not received worthy attention to date. Hence it is highly satisfying and timely to see the critical links between CSR, sustainability, and leadership being explored in a single volume. This connection involves a systems approach and an acknowledgement that all domains are implicated in the design and implementation of sustainable policies. This means that leadership, in its broadest sense, is vitally important to the effective implementation of socially responsible and environmentally sustainable business strategies. Ghandi conveyed this wisdom in the following words: "Be the change you wish to see in the world".

Gabriel Eweje and Ralph Bathurst have carefully crafted this book, which links these fundamental elements into a coherent whole. Further, the contributors have introduced a variety of fresh perspectives to highlight that sustainability needs to be viewed holistically, thereby taking a systemic approach. It is long overdue that these issues are canvassed within a global context and that CSR, sustainability, and leadership act together to ensure thriving societies.

This book is a must read and a valuable companion to scholars, students, and leaders seeking to find productive ways forward to a sustainable future!

Kambiz Maani

Section A

Leading for Sustainability

1 Introduction

Leading for Corporate Social Responsibility and Sustainability

Gabriel Eweje and Ralph J. Bathurst

Introduction

In the quest for sustainable business and socially responsible corporations, it seems increasingly the case that leadership is *both* the solution *and* the problem. Leaders are at the heart of the organization's strategy, designing plans for future growth and expansion, settling policies and procedures to smooth the pathway for stakeholders to embrace the purposes of the enterprise fully, and protecting the rhetorical environment so that staff remain motivated and persuaded about the value of their work. This resonates with the argument that

> the fundamental challenge facing business in the 21st century will be meeting the needs of consumers and shareholders . . . in a way that balances economic, environment, and social requirements . . . Companies must behave differently in the next century, and will require new leadership.
>
> (cited by Defee, Esper, & Mollenkopf, 2009, p. 87)

Yet as has been observed, public proclamations about the sustainability of businesses in the environment within which they operate appear to be mere puffery (Ditlev-Simonsen & Wenstøp, 2011). There is a will to change the face of business away from the pure profit motive towards a more inclusive sustainable future. However, in their desire to ensure the survival and growth of business, leaders become guardians and protectors of practices that continue to deplete resources and in effect become blockers rather than enablers of development and transformation.

In this book, corporate social responsibility (CSR), sustainability, and leadership are inextricably linked. CSR and sustainability have attracted greater global attention, as various stakeholders exert enormous pressure on corporations to change the way they operate and focus on the triple bottom line (see Elkington, 1997)—which measures corporations' corporate social responsibility, economic value, and environmental impact—and move towards a focus that is against profitability being the sole aim of business.

Thus, with the acceptance of CSR and sustainability as important business performance indicators, it is now timely to assess the impact that leadership has on the global development of these processes. The challenges of integrating these three interconnected areas demand that we think of the role leadership has in promoting CSR and sustainability as a key element to sustainable business. How might leaders in the global business context transform their enterprises from playing catch-up and bemoaning missed opportunities, to proactively seeking changes in attitudes, behaviours, and reputation? This introductory chapter sets up the text for explorations of leadership within a profoundly important field for humanity by incorporating the CSR and sustainability paradigms into decision making in the quest for competitive advantage.

Prognosticators warn us that the planet is on the brink of disaster and that business must play its part in reducing pollutants and unsustainable practices. Proponents of growth and increasing prosperity counter by reaffirming Friedman's now famous aphorism that the social responsibility of business is business, and it is the role of social networks and governments to attend to the environment within which business functions.

Is business a separate branch of society, operating on its own account with references only to itself, or does it grow organically from the roots, ensuring the prosperity of all?

In this book, we inquire into the question by exploring the intersections of three essential elements: corporate social responsibility (CSR), sustainability, and leadership. That they come together in this book is both unremarkable and yet innovative. The intersection of these three elements is, we think, where the contestations over the future of business in society are found.

The opening ceremony of the 2016 Olympic Games in Rio de Janeiro, witnessed by an estimated television audience of 900 million, revealed in dramatic form the effects of climate change on the planet. Coastlines inundated by rising tides endanger most of the planet's population and, by inference, the economic centres that support humanity. The underlying message of the Brazilian hosts is that the risks to life as we know it cannot be underestimated. Such large-scale events of international significance are opportunities to reiterate the urgency of the sustainability agenda. But are we listening?

If ever there was a need for wise and decisive leadership, it is now. Yet the leadership practices that we continue to advocate are the same ones that have brought us to this place of unsustainability. Leaders are needed, but of what kind? Certainly, our current preferences for hierarchies of control within organizations have led to stasis with leaders lacking the ability to innovate beyond maintaining existing power dynamics. For instance, Grint (1997) claims that leadership will not be found in individuals who control enterprises but rather within the mobilization of entire groups. For those individuals who may have demonstrated creativity and innovation in more junior positions in their organizations, the same qualities work against them when in senior leadership roles. Grint argues that organizations are simply too conservative to risk taking courageous steps outside the certainties of the profit motive alone.

It may be that events such as the openings of global sporting events are occasions to draw the attention of political and business leaders to the sorry plight of the planet. There seems to be little else of such universal appeal that captures the desire of the public to preserve their way of life for future generations.

The new millennium has put leadership into the microscope, as various companies strive to make CSR and sustainability as vital as profit making. There is no doubt that the 2008 economic crisis which led to huge financial constraints on businesses tested the true meaning of operating responsibly and sustainably in the face of limited resources. Thus we argue that it takes leadership—a certain kind of leadership—to transform a business into a sustainable business. It is about courage, determination, and truth. Similarly, as Ferdig (2007) posits, "Sustainability leaders recognize that the experience of change itself, and the dissonance it creates, fuels new thinking, discoveries, and innovations that can revitalize the health of organizations, communities, and the earth" (p. 25). Corporations wish to not only participate in responsible behaviour but also actively lead within their local environments. However, businesses are failing in their execution of CSR because of ineffective leadership. Therefore, until CSR and sustainability initiatives are directly linked and integrated to overall business strategy, there will continue to be a question mark over the competencies of those tasked with leading in today's business world.

So where is the leadership necessary to make the significant changes needed to bring sustainable business operations and CSR together and to guide citizenry across the planet to a better future? Business leaders are central to an organization's purpose in the world, and this book will inform a robust discussion on issues which are pressing.

Objectives of the Book

It is important to mention quickly that it is not the aim of this book to redefine the notions of CSR, sustainability, and leadership. There are numerous definitions and information available in prints on the three concepts. The challenge we faced as academics, practitioners, policymakers, leaders, and students is how to integrate, theorize, and conceptualize these three important concepts. This book will fill the gap in the existing material in these subject areas. The main themes and objectives are to bring new perspectives into CSR, sustainability, and leadership by integrating these themes into an overarching discussion about the role of corporations in the contemporary business environment. In particular, this book examines the latest thinking, empirical, and conceptual work from various perspectives, and how they are perceived, discussed, and understood. Hence this book is timely; it explores in detail the current trends in CSR, sustainability, and leadership within the context of today's challenges. This book provides the reader with a new perspective on the important role leadership can play in making CSR and sustainability work for their organizations.

Plan of the Book

The chapters in this book are relevant in sustainability research and focus on issues that are critical, topical, and needed at this stage of the discussion. Thus the chapters bring different techniques and analyses together to arrive at new information that identifies trends in CSR, sustainability, and leadership discourse.

The main chapters are divided into two sections (Section A "Leading for Sustainability", and Section B "Global Challenges and Concerns").

Section A: Leading for Sustainability

McGhee and Grant (Chapter 2) argue that much of the management literature prioritizes a market approach to business that seeks to maximize economic gain often at the expense of society and the natural environment. They further assert that leadership within business often portrays this dominant paradigm and thus is unlikely to foster the transformation required to create a future sustainable world. Their chapter briefly outlines leadership theory, noting that its development reflects this paradigm and ultimately contributes to unsustainability. It then offers alternative approaches to leadership that may provide a means to overcome current limitations. Finally, the chapter provides some practical steps on how best to encourage proper sustainability leadership within business.

Jamali, Mohanna, and Panossian (Chapter 3) examine the recent manifestations of responsible leadership by showcasing the responsible practices and strategies of five sustainability champions from the Arab world. The five case studies reveal that responsible leaders can serve as important drivers of change with respect to social and developmental issues by catalyzing various efforts, platforms, and organizations that address specific social challenges facing Arab society. Thus their findings validate that responsible leadership's positive spillovers transcend the boundaries of their organizations and shape the sustainable growth of stakeholders and communities across the globe. They present some implications in relation to the construct of responsible leadership both in theory and in application.

Wu and Ma (Chapter 4) investigate how corporate sustainability integrates social, environmental, and economic aspects as a whole, which they believe is crucial to a firm's long-term success and survival. Drawing on the literature on sustainability, leadership, organizational learning, and change, from an organizational learning perspective, they propose a framework linking the styles of leadership with strategic change towards corporate sustainability. They conclude that leadership plays an important role in leading organizations to sustainability in a dynamic environment and that the journey of a company towards sustainability involves a multi-loop learning process, and in each phase, there is a need for an appropriate leadership style to fit the specific situation.

Bolton and Landells (Chapter 5) explore decision making as an underacknowledged aspect of sustainable and responsible leadership. Specifically, this chapter explores decision making in volatile, uncertain, complex, and ambiguous environments against which CSR and sustainability agendas take shape. They argue that these dynamic agendas confront leadership and decision makers by challenging rational decision-making processes and associated power relations characterized by the transient nature of key decision-choices in multi-stakeholder environments, leveraging emergent knowledge from dynamic stakeholder interactions. In this chapter, Cohen, March, and Olsen's (1972) garbage can model of decision making is extended to better identify decision-making environments characterized by the increasing ambiguity of strategic goals often in contention with cultures committed to order, rationality, control, and predictability; new and diverse forms of transient stakeholder involvement in the decision-making process; and the subjective and political impact of attempts to restore or create order. This framework is then used to explore three different levels of decision making associated with CSR and sustainability agendas.

Tench and Topić (Chapter 6) analyze the corporate website of Waitrose and the policy documents of the John Lewis Partnership. The chapter demonstrates how a successful business model works and to what extent the company's success can be attributed to leadership. They posit that John Lewis's leadership model is centred on shared business responsibility, and participation of all partners in setting organizational goals has contributed towards sustainable growth and policies of environmental protection. They conclude that the John Lewis Partnership presents a successful model of sustainable business that achieved profit growth even during a time of crisis for the retail sector when many competitors were struggling to preserve their market position. Accordingly, the John Lewis model seems to be a clear example of a textbook definition of a sustainable business. Whereas this model does not necessarily work for every company, some policies of the John Lewis partnership can be used for designing other leadership and sustainability policies—i.e. ensuring that management cannot act according to their own beliefs without taking into consideration the interests of employees and the corporation at large.

Hakimian, Farid, Ismail, and Nair (Chapter 7) argue in their chapter that the art of good leadership is, or should be, the foundation of CSR. In this regard, leadership, not only the 'leaders', should be examined to indicate the significant and direct association with CSR. And it should be noted that leadership is not only about and recognized as a title, status, or a job position; it is about influencing, changing, managing, and encouraging people to stay on the right path to reach their goals. In today's business world, globalization has increased the movement of individuals, ideas, goods, and corporate activities across borders, which means there is a need for organizations which apply equal respect to people and the environment all around the world. This chapter reviews the interplay between leadership styles and CSR, as well as the previous research and case studies.

Section B: Global Challenges and Concerns

Hui (Chapter 8) examines the practice of CSR by a large governmental development agency cum municipal services provider in fulfilling its economic self-interests and societal expectations. In particular, the chapter examines the embeddedness of CSR in the organization's strategic planning processes, which also underscores the crucial roles top management played in enabling the CSR adoptions as well as the related triple-bottom-line results generated. The findings suggest that CSR can be an organizational routine of value that is hard to emulate when it is tightly embedded in firms' core value creation routines and reward mechanisms.

Heenetigala, Armstrong, Lokuwaduge, and Ediriweera (Chapter 9) investigate ESG (environmental, social, and governance) reporting in the mining sectors. The purpose of the study was to fill a gap in research into sustainability reporting in Australia. The sample consisted of 30 top companies rated by market capitalization listed on the Australian Securities Exchange (ASX) divided into two groups of 12 (top companies) and the next 18 companies. The research questions were as follows: What kinds of ESG measures are used in the mining industry? How many and what kinds of reports are issued? Are there differences in reporting between the 'top' tier companies and other listed companies? The data were obtained from annual and sustainability reports. Environmental measures that were reported were renewable/non-renewable material, fuel consumption, emissions, and hazardous material. Social indicators included data on employees, gender, occupation health and safety, indigenous employment, local community engagement. The results indicate that the entire 'top' group used the GRI guidelines. In addition, either companies failed to mention information that might send a negative message to stakeholders or they mentioned the information with the purpose of providing an optimistic picture to the stakeholders. A result is that perhaps the materiality of ESG performance data to actual corporate decision makers and its contribution to the value chain was not always evident.

Mizuo (Chapter 10) argues that a BOP company (bottom-of-the-economic-pyramid, where people live on no more than US$3,000 per year) leads to growth strategies aiming at the company's own sustainability. He further posits that the leadership with strategic CSR to BOP business leads to organizational innovation in creating new business opportunities that can lead to diverse innovation, product development, and technological development;

improvements in competitiveness; and empowerment of human resources. He concluded that leaders within the BOP businesses can lead to sustainable growth.

Ali and Huda (Chapter 11) consider how consumer goods have driven economic growth and poverty alleviation in much of the developing world and the need to balance environmental ethics with the moral imperative of human well-being in all its various manifestations. Corporate leadership is considered in the context of multinationals that have grappled directly with issues of consumption of their products, considering both environmental and social aspects of their decisions. The chapter explores issues such as the sharing economy, and it evaluates sustainable practices that align socio-economic activities with natural processes by integrating traditional knowledge with modern science. They further examined the underlying drivers of mass consumption, the political history behind materialism, and the relationship between happiness and consumption. They concluded that providing consumers and political systems with such information can be helpful in decision making and may help to build consensus around development paths that best balance ecological goals with social aspirations for material consumption.

Riot (Chapter 12) offers a portrait of Bernard Arnault, head of the LVMH Empire, at the occasion of the opening of the Louis Vuitton Art Foundation in Paris. In the media, the foundation was officially presented as a gesture towards corporate social responsibility (CSR) and an act of philanthropy in favour of contemporary art and artists, as well as the general public. However, questions may be raised as to what this gesture, coming from a very influential leader, intends to represent. Is it a gift from a business leader or a communication strategy by a global fashion group? Is it a major step in the direction of a more sustainable dimension for a luxury goods empire or just a regular fashionable event where CSR is only a marginal dimension, a green shade in contrast with the red carpet? She crafted this case as emblematic of CSR, art, and leadership in association with the present age. She further examined the meaning of the foundation, presented as a gift to the Parisians and all art lovers ready to visit Paris. She wonders what it is intended to represent and what may be its purpose. More specifically, the issue of what CSR stands for in terms of representation, and how it relates to art, is missing in the debate about corporate commitments to CSR. Offering a vivid picture of CSR may be the occasion to redefine what it is to be a CSR leader in Paris about a year before the Paris Climate Conference. It is also an opportunity to measure the significance of art in bridging business activities, such as luxury and fashion and CSR, and to understand why the media preferred to describe the building, the dresses, and the food at the party rather than deal with the issue.

Eweje and Bathurst (Chapter 13) summarize the collection by linking the key ideas of CSR, sustainability, and leadership explored in the book. Furthermore, they make some theoretical arguments about the field going forward by exploring future research imperatives. They also examine the implications for academics, practitioners, and supranational organizations on the centrality of leadership to address pressing issues which will lead to innovation and creativity.

References

Cohen, M. D., March, J. G., & Olsen, J. P. (1972). A garbage can model of organizational choice. *Administrative Science Quarterly, 17*(1), 1–25.

Defee, C. C., Esper, T., & Mollenkopf, D. (2009). Leveraging closed-loop orientation and leadership for environmental sustainability. *Supply Chain Management: An International Journal, 14/2*, 87–97.

Ditlev-Simonsen, C. D., & Wenstøp, S. (2011). Companies' ethical commitment: An analysis of the rhetoric in CSR reports. *Issues in Social & Environmental Accounting, 5*(1/2), 65–81.

Elkington, J. (1997). *Cannibals with forks: The triple bottom line of twenty-first century business.* Oxford, UK: Oxford University Press.

Ferdig, M. A. (2007). Sustainability leadership: Co-creating a sustainable future. *Journal of Change Management, 7*(1), 25–35.

Grint, K. (1997). Introduction. In K. Grint (Ed.), *Leadership: Classical, contemporary and critical approaches* (pp. 1–17). Oxford, UK: Oxford University Press.

2 Sustainability Leadership

It's Not About Heroes

Peter McGhee and Patricia Grant

Introduction

How is it that our Western liberal values combined with modern scientific knowledge have led us to a place where economic growth has become the panacea for all that ails us (Hamilton, 2003) while we stumble from one financial crisis to the next (Wilbur, 2009), where materialism, consumption, affluenza, and associated ills are rampant (Hamilton & Denniss, 2005; James, 2007; Kasser, 2002); where inequality is at unprecedented levels (Wade, 2013; Wilkinson & Pickett, 2010); and where the environment is at significant risk (Klein, 2014; Pearce, 2007)?

The answer, in part at least, is that reason itself has become irrational (Horkheimer & Adorno, 1947/2002). An over-emphasis on calculative rationality, technocratic thinking, and formal bureaucracy has come to permeate society and organizations. Unfortunately, such approaches leave little room for moral considerations, emotion, and intuition—the very things that make us human (Roberts, 2004). This is most evidenced in the rise of market liberalism, with its emphasis on utility, efficiency, and self-interest (Dierksmeier, 2012; Frank, Gilovich, & Regan, 1993; Rosanas, 2008), often at the expense of substantive goals that conceivably are more important for human flourishing (Moore, 2008).

Certainly, incremental thinking and action over the last 30 years have endeavoured to produce a more flourishing and sustainable world (see e.g. Assadourian & Renner, 2012; Pepper & Wildy, 2008; UNCED, 1992; WCED, 1987). Many CEOs, and the corporations they oversee, want to become "more sustainable" (Accenture, 2010; Gladwin, Kennelly, & Krause, 1995), and interest from society about sustainability continues to grow. In New Zealand, for example, a recent survey by Colmar Brunton (2014) found a growing concern for such issues. Yet despite these positive developments, the world continues towards potential calamity (Foster, 2015; Klein, 2014).

Unfortunately, according to Ehrenfeld and Hoffman (2013), such incremental change is "merely a Band-Aid approach that masks deeper cultural roots of our sustainability challenge" (p. 1). Much of what occurs in the name of sustainability is still based on a view of economics that only minimizes unsustainability rather than advancing sustainable practices. According to Ehrenfeld and Hoffman, we "need a deep shift in values" (p. 4) that results in a "transformational change in the foundational [behavioural, cultural, institutional] structures of our society" (p. 5).

The recent International Academy for Business in Society's conference held at Cambridge University's Institute for Sustainability Leadership noted that the leadership needed for such change does not yet exist (Bendell & Little, 2015). Correspondingly, only a third of CEOs from the world's largest companies think business is heading in the right direction when it comes to sustainability (Accenture, 2013). Consequently, Bendell and Little ask, "What type of business leadership is needed to deal with these issues?" and, "Where will such leaders come from?" Whereas such questions remain to be answered, one thing is certain. These leaders cannot come from within the same paradigm that led us down this untenable path in the first place. If much of what occurs in the name of corporate sustainability "casually dismisses the finiteness of the world and our essential interconnections within it" (Ehrenfeld & Hoffman, 2013, p. 25) and reflects a market approach seeking to maximize economic gain (Gladwin et al., 1995), then we need a different way of thinking about how we do business, and we need business leaders who can progressively shift our focus towards a *telos* that reflects what is best for humanity and the world in which we live.

First, this chapter will briefly outline leadership theory, noting that its development often reflected a rational, technocratic, and economic worldview. Second, and more specifically, it explores the relationship between leadership and unsustainability. Third, the chapter offers alternative approaches to leadership that may provide us with a way out of this quagmire. Fourth, and finally, it concludes by offering some practical steps on how best to encourage sustainability leadership in an organization.

Leadership Development

Leadership is an important topic. A recent study by Gagnon and Collinson (2014) cited US$45 billion annual expenditures in the United States alone for leadership development. The same study found that European CEOs were also "extremely committed to leadership development" (p. 648). Many universities offer courses on leadership—the focus of which is usually personal development in preparation for senior management in an organization. There are, moreover, several journals dedicated to the topic.

We offer a brief survey of leadership development since the turn of the century. We hope this will elucidate the strong relationship between leadership, rational technocratic thinking, and the economic growth paradigm, which combined have contributed to simply minimizing unsustainability as opposed to being sustainable.

Western (2010) contends that three discourses have dominated leadership development over the past century. These, he writes, show how organizational leadership has been constructed and enacted during that time. A discourse is a "linguistic and cultural set of normative assumptions, an institutional way of thinking" (p. 37) that we cannot easily think or act outside of. Once we identify the discourses that dominate leadership thinking, then we can unravel from them. This, states Western, "enables us to change what we previously took for granted and explore new possibilities" (p. 37). It is also important to understand that these "discourses are not time-bound . . . They all remain with us, and contemporary organizations can still be dominated by any one [or all] of them" (p. 41). Table 2.1 summarizes each of these discourses' main characteristics, their limitations, and the authors who developed these ideas.

The first discourse is that of the controller who seeks to maximize efficiency. The job of this leader was to shift power to management, use modern techniques to ensure work was carried out efficiently, choose the best people for the job and make certain they were trained correctly, and then monitor them closely to ensure the work was done competently (Morgan, 1997). It was within this discourse that Max Weber (1947) developed his ideas about bureaucracy as the best fitting form of organization. Hierarchal supervision, regulatory control, and technocratic thinking, as well as

Table 2.1 Leadership Discourses (1900–2000) (adapted from Western (2010), pp. 38–41)

Leadership Discourses	Characteristics	Limitations	Main Authors
Controller *(Scientific Management)*	Organizations as machines, hierarchical bureaucracy, emphasis on formal goals	Dehumanizing, displaces substantive goals, erodes freedom and creativity	Frederick Taylor (1947), Henri Fayol (1949), Max Weber (1947)
Therapist *(Human Relations Movement)*	Organizations as organisms, focus on worker's needs, emphasis on self-actualization	Individualistic, manipulative, creates "organization men"	Elton Mayo (1949), Carl Rogers (1951), Abraham Maslow (1954)
Messiah *(Culture and Organization)*	Organizations as cultures, charismatic leadership, focus on teams, links company success to personal success	Employee worship of leader, engineered cultures, designer employees devoted to organization	Burns (1978), Conger & Kanungo (1987), Bass (1985, 1990)

formalism and power, characterized his 'spirit' of rational bureaucracy (i.e. the unifying rationalist principle). Interestingly, Weber also noted the strong connection between bureaucracy and the market. Capitalism, he wrote, needs productive organizations that have a "stable, strict, intensive, and calculable administration" (p. 338). At the same time, capitalism "is the most rational economic basis for bureaucratic administration and enables it to develop in the most rational form, especially because, from a fiscal point of view, it supplies the necessary money resources" (p. 338).

In the 1930s and 1940s, a new understanding of leadership developed, which Western (2010) labelled the therapist discourse. The focus here was on self-actualizing employees through their work, thereby increasing motivation and commitment. This perspective remains popular today. Much of current leadership development is based on individual enhancement and/or modifying high-potential individuals' behaviour to fit the organization's needs. Whereas it is an improvement in engaging employees, this discourse has significant limitations. First, its focus tends to shift problems back to individuals rather than systems, while also downplaying the potential of the vast majority without leadership roles, thus implying that they have little or no influence over outcomes (Bendell & Little, 2015). Second, it becomes an alternative means of manipulative control, using tools such as coaching, psychometrics, and emotional intelligence (EQ) to shape employees to fit company norms, values, and goals (Western, 2010). These, of course, mirror Weber's (1947) 'spirit' of rational bureaucracy and are concerned primarily with maximizing economic returns (Ehrenfeld & Hoffman, 2013).

A third discourse, messiah leadership, arose during the 1970s (Western, 2010). This new leadership style "emerged with the aim to create strong, dynamic organizational cultures under the vision and charisma of a transformational leader" (p. 40). Interestingly, Max Weber (1947) discussed charisma as one of the three types of legitimate authority.[1] The followers of charismatic leaders, stated Weber, attributed extraordinary qualities to them on the basis of "specific and exceptional sanctity, heroism or exemplary character of the person, and of normative patterns or order revealed or ordained by him" (p. 3). Unfortunately, Yukl (1999) notes, as did Weber (1947) before him, that 'worshipping' such leaders hands over substantial power and control that is frequently misused (see e.g. Duchon & Burns, 2008; Schwartz, 1991).

Transformational leadership theory builds on these earlier ideas. For example, Bass (1990) describes transformational leaders as

> broadening and elevating the interests of their employees, when they generate awareness and acceptance of the purposes and mission of the group, and when they stir their employees to look beyond their own self-interests for the good of the group.
>
> (p. 21)

However, at its core, transformational leadership is still about the ability of an individual to control the group. For example, Stevens, D'Intino, and Victor (1995) argue that transformational leadership often favours other stakeholders (e.g. shareholders and customers) to the detriment of employees. Along similar lines, Axtell-Ray (1986) argued that this modality inspires workers to *love* the organization, its values, and its goals, which are usually instrumentalist, technocratic, and profit oriented. Employees are encouraged to act this way even if at significant cost to themselves.

Unfortunately, the consequence of interpreting leadership through such lenses may have encouraged a current approach in business that at best minimizes unsustainability. Such leadership, with its focus on control and formal organizational goals, is unlikely to provide the kind of guidance necessary to engage with wider issues such as climate change or social inequality. The next section identifies several features inherent in contemporary leadership theory and demonstrates their connection with the aforementioned paradigms and their contribution to unsustainability.

Leadership and Unsustainability

In a recent article published in the *Journal of Corporate Citizenship*, Bendell and Little (2015) discuss several ways in which current approaches to leadership contribute to unsustainability. The first aspect, they argue, inherent within much of the leadership literature, is the notion of personal development, which often functions as a pretence for validating the self. Whereas this idea finds its genesis in the therapist discourse, contemporary approaches also incorporate the messiah discourse. Take, for example, the currently popular authentic leadership paradigm (Luthans & Avolio, 2003). To discover their authentic leadership style, George et al. (2007) state, individuals are encouraged to think about their life stories while answering questions such as how they became self-aware, where their most deeply held values come from, how integrated their lives are, and what motivates them intrinsically, all within the context of seeking or occupying a senior role in a firm. Rather than self-exploratory, these processes could also be characterized as self-justification, "as the exploration of self is framed by the aim of constructing narratives that explain one's right to seniority within a corporation—an almost 'divine' right to lead" (Bendell & Little, 2015, p. 19).

Unfortunately, state Bendell and Little, such approaches ignore sociological insights that demonstrate how language, discourse, and structures functioning through mass media and other forms of transmission influence our ability to individuate (see e.g. Berger & Luckmann, 1991; Fairclough, 2013; Goffman, 1959). Many leaders' sense of self is influenced by their organization's norms and goals, which in turn often reflect market ideology. If a business's current unsustainability is an outcome of these same factors, then any type of leadership development ignorant of this will be of little worth in achieving sustainability because it will likely reinforce similar conduct. In fact, 'true' authentic leadership might involve helping others free themselves from contemporary beliefs about reality and success (Bendell & Little, 2015) and enacting practices that resist the current economic dogma (Lips-Wiersma & Algera, 2012).

The second aspect of the leadership literature which, according to Bendell and Little (2015), may exacerbate unsustainability is its focus on traits. Again, this idea can be found in all the previous leadership discourses, but it is in the messiah discourse where it achieves its zenith. The idea that leaders have certain traits, characteristics, or qualities that non-leaders do not have has been popular in the academic literature for quite some time (see e.g. Bono, Shen, & Yoon, 2014; Cowley, 1928; Gibb, 1947; Jago, 1982; Judge & Bono, 2000; Kirkpatick & Locke, 1991).

Trait theory has been the subject of much criticism (Andersen, 2006; House & Aditya, 1997; Morgeson et al., 2007; Pervin, 1994). A seminal piece of research by Meindl, Ehrlich, and Dukerich (1985) found that people over-attribute the significance of leader's qualities and influence, "particularly when the event or outcome in question is especially significant" (p. 97), when compared with other potential factors shaping outcomes. Recent work by Khuruna (2003) supports these findings. Interestingly, Meindl et al. (1985) also note that this romanticized view of leadership reflects "a general belief in organisations as potentially effective and efficient value-producing systems that fulfil the various interest of their participants and society as a whole" (p. 97). This faith in leadership is "symbolized in the formal hierarchy of authority and the officials who occupy the elite positions of power and status", which may be "one manifestation of internalized values about the validity of organizations and therefore by implication, the roles occupied by people who are charged with the responsibility to maintain & control them" (p. 97)

A focus on traits encourages unsustainability in several ways. First, certain qualities supposedly important to leadership such as empathy and self-awareness (Goleman, 2004), intelligence (DeRue, Nahrgang, Wellman, & Humphrey, 2011), or openness and conscientiousness (Judge, Bono, Ilies, & Gerhardt, 2002) are key for anyone who is even remotely capable. Bendell and Little (2015) argue that limiting these traits to leaders alone downplays the role of supposed non-leaders in analyzing and solving the sustainability challenge. This restricts capacity for new ideas, and it constrains answers to a small pool of people who are usually entrenched in the paradigm that caused these problems in the first place.

Second, if as some have argued (see e.g. Fairclough, 2013), the self is socially constructed, then these supposed "fixed leadership traits" may reflect certain values and beliefs that are, in turn, underpinned by a specific paradigm (Bendell & Little, 2015). In other words, they may be useful for leaders "to exert control over the meanings and interpretations important constituencies give to whatever events and occurrences are considered relevant for the organisation's functioning and success" (Meindl et al., 1985,

p. 99). Along similar lines, Gemmill and Oakley (1992) have argued that leadership is simply a myth we tell ourselves to justify existing perspectives about hierarchy and power in organizations. This myth, they argue, creates a psychic prison of learned helplessness, whereby individuals become incapable of imagining or perceiving other alternatives. This idea can generate "feelings of despair and resistance to initiating any form of action" (p. 114). To state that these traits are found in leaders alone is to provide the majority of humanity with an excuse not to act. We wait for those deemed 'leaders' to solve our problems while we grow more despondent about our current situation.

Third, if we are not fixed beings but instead act in different ways in different contexts while changing over time, then we should be considering what forms of leadership best suit the situation and that can elicit the best group behaviours to achieve desired goals (Bendell & Little, 2015). An individual may be good in some situations, but leadership itself is usually developing, dispersed, and discontinuous with diverse people foremost at different times (Gastil, 1994; Raelin, 2003).

The final aspect of the leadership literature which may contribute to unsustainability, and which naturally follows on from the earlier discussion, is our susceptibility to the idea of the "Great Man" myth (Bendell & Little, 2015). The Scottish philosopher Thomas Carlyle (1997 [1840]) was an early proponent of such thinking:

> For, as I take it, universal history, the history of what man has accomplished in this world, is at bottom the history of the great men who have worked here. They were the leaders of men, these great ones . . . the soul of the whole world's history, it may justly be considered, were the history of these.
>
> (p. 1)

Perhaps this myth derives from our childhood, as many of us were brought up with stories of heroes achieving magnificent feats of endeavour or great leaders who helped shape history. Often these individuals are extolled as unique—someone the rest of us could only hope to be a pale imitation of. Whatever the reason, this myth continues to be perpetuated today (see e.g. Alain, September, 2011; Breen, September, 2005; Kitroeff, October, 2014).

This myth acts as a buffer to legitimate criticism, often allowing corporate leaders the luxury of advocating for sustainability, while acting in ways that are inherently unsustainable. Take, for example, Warren Buffet, who, in 2007, while discussing global warming, stated,

> You have to build the ark before the rains come . . . If you have to make a mistake, err on the side of the planet . . . Build a margin of safety to take care of the only planet we have.
>
> (cited in Klein, 2014, p. 233)

Unfortunately, such admirable words have not stopped Buffet from owning several coal-burning utilities, shares in Exxon Mobil and tar sands giant Suncor, or from buying the Burlington Northern Railroad, which is one of the biggest coal haulers in the United States (Klein, 2014). Richard Branson is another example of a 'great business leader' who has been lauded for his funding of renewable energy initiatives and his work in setting up the celebrated B Corporations (Cofino, June, 2013). Yet, despite all this, he continues to expand his business aggressively in the world's most carbon-intensive form of transportation and one of the most pollutive industries.

Arguments for such leadership "reinforce and reflect the widespread tendency of people to deskill themselves and idealise leaders by implying only a select few are good enough to exercise initiative" (Gemmill & Oakley, 1992, p. 120). According to Bendell and Little (2015), this ultimately creates a 'them versus us mindset'—the 'them' being the managers who need to control and exercise power, and the 'us' being the workers who need to be controlled to achieve organizational goals. This mindset alienates us from each other and nature. It is the same mindset at the root of our current unsustainability (Ehrenfeld & Hoffman, 2013). Unfortunately, such ideas about leadership become self-fulfilling truths. Theoretical propositions become beliefs shaping individuals, organizations, and societies. As beliefs are reinforced by their seeming truthfulness, they become normative rules of behaviour, which in turn create actions in accordance with their theories' primary assumptions (Ferraro, Pfeffer, & Sutton, 2005). For example, it does not matter how artificial the 'Great Man' myth is. The idea is so entrenched in our language that it has become a reality.

Following Bendell and Little (2015), it is this chapter's premise that current leadership thinking reflects a "panoptic managerialism" (p. 19), an emphasis on powerful individuals, and a service to market-oriented ends. Combined, these form a "common sense" (p. 19) perspective of leadership that has become entrenched in our organizations. Unfortunately, such thinking resonates with what Goodpaster (1994) has labelled a *teleopathic* disease that is plaguing contemporary organizations. This malady ensures a fixation on narrow short-term material goals pursued thoughtlessly, rationalization whereby immoral actions are justified by appeal to constructs such as loyalty and legality, and detachment that promotes a kind of callousness. Actors entrenched in this worldview seem less likely to guide us towards sustainability.

Alternative Approaches to Sustainability Leadership

If leadership that encourages unsustainability is controlling, power focused, hero oriented, and market dominated, then sustainability leadership perhaps should be dissimilar in nature. Such leadership should be distributed across the group as opposed to being centralized. It would be often episodic, arising to suit the context and not necessarily permanently conceived within a role or position. Such leadership would emerge from interactions between agents, ideas, and the environment, and it would be more adaptive in nature. Finally, sustainability leadership would be more about the hosting of leadership activity and leader actors than being heroic.

Sustainability leadership challenges the modernist slogan *form follows function* (Western, 2010). Instead of organizations fit for their rational, technocratic, and utilitarian function, we need structures and leadership that fit the goal of being fully sustainable. Ultimately, sustainability leadership is about the whole; it's about how *we* define the situation that needs addressing and then how *we* act accordingly. It is not about an individual informing us about the nature of the situation and then telling us how to act. With these broad thoughts in mind, we summarize several ideas from the literature in the following sections to inform what such leadership might entail.

Sustainability Leadership Is Distributed

Spillane's (2004) theory of distributed leadership echoes some of these ideas. He asserts leadership activity is more important than the actual leaders themselves. In other words, rather than interpreting leadership as a function of capabilities, competencies, or character, it is best understood as a practice "stretched over leaders, followers, and the material and symbolic artifacts in a situation" (p. 27). Applied to sustainability leadership, this theory suggests it is not about setting direction, creating alignment, and maintaining commitment (Quinn & Dalton, 2009), which are all top-down actions. Rather, it is the outcome of the dynamics of a particular context, the interpersonal relationships of all involved in that context, and interactions between them (Pepper & Wildy, 2008).

Such groups are not leaderless; rather, they are leaderful, with everyone empowered to engage, challenge, lead, or follow (Gastil, 1994). Indeed, if we think of unsustainability as a problem shared by all, then such modes of thinking may be the only way to move organizations towards sustainability. This resonates with Ferdig (2010) who states "rather than providing all the answers, sustainability leaders create opportunities for people to come together and generate their own answers—to explore, learn, and devise a realistic course of action to address sustainability challenges" (p. 31).

In UK public service, for example, distributed leadership was implemented "to combat social exclusion, facilitate joined-up government, build relationships with multiple stakeholders and engender citizen and user participation" (Currie & Lockett, 2011, p. 293). In their analysis of health providers, Currie and Lockett found that distributing authority to front-line staff and developing actor-networks resulted in a more collective leadership approach. This equated to a set of practices performed by actors at all levels of the organization rather than just qualities located in senior-level managers. Moreover, all actors played a role in creating and influencing leadership and in developing the skills required to generate conditions in which collective learning (around such issues as sustainability) could occur.

A more radical illustration of distributed leadership comes from social movement organizations. Using examples such as the uprisings in parts of the Middle East and the Occupy Wall Street movement, Sutherland, Land, and Bohm (2013) argue that leadership is a social process of constructed meaning-making and distributed communal interaction. Within an organizational context, this entails actors constructing interpretations that "foster commitment from other organisational actors, so that they feel the action is meaningful and important" (p. 763). Some actors may manage meaning more than others, but these "meanings must be shared, common and valued by all in the organisation before collective action can occur" (p. 763). Thus understood, leadership need not stabilize in hierarchies or inhere in specific individuals, but rather it emerges from the collective performance of the group. Consequently, if leadership is not fixed within a stable individual, then leadership can exist without 'leaders'.

Given this shift in focus, Sutherland et al. assert that we should not be discussing individual leaders (as per the mainstream literature) but rather should utilize the phrase leadership actors (and leaderful groups, Gastil, 1994). In an organization, this would be any actor or group who "exercises power by managing meaning, defining reality and providing a basis for organizational action" (p. 764). These leadership actors don't consciously compel others to act, rather they exercise "the kind of power that occurs in a group of equals; that is the power not to command, but to suggest and to be listened to, to begin something and see it happen" (Starhawk, 1987, p. 10). This power is a subtle, dynamic feature of social processes. Thus leadership becomes a "shared activity that creates social meanings, which may be temporarily stable but always open to consternation, change and reinterpretation" (p. 764).

Again, an example may help. Elsen-Ziya and Erhart's (2015) case study of the Gezi Park protest in Turkey in 2013, initiated as a reaction to government policies infringing upon civil liberties, found the "movement's most unique feature was its horizontal, mostly post-heroic, and in some instances leaderless configuration" (p. 483) combined with increasing use of social media and unconventional ways of organizing. As one participant noted,

> We do not need hierarchical structures, leaders and forerunners anymore. This is a jump of consciousness. Women from all around Turkey are arriving. They are uniting against violence. They pick up the megaphone and shout out their ideas.
>
> (p. 483)

This new form of leadership sought to "replace the current rule (of Turkey) with a democratic, civil, and inclusive model where hierarchizes were flatter" (p. 483). Consequently, the park became a utopian pluralist space where no one voice could dominate and in which common ideas or goals served as the leader, as opposed to any one individual or 'great person'.

Sustainability Leadership Is Emergent

As discussed earlier, much of current leadership reflects the industrial age (Uhl-Bien, Marion, & McKelvey, 2007). This is not surprising given the still overwhelming influence of economic rationalism and technocratic thinking (Casey, 1995; Morgan, 1997; Weber, 1947). Recent literature, however, fosters a perspective which understands organizations as complex adaptive systems (Stacey, 2001; Stacey, Griffin, & Shaw, 2002). This theory views "organisations as non-linear dynamic systems that exhibit self-organising and emergent phenomena" (Metcalf & Benn, 2013, p. 375). Using this lens, organizations are not linear hierarchical systems, rather they are chaotic interrelated entities that cannot be controlled (Wheatley, 2011). Elements within an organization (e.g. actors, thoughts and outcomes) interact unpredictably with one another to produce emergent change (Marion & Uhl-Bien, 2001). This change occurs non-linearly and in unexpected places. Foreseeably, the result of trying to control such chaotic systems is to create more structures which are ultimately uncontrollable (Wheatley, 2011).

The environment of complex adaptive systems produces "a system's dynamic persona" (Uhl-Bien et al., 2007, p. 299). For organizations, this refers to the exchanges and connections between elements in the internal as well as the external environment. Sustainability leadership is socially constructed in and from this context (Marion & Uhl-Bien, 2001). In this way, such leadership is an emergent property that arises as a result of, and in response to, these interactions and interdependencies. This differs from managerial (or hierarchical) leadership, which reflects the more rational bureaucratic approach discussed earlier in this paper. Marion and Uhl-Bien label this type of leadership *adaptive* in that it "occurs in emergent, informal adaptive dynamics throughout the organisation" (p. 300).

Interestingly, Marion and Uhl-Bien (2001) assert that leadership in complex systems "occurs in the face of adaptive challenges (typical of the Knowledge Era) rather than technical problems (more characteristic of the Industrial Age)" (p. 300). Sustainability is the adaptive challenge of our age, and it requires new learning, innovation, and different forms of behaviour. Existing styles of leadership may be ineffective because they use knowledge and procedures already in hand and, therefore, are potentially doomed to repeat mistakes of the past while offering little that is new. Anyone taking up the sustainability challenge needs to understand this. You cannot corral complex organizations (and the agents within them) into being more sustainable; all one can do is set up the conditions that encourage and allow emergent change and then let the system determine where it wishes to go and how it wishes to get there (Uhl-Bien et al., 2007). Any outcomes occurring as a result of such a process will be, to some extent, unpredictable, but they will also be self-organizing (from within the group itself), novel, and adaptive while exhibiting sufficient significance and impact to create change.

Bendell and Little (2015) refer to Ray Anderson (the late CEO of Interface Inc.) as an example of a leader with an approach to sustainability that reflected aspects of distributed leadership and complex adaptive systems theory. At a presentation given in 2009 in the United Kingdom, Anderson discussed how the existing hierarchy and systems within Interface would limit their ability to achieve the company's stated goal of zero emissions. He noted that people were inspired once they realized that sustainability was about their families and their communities (i.e. they developed a shared meaning) and that his main role was to make sure the bureaucracy got out of the way. He encouraged an environment where nothing would prevent people from taking this mission on, coming together, and using their imaginations. He was prepared for this process to be unpredictable, novel, and, especially, destructive of old ways of thinking.

Sustainability Leadership Is About Hosting

Who is best suited for the sustainability challenges facing organizations in the twenty-first century? Perhaps not leaders conceived as 'great men' or heroes. As Wheatley (2011) so eloquently states,

> It's time for all the heroes to go home . . . It is time for us to give up these hopes and expectations that only breed dependency and passivity, and that do not give us solutions to the challenges we face. It's time to stop waiting for someone else to save us. It's time to face the truth of our situation—that we're all in this together, that we all have a voice—and figure out how to mobilize the hearts and minds of everyone in our workplaces.
>
> (n.p.)

This focus on heroes is limited. It reinforces existing unsustainability while minimizing the incentive for followers to embrace change.

Another approach importing many of the qualities of sustainability leadership discussed earlier might conceive of people in organizations hosting leadership activity as opposed to being heroes. According to Wheatley (2011), hosting involves nurturing the conditions and group processes, and providing the resources for people to have leaderful groups, to generate leadership activity, and to be leadership actors. Hosting recognizes sustainability as a complex problem with all parts of the system needing to be involved. As Pepper and Wildy (2008) note, such an approach demonstrates deep systemic understandings. It recognizes that leadership is an emergent property of the interactions between all parts of the organization. Enacting a model of "power with" that is characterized by "fluid expertise, the willingness to show, and acknowledge interdependence and need for input" (p. 653), the kind of power that reflects equals within a group, as opposed to "power over" (Fletcher, 2004), is more reflective of this approach.

Wheatley (2011) talks about creating spaces where potential leadership activity and/or actors are unencumbered by the senseless demands of bureaucracy. Using an idea initially conceived by the Japanese philosopher Kitaro Nishida (1990), Nonaka and Konno's (1998) concept of *ba* or a "a shared space for emerging relationships" (p. 40) reflects this idea. For Nonaka and Konno, this mutual space is essential in the creation of knowledge because it "provides the energy, quality, and place to perform the individual conversions and to move along the knowledge spiral" (p. 41). Interestingly, *ba* may not be an actual place; it could also be a mental state, a sense of flow (Csikszentmihalyi, 1990), where knowledge emerges as we make sense of the world (Nonaka & Toyama, 2003). Hosting plays a vital role in setting up and facilitating such spaces. They recognize that knowledge needs to be cultivated, sustained, enriched, and cherished. Becoming activists in support of *ba*, they commit "themselves to new ideas, experiments, and [their] fellow human beings" (p. 54).

Another feature of hosting is the ability to keep at bay stifling bureaucracies (Wheatley, 2011). As Ray Anderson specified earlier, formal bureaucracy tends to get in the way of new emergent learnings and behaviours. Part of this involves defending the conditions, spaces, and actors from traditional leadership who typically want control and who are wary of providing workers with too much liberty. This happens in organizations frequently when senior 'leaders' justify their opposition to legitimate change, arguing that employees, if given to such freedom, will simply use it to take advantage of the organization, or they will overstep their bounds (Maccoby, Gittel, & Ledeen, 2004). Wheatley (2011) contends that this is about fear of losing power and control. Opposing such demands is an important opportunity for sustainability leadership: they must not compromise the moral grounding by which to facilitate transformation (Middlebrooks, Miltenberger, Tweedy, Newman, & Follman, 2009).

Finally, hosting is something that one does rather than something that one is (McKergow, 2009). Host and guest are co-defining; together they construct the context, and without both nothing can be achieved. Moreover, these roles are interchangeable—sometimes you host, sometimes you are a guest. Depending on the situation, both have responsibility to ensure an event is a success. This reflects much of what was written earlier about sustainability leadership: it is distributed (between the hosts and the guests with these roles being interchangeable), episodic (a host exists for a specific event after which he or she is no longer needed), and emergent (the host facilities the conditions for leadership activity, actors, and new knowledge to develop).

If we return to Sutherland et al.'s (2013) analysis of grassroots social movement groups, we can see examples of hosting leadership. Sutherland et al. do not label this as such, but it is effectively what occurred. Different individuals would facilitate events depending on their experience, their skill level, and the context. However, Sutherland et al. also note that whereas leadership actors emerged in certain situations, the focus was still on "ensuring that all were able to contribute to the leadership of the organisation by building collective power through the distribution of skills, knowledge and expertise" (p. 13). In the four social movements they analyzed (two environmental groups, one alternative media group, and one anarchist student group), experienced individuals were often invited to host events, but efforts were made to ensure that they did not become permanent leaders. One means of achieving this was by rotating formal roles, with every member being expected to take on hosting at some point. This rotation also ensured equality of participation and reduced the passivity of group members. Moreover, "role rotation encouraged accountability through increasingly symmetrical power relations" (p. 14). In other words, the host and the guests became interchangeable: the temporary leadership actors became accountable to the group and vice versa. This ensures that power is distributed and further supports more democratic forms.

Conclusion

The nature of sustainability leadership is such that organizations would do well to focus on three areas of development. The first involves cultivating critical self-reflection as opposed to self-validation in potential leadership actors (Bendell & Little, 2015; Spillane, 2004). Such reflection occurs when individuals question their presuppositions and evaluate the suitability of their worldview in their present context (Mezirow, 1990). For example, stimulating potential leadership actors or leaderful groups to recognize the connection between mainstream economic dogma and its negative outcomes (such as climate change, biodiversity loss, and social inequality), along with the anguish this generates for human beings, is essential for transformation. For it is in these moments, where past assumptions are let go, that self-exploration occurs.

The second area of development is relationship building. Interaction with others, working with groups, and nurturing networks are central to sustainability leadership; consequently, cultivating interpersonal and group facilitation competencies is a necessity (Pepper & Wildy, 2008). Sustainability challenges are caused by, and effect, multiple actors. Solving such problems and generating future opportunities requires "the capacity to understand, compare, and critically evaluate different positions, perspectives and preferences" (Wiek, Withycombe, & Redman, 2011, p. 211). This interpersonal competence is especially important when it comes to the various stakeholder negotiations and collaborations required to bring about lasting change.

The third, and final, area of leadership development is systems-thinking competence (Wiek et al., 2011). Given the nature of complex adaptive systems, sustainability leadership must be able to

> collectively analyze complex systems across different domains (society, environment, economy, etc.) and across different scales (local to global), thereby considering cascading effects, inertia, feedback loops and other systemic features related to sustainability issues and sustainability problem-solving frameworks.
>
> (p. 207)

The ability to analyze such systems includes comprehending, empirically verifying, and articulating their structure, key components, and dynamics. Because of the complexity involved here, it is unlikely that a single leader would be able to carry out this role. Hence shared leadership across a group is considered the best approach in such an environment (Metcalf & Benn, 2013). Developing leadership activity with such a group should refrain from promoting control and direction and instead facilitate individuals "to become aware of the complex systems in which we are embedded, and care for the systemic changes that, though distant and difficult to discern, threaten the web of connections that sustain us" (Satterwhite, 2010, p. 239).

Shirberg and MacDonald (2013) argue that "sustainability leadership cannot be taught solely with traditional leadership theory" (p. 18). Such theory is problematic for the reasons addressed earlier, the most relevant of which is its embeddedness within a rational technocratic and economic paradigm. Taking a different view of leadership enables us to offer alternative approaches and models that are more likely to encourage sustainability within organizations and society. Without such an analysis, leadership theory is prone to repeat previous mistakes that have so far led to sustainable business efforts being largely ineffectual (Bendell & Little, 2015). As noted by Ehrenfeld and Hoffman (2013), such 'Band-Aids' tend to minimize unsustainability rather than effecting lasting change.

We need leadership that is more democratic and that distributes leadership activity and actors across the organization. This type of leadership is episodic, *arising for* a specific problem and context. It is also emergent, *arising from* the interactions between ideas, agents, and environments that relate to a specific problem and context. Ultimately, such leadership needs to be highly adaptive. Finally, we need individuals in organizations hosting others in such a way that widespread sustainability leadership activity and actors can develop. In order to develop such individuals, organizations should encourage critical self-reflection about (un)sustainability as opposed to self-justification of one's status. Organizations should also develop actors' interpersonal skills and systems-thinking competency. This approach to leadership is reflective of sustainability itself, and while not a panacea to all that ails us, it may be a significant improvement on our current maladaptive practices.

Note

1 The others being rational, legal, and traditional authority.

References

Accenture. (2010). *A new era in sustainability: UN Global Compact-Accenture CEO study 2010*. Retrieved from: https://www.unglobalcompact.org/library/230

Accenture. (2013). *The UN Global Compact-Accenture CEO study on sustainability 2013: Architects of a better world*. Retrieved from: http://www.accenture.com/Microsites/ungc-ceo-study/Documents/pdf/13–1739_UNGC%20report_Final_FSC3.pdf

Alain, P. (September 2011). *10 must-have leadership traits: What world leaders have said about leadership*. Retrieved from: http://www.industryleadersmagazine.com/10-must-have-leadership-traits-what-world-leaders-have-said-about-leadership/

Andersen, J. A. (2006). Leadership, personality and effectiveness. *The Journal of Socio-Economics, 35*, 1078–1091.

Assadourian, E., & Renner, M. (2012). *State of the world 2012: Moving towards sustainable prosperity*. Washington: Worldwatch Institute.

Axtell-Ray, C. (1986). Corporate culture: The last frontier of control. *Journal of Management Studies, 23*(3), 286–295.

Bass, B. M. (1985). *Leadership & performance beyond expectations*. New York: Free Press.

Bass, B. M. (1990). From transactional to transformational leadership: Learning to share the vision. *Organizational Dynamics, 18*(3), 19–31.

Bendell, J., & Little, R. (2015). Seeking sustainable leadership. *The Journal of Corporate Citizenship, 60*, 13–26. doi:10.9774/GLEAF.4700.2015.de.00004

Berger, P. L., & Luckmann, T. (1991). *The social construction of reality: A treatise in the sociology of knowledge*. London: Penguin.

Bono, J. E., Shen, W., & Yoon, D. J. (2014). Personality and leadership: Looking back, looking ahead. In D. V. Day (Ed.), *The Oxford handbook of leadership and organizations* (pp. 199–220). New York: Oxford University Press.

Breen, B. (September 2005). The 3 ways of great leaders. *Fast Company*, (98), 49–52.

Burns, J. (1978). *Leadership*. New York: Harper Row.

Carlyle, T. (1997 [1840]). *Heroes and hero worship*. Retrieved from: www.gutenberg.org

Casey, C. (1995). *Work, self and society*. London: Routledge.

Cofino, J. (June 2013). Richard Branson and Jochen Zeitz launch the B Team challenge. *The Guardian*. Retrieved from: http://www.theguardian.com/sustainable-business/blog/richard-branson-jochen-zeitz-b-team

ColmarBrunton. (2014). *Better business, better future*. Retrieved from: http://www.colmarbrunton.co.nz/index.php/polls-and-surveys/better-business-better-future/better-business-better-world-report

Conger, J. A., & Kanungo, R. (1987). Toward a behavioral theory of charismatic leadership in organizational settings *Academy of Management Review, 12*, 637–647.

Cowley, W. H. (1928). Three distinctions in the study of leaders. *The Journal of Abnormal and Social Psychology, 23*(2), 144–157. doi:10.1037/h0073661

Csikszentmihalyi, M. (1990). *Flow: The psychology of optimal experience.* New York: Harper & Row.

Currie, G., & Lockett, A. (2011). Distributing leadership in health & social care: Concertive, conjoint or collective? *International Journal of Management Reviews, 13*, 286–300. doi:10.1111/j.1468–2370.2011.00308.x

DeRue, D. S., Nahrgang, J. D., Wellman, N., & Humphrey, S. E. (2011). Trait and behavioral theories of leadership: An integration and meta-analytic test of their relative validity. *Personnel Psychology, 64*, 7–52. doi:10.1111/j.1744–6570.2010.01201.x

Dierksmeier, C. (2012). Deconstructing the neoclassical economic paradigm In D. Mele & C. Dierksmeier (Eds.), *Human development in business: Values & humanistic management in the encyclical Caritas in Veritate* (pp. 21–44). London: Palgrave Macmillan.

Duchon, D., & Burns, M. (2008). Organizational narcissism. *Organizational Dynamics, 37*(4), 354–363. doi:10.1016/j.orgdyn.2008.07.004

Ehrenfeld, R., & Hoffman, A. J. (2013). *Flourishing: A frank conversation about sustainability.* Stanford, CA: Stanford Business Books.

Eslen-Ziya, H., & Erhart, I. (2015). Toward a post-heroic leadership: A case study of Gezi's collaborting multiple leaders. *Leadership, 11*(4), 471–488. doi:10.1177/1742715015591068

Fairclough, N. (2013). *Language & power.* Abingdon, Oxon: Routledge.

Fayol, H. (1949). *General & industrial management* (C. Storrs, Trans.). New York: Pitman.

Ferdig, M. A. (2010). Sustainability leadership: Co-creating a sustainable future. *Journal of Change Management, 7*(1), 25–35. doi:10.1080/14697010701233809

Ferraro, F., Pfeffer, J., & Sutton, R. I. (2005). Economics language and assumptions: How theories can become self-fulfilling. *Academy of Management Review, 30*(1), 8–24. doi:10.5465/AMR.2005.15281412

Fletcher, J. (2004). The paradox of post-heroic leadership: An essay on gender, power & transformational change. *Leadership Quarterly, 15*(5), 647–661.

Foster, J. (2015). *After sustainability.* London: Earthscan.

Frank, R. H., Gilovich, T., & Regan, D. T. (1993). Does studying economics inhibit cooperation? *Journal of Economic Behaviour and Organization, 43*, 101–113.

Gagnon, S., & Collinson, D. (2014). Rethinking global leadership development programmes: The interrelated significance of power, context and identity. *Organisation Studies, 35*, 546–975.

Gastil, J. (1994). A definition and illustration of democratic leadership. *Human Relations, 47*(8), 953–975.

Gemmill, G., & Oakley, J. (1992). Leadership: An alienating social myth. *Human Relations, 45*(2), 113–129. doi:10.1177/001872679204500201

George, B., Sims, P., McLean, A. N., & Mayer, D. (2007). Discovering your authentic leadership. *Harvard Business Review, February*, 1–8. (Reprinted from www.hbr.org).

Gibb, C. A. (1947). The principles and traits of leadership. *The Journal of Abnormal and Social Psychology, 42*(3), 267–284. doi:10.1037/h0056420

Gladwin, T. N., Kennelly, J. J., & Krause, T.-S. (1995). Shifting paradigms for sustainable development: Implications for management theory and research. *Academy of Management Review, 20*(4), 874–907.

Goffman, E. (1959). *The presentation of self in everyday life.* London: Penguin.

Goleman, D. (January, 2004). What makes a leader? *Harvard Business Review,* 1–10. (Reprinted from www.hbr.org)

Goodpaster, K. E. (1994). Work, spirituality and the moral point of view. *International Journal of Value-Based Management, 7*(1), 49–62. doi:10.1007/BF00 892148

Hamilton, C. (2003). *Growth fetish.* Crows Nest, NSW: Allen & Unwin.

Hamilton, C., & Denniss, R. (2005). *Affluenza: When too much is never enough.* Crows Nest, NSW: Allen & Unwin.

Horkheimer, M., & Adorno, T. W. (1947/2002). *Dialectic of enlightenment: Philosophical fragments* (E. Jephcott, Trans.). Stanford: Stanford University Press.

House, R. J., & Aditya, R. N. (1997). The social scientific study of leadership: Quo vadis? *Journal of Management & Organization, 23,* 409–473.

Jago, A. G. (1982). Leadership: Perspectives in theory and research. *Management Science, 28*(3), 315–336. doi:10.1287/mnsc.28.3.315

James, O. (2007). *Affluenza.* Reading, UK: Vermilion.

Judge, T. A., & Bono, J. E. (2000). Five-factor model of personality and transformational leadership. *Journal of Applied Psychology, 85*(5), 751–765. doi:10.1037/0021-9010.85.5.751

Judge, T. A., Bono, T. E., Ilies, R., & Gerhardt, M. (2002). Personality and leadership: A qualitative and quantitative review. *Journal of Applied Psychology, 87,* 765–780.

Kasser, T. (2002). *The high price of materialism.* Cambridge, MA: MIT Press.

Khuruna, R. (2003). *Searching for the corporate savior: The irrational quest for charismatic CEO's.* Princeton, NJ: Princeton University Press.

Kirkpatick, S. A., & Locke, E. A. (1991). Leadership: Do traits matter? *Academy of Management Perspectives, 5*(2), 48–60. doi:10.5465/AME.1991.4274679

Kitroeff, N. (October 2014). A professor thinks leaders should be like Christopher Columbus. *Business Week.* Retrieved from: http://www.bloomberg.com/bw/articles/2014-10-14/professor-wants-leaders-to-follow-lessons-from-christopher-columbus

Klein, N. (2014). *This changes everything.* New York: Simon & Schuster.

Lips-Wiersma, M., & Algera, P. M. (2012). Radical authentic leadership: Co-creating the conditions under which all members of the organisation can be authentic. *The Leadership Quarterly, 23,* 118–131. doi:10.1016/j.leaqua2011.11.010

Luthans, F., & Avolio, B. (2003). Authentic leadership: A positive developmental approach. In K. S. Cameron & J. E. Dutton (Eds.), *Positive Organizational Scholarship: Foundations of a New Discipline* (pp. 241–258). San Francisco, CA: Berrett-Koehler.

Maccoby, M., Gittel, J. H., & Ledeen, M. (2004). *Leadership and the fear factor* (Vol. 4). Retrieved from: http://sloanreview.mit.edu/article/leadership-and-the-fear-factor/

Marion, R., & Uhl-Bien, M. (2001). Leadership in complex organizations. *The Leadership Quarterly, 12,* 389–418.

Maslow, A. H. (1954). *Motivation and personality.* New York: Harper & Row.

Mayo, E. (1949). *The social problems of an industrial civilization.* Abingdon, Oxon: Routledge.

McKergow, M. (2009). Host leadership: Towards a new yet ancient metaphor. *The International Journal of Leadership in Public Services*, *5*(1), 19–24.

Meindl, J. R., Ehrlich, S. B., & Dukerich, J. M. (1985). The romance of leadership. *Administrative Science Quarterly*, *30*, 78–102.

Metcalf, L., & Benn, S. (2013). Leadership for sustainability: An evolution of leadership ability. *Journal of Business Ethics*, *112*, 369–384. doi:1007/s10551–012–1278–6

Mezirow, J. (1990). How critical reflection triggers transformative learning. In J. Mezirow (Ed.), *Fostering Critical Reflection in Adulthood* (pp. 1–20). San Francisco: Jossey-Bass Publishers.

Middlebrooks, A., Miltenberger, L., Tweedy, J., Newman, G., & Follman, J. (2009). Developing a sustainability ethic in leaders. *Journal of Leadership Studies*, *3*(2), 31–43. doi:10.1002/jls.20106

Moore, G. (2008). Re-imagining the morality of management: A modern virtue ethics approach. *Business Ethics Quarterly*, *18*(4), 483–511. doi:10.5840/beq200818435

Morgan, G. (1997). *Images of organisation*. Thousand Oaks, CA: Sage Publications.

Morgeson, F. P., Campion, M. A., Dipboye, R. L., Hollenbeck, J. R., Murphy, K., & Schmitt, N. (2007). Are we getting fooled again? Coming to terms with limitations in the use of personality tests for personnel selection. *Personnel Psychology*, *60*, 1029–1049.

Nishida, K. (1990). *An inquiry into the good* (M. Abe & C. Ives, Trans.). New Haven: Yale University Press.

Nonaka, I., & Konno, N. (1998). The concept of "Ba": Building a foundation for knowledge creation. *California Management Review*, *40*(3), 40–54.

Nonaka, I., & Toyama, R. (2003). The knowledge-creating theory revisited: Knowledge creation as a synthesizing process *Knowledge Management Research & Practice*, *1*, 2–10.

Pearce, F. (2007). *The last generation: How nature will take her revenge for climate change*. London: Transworld Publishers.

Pepper, C., & Wildy, H. (2008). Leading for sustainability: Is surface understanding enough? *Journal of Educational Administration*, *46*(5), 613–629. doi:10.1108/09578230810895528

Pervin, L. A. (1994). A critical analysis of current trait theory. *Psychological Inquiry*, *5*(2), 103–113. doi:10.1207/s15327965pli0502_1

Quinn, L., & Dalton, M. (2009). Leading for sustainability: Implementing the tasks of leadership. *Corporate Governance*, *9*(1), 21–38. doi:10.1108/14720700910936038

Raelin, J. A. (2003). *Creating leaderful organisations: How to bring out leadership in everyone*. San Francisco: Barrett-Koehler.

Roberts, J. (2004). The dialectic of the enlightenment In F. Rush (Ed.), *The Cambridge Companion to Critical Theory* (pp. 57–73). Cambridge, UK: Cambridge University Press.

Rogers, C. (1951). *Cleint-centered therapy: Its current practice, implications & theory*. London: Constable.

Rosanas, J. M. (2008). Beyond economic criteria: A humanistic approach to organizational survival. *Journal of Business Ethics*, *78*(3), 447–462. doi:10.1007/s10551–006–9341–9

Satterwhite, R. (2010). Deep systems leadership: A model for the 21st century. In B. W. Redekop (Ed.), *Leadership for environmental sustainability* (pp. 230–242). New York: Routledge.

Schwartz, H. (1991). Narcissism project and corporate decay: The case of general motors. *Business Ethics Quarterly, 1*(3), 249–268.

Shirberg, M., & MacDonald, L. (2013). Sustainability leadership programs: Emerging goals. methods and best practices. *Journal of Sustainability Education, 5*, 1. Retrieved from: http://www.jsedimensions.org.ezproxy.aut.ac.nz/wordpress/content/sustainability-leadership-programs-emerging-goals-methods-best-practices_2013_06/

Spillane, J. (2004). Towards a theory of leadership practice: A distributed perspective. *Journal of Curriculum Studies, 36*(1), 3–34.

Stacey, R. D. (2001). *Complex responsive processes in organizations*. London: Routledge.

Stacey, R. D., Griffin, D., & Shaw, P. (2002). *Complexity & management*. London: Routledge.

Starhawk. (1987). *Truth or dare: Encounters with power, authority & mystery*. San Francisco: Harper.

Stevens, C. U., D'Intino, R. S., & Victor, B. (1995). The moral quandary of transformational leadership: Change for whom? *Research in Organizational Change and Development, 8* 123–143.

Sutherland, N., Land, C., & Bohm, S. (2013). Anti-leaders(hip) in social movement organizations: The case of autonomous grassroots groups. *Organization, 21*(6), 759–781. doi:10.1177/350508413480254

Taylor, F. (1947). *Scientific management*. New York: Harper & Row.

Uhl-Bien, M., Marion, R., & McKelvey, B. (2007). Complexity leadership theory: Shifting leadership from the industrial age to the knowledge era. *The Leadership Quarterly, 18*(4), 298–318. doi:http://dx.doi.org/10.1016/j.leaqua.2007.04.002

Wiek, A., Withycombe, L., & Redman, C. L. (2011). Key competencies in sustainability: A reference framework for academic program development. *Sustainability Science, 6*(2), 203–218. http://10.1007/s11625-011-0132-6

Wilbur, C. (2009). Financial crises and self-interest. *Cultura Economica, 73–74*, 17–22.

Wilkinson, R., & Pickett, K. (2010). *The spirit level: Why greater equality makes societies stronger*. London: Bloomsbury.

Yukl, G. (1999). An evaluation of conceptual weaknesses in transformational and charismatic leadership theories. *Leadership Quarterly, 10*(2), 285–305.

3 Responsible Leadership in Times of Change

Champions From the Arab Region

Dima Jamali, Nadine Mohanna, and Hagop Panossian

Introduction

Sustainability is the new hype in the business context, but what fuels sustainable innovations and sustainable practices? The short answer is responsible leadership. In this chapter, we delve into the recent writings on responsible leadership to try to elucidate the core of this concept and what it is about. Whereas sustainability has received resonating attention in recent years, much less is known about responsible leaders—the decision makers who are the architects of change within responsible organizations and their role in formulating and executing such initiatives. Therefore, we delve in this chapter into various recent formulations of responsible leadership, what it means, and what it entails, and report in the second half of the chapter on the responsible practices and strategies of five sustainability champions from the Arab world, thus illustrating what they have done to drive change in relation to sustainability by placing sustainability at the very heart of the businesses they have created.

The concept of responsible leadership has emerged in light of evidence that the decisions of senior leaders have significant impacts on their firms and the societies within which they operate (Aguilera et al., 2007; Crilly, 2011; Kakabadse et al., 2005; Waldman & Galvin, 2008). Across the globe, there is an important metamorphosis in terms of heightened awareness of sustainability issues, and there is growing attention to the need for the kinds of leaders who are sensitized to the importance of reconciling multiple demands and tensions, including economic and social interests. Responsible leadership is thus a construct that lies at the intersection of two fields—namely, leadership and corporate social responsibility, or sustainability, and which has been attracting increasing attention in recent years, given growing and compelling social and environmental problems, as well as increasing pressure on business organizations of various types and sizes to pull their weight and assume more responsible orientations and operations.

Whereas traditional leadership is about the ability to influence others and to facilitate the achievement of collective objectives, responsible leadership is concerned with the galvanizing of these efforts in pursuit of social and economic goals and objectives. Responsible leadership, in fact, has a comprehensive and inclusive connotation, inviting attention and consideration of the impacts and spillovers of leadership beyond traditional organizational boundaries. Based on recent writings, a definition of responsible leadership can be synthesized as intentional decisions and actions taken by leaders in the interest of the stakeholders of the company, and the promotion of positive social change for society as a whole (Stahl and de Luque, 2014; Voegtlin et al., 2012). This definition resonates with the frameworks presented in this chapter, turning attention to the need to reconcile economic, social, and environmental responsibilities and attending to the needs of various stakeholders both within and outside the organization.

Leaders play a significant role as architects of change, whereas responsible leaders serve as drivers and architects of sustainable change that successfully strikes a balance among economic, environmental, and social bottom lines. According to Szekely and Knirsch (2005), effective sustainability performance cannot be achieved without the commitment of leadership to sustainability and the adoption of an appropriate management incentive scheme. Responsible leaders thus ensure that sustainable development values and vision are not only integrated into business strategy, policies, and culture but also communicated to all employees. Responsible leadership thus entails setting appropriate sustainability and CSR goals, developing a coordinated sustainability approach, and monitoring and evaluating progress and tracking the impact of such initiatives (Szekely and Knirsch, 2005). Accordingly, the engagement of leaders is crucial to set the firm on a path to long-term sustainability (Wood et al., 1986) and to carve a competitive edge for the firm by proactively institutionalizing and managing sustainable performance.

Responsible leadership is certainly gaining traction globally, but little attention has been accorded to how it manifests itself in practice and in specific locales. We embark in this chapter on analyzing responsible leadership in an under-studied context—namely, the Middle East and North Africa (MENA) region. This is both timely and important, given the myriad socio-economic challenges that have been exposed in the aftermath of the Arab Spring, starting with youth unemployment (there is an estimated 20 million unemployed youth across this region, mostly females), elitist access to health care and education, and gender inequality. Poverty, for example, is a growing problem across the region, afflicting 30 per cent to 40 per cent of non-oil-producing countries (Ghandour, 2013). According to recent statistics, 23 per cent of the 345 million MENA residents live on less than US$2 per day (World Bank, 2011). Public health coverage extends to just about 30 per cent to 40 per cent of the population in non-oil-producing countries (Jawad, 2014). Female labour force participation is one of the lowest in the world, estimated at 26 per cent, which is half of the global average of 51 per cent (Jamali & Lanteri, 2015; Jamali & Sidani, 2012).

Responsible leadership is particularly important in this difficult context with mounting economic and social challenges, haunting future generations of Arab citizens. We wish to showcase the important role that leaders can play in serving as conduits for positive social change with long-term implications for future generations. By shedding light on prominent leaders from across MENA, and the concrete actions they have taken to champion change, both within and outside their organizations, we provide evidence that responsible leaders can serve as important architects of change and go a long way in making a difference with respect to relevant and thorny social and developmental issues. We start the chapter by providing a brief description of the literature and key frameworks on the topic. We next illustrate responsible leadership in practice by examining and showcasing five successful champions from the Arab world. The findings are fleshed out and implications synthesized in relation to frameworks presented and the opportunities and constraints facing responsible leadership in times of change.

Literature Overview

Stahl and de Luque (2014) provided a simple framework for explaining responsible leadership revolving around two leadership behaviours—namely, 'doing good' and 'avoiding harm'. The latter behaviour (proscriptive morality) consists of decisions taken by socially responsible leaders to deter or refrain from actions that have harmful consequences. 'Doing good' behaviours (prescriptive morality) include activities directed to improve social welfare. Crilly et al. (2008) addressed the implications of the two behavioural dimensions and concluded that values, affect, and reasoning all matter to socially responsible behaviour. These authors suggested that 'doing good' actions are governed by self-transcendence values and positive affect cognition, as well as moral and reputation-based reasoning while 'avoiding harm' activities are better explained by cognition (moral reasoning). Accordingly, responsible leadership behaviour is defined as "intentional actions taken by leaders to benefit the stakeholders of the company and/or actions taken to avoid harmful consequences for stakeholders and the larger society" (Stahl & de Luque, 2014, p. 238). Additionally, Stahl and de Luque (2014) suggest that situational aspects may mediate the relationship between the contextual influence and the leaders' responsible behaviour. For example, responsible leadership is facilitated when leaders operate in an environment where stakeholders' rights are respected and laws and regulations are strictly enforced. Paradoxically, they also note that the need for responsible leadership is less acute precisely in such situations.

Miska et al. (2014) identified three competing perspectives on responsible leadership: agent, stakeholder, and converging views (Figure 3.1). Under the agent theory, responsible leadership is aligned with Friedman's (2007) notion that social responsibility is an implicit component of the goal of increasing profits. By increasing profits, companies also create jobs and new

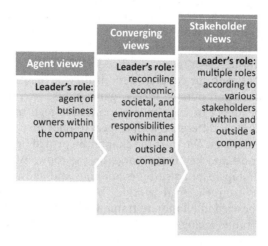

Figure 3.1 Overview of Perspectives on Responsible Leadership
(Source: Miska et al., 2014)

goods and services. Accordingly, the main objective of business leaders is to generate economic returns within the boundaries of societal law and ethical customs. Alternatively, stakeholder theory focuses on how business leaders affect the social systems in which their companies operate, having manifold spillovers on multiple stakeholders (Komives and Dugan, 2010). The stakeholder view denotes that business leaders can promote stakeholder inclusion and sustainable societal development by addressing pressing problems such as poverty and global warming (Maak and Pless, 2006). The third perspective is the converging view, which combines both the economic perspective and the stakeholder view (Waldman and Siegel, 2008). According to this perspective, leaders should only select those social issues that lie within their realm of influence and that their companies can in turn tackle, effectively creating an alignment of interest and long-term competitive advantage (Porter and Kramer, 2006).

The converging views perspective illustrated earlier is consistent with the notion of Creating Shared Value (CSV), introduced and advanced by Porter and Kramer (2006, 2011). CSV has gained momentum in recent years, representing a new leadership philosophy that consists of identifying "policies and operating practices that enhance the competitiveness of a company while simultaneously advancing the economic and social conditions in the communities in which the company operates" (Porter & Kramer, 2011). In a nutshell, CSV is a modern version of CSR that expands the connections between societal and economic spheres through tackling only social problems that intersect with the business. CSV challenges business leaders to focus on areas of intersection that reconcile economic and social progress. CSV is thus a new integrated conception of CSR, which invites managers to think beyond discretionary philanthropy and doing good, to avenues for joint company and community value creation which can be integral to the company's growth and competitiveness over time (Figure 3.2). By expanding the pool of economic and social value creation, CSV offers potential for innovative sustainable growth of companies in their particular environments; however, achieving shared value objectives requires leaders to nurture new skills and knowledge, such as developing a far deeper appreciation of societal needs, viewing the corporation as socially embedded, and actively uncovering avenues for shared value creation (Porter & Kramer, 2011).

Waddock and Bodwell (2002) proposed the Total Responsibility Management framework, which in turn channels attention to three important aspects of responsible management (Figure 3.3) including inspiration, integration, and innovation. Inspiration comprises vision setting, management commitment, and leadership tone, where senior managers need to prioritize responsibility both in discourse and in practice as part of the regular lexicon of the organization (Waddock & Bodwell, 2002). Integration deals with the incorporation of the values driving responsibility into business strategy, employee relationships, and operating practices and management systems. The innovation component is concerned with embracing a progressive upgrading orientation towards continuous innovation and improvement. Although the model was not tailored to address responsible leadership per se, it directs attention to the important role of leaders in articulating a clear

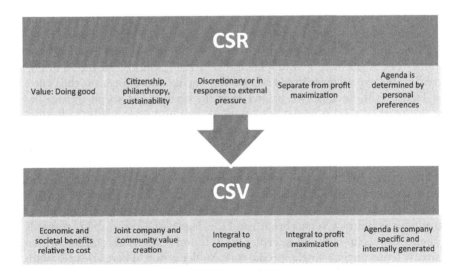

Figure 3.2 The Total Responsibility Management (TRM) Framework

(Source: Adapted from Waddock & Bodwell, 2002)

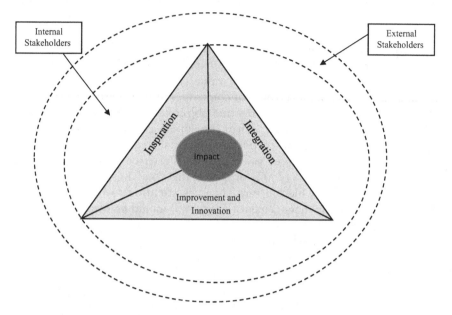

Figure 3.3 Total Responsibility Management
(Adapted from Waddock & Bodwell, 2002)

and compelling vision of responsibility and communicating this effectively to ensure that responsibility management is accorded the attention it deserves and that it is understood and embraced by employees and integrated into corporate systems and practices including long-term improvement, remediation, and assessment systems. The Total Responsibility Management framework suggested by Waddock and Bodwell (2002) is illustrated in Figure 3.3, but we adapt it here and add the impact component (at the centre of Figure 3.3), because we believe that the creation of social impact lies at the heart of total responsibility management and responsible leadership. Responsible leaders thus drive and catalyze total responsibility management in practice by according attention to the 4Is illustrated in Figure 3.3, including inspiration, integration, improvement and innovation, and impact.

Pless et al. (2012) also considered responsible leadership in what concerns the interactions with stakeholders (Figure 3.4). They categorized leaders based on the extent to which they differ in terms of breadth of stakeholder group focus (narrow versus broad) and the degree of accountability towards others (low versus high). Pless et al. (2012) found that business leaders with a narrow focus target a single specific stakeholder group, whereas leaders with a broader focus take into consideration the needs of multiple-stakeholder groups. As for the accountability dimension, Pless et al. (2012) characterize the low-accountability leaders as those with direct responsibility towards shareholders, whereas leaders with a high-accountability embrace a sense of

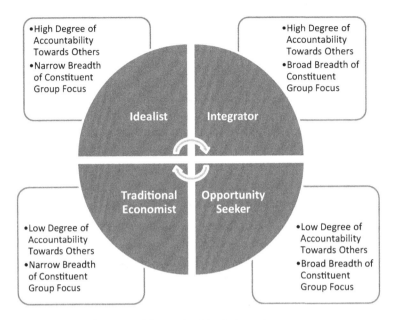

Figure 3.4 Matrix of Responsible Leadership Orientation
(Source: Pless et al., 2012)

accountability that goes well beyond the shareholders and profit maximization outcomes. By mapping the two aforementioned dimensions, they then introduce four orientations towards responsible leadership, including (1) the traditional economist (low accountability, narrow breadth of stakeholder focus), (2) the opportunity seeker (low accountability, broad breadth), (3) the integrator (high accountability, broad breadth), and (4) the idealist (high accountability, narrow breadth). Each of the former orientations represents a different type of leadership for CSR. Whereas the traditional economist corresponds to leaders with little commitment to CSR, the opportunity seeker will promote socially responsible initiatives only if there are instrumental motives for doing so. Idealists are typically equivalent to social entrepreneurs with a narrow focus on a limited circle of stakeholders, whereas integrators are equivalent to responsible leaders engaging with multiple constituent groups and delivering results along multiple bottom lines.

The literature on responsible leadership thus turns the spotlight to the role of leaders as important architects and stewards of their organizations, and how they can initiate change not as individual entrepreneurs but by mobilizing their firms' resources, utilizing and even going beyond various mechanisms of firm-level governance (Scherer et al., 2013). Responsible leaders make important decisions that have multiple spillover effects for internal and external stakeholders within existing governance channels (Filatotchev, 2012). As demonstrated through the various frameworks reviewed earlier, responsible leaders constitute a breed of leadership grounded in norms of inclusiveness and doing good, a heightened sense of accountability, serving as protagonists of increasingly converging or integrative views of business and society, focusing on reconciling economic and social interests, and making a difference beyond the boundaries of their corporations with positive spillovers for multiple stakeholders along multiple bottom lines. In the next section, we turn to concrete illustrations of responsible leadership from the MENA context by showcasing examples of leaders who have been successful champions of sustainability and shared value creation in the Arab context. We then derive from these cases lessons and implications that are likely to have wider relevance and applicability.

Champions of Responsible Leadership in the Arab Region

This section presents brief descriptions of the responsible leaders who have been selected for inclusion in this chapter. The studied champions consist of five leaders in the MENA region who have served as role models in promoting sustainable development in their organizations. We seek to address how the selected champions contribute to CSR strategy and sustainable development in their companies and communities. We start by presenting a brief description of each leader's profile (Table 3.1) and then dwell in more detail on their contributions to CSR and sustainability in the next section.

Table 3.1 Biographies of Responsible Leadership Champions

Fadi Ghandour	Fadi Ghandour is the founder and vice chairman of Aramex International, where he served as the company's CEO for 30 years. Aramex International is one of the leading global providers of comprehensive logistics and transportation solutions in the Middle East and South Asia, employing more than 13,900 people in over 354 locations across 60 countries. In 2005, Aramex went public on the Dubai Financial Market as Arab International Logistics. Mr Ghandour is also the co-founder and director of MENA Venture Investments, a seed-capital fund that provides capital, access to networks and technical expertise to start-up tech companies in the MENA region and beyond. He is a member of the board of the Abraaj Group and the chairman of Wamda, a platform of programs and networks that aims to accelerate entrepreneurship ecosystems across MENA. Ghandour is also a founding investor in Maktoob.com, an Arab Internet services company which was acquired by Yahoo; a member of the board of trustees of the American University of Beirut; a board member of Endeavor Global; and a board member of Oasis 500, a leading early stage and seed investment company.

(Continued)

Naseer Homoud	Dr Naseer Shahir Homoud is a well-known Arab leader who has made significant contributions in diverse fields ranging from dental health care to real estate, sports, and philanthropy. The Arabian Business Network ranked him 44 among the 500 most powerful Arabs in the world. Dr Naseer established the Consultant Dental Center in Doha, one of the best centres of dental health care and cosmetic dentistry in Qatar. Dr Naseer also entered the real estate sector by establishing the Wall Investment & Real Estate Development. The success of the Wall has not only contributed to the growth of Qatar's economy but also quickly transformed into a real estate empire covering many countries of the region. In 2008, Dr Naseer established Spanish International Business and Trading Center to promote bilateral trade between the Middle East region and Spain.
Talal Abu-Ghazaleh	Dr Talal Abu-Ghazaleh is the chairman and founder of Talal Abu-Ghazaleh Organization (TAG-Org), a leading global provider of professional and educational services in 80 offices worldwide including the Middle East, North Africa, Pakistan, India, Cyprus, and China. He is recognized as one of the most influential leaders in the Arab world, with seminal contributions in professional services, intellectual property, education, knowledge economy, information technology, and many other fields. Dr Talal Abu-Ghazaleh is currently chairman of the Arab Coalition of Services and a member of the World Trade Organization Panel on Defining the Future of Trade. He also chairs the Economic Policy Development Forum, the Arab States Research and Education Network, the Arab Organization for Quality Assurance in Education, the Arab Intellectual Property Mediation and Arbitration Society, the Licensing Executives Society-Arab Countries, the Arab Knowledge Management Society, and the Arab Society for Intellectual Property.
Rana Salhab	Rana Salhab is partner in charge of talent and communications at Deloitte in the Middle East region, which spans 16 countries and 25 offices. She holds an MBA degree from the American University of Beirut. Before joining Deloitte in 2003, she was the human resources director in the EMEIA (Europe, Middle East, India, and& Africa) and Growing Economies (Russia, Central and Eastern Europe, Middle East) regional management teams at Andersen. During her career, she provided human capital consulting services to multinational and leading companies in the region. She also lectured at the university level in educational management. At the beginning of her career, Salhab worked in the education and corporate sectors in Lebanon, Saudi Arabia, Egypt, and Switzerland.
Adnan Kassar	Adnan Kassar is the chairman and major shareholder of Fransabank SAL, chairman of Fransa Holding (Lebanon) SAL, and founder and co-owner of A. A. Kassar SAL, a leading trading company headquartered in Beirut. Kassar

(Continued)

Table 3.1 (Continued)

successfully expanded Fransabank Group into one of the largest and leading banks in Lebanon, and the most prominent one with regard to its international affiliations. Today, Fransabank Group has the largest branch network in Lebanon in addition to an international presence in 10 countries. Adnan Kassar was the first Arab personality to head, in 1999, the International Chamber of Commerce (ICC) based in Paris for a two-year term. He held the position of president of the Beirut Chamber of Commerce and Industry for over 30 years and successfully established the Federation of Chambers of Commerce, Industry and Agriculture in Lebanon. Kassar also served as minister of economy and trade of the Republic of Lebanon in 2004 and 2005, and minister of state from 2009 to 2011. Today, he is a major industrial and real estate investor and the chairman of the General Union of Arab Chambers of Commerce, Industry and Agriculture.

Responsible Leadership in Action in the Arab Region

Beyond the earlier brief introduction, in this section, we dwell on responsible leadership in practice as well as how these various leaders have exhibited and enacted responsible leadership using the weight of their respective organizations to mobilize and effect positive social change. Each of the leaders chosen represents an embodiment of different aspects of responsible leadership and combined serve to restore hope that responsible leadership can be an effective mechanism for making change happen, even in the most difficult contexts.

Fadi Ghandour

Fadi Ghandour is known for his passion for CSR and as a strong advocate of a more public-spirited and decisive presence for the Arab private sector in the sustainable development of the region. In addition to being a member of the Dean's Advisory Council of the Columbia University School of Social Work, Fadi serves as a regional board member of Injaz Al-Arab, a non-profit organization that strives to create viable work opportunities for young people in the Arab world. Ghandour also serves as a member of the board of Business for Social Responsibility and a vice chair of the board of trustees of the Jordan River Foundation. Under his management, Aramex adopted sustainability as a strategy where corporate activism is embedded in the business model. Actually, in 2006, Aramex was the first company in the region to report on its CSR and sustainability practices. The 2006 sustainability report in fact included a clear commitment from Ghandour, back then the CEO of Aramex, who stated,

> Sustainability will transform the way we think about our business. It will lead to new types of services, new levels of understanding, new

ways of collaboration, renewed respect for our place in the world, and a profound commitment to ecological preservation through sustainability innovation, all of which will benefit shareholders and stakeholders alike.

(Aramex Sustainability Report, 2006)

In his last year as the company's CEO, Ghandour reconfirmed his personal and professional commitment to sustainable development in the company's sustainability orientation.

We belong to the communities we serve and their interests are always a priority. We knew early on that we cannot prosper if our bottom line is divorced from our societies. This commitment to our stakeholders is reflected in everything we do: in the way we run the company, partner with suppliers, deliver for customers, collaborate with communities and work so hard to lighten our footprint on the environment.

(Aramex Sustainability Report, 2012)

Anchored in the vision and philosophy of its founder, Aramex continues to play a leading and active citizenship role in the development of the social environment in the various communities in which it operates. Aramex instituted a CSR program targeting diverse areas such as education and youth empowerment, entrepreneurship, community development, emergency relief, sports, and environment. Aramex also took many active steps and initiatives to preserve the natural environment. The company is becoming a leader in neutralizing carbon emissions through the use of hybrid vehicles. The sustainability report of 2013 stated that Aramex is

committed to finding measures to reduce our energy intensity and carbon footprint, from being one of the first companies in the region to measure our footprint, to joining the WEF's working group on the decarbonization of the logistics industry

(Aramex Sustainability Report, 2013)

Responsible leadership was also enacted through the active involvement of Aramex in various aspects of community development. One of the key illustrations was the incubation of Ruwwad in Jordan, a non-profit organization that helps disadvantaged communities overcome marginalization through youth activism, civic engagement, and education. Ghandour established this organization in 2005 by bringing together a group of social entrepreneurs with the aim of deploying entrepreneurship in the service of communities' needs. Today, Ruwwad for Development is a regional private sector–led community empowerment initiative that helps disadvantaged communities overcome marginalization through youth activism, civic engagement, and education, and it provides access to capital for microbusinesses. The organization expanded to reach Jordan, Egypt, Lebanon, and Palestine, and it operates through a strong network of partnerships with civil society and governmental agencies.

Today, having stepped down as CEO of Aramex, Ghandour continues to focus on other aspects of sustainability and social development through various new ventures and investments. Ghandour is currently serving as the executive chairman of Wamda, a platform of programs and networks that aims to accelerate entrepreneurship ecosystems across MENA. In this respect, Ghandour recently launched Corporate Entrepreneurship Responsibility, a collaborative movement under the umbrella of Wamda aiming to lobby, mobilize, and organize the private sector in the region to bolster the entrepreneurship ecosystem. Ghandour considered that "these ecosystems would be the bedrock of the sector's developmental strategies and the nexus around which new public-private partnerships would pivot" (Ghandour, 2013). To ensure a sustainable society moving forward, Ghandour called upon the participation of private wealth and corporations in enhancing start-up access to capital and expanding entrepreneurship networks. Ghandour also emphasized the role of CEOs in providing access to knowledge and mentorship to a new generation of entrepreneurs. Ghandour is also the co-founder and director of MENA Venture Investments, a seed-capital fund that provides capital, access to networks, and technical expertise to start-up tech companies in the MENA region and beyond. The venture works with entrepreneurs to help them grow their start-ups at early stages and offers assistance through a cross-border operational support network. Across these ventures, Ghandour is obsessively concerned with a priority social issue facing the Arab region—namely, job creation about which he recently reiterated,

> Job creation needs to be at the core of every stakeholder program, be it a policy, national strategy, private-sector initiative or social activity. It is time we pool our knowledge, resources, capital and networks to turn entrepreneurship into a development tool for our societies and economies.
>
> (Ghandour, 2014)

Naseer Homoud

Dr Naseer Shahir Homoud is a well-known Arab leader who has made significant contributions in diverse fields ranging from dental health care to real estate, sports, and philanthropy. He is mostly known for establishing the Wall Investment & Real Estate Development. Led by Dr Naseer Shahir Homoud as its CEO and chairman, the Wall became a successful example of reconciling business interests with a sense of responsibility and accountability vis-à-vis society. Homoud established his personal philosophy regarding helping society at the core of the Wall's culture. As a visionary of social responsibility, Homoud believes that charity must change and evolve to something more systematic and institutionalized to meet the country's changing requirements. The company's website clearly states, "The CSR wing at The Wall ensures that the long cherished dream of its founder is realized under any adverse circumstances" ("Our Achievements & CSR", n.d.). Accordingly, CSR is at the heart of the Wall's mission statement, where contributing to the well-being of the community is a core value. Strict adherence to social duties and respect to all community, environmental, and legal requirements form a crucial component of the inherent business philosophy under which the company operates.

Today, the Wall's sense of social responsibility is reflected in practices that support key communities in which the company operates such as organizations, industries, and society. The Wall utilizes its strength and competitive advantages for broader social goals including environmental responsibility, ethical behaviour, and heightened transparency and accountability. Such CSR initiatives cover different areas, including issues pertaining to hunger and malnutrition, HIV/AIDS, disaster response, education, and water. The company also adheres to international standards of governance and employs eco-friendly and safety policies to safeguard its employees and working environment. As a responsible corporate citizen, the Wall is one of the few companies in the construction industry that provides structured industrial training to students from different engineering and management institutes as a way of helping participants develop their professional skills and abilities.

In recognition of the effective corporate practices of his business empire, Homoud has been conferred the CEO Middle East Award 2012 for Corporate Social Responsibility. The prestigious award acknowledges outstanding success, ethical practices, and the vital contribution made by individuals and their companies to the intertwined vibrancy of business and society in the region. In this respect, Homoud commented,

> I do not view it as recognition of my personal accomplishments rather as an affirmation of the work which we are doing for ultimate benefit of mankind; this award is not simply about my work rather it is to be shared with everyone who strives for an egalitarian society.
>
> (Khan, 2012)

Homoud is also known for his involvement in various charitable work and philanthropic programs and activities. He served in several humanitarian organizations in different positions such as the external relations advisor of the Arab Non-Violence Society, honorary member of the Arab Youth Media Forum, and vice president of the World Health Fund. He also served for three years as the goodwill ambassador and regional director of the Intergovernmental Institution for the Use of Micro-Algae Against Malnutrition and the permanent observer to the United Nations Economic and Social Council, which works for eradication of malnutrition and hunger. Homoud founded the Ideon Charity Association, which provides both financial and medical aid to families in need. He has also contributed to replanting one of the most important historical forests in Jordan. In addition, he has supported many athletes in Jordan in addition to launching a campaign to aid the people of the Gaza Strip and victims of natural calamities in Japan, Haiti, and many regions of Africa. Homoud's other philanthropic activities include providing scholarships to students in need, free dental services to orphans under the Directorate of Education in the Irbid Governorate, distribution of food during the month of Ramadan, and arrangement of the Annual International Sport Camp in Doha and Amman for children.

Talal Abu-Ghazaleh

Abu-Ghazaleh has created a unique hybrid: a for-profit private firm, Talal Abu-Ghazaleh Organization (TAG-Org), with a mission statement that declares that it aims to contribute to economic, social, and cultural development worldwide. The company, which operates in 80 offices and with 180 representatives worldwide, implements CSR initiatives covering the fields of education and scientific research, community service, and awareness building and sensitization.

Abu-Ghazaleh is also a board member of the Global Social Responsibility Ambassador of CSR Regional Network, and he served on the board of the UN Global Compact and as chairman of the UN Global Alliance for ICT and Development. In this respect, Abu-Ghazaleh declared his organization to be "a proud member of the United Nations Global Compact, supporting the compact ten founding principles within the areas of human rights, labor, environment and anti-corruption" (Abu-Ghazaleh, 2015). The UN Global Compact members are expected to embrace, support, and enact within their sphere of influence a set of core values in the areas of human rights, labour, the environment and anti-corruption. Abu-Ghazaleh made sure that TAG-Org is fully committed to those principles by making them a core part of the organizational culture and day-to-day operations.

Exhibiting responsible leadership at its best, Abu-Ghazaleh took an additional step by establishing Talal Abu-Ghazaleh Foundation, a non-profit organization funded by TAG-Org for promoting sustainable development through social and economic initiatives with the aim of enhancing capabilities of individuals, groups, institutions, and societies worldwide. The foundation includes a large number of educational institutions, research centres, news agencies, professional associations, and Arab and international organizations. Envisioned by Mr Abu-Ghazaleh, one of the CSR initiatives supported by TAG Foundation is Talal Abu-Ghazaleh Knowledge Society, which aims to support Jordanian university students by providing them with a professional and friendly learning environment and enabling them to enter the job market and competing for the best opportunities available. Another member of the TAG Foundation is the Arab States Research and

Education Network, which was founded by Abu-Ghazaleh with an objective to connect existing Arab research and education networks with each other and to their counterparts across the globe and to act as a catalyst for e-infrastructures in Arab countries where they are not yet instituted. The foundation supported the Electronic Project Center (eNabler), which provides users around the world with all the resources and data to reinforce their progress towards achieving the Millennium Development Goals.

The role of Abu-Ghazaleh in promoting CSR goes beyond the frontiers of his organizations and foundation. Under the umbrella of the TAG Foundation, Talal Abu-Ghazaleh International Institute for Social Responsibility aims to introduce the concept of social responsibilities (SR) to companies by offering the required training, skills, and resources to ensure its application for corporate and societal sustainability. The services provided by the institute include platforms for sharing SR best practices, implementing SR development projects, and organizing workshops, conferences, and seminars on SR at the local, regional, and international levels. In 2014, Dr Talal Abu-Ghazaleh was named the "International Ambassador for Corporate Social Responsibility" in a ceremony held in Manama under the patronage of the Bahraini Ministry of Social Development in appreciation of his contributions in the societal, humanitarian, and charitable fields. The high-level ceremony also witnessed the launch of the Talal Abu-Ghazaleh Award for Social Initiatives, which was attended by officials, businessmen, and civil society and media leaders. The forum aimed to honour Abu-Ghazaleh's distinguished efforts in the field of social service, sustainable development, and corporate social responsibility.

Rana Salhab

As partner in charge of talent and communications at Deloitte, the world's largest professional services firm, Salhab has a wide range of Middle East regional responsibilities. Salhab's role includes overseeing corporate responsibility strategies and practices for Deloitte in the region. "Historically, the emphasis has been around community and 'giving,'. . . We now have a wide agenda for corporate responsibility with main focus areas that we view as integral to our business strategy" remarked Salhab (Kamel, 2011). Today, Deloitte's sustainability strategy focuses on key values aiming to utilize the firm's resources and capabilities to support ethical behaviour and operational sustainability, and advance culture and education. Additionally, Salhab had repeatedly explained that because Deloitte's core competency is intellectual capital, their corporate responsibility program is based on utilizing the skills and know-how of the firm's team. The company requires its employees to engage in pro bono and volunteer work to contribute to community development.

One of the key targets of Deloitte's corporate responsibility program is female empowerment. Actually, Salhab herself is a strong advocate of women's advancement. She is a member of the global Deloitte Women Advisory Council, and she created Deloitte Retention and Advancement of Women (DRAW)—a program that supports the professional development of women in the Middle East. DRAW has been successful in establishing grounds for mothers in business by allowing flexible working hours and other workplace accommodations. Salhab herself faced some difficulties in her career as a result of being a woman. One of Salhab's biggest achievements was becoming Deloitte's first female partner in the Middle East region.

Salhab is also a promoter of youth skills-building programs. Deloitte is working across many countries with Injaz al-Arab, a non-governmental organization (NGO) fostering entrepreneurship skills, by implementing "Be Entrepreneurial" curriculum. The aim of the program is to provide high school and university students with entrepreneurship skills. Salhab explained the choice of the NGO by stating, "This NGO is intriguing to us because it exists across the region . . . and we want to think regionally and not country by country" ("Investing in Talent: Rana Ghandour Salhab", 2013). Salhab is also a judge for the Injaz Al-Arab Young Entrepreneurship Competition.

Salhab is co-chair of the MENA Entrepreneurship Action Group of the World Economic Forum (WEF), a member of the board of directors of Injaz Lebanon, and a judge on the MIT Enterprise Forum Arab Business Plan Competition. Additionally, Salhab is on the advisory committee of Reach, a non-profit mentoring program based in the UAE devoted to helping young female professionals in the region to develop their skills and potential through professional mentoring and support. Salhab commented on her role in Reach by stating, "Being a member of the Reach Advisory Committee gave me a unique insight into the impact such a pioneering organization could make in the advancement of UAE women leaders" ("25 Professional Women Mentored by Reach in Year 1", 2015)

Adnan Kassar

Under the leadership of Mr Adnan Kassar, Fransabank Group adopted responsible business practices and social investments to create long-term value and sustainability for its shareholders and communities. The group's commitment to CSR is at the core of its organizational values and mission statement. Fransabank Group's CSR strategy has earned the group a leading role in the country's corporate landscape, where its CSR activities continue to support various sectors including the economy, environment, and social, cultural, and humanitarian events. Such achievements are the result of the energetic role played by Mr Kassar in the establishment and development of the group's CSR initiatives. As Kassar put it,

> I have always called on companies to act as responsible citizens and
> confirmed that this was a winning strategy for companies enabling them

to gain the loyalty of their customers, the trust of their partners and shareholders, and the devotion of their employees.

(Kassar, n.d.)

Fransabank Group's CSR strategy is based on three principles: to promote effective public-private partnerships, to promote economic development, and to enhance civil society's capacities and aspirations. Such commitment translates into a diverse range of social activities that advocate Fransabank's image as a sustainable contributor to the Lebanese economy. As stated in the group's CSR report, the ultimate goal behind this CSR strategy is

to remove the barriers between "us" as a business and "them" as society and demonstrating that we are all part of the greater picture and that through passion, effort and generosity, we can change the world around us for the better.

("Touching Lives, Inspiring Communities", 2012)

In addition, during his position as president of the International Chamber of Commerce, Kassar developed a strong relationship between the United Nations and his business, which translated in the pursuit of mutually supported goals and objectives. In particular, Kassar is a strong advocate of the UN Global Compact, which he signed in 1999 with then UN Secretary-General Kofi Annan. Within the context of the Global Compact, Fransabank Group established a commitment to promote the Compact's values in the areas of environment, human rights, labour, and anti-corruption, and set itself as a role model that other businesses may follow.

Kassar's social impact expanded to reach the Arab world, where he is recognized for his distinguished contributions to the promotion of inter-Arab trade and investment, as well as advancing the role of the private sector as an important partner in development in the Arab world. His efforts played an instrumental role in the creation of the Greater Arab Free Trade Area, which will serve as a preliminary step for the establishment of the Arab Common Market. On a more personal level, Kassar is an active admirer of culture and art in Lebanon and internationally. He is a member of the Distinguished Board of International Advisors of the White Nights Foundation of America, which aims to strengthen cultural, educational, and business aspects in an apolitical environment. Kassar's distinguished economic accomplishments on the international and Lebanese fronts earned him many official orders of merit, including the Lebanese National Cedar Order of Merit and the Order of National French Merit (officer). Kassar also received recognition for his CSR initiatives, including being named Business for Peace Honouree by the Business for Peace Foundation's independent award committee, an award from the executive director for the UN Global Compact, and the ICC Merchant of Peace Award.

Discussion and Implications

The five examples present prototypes of responsible leaders from the Arab context, representing both the embodiment and enactment of responsible leadership in practice. Whereas each is successful in pursuing his or her own passion in a particular line of business, all five leaders are united in their philosophy of activism and doing good, values of self-transcendence and working for the betterment of society, and for sparking the development of various platforms and organizations that attend to specific social challenges facing Arab society at this particular juncture.

Revisiting the findings in light of the frameworks presented at the beginning of this chapter, it is clear that all five responsibility champions recognize their broad responsibility to society beyond the immediate confines of their businesses and that they have been successful in mobilizing their businesses to better serve broad societal and developmental objectives. The findings suggest also that all five leaders represent 'doing good behaviour' dimensions of responsible leadership identified by Stahl and de Luque (2014). All five leaders have also developed business models and processes that use their companies' core competencies to address social needs. They appear to go beyond their economic and legal obligations to enhance social welfare. They seem also more concerned with the 'doing good' aspects of leadership than avoiding harm, possibly in light of the positive momentum provided through the former.

Returning to Miska et al.'s (2014) perspectives on responsible leadership, Homoud and Kassar mostly and, to some extent, Abu-Ghazaleh adhere to the converging theory portrayed by Waldman and Siegel (2008) and Porter and Kramer (2006), as they appear to tackle issues their companies can address efficiently while gaining a competitive advantage. These leaders seem to embrace the converging or shared value creation models of leadership discussed at the beginning of the chapter, looking actively to expand the pie and to reconcile economic and social value creation. On the other hand, Ghandour and Salhab seem to belong to the stakeholder view as presented by Maak and Pless (2006). These leaders are addressing sustainable social and environmental development by creating developmental programs targeting specific stakeholders (small-scale entrepreneurs in the case of Fadi Ghandour and female advancement in the case of Rana Salhab). Additionally, our content analysis revealed that, from the perspective of these leaders, responsible leadership does not necessarily involve a trade-off between financial performance and social objectives.

In terms of the Total Responsibility Management framework, it is clear that all five leaders resonate with passion, commitment, and a heightened sense of accountability towards society or specific constituent groups (e.g. youth, in the case of Fadi Ghandour, and women in the case of Rana Salhab). Their visions and values have permeated their businesses and successfully reflected in their firms' strategies, mission statements, and core values. All have gone a long way in terms of inspiration, institutionalization, and driving impact—beyond the boundaries of the business, with manifold positive spillovers on society. All five leaders also fit the description of integrators, with a sense of accountability towards multiple constituent groups and overriding concern to delivering results along multiple bottom lines. In specific, Ghandour, Salhab, and Abu-Ghazaleh created programs that tried to mobilize other companies and organizations towards social value creation beyond the boundaries of their businesses.

With respect to Pless et al.'s (2012) Matrix of Responsible Leadership Orientation, the selected CSR champions were found to follow the integrator dimension by having a high degree of accountability and a broad breadth of constituent group focus. Ghandour impacted a wide spectrum of stakeholders from across the region, working initially through his company, Aramex, and gradually expanding his positive spillovers through Wamda and Maktoob.com to reach a wider spectrum of young Arab entrepreneurs. Homoud pioneered the Wall and turned it into an exemplary socially oriented organization that touches the lives of Arab youth on various salient social issues across the region including hunger, water, and education. Abu-Ghazaleh has possibly wielded the widest sphere of influence through his TAG-Org and TAG Foundation, thus influencing generations of Arabs working primarily in the fields of research and education. With an acute sense of responsibility, Salhab has reached out and influenced a broad array of stakeholders working in the women empowerment space across the region. Kassar has also influenced a wide range of stakeholders through his company and the variety of CSR activities spearheaded pertaining to social, cultural, and humanitarian events.

The responsible leaders showcased in this chapter therefore reveal through concrete examples that there is room and scope for responsible leadership to forge ahead and make a concrete and positive difference in various communities across the globe. They are examples of individuals exerting leadership influence in their particular companies, communities, and societies, and mobilizing their political and social influence, their networks, and their social capital (e.g. trust, ownership, commitment) to make positive social change. All five leaders have transcended the boundaries of their organizations, and they have had multiple positive spillovers on various stakeholders within the Arab region by focusing on salient and important issues ranging from education to sanitation to youth and women empowerment and employment.

Stepping back and deriving implications for the ongoing wider discourse on responsible leadership, there is much to learn from what is presented in this chapter and also various questions and gaps that arise and remain to be addressed and filled. For example, we only began to touch the surface on how leadership behaviour, corporate governance mechanisms, and institutional and contextual forces can shape particular expressions of responsible leadership, but the interplay of these different factors needs to be explored more. As suggested by Waldman and Balvin (2014), specific contextual factors may increase the psychological strength and moral intensity of the situations facing managers, and they can thus serve to promote or hinder responsible behaviour. Certainly, the difficult regional environment post-Arab Spring and the accumulation of social challenges may have provided an additional impetus for the manifestations of responsible leadership documented in this chapter.

The other important and interesting question to consider is how do responsible leaders prioritize and balance different stakeholder issues and concerns, and how do they mobilize processes of influence to create an organizational climate of responsibility that transcends the influence and capability of specific individuals? Whereas there are clearly psychological processes and values at play in the selection of social issues that the different leaders have decided to pursue and give attention to (e.g. entrepreneurship and employment creation in the case of Ghandour; women empowerment and advancement in the case of Salhab; research and education in the case of Abu-Ghazaleh), they have all been successful in integrating those value preferences into the CSR processes and orientations of their respective companies. Hence they have mobilized managerial, intellectual, and financial capital that far exceeds the capability of any specific individuals. This is the art of responsible leadership and in fact speaks to the successful reconciliation of leadership and CSR as outlined at the outset of this chapter.

This chapter constitutes a first step in enhancing our understanding of how responsible leadership works in practice by taking examples of a few prominent leaders from the Arab region. Clearly, there is more work to do to understand the complex dynamics of responsible leadership and its antecedents and outcomes, and to bridge the gap between the microprocesses of leadership and macroprocesses of CSR. This is certainly a fertile area for future research that could attract interest from researchers from multidisciplinary fields, including sociology, psychology, corporate governance, and ethics and sustainability, among others. It could also shed light on the role of individual leaders in catalyzing meaningful change. We call for and encourage future research that can help shed light on responsible leadership and its dynamics in various contexts, given its uncontested influence in wielding positive change.

References

25 professional women mentored by reach in year 1. (April 5, 2015). Retrieved from: http://www.reachmentoring.org/news/25-professional-women-mentored-by-Reach-in-year-1

Abu-Ghazaleh, T. (2015). *Communication on progress*. Retrieved from: https://www.unglobalcompact.org/system/attachments/cop_2015/185741/original/cop2015.pdf?1441185901

Aguilera, R., Rupp, D. E., Williams, C. A., & Ganapathi, J. (2007). Putting the S back in corporate social responsibility: A multilevel theory of social change in organizations. *Academy of Management Review*, 32(3), 836–863.

Aramex Sustainability Report. (2006). Retrieved from: https://www.aramex.com/content/directory/Sustainability_Reports/Aramex%20Sustainability%20Report%202006%20(Web%20quality).pdf

Aramex Sustainability Report. (2012). Retrieved from: https://www.aramex.com/content/uploads/100/55/46280/Aramex%20Annual%20Report%202012_ENG_complete_final_LR.PDF

Aramex Sustainability Report. (2013). Retrieved from: https://www.aramex.com/news/item.aspx?id=8cb52aff-efc9–48a3–8afa-77a3e582b193

Crilly, D. (2011). Predicting stakeholder orientation in the multinational enterprise: A mid-range theory. *Journal of International Business Studies*, 42(5), 694–717.

Crilly, D., Schneider, S. C., & Zollo, M. (2008). Psychological antecedents to socially responsible behavior. *European Management Review*, 5(3), 175–190.

Filatotchev, I. (2012). Corporate governance issues in competitive strategy research. In G. Dagnino (Ed.), *Handbook of research on competitive strategy* (pp. 300–324). Cheltenham, UK: Edward Elgar.

Friedman, M. (2007). The social responsibility of business is to increase its profits. In W. C. Zimmerli, K. Richter, & M. Holzinger (Eds.), *Corporate ethics and corporate governance* (pp. 173–178). Berlin: Springer.

Ghandour, F. (2013). Corporate entrepreneurial responsibility (CER). Retrieved from: http://www.wamda.com/2013/01/corporate-entrepreneurship-responsibility-by-fadi-ghandour

Ghandour, F. (2014). Breaking barriers to scale for Arab entrepreneurs. *Al Arabiya News*. Retrieved from: http://english.alarabiya.net/en/views/business/2014/05/01/Breaking-barriers-to-scale-for-Arab-entrepreneurs.html

Investing In Talent: Rana Ghandour Salhab. (April 5, 2013). Retrieved from: http://csrmiddleeast.org/profiles/blogs/investing-in-talent-rana-ghandour-salhab

Jamali, D., & Lanteri, A. (2015). *Social entrepreneurship in the Middle East*. New York, NY: Palgrave McMillan.

Jamali, D., & Sidani, Y. (2012). *CSR in the Middle East: Fresh perspectives*. New York, NY: Palgrave McMillan.

Jawad, R. (2014). *Social protection in the Arab region: Emerging trends and recommendations for future social policy*. United Nations Development Programme, Regional Bureau for Arab States, Arab Human Development Report, Research Paper Series. Retrieved from: http://www.arab-hdr.org/publications/other/ahdrps/Final_Rana%20Jawad_Social%20Policies%20(ENG).pdf

Kakabadse, N., Rozuel, C., & Lee-Davis, L. (2005). Corporate social responsibility and stakeholder approach: A conceptual review. *International Journal of Business Governance and Ethics*, 1(4), 277–302.

Kamel, L. (June 23, 2011). *Alumna Rana Salhab promotes corporate responsibility at Deloitte*. Retrieved from: http://align.aub.edu.lb/2011/06/alumni-rana-ghandour-salhab-csr/

Kassar, A. (n.d.). *A socially committed group*. Retrieved from: https://www.fransabank.com/English/SociallyCommittedGroup/Pages/Corporate-Social-Responsibility-Strategy.aspx

Khan, F. (September 23, 2012). *Dr. Naseer Homoud conferred CEO Middle East award 2012*. Retrieved from: http://www.prnewswire.com/news-releases/dr-naseer-homoud-conferred-ceo-middle-east-award-2012-170869191.html

Komives, S. R., & Dugan, J. P. (2010). Contemporary leadership theories. In R. A. Couto (Ed.), *Political and civic leadership: A reference handbook* (Vol. 1, pp. 111–120). Los Angeles, CA: Sage.

Kramer, M. R., & Porter, M. (2011). Creating shared value. *Harvard Business Review, 89*(1/2), 62–77.

Maak, T., & Pless, N. M. (2006). Responsible leadership in a stakeholder society: A relational perspective. *Journal of Business Ethics, 66*(1), 99–115.

Miska, C., Hilbe, C., & Mayer, S. (2014). Reconciling different views on responsible leadership: A rationality-based approach. *Journal of Business Ethics, 125*(2), 349–360.

Miska, C., Stahl, G. K., & Fuchs, M. (2014). *Unethical managerial behavior: The moderating roles of moral intensity and situational strength.* Presented at the 74th Annual Meeting of the Academy of Management, August 1–5, Philadelphia.

Our Achievements & CSR. (n.d.). Retrieved from: http://www.thewallholding.com/service.php?id=53

Pless, N. M., Maak, T., & Waldman, D. A. (2012). Different approaches toward doing the right thing: Mapping the responsibility orientations of leaders. *Academy of Management Perspectives, 26*(4), 51–65.

Porter, M. E., & Kramer, M. R. (2006). Strategy & society: The link between competitive advantage and corporate social responsibility. *Harvard Business Review, 84*(12), 78–92.

Porter, M. E., & Kramer, M. R. (2011). Creating shared value. *Harvard Business Review, 89*(1/2), 62–77.

Scherer, A. G., Baumann-Pauly, D., & Schneider, A. (2013). Democratizing corporate governance: Compensating for the democratic deficit of corporate political activity and corporate citizenship. *Business and Society, 52*(3), 473–514.

Stahl, G. K., & de Luque, M. S. (2014). Antecedents of responsible leader behavior: A research synthesis, conceptual framework, and agenda for future research. *The Academy of Management Perspectives, 28*(3), 235–254.

Sully de Luque, M. F., Washburn, N. T., Waldman, D. A., & House, R. J. (2008). Unrequited profit: How stakeholder and economic values relate to subordinates' perceptions of leadership and firm performance. *Administrative Science Quarterly, 53*(4), 626–654.

Szekely, F., & Knirsch, M. (2005). Responsible leadership and corporate social responsibility: Metrics for sustainable performance. *European Management Journal, 23*(6), 628–647.

Touching Lives, Inspiring Communities. (2012). Retrieved from: file:///C:/Users/New%20Nadine/Downloads/Final%20CSR%20Book%20-%20April%202012.pdf

Voegtlin, C., Patzer, M., & Scherer, A. G. (2012). Responsible leadership in global business: A new approach to leadership and its multi-level outcomes. *Journal of Business Ethics, 105*(1), 1–16.

Waddock, S., & Bodwell, C. (2002). From TQM to TRM. *Journal of Corporate Citizenship*, (7), 113–126.

Waldman, D. A., & Balven, R. M. (2014). Responsible leadership: Theoretical issues and research directions. *The Academy of Management Perspectives, 28*(3), 224–234.

Waldman, D. A., & Galvin, B. M. (2008). Alternative perspectives of responsible leadership. *Organizational Dynamics, 37*(4), 327–341.

Waldman, D. A., & Siegel, D. (2008). Defining the socially responsible leader. *The Leadership Quarterly*, *19*(1), 117–131.

Wood, V. R., Chonko, L. B. & Hunt, S. D. (1986). Social responsibility and personal success: Are they incompatible? *Journal of Business Research*, *14*(3), 193–212.

The World Bank. (2011). *Data: Middle East & North Africa*. Retrieved from: http://data.worldbank.org/region/MNA

4 The Role of Leadership in Leading Organizations Towards Sustainability

An Organizational Learning Perspective

Minyu Wu and Angela Ma

For the past several decades, there has been increasing pressure from multiple stakeholders for business organizations to go above and beyond economic performance. Corporate sustainability, which integrates social, environmental, and economic dimensions as a whole, is not empty rhetoric; it is crucial to a firm's long-term success and survival. Although the concept of corporate sustainability evolves constantly, along with different stakeholder claims, it could be referred to as the notion of sustainability at the corporate level (Dentchev, 2009; Steurer, Langer, Konrad, & Martinuzzi, 2005). Indeed, business organizations are the most important actors in achieving the goal of sustainable development. It is because, on the one hand, business entities and their activities within the value chains related to the production-consumption system are arguably among the major factors that cause sustainability issues, whereas on the other, businesses may also be a main source of innovative activities, which are able to mitigate environmental pollution as well as improve the eco-efficiency of products and production processes. In addition, business organizations could play a role in shaping continuous fundamental structural changes in current socio-technical systems (Twomey & Gaziulusoy, 2014). Just as former UN secretary-general Kofi Annan (2002) put it,

> We now understand that both business and society stand to benefit from working together. And more and more we are realizing that it is only by mobilizing the corporate sector that we can make significant progress. The corporate sector has the finances, the technology and the management to make all this happen. The corporate sector need not wait for governments to take decisions for them to take initiatives.

Corporate sustainability requires not only a holistic approach for a firm to generate value for its critical stakeholders but also a learning process of continuously developing and maintaining relationships with both existing and new stakeholders (Wu, 2011; Post, Preston, & Sachs, 2002). This perspective also views corporate sustainability as a process of change in an organization fully supported by senior leaders. Given that those in positions of leadership sponsor change initiatives, the ways in which leadership is conducted is one of the most important factors that align and further integrate sustainability into the company's overall strategy (VOX Global et al., 2012; Waddock & Bodwell, 2007). Therefore, leadership is critical to help businesses become sustainable. For example, General Electric has been the leader in several business sectors since its CEO, Jeff Immelt, declared that the company would devote every effort towards sustainability (Nidumolu et al., 2009). Commitment to a sustainable future on the part of senior leaders calls for an exploration of the styles which might be most appropriate for achieving the necessary strategic change.

This chapter is organized as follows: we first describe the concept of corporate sustainability and its implications for strategic change. This is followed by an examination of the relationship between leadership and strategic change. A framework of organizational learning introduces the relationship between styles of leadership, and organizational learning is examined. Finally, there is a discussion and a conclusion is drawn.

Moving Towards Sustainability as a Strategic Change

The concept of corporate sustainability was derived from the notion of sustainable development that was defined as "development which meets the needs of the present without compromising the ability of future generations to meet their own needs" (WCED, 1987, p. 42). At the firm level, corporate sustainability was referred to as "meeting the needs of a firm's direct and indirect stakeholders (such as shareholders, employees, clients, pressure groups, and communities) without compromising its ability to meet the needs of future stakeholders as well" (Dyllick & Hockets, 2002, p. 131). In addition, Elkington (1999, p. 397) suggested that "sustainable development involves the simultaneous pursuit of economic prosperity, environmental quality, and social equity", and business organizations that promote corporate sustainability "need to perform not against a single, financial bottom line but against a triple bottom line". Both sustainable development and corporate sustainability are in line with the meaning of the green economy, which "results in improved human well-being and social equity, while significantly reducing environmental risks and ecological scarcities" (UNEP, 2010, p. 3). In other words, corporations need to adopt a new way of doing their business that ensures the long-term survival of human communities.

The journey of a company towards sustainability is a typical case of strategic change, which refers to a major strategic reorientation, including change in existing organizational goals and strategies, as well as structural and organizational changes that support the new strategic focus (Eccles, 1996; Worley, Cummings, & Mobley, 2000). Moving into a new era of doing business, making decisions, and solving problems in support of the principles of sustainability could be a set of complex undertakings, compared to the traditional commercial approach that was driven by the single objective of profit maximization. As a wide variety of stakeholders are involved, dealing with a sustainability issue requires a more systematic or holistic approach, in which multiple objectives could be addressed simultaneously (Theis & Tomkin, 2012). In this sense, business decisions recognize the necessity of considering different stakeholder demands.

A stream of research argues that pursuing corporate sustainability helps firms gain strategic advantage against their competitors. For example, Porter and van der Linde (1995) argued that stringent environmental regulations, if properly designed, would stimulate innovation activities in companies to advance sustainability. Empirical studies were conducted by other researchers and supported this argument (Greenstone, 2003; Taylor, Rubin, & Hounshell, 2005). In particular, Nidumolu, Prahalad, and Rangaswami (2009) pointed out that corporate sustainability is a key driver for innovation in companies. Nonetheless, corporations initiate a shift of their business practices from traditional styles to more sustainable modes that can be regarded as a response to the pressure of multiple stakeholders. Nidumolu et al. (2009) described this phenomenon as a five-stage journey towards corporate sustainability, which includes viewing compliance as an opportunity, making value chains sustainable, designing sustainable products and services, developing new business models, and creating next-practice platforms. They argued that firms need to develop key capabilities at each stage to deal with different challenges and opportunities they face, along with the journey moving toward sustainability.

In a similar vein, Gaziulusoy and Twomey (2014) used a three-wave typology to portray how business organizations respond to sustainability issues. In the first wave of response, business organizations tend to adopt risk management to minimize its compliance risk. At the same time, cost reduction or operational efficiency may be achieved while pursuing sustainability compliance. In the second wave of response, firms may go beyond compliance and risk management. They can gain competitive advantage in their current markets through improvement schemes of the operations such as eco-efficiency, compliance leadership, or eco-branding. In addition, business organizations may develop a unique value proposition that could create value for customers and for the society as a whole, while maintaining economic efficiency and minimizing environmental impacts. Firms may focus on the creation of new markets through developing and deploying new products and services or creating new business models. The third wave of business response to sustainability issues includes the corporations that go beyond self-interest. These corporations regard themselves as part of a greater ecosystem and acknowledge the limits of the resources in the world. In other words, corporate strategies are moved beyond an instrumental (win-win) approach, and business leaders of sustainable organizations are expected to develop innovations leading to the next phase of business practices.

To sum up, sustainability has been a driver for innovation and change in strategic orientations. If we regard corporate sustainability as a specific strategic change initiative, the next question would be how do business organizations make it happen? In the following section, we will discuss the role of leadership on this issue.

The Relationship Between Leadership and Strategic Changes

In this chapter, we are interested in how leadership can lead an organization moving towards sustainability. Therefore, we not only focus on strategic leadership, which concentrates on influences of the dominant coalition on the strategic process of the firm (Vera & Crossan, 2004), but also on the relationship between leaders and their followers. According to Vera and Crossan (2004), Bass's (1990) approach of transactional/transformational leadership is useful to illustrate how strategic change might occur. However, in our view, as multiple stakeholders are involved, we suggest that servant leadership (Greenleaf, 2002) is also an important leadership style, whereas we consider that strategic change may be initiated from the bottom up.

Bass (1990) described transformational leadership as the style of leadership that helps individuals transcend their self-interest for organizational benefits. Transformational leaders demonstrate idealized influence, which serves as a role model to the followers whose behaviours are consistent with the values the leader embraces; inspirational motivation, which involves articulating a clear and appealing vision of the organization to inspire the followers; intellectual stimulation, which enhances followers' creativity by re-examining assumptions about their work and challenging how it can be performed; and individual consideration, which respects followers and supports their individual feelings and needs (Bass, 1990).

On the other hand, transactional leadership is generally described as a kind of leadership "which is based on transactions between manager and employees (Bass, 1990, p. 20)". Transactional leaders also display four characteristics: contingent reward, which is based on contractual exchange of rewards for effort, rewards for good performance, or accomplishment recognition; management by exception (active), which monitors deviations from standards and takes appropriate actions; management by exception (passive), which takes an action only if there is something wrong; and laissez-faire, which tends to abdicate responsibilities and avoid making decisions (Bass, 1990). Some researchers suggested that the characteristics of both transformational and transactional leadership possibly coexist in the same individuals but to a different extent (e.g. Bass, 1998; Vera & Crossan, 2004).

Robert Greenleaf coined the term servant leadership, which portrays a leader who puts the concerns of followers first instead of the goals of the team or organization (Greenleaf, 2002). Servant leaders are concerned with others and demonstrate their influence on staff needs, job satisfaction, personal development, empowerment, and task performance. According to Johnson (2015), servant leadership exhibits a few attributes: stewardship, obligation, partnership, emotional healing, and elevating purpose. In other words, whereas traditional leadership generally involves the accumulation and exercise of power by one at the "top of the pyramid", a servant-leader focuses primarily on the growth and well-being of people and the communities to which they belong.

Successful sustainability initiatives within an organization are usually determined by a shared commitment of each member involved. A significant challenge that most business organizations may face is how to integrate employees in their sustainability initiatives effectively. As a strategic change, the goal of corporate sustainability requires leadership that mobilizes people towards a new vision. Interestingly, some large corporations have recently introduced corporate sustainability positions, such as 'chief sustainability officers', into their senior management teams (Strand, 2014). Although the success or failure of such initiatives still needs further investigation, the position implies that the strategic leadership of corporate sustainability is significantly important. Benn, Dunphy, and Griffiths (2004) posited that firms might demonstrate two different types of change for sustainability: transformational and incremental change. For some business organizations, moving towards sustainability needs to redefine their core business scopes or key relations with their multiple stakeholders. On the other hand, some organizations only rely on the accumulation of small changes over time, which may result in a large change afterwards. Benn et al. (2004) argued that to become a sustaining organization involves both internal and external stakeholders and requires competent change agents to promote and manage organizational changes towards sustainability objectives. They also maintained that leadership plays an important role in fostering such changes and further suggested that different styles of leadership are needed to deal with the complexity of the situations as they arise. Hence different styles of leadership may have significant implications for strategic change.

A few writers have linked corporate strategy to organizational learning. For instance, Mintzberg (1978) argued that learning plays an important role in the strategic planning process, and strategies comprise both deliberate efforts and emergent involvement. According to Mintzberg (1978), all strategy making walks on two feet, one deliberate, the other emergent; he further asserted that purely deliberate strategy making may miss learning, and purely emergent strategy making pays little attention to control. Pushed to the limit, neither approach makes much sense. Hence a strategy must be coupled with both learning and control. In a similar vein, Ingley and Wu (2007) recognized the strategy process as twofold. Initially, the strategy is the result of a stream of decisions and actions influenced by cognitive, political, organizational, and emergent factors. At the same time, a corresponding learning process occurs. When environmental change takes place, both strategic decision-making and organizational learning processes will proceed simultaneously. Following this theme, we argue that the concept of organizational learning can enhance our understanding of strategic change.

A Missing Link in Strategic Change and Leadership: Organizational Learning

There is a wide range of definitions of organizational learning in the literature. Chiva and Alegre (2005) indicated two main perspectives: one is the cognitive possession and the other is the social process. The cognitive-possession perspective of organizational learning includes two groups with distinctive perspectives (Cook & Yanow, 1996). One conceived of organizations as individuals, possessing similar capabilities to learn; the other suggested that it is the individual who learns in an organizational context, thus constructing 'organizational learning'. By contrast, the social-process approach emphasized that organizational learning is a social process of organizational members, based on their participation in a (community of) practice (Gherardi, 1999; Lave & Wenger, 1991). In order to demonstrate the impacts from leadership on organizational learning, and thereby its further influence on strategic change, we take a view which is in line with the social-process approach. In particular, Crossan, Lane, and White's (1999) 4I learning framework, which is one of the most cited among the literature, provides insights to our understanding of the link between leadership, organizational learning, and strategic change (Crossan & Bedrow, 2003; Vera & Crossan, 2004).

The 4I Learning Framework

The 4I learning framework involves four psychological and social processes: intuiting, interpreting, integrating, and institutionalizing (Crossan et al., 1999). It acknowledges the interactions between cognitions and actions at three levels within an organization: intuiting and interpreting at the individual level, interpreting and integrating at the group level, and institutionalizing at the organization level. Crossan et al. (1999) defined the four processes of organizational learning as follows: first, intuiting is the knowing of a truth or fact by personal stream experience; second, interpreting is the process by which individuals clarify a new insight or idea in order to ensure understanding by others; third, integrating refers to the process that individuals develop and share their comprehension, and make mutual adjustments as a result of coordination; lastly, institutionalizing refers to the process that behavioural patterns and routinized actions occur within the organization by way of learning. As a result, policies, strategies, and procedures are formalized by the organization based on the learning that has been achieved at the individual and group levels.

Crossan et al. (1999) highlighted two notions of organizational learning. One refers to *learning flows* and the other refers to *learning stocks*. In addition, Crossan et al. (1999) indicated two distinctive types of learning flows: feedforward and feedback learning flows. Feedforward learning flows signify knowledge creation where cognitions and actions change across levels from the individual to the group and then to the organization—from intuiting to interpreting and, in turn, from integrating to institutionalizing. Feedback learning flows indicate existing knowledge where cognitions and actions transfer across levels from the organization to the group and then to the individual—from institutionalizing to integrating and, subsequently, from interpreting to intuiting. Crossan et al. (1999) further argued that the interplays of the two types of learning flows in an organization may create a tension between them, similarly corresponding to the tension between exploration and exploitation (March, 1991).

Crossan et al. (1999) suggested that learning stocks exist at each organizational level as mentioned earlier; they serve as the inputs to one learning flow and the outcomes of it at another level. At an individual level, learning stocks refer to "individual competence, capability and motivation to undertake the required tasks"; at a group level learning stocks refer to "group dynamics and the development of shared understanding"; at an organization level learning stocks refer to "alignment between the non-human storehouses of learning including systems, structure, strategy, procedure, given the competitive environment" (Bontis, Crossan, & Hulland, 2002, pp. 443–444). A similar concept to describe learning stocks is 'dominant logic' suggested by Prahalad and Bettis (1986). They defined dominant logic as a set of beliefs, norms, and assumptions shared by the senior management team and used for strategic decision making. The notion of learning stocks is also similar to the term 'strategic cognitive structures', which was coined by Porac and Thomas (2002), referring to top management's assumptions and beliefs about the environment, strategy, and stage of organization. According to Porac and Thomas (2002), the strategic cognitive structures could be analyzed at four levels: individual, group, organization, and industry. An organization's dominant logics or strategic cognitive structures have significant influences on the strategy process, such as identifying and defining key problems, providing and evaluating strategic alternatives, and making strategic decisions. In addition, according to Bettis and Prahalad (1995), dominant logic can be viewed as 'organizational intelligence', which determines an organization's ability to learn. To sum up, learning stocks play a role as the mental model of an organization that has strong influences on its strategic decision making. It selects and interprets the information that is in conformity with its underlying assumptions and values. It also represents an organization's capacity to learn, which is accumulated by the aforementioned types of learning flows.

The Relationship Between Organizational Learning and Strategic Change

We move on to the discussion on the relationship between organizational learning and strategic change. Organizational learning has also been used to describe the process of strategic change, whereas the path of strategy may be different for each case. In the field of sustainable development, Pahl-Wostl (2009) developed a multi-loop learning framework to analyze how learning processes at different levels influence the adaptive capacity of resource governance and management systems. The multi-loop learning framework includes three levels of learning: single-loop, double-loop, and triple-loop learning.

Single-loop learning means members of an organization adapt to the environment within fixed goals, norms, and assumptions (Argyris & Schön, 1978). Hence single-loop learning corresponds to 'evolution' or 'convergent change'. Dierkes, Marz, and Teele (2003) indicated that single-loop learning occurs when a strategic event comes into being and the organizational vision remains the same. Because a company's vision stands for the domain of business and the future development, it is similar to "a company's theory of the business". It not only shapes strategic behaviour but also dominates the contents of its strategic decision making and determines the objectives of the organization (Drucker, 1994). We may hold that single-loop learning or convergent change suits organizations only in a relatively stable environment.

By contrast, a double-loop learning approach is needed for firms in more turbulent surroundings. Double-loop learning takes place when underlying norms or assumptions change and result in transformation or reorientation (Argyris & Schön, 1978). In other words, double-loop learning concurs with 'revolution' or 'frame-breaking change'. Burgelman and Grove (1996) suggested that organizational renewal requires that top managers conduct strategic recognition and articulate a new vision. This means that leaders need to develop a cognitive map regarding the future of the industry and the right position of that company while they are confronted with discontinuous change. As a vision is an influential guiding philosophy, to challenge a firm's underlying belief systems means to challenge its vision and interrelated mission simultaneously. Initiating double-loop learning requires challenging and altering the existing belief systems of the organization. Achieving this goal requires abandoning some, if not all, of what has been learned by the organization. "Unlearning" becomes a necessary activity at this stage. According to Hedberg (1981), unlearning refers to "a process through which learners discard knowledge" and "makes way for new responses and mental maps" (p. 18). Unlearning is required of managers to remove the existing operations that have been successful in the past (McGill & Slocum, 1993) and to catch-up with a new strategic focus through relearning within the organization (Johnson, 1990).

Many researchers treat organizational learning as a two-level approach: such as single-loop and double-loop learning (Argyris & Schön, 1978), first order and second order (Arthur & Aiman-Smith, 2001), and exploitation and exploration (Levinthal & March, 1993). However, recent scholarship has suggested incorporating an additional type called 'triple-loop' learning (e.g. Pahl-Wostl, 2009; Tosey, Visser, & Saunders, 2012) to give insight into the levels of organizational learning. According to Eilertsen and London

(2005), triple-loop learning encompasses and transcends both single- and double-loop learning. They further argued that triple-loop learning also refers to the capability of an organization that can effectively perform single- and double-loop learning. Hence it may not only challenge existing goals, norms, beliefs, and assumptions of an organization but also question its current learning system. In other words, it is about the organization and its members learning how to learn by utilizing shared knowledge and contributing to collective knowledge generation. Pahl-Wostl (2009) argued that triple-loop learning concerns the changes in the structural context and factors that determine organizational beliefs and assumptions, which are related to regulatory frameworks, practices in risk management, and dominant value structure; in terms of strategic renewal, triple-loop learning is a concept of transformational change.

Because corporate sustainability is a complex issue, it is useful to use the multi-loop learning framework to describe strategic change towards sustainability. As we mentioned earlier, strategic changes in different situations may require distinctive styles of leadership. We are interested in how distinctive styles of leadership would influence organizational learning and thereby impact strategic change towards corporate sustainability.

Styles of Leadership, Organizational Learning, and Strategic Change

In this section, we will discuss the relationship between styles of leadership and organizational learning—how leadership affects different organizational learning flows and stocks. In an organizational context, learning emerges while individuals interact with other individuals, groups, functions, rules, policies. However, there are two distinctive views among scholars: the top-down and bottom-up approaches. Some researchers viewed organizational learning as a traditional top-down process, which was initiated and controlled by senior leaders (see Van de Ven & Poole, 1995). According to Mulholland, Zdrahal, and Domingue (2005), the top-down approach is strategically driven and motivated by critical factors such as technological change, market turbulence, mergers and acquisitions, and emerging issues proposed by top management. The introduction of new programs generally initiates this type of learning, including a training agenda, recruitment policy, and knowledge management strategies. On the other hand, some commentators maintained that although leaders play an important role in guiding or supporting organizational members in their learning, their function is to provide an appropriate and favourable environment to facilitate learning, not to determine what should be learned (see Marion & Uhl-Bien, 2001). Mulholland et al. (2005) describe this type of organizational learning as local and continuous learning, which occurs frequently with the front-line employees through communication and interaction with colleagues. Hannah and Lester (2009) argued that for firms in a complex environment involving both dynamic and discontinuous forces, neither the top-down nor the bottom-up approach will be adequate. Therefore, effective organizational learning requires leaders to adopt a comprehensive strategy that develops the capacity to encourage and empower employees across different levels to learn. Hence to encourage learning may require leaders to adopt different styles of leadership. We will focus on the three styles of leadership that have been discussed: transformational, transactional, and servant leadership.

Leadership and Learning Flows—Feedforward Learning

Based on the 4I learning framework (Crossan et al., 1999), feedforward flows refer to the learning process initiated from organizational members' intuitive cultivation, knowledge, and experiences. At the beginning, individual perceptions or mental models screen and interpret new insights and then shape them through group communications; through collective action, new insights are integrated as shared beliefs or understanding among organizational members; over time, through integrative collective actions, new insights are institutionalized as routines, rules, and procedures—being a part of formal organizational systems.

As for transformational leaders, their agenda usually involves developing a team's vision of change and institutionalizing such change; they also need to foster their colleagues to accept the new vision as a group goal (Podsakoff, MacKenzie, Moorman, & Fetter, 1990; Tichy & Ulrich, 1984). Transformational leaders often inspire and facilitate individual and group learning by way of the following approaches: challenging the assumptions through encouraging them to think creatively and innovatively, taking more risks through respecting followers and supporting their individual feelings and needs, and sharing information across the organization through fostering individual and group participation (Podsakoff et al., 1990; Vera & Crossan, 2004). In addition, transformational leaders also help learning flow from the group to the institutional level. Tichy and Devanna (1986) argued that institutionalizing change is one of the important tasks of transformational leaders who motivate organizational members to contribute their ideas to fit into the new vision. As organizational members have been involved in the strategic planning process, through effective communication and group interaction, they are encouraged to participate in the new strategy formulation, including changes in values, rules, procedures, and policies. Before new ideas are institutionalized, they must be evaluated, tested, and accepted by the organization members, including the organizational procedure for approval. Leaders have the legitimate power and responsibility to facilitate organizational learning at the integrating stage by focusing on new ideas within the domains of planned vision and mission. According to Crossan et al. (1999), at the institutionalizing stage, organizational learning will result in creating new institutional factors (including the organizational system, structure, procedures, and routines). Transformational leaders reinforce the new built institutional factors by using high-performance expectations and behaving as role models for their followers (Podsakoff et al., 1990). Over time, new ideas will be institutionalized in the reformed strategies, routines, and day-to-day practices.

In the case of transactional leaders, they tend to emphasize control, standardization, formalization, and efficiency (Bass, 1985). For example, they usually motivate followers by payoffs as well as compliance and performance. In addition, they use positive and negative contingent rewards to reinforce followers' behaviours so that they are in line with organizational visions. Moreover, according to Bass (1985, 1990), transactional leaders who adopt 'management by exception' would actively monitor their followers' performance and take corrective actions if any case is not in conformity with organizational goals, rules, or procedures. Therefore, transactional leadership generally plays a limited role in facilitating feedforward learning at the levels of intuiting and interpreting. On the other hand, transactional leadership plays an important role in the institutionalization of learning in order to share the new vision, actions, and practices so that changes are institutionalized. Thus, effective leaders commonly fulfill their followers' expectations (as a kind of 'exchange').

Vera and Crossan (2004) suggested that there are conditions under which top management's transformational and transactional leadership behaviours support the feedforward flow of learning. Although transactional and transformational leadership styles appear to be on the two opposite ends of the spectrum, they are only best suited for the top-down nature of organizational learning. In other words, both styles of leaders focus on how to direct followers towards the planned vision, regardless of old or new ones. We argue that both styles of leadership do not fully cover the bottom-up nature of organizational learning, which is initiated by lower-level employees. In this regard, servant leadership is the appropriate style of leadership for the bottom-up learning approach. According to Johnson (2015), servant leaders view followers as partners and empower them by sharing information and powers; this would certainly encourage organizational learning, which occurs from a bottom-up approach, in terms of intuiting and interpreting at the individual and group levels of the 4I framework (Crossan et al., 1999). In addition, through collaboration and persuasion, servant leaders act as the agents of followers and achieve the goals of the common good; this will facilitate organizational learning in the stages of integrating and institutionalizing. Thus servant leadership facilitates feedforward learning flows.

Leadership and Learning Flows—Feedback Learning

Feedback learning flows refer to how institutional factors, such as organizational systems, structures, routines, and cultures, affect individuals and groups. The leadership refreshes and reinforces routines and policies to ensure that members behave and perform in a manner consistent with the organizational vision and values. Once new ideas are institutionalized, feedback learning flows help them last for a certain period of time (Crossan et al., 1999). Feedback learning flows commonly start from the organizational level through to the group and then to individuals, with processes from institutionalizing to integrating and, then, from interpreting and intuiting. In the institutionalizing process, institutional factors, such as routines, serve the function as gatekeepers to direct and shape how organizational members make decisions and take actions within an organization. Feedback learning reinforces through influencing organizational members' cognitions and behaviours as individuals and groups continue to make sense of institutional factors, such as routines (Vera & Crossan, 2004).

Transformational leadership has a positive impact on feedback learning in a context of change, as it is the style that is suitable to promote a new vision for strategic change (Tichy & Ulrich, 1984). Transformational leaders support feedback learning by not only identifying and articulating a vision in the first instance but also by fostering the acceptance of group goals after the new vision is introduced. They are able to cultivate a sense of group coherence and team spirit through effective communication and individualized support to inspire staff to make a commitment to the firm's new vision and to work together to achieve new shared goals (Podsakoff et al., 1990). During the process of developing new routines, through fostering the development of followers' needs and using high-performance expectations, transformational leaders motivate staff to overcome resistance to change. They also help staff perform the new institutionalized learning and establish new routines to replace old ones (Vera & Crossan, 2004).

Transactional leadership facilitates feedback learning by refreshing and refining current learning, which is usually characterized as incremental changes in institutionalized learning. Transactional leaders influence feedback learning through their control role by focusing on current values and vision, as well as enhancing efficiency in existing routines and practices (Vera & Crossan, 2004). As an organization's control system is normally embedded in its institutional factors (including culture, structure, strategy, procedures, and routines), transactional leaders play the role of gatekeeper to ensure standardization, formalization, and efficiency (Bass, 1998). Hence transactional leadership is best suited for feedback learning that reinforces existing institutional factors. As mentioned earlier, transactional leaders focus on compliance and performance, as well as 'management by exception'; they monitor and control organizational members' behaviors and actions, and ensure that organizational members are in line with the institutional requirements and expectations. Through training programs and formal systems, transactional leaders encourage the flow of learning from the organizational level to individual and group levels by using 'carrots and stick' that link personal interest to organizational goals (Vera & Crossan, 2004).

As for the bottom-up learning approach, if servant leaders support feed-forward learning flows from the individual to the group and then from the group to the organizational level, it plays an equally important role that facilitates the feedback learning flows from the institution to the group and the individual. According to Johnson (2015), servant leaders make meaning of followers' work and their lives by emphasizing the visions, missions, and ideas of the institutions, which are linked to the followers' growth and well-being.

This would certainly support organizational learning in terms of institutionalizing and integrating at the group and individual levels of the 4I framework (Crossan et al., 1999), as the organizational members are more willing to accept and learn institutional factors. Moreover, servant leaders take the responsibilities for their followers and institutions seriously. In addition, together with emotional healing and active participation (Johnson, 2015), servant leadership helps organizational members take ownership of forming and accepting institutional factors at the group and individual levels as well. Thus servant leadership facilitates feedback learning flows, which occur from a bottom-up approach.

Leadership and Learning Stocks

We move on to consider how different styles of leadership affect learning stocks. According to Crossan et al. (1999), learning stocks refer to the outcomes of learning flows at each level of the organization (individual, group, and organizational). As discussed earlier, learning stocks represent an organization's capacity to learn, which is accumulated by feedforward and feedback learning flows. How the features of transformational leadership affect learning stocks can be described by four typical behaviors of transformational leaders (Vera & Crossan, 2004). First, they are role models for followers and motivate individuals and groups to learn. Second, they encourage innovation and creativity, thus supporting followers in challenging the underlying assumption and belief systems of the organization. Third, they motivate individuals and groups by providing meaning and challenges at work. Fourth, they offer followers individual support, such as mentoring and coaching; this could help followers in personal development and inspire them to take more risks. All these behaviors show that transformational leaders support organizational members in questioning the existing belief systems and exploring new ones. This is a typical situation of double-loop learning and will result in significant change in organizational learning stocks—strategic cognitive structures (Dierkes et al., 2003).

On the other hand, transactional leaders focus on standardization, formalization, and efficiency (Bass, 1985). They required organizational members to refine, modify, or improve their performance within the existing belief systems. As transactional leaders tend to emphasize compliance and efficiency that minimize risks or waste, they monitor and control organizational members' behaviors and actions to make sure that there will be no deviations from the current practices, norms, values, and visions of the organization. In other words, transactional leadership supports and reinforces the current belief systems. This is a typical situation of single-loop learning, and it will result in only minor or incremental change in organizational learning stocks. Therefore, the belief systems of the top managers, the decision rules, leadership strategy, and organizational structure, will not differ significantly under the same organizational vision (Dierkes et al., 2003).

As mentioned earlier, servant leadership is best suited for the bottom-up learning approach. Servant leaders share information and power with the followers and help them develop themselves and perform at their best (Johnson, 2015). In this way, servant leadership supports organizational members in developing their capacity to learn. In addition, servant leaders motivate followers by supporting their need for self-actualization (Smith, Montagno, & Kuzmenko, 2004). As servant leadership emphasizes personal development and empowerment of organizational members, this provides important implications for organizational learning in terms of learning stocks. Continuous personal development would bring changes to the mental models of organizational members. For servant leadership, Greenleaf (1998) suggested, "The leader knows some things and foresees some things which those one is presuming to lead do not know or foresee as clearly" (p.124). Working together with other organizational members, servant leaders will co-create a shared vision, encourage sharing knowledge with each other, and foster a collaborative learning culture. Furthermore, we argue that servant leadership supports triple-loop learning, which involves a process of transformation that always generates a shift in context or perspectives (Medemaa, Walsb, & Adamowski, 2014). Triple loop learning is about learning how to learn and reviewing the norms, values, and protocols that shape organizational members' learning and decision-making processes (Pahl-Wostl, 2009). Senge (1990) posited that in a learning organization, leaders are designers, teachers, and stewards. Their roles are significantly different from that of a charismatic leader.

From the earlier discussion, we can argue that there is no one best style of leadership and different styles of leadership do have impacts on organizational effectiveness, depending on different contexts (Avery, 2004; Yukl, 1999). In some situations, transactional leadership may be a good facilitator of effective learning; in some other situations, transformational leadership may be more desirable. There are still more situations in which servant leadership is more appropriate. In addition, Tushman and O'Reilly (1996) argued that to be successful in the long run, managers must be able to carry out both incremental and revolutionary change. In other words, they need to pursue different approaches simultaneously, such as feedforward and feedback learning, exploration and exploitation, and flexibility and control. Tushman and O'Reilly (1996)'s argument is in line with Rowe's (2001) argument that successful firms need strategic leaders who possess a combination of visionary leadership—future oriented and managerial leadership—short-term oriented. We conclude that it requires a mix of different styles of leadership to encourage organizational learning.

Discussion and Conclusion: Styles of Leadership and Strategic Change Towards Sustainability

We have identified three styles of leadership that are relevant to strategic change: transactional, transformational, and servant leadership. As for the relationships between organizational learning and strategic change, we have also summarized three types of organizational learning that may have different implications for strategic change: single-, double-, and triple-loop learning. If we view the journey of a corporation towards sustainability as a strategic change, an organizational learning perspective can describe it. In fact, Gaziulusoy and Twomey's (2014) three-wave typology of business response to sustainability issues could include Nidumolu et al.'s (2009) five-stage journey towards corporate sustainability. In addition, both of them cover all of the three levels of learning: single-loop, double-loop, and triple-loop learning.

According to Gaziulusoy and Twomey's (2014), in the first wave of response, business organizations tend to adopt risk management to minimize its compliance risk. This is in line with Nidumolu et al.'s (2009) stage 1, viewing compliance as opportunity, and stage 2, making value chains sustainable. In this phase, firms need to enhance their competence in company operations and the value chain; they enjoy cost reduction or operational efficiency while pursuing sustainability. In other words, they are trying to correct unacceptable outcomes or to make improvements (such as reduction of pollution and energy savings). This wave is obviously a kind of single-loop learning, which is performed without questioning or challenging underlying beliefs and assumptions. Transactional leadership is suitable in this stage. For example, DuPont appointed Linda Fisher as its first chief sustainability officer in 2004. Under her leadership, a sustainable growth review with each of DuPont's 13 business units has been conducted every year, including a comprehensive investigation of the business's environment, safety and health performance, product stewardship, product regulatory analysis, and a trends analysis, which identified the key sustainability challenges and issues the company is facing (VOX Global et al., 2012).

In the second wave of response, apart from striving for economic efficiency and minimizing environmental impacts, business organizations tend to develop a value proposition that creates value for customers as well as for the society as a whole. They could achieve this by the activities similar to those of Nidumolu et al.'s (2009) stage 3, designing sustainable products and services, and stage 4, developing new business models. In this phase, firms need to develop and deploy new products and services, as well as reformulate their marketing strategies, supply chains, or customer service operations in order to achieve corporate sustainability. At the same time, organizational members not only examine the deviations from the rules or norms and take corrective actions, if necessary, but also review whether the rules or norms should be altered. This wave is a kind of double-loop learning, as it needs to challenge the underlying beliefs and assumptions of doing things, as well as patterns of thinking. In this stage, transformational leadership is required to transform the firm by changing the values, mindsets, and behaviours of the members of the whole organization. For example, Muhtar Kent, the CEO of Coca-Cola, regarded himself as the chief sustainability officer of the company. Under his transformational leadership, the company developed a comprehensive sustainability initiative, 'Live Positively', which was further integrated into its overall strategy. It was also a part of the company's 2020 vision and had significant influence on the leadership's processes, thinking, and investments, including sustainable innovation, such as the PlantBottle, to lighten the footprint on the planet by developing partially bio-plastic bottles to replace the functions of traditional PET plastic bottles (Shapiro, 2010).

In the third wave of response, Gaziulusoy and Twomey (2014) suggested that business corporations will redefine the notion of the firm in the society and in the ecological system; in other words, as part of the whole society and its greater ecosystem, firms need to develop innovations that lead to new kinds of practices. This wave is similar to Nidumolu et al.'s (2009) stage 5: creating next-practice platforms. Business organizations need to know how non-renewable and renewable resources influence the industries and the ecosystem, and they need to integrate business models, technological changes, and relevant laws and regulations. Based on the sustainability perspective, the key issue in this stage is to question the dominant logic behind business today, including the purpose of the firm as well as its governance system. This wave is a kind of triple-loop learning. At this stage, stakeholder engagement would play an important role of organizational learning. It requires organizational members to interact actively with both internal stakeholders (other employees) and external stakeholders (e.g. policymakers, investors, and communities). As we argued, servant leadership would be more desirable in this stage. For example, Ray Anderson, the former CEO and founder of Interface, Inc., demonstrated his servant leadership through valuing natural resources as much as the products produced by the company, which accentuates the importance of stewardship and community development. Under his servant leadership, Interface introduced innovative ways of doing business through engaging internal and external stakeholders. Accordingly, Interface replaced many of its operation processes and procedures with more environmentally friendly approaches, and the company was run both profitably and sustainably (Kincaid, 2012). As shown in Table 4.1, based on the earlier discussion, we summarize the relationships between phases of strategic changes, types of learning, and different styles of leadership.

Table 4.1 A Development Model of Corporate Sustainability—Relationships Between Leadership Styles, Organizational Learning, and Strategic Changes

Phase	Strategic Changes Towards Sustainability	Types of Learning	Styles of Leadership
1	To adopt risk management to minimize its compliance risk and enhance cost reduction or operational efficiency	Single-loop learning	Transactional leadership
2	To address sustainability issues as a strategic requirement/opportunity and to develop a value proposition that creates value for customers as well as for the society as a whole	Double-loop learning	Transformational leadership
3	To redefine the notion of the firm as an integral element of the whole social society and its ecological system	Triple-loop learning	Servant leadership

This table shows a development model of corporate sustainability in terms of three phases of strategic change. We argue that the journey of a company towards sustainability involves the multi-loop learning process, and in each phase, there is a need of an appropriate leadership style to fit the specific situation. In the first phase, transactional leadership is desirable, as it can well facilitate single-loop learning. In the second phase, transformational leaders are the most effective, as they are able to initiate double-loop learning. In the third phase, servant leadership is the best, as it plays an important role in fostering triple-loop learning. Because there is no guarantee that a corporation will always proceed clearly from one stage to the next, it is desirable to adopt a mix of leadership styles to encourage organizational learning.

References

Annan, K. (August 31, 2002). *World summit on sustainable development—Secretary-general remarks to Business Day event.* Retrieved from: http://www.un.org/events/wssd/summaries/envdevj15.htm

Argyris, C., & Schön, D. (1978). *Organizational learning: A theory of action perspective*, Reading, MA: Addison Wesley.

Arthur, J. & Aiman-Smith, L. (2001) Gainsharing and organizational learning: An analysis of employee suggestions over time. *Academy of Management Journal*, 44, 737–754.

Avery, G. C. (2004). *Understanding leadership: Paradigms and cases.* London: Sage.

Bass, B. M. (1985). *Leadership and performance beyond expectations.* New York: Free Press.

Bass, B. M. (1990). From transactional to transformational leadership: Learning to share the vision. *Organizational Dynamics*, *18*(3), 19–31.

Bass, B. M. (1998).*Transformational leadership: Industry, military, and educational impact*. Mahwah, NJ: Lawrence Erlbaum Associates.

Benn, S., Dunphy, D., & Griffiths, A. (2004). Integrating human and ecological factors: A systematic approach to corporate sustainability. In D. Marinova, D. Annandale, & J. Phillimore (Eds.), *The International Handbook on Environmental Technology Management* (pp. 222–240). Cheltenham, UK: Edward Elgar.

Bettis, R. A., & Prahalad, C. K. (1995). The dominant logic: Retrospective and extension. *Strategic Management Journal*, *16*, 5–14.

Bontis, N., Crossan, M. M., & Hulland, J. (2002). Managing an organizational learning system by aligning stocks and flows. *Journal of Management Studies*, *39*, 437–469.

Burgelman, R. A., & Grove, A. S. (1996). Strategic dissonance. *California Management Review*, *38*(2), 8–28.

Chiva, R., & Alegre, J. (2005). Organizational learning and organizational knowledge: Towards the integration of two approaches. *Management Learning*, *36*, 49–68.

Cook, S., & Yanow, D. (1996). Culture and organizational learning. In M. Cohen & L. Sproull (Eds.), *Organizational learning* (pp. 430–459). London: Sage.

Crossan, M. M., & Bedrow, I. (2003). Organizational learning and strategic renewal. *Strategic Management Journal*, *24*, 1087–1105.

Crossan, M. M., Lane, H. W., & White, R. E. (1999). An organizational learning framework: From intuition to institution. *Academy of Management Review*, *24*, 522–537.

Dentchev, N. A. (2009). To what extent is business and society literature idealistic? *Business & Society*, *48*, 10–38.

Dierkes, M., Marz, L., & Teele, C. (2003). Technological vision, technological development, and organizational learning. In M. Dierkes, A. B. Antal, J. Child, & I. Nonaka (Eds.), *Handbook of organizational learning and knowledge* (pp. 428–445). New York: Oxford University Press.

Drucker, P. F. (1994). The theory of the business. *Harvard Business Review*, *72*(5), 95–104.

Dyllick, T., & Hockerts, K. (2002). Beyond the business case for corporate sustainability. *Business Strategy and the Environment*, *11*, 130–141.

Eccles, T. (1996). *Succeeding with change*. London: McGraw-Hill.

Eilertsen, S., & London, K. (2005). Modes of organizational learning. *Kollner Group*. Retrieved from: http://www.kollnergroup.com/wp-content/uploads/2009/11/Modes-of-Organizational-Learning.pdf

Elkington, J. (1999). *Cannibals with forks: The triple bottom line of 21st century business*. Oxford: Capstone.

Gaziulusoy, A. I., & Twomey, P. (2014). *Emerging approaches in business model innovation relevant to sustainability and low-carbon transitions*. Working paper for the Visions & Pathways project. Retrieved from: http://www.visionsandpathways.com/wp-ontent/uploads/2014/10/Gaziulusoy_Twomey_NewBusinessModels.pdf

Gherardi, S. (1999). Learning as problem-driven or learning in the face of mystery? *Organization Studies*, *20*, 101–124.

Greenleaf, R. K. (1998). *The power of servant-leadership: Essays*. San Francisco, CA: Berrett-Koehler Publishers.

Greenleaf, R. K. (2002). *Servant leadership: A journey into the nature of legitimate power and greatness* (25th anniversary edn.). New York: Paulist Press.

Greenstone, M. (2003). Estimating regulation-induced substitution: The effect of the clean air act on water and ground pollution. *American Economic Review*, 93, 442–448.

Hannah, S. T., & Lester, P. B. (2009). A multilevel approach to building and leading learning organizations. *The Leadership Quarterly*, 20, 34–48.

Hedberg, B. (1981). How organizations learn and unlearn. In P. C. Nystrom, & W. H. Starbuck (Eds.), *Handbook of organizational design, volume 1* (pp. 3–27). New York: Oxford University Press.

Ingley, C., & Wu, M. (2007). The board and strategic change: A learning organisation perspective. *International Review of Business Research Papers*, 3, 122–143.

Johnson, C. E. (2015). *Meeting the ethical challenges of leadership: Casting light or shadow.* (5th edn.). London: Sage.

Johnson, G. (1990). Managing strategic change: The role of symbolic action. *British Journal of Management*, 1, 183–200.

Kincaid, M. (2012). Building corporate social responsibility through servant-leadership. *International Journal of Leadership Studies*, 7(2), 151–171.

Lave, J., & Wenger, E. (1991). *Situated learning: Legitimate peripheral participation.* New York: Cambridge University Press.

Levinthal, D., & March, J. (1993). The myopia of learning. *Strategic Management Journal*, 14, Special issue, 95–112.

March, J. (1991). Exploration and exploitation in organizational learning. *Organizational Science*, 2, 71–87.

Marion, R., & Uhl-Bien, M. (2001). Leadership in complex organizations. *The Leadership Quarterly*, 12, 381–556.

McGill, M. E., & Slocum, J. W. Jr. (1993). Unlearning the organization. *Organizational Dynamics*, 22(2), 67–79.

Medemaa, W., Walsb, A., & Adamowski, J. (2014). Multi-Loop social learning for sustainable land and water governance: Towards a research agenda on the potential of virtual learning platforms. *NJAS—Wageningen Journal of Life Sciences*, 69, 23–38.

Mintzberg, H. (1978). Pattern in strategy formation. *Management Science*, 24, 934–948.

Mulholland, P., Zdrahal, Z., & Domingue, J. (2005). Supporting continuous learning in a large organization: The role of group and organizational perspectives. *Applied Ergonomics*, 36, 127–134.

Nidumolu, R., Prahalad, C. K., & Rangaswami, M. R. (2009). Why sustainability is now the key driver of innovation. *Harvard Business Review*, 87(9), 56–64.

Pahl-Wostl, C. (2009). A conceptual framework for analyzing adaptive capacity and multi-level learning processes in resource governance regimes. *Global Environmental Change*, 19, 354–365.

Podsakoff, P. M., MacKenzie, S. B., Moorman, R. H., & Fetter, R. (1990). Transformational leader behaviors and their effects on followers' trust in leader, satisfaction, and organizational citizenship behaviors. *The Leadership Quarterly*, 1, 107–142.

Porac, J. F., & Thomas, H. (2002). Mapping cognition and strategy: Issues, trends and future directions. In A. Pettigrew, H. Thomas and R. Whittington (Eds.), *Handbook of strategy and management* (pp. 165–181). London: Sage.

Porter, M. E., & van der Linde, C. (1995). Green and competitive: Ending the stalemate. *Harvard Business Review, 73*(5), 120–113.

Post, J. E., Preston, L. E., & Sachs, S. (2002). *Redefining the corporation: Stakeholder management and organizational wealth*. Stanford, CA: Stanford Business Books.

Prahalad, C. K., & Bettis, R. A. (1986). The dominant logic: A new linkage between diversity and performance. *Strategic Management Journal, 7*, 485–501.

Rowe, G. (2001). Creating wealth in organizations: The role of strategic leadership. *Academy of Management Executive, 15*(1), 81–94.

Senge, P. M. (1990). *The fifth discipline: The art and practice of the learning organization*. New York: Doubleday.

Shapiro, A. L. (2010). *Coca-Cola goes green*. Retrieved from: http://www.forbes.com/2010/01/29/muhtar-kent-coca-cola-leadership-citizenship-sustainability.html

Smith, B. N., Montagno, R. V., & Kuzmenko, T. N. (2004). Transformational and servant leadership: Content and contextual comparisons. *Journal of Leadership and Organizational Studies, 10*, 80–91.

Steurer, R., Langer, M. E., Konrad, A., & Martinuzzi, A. (2005). Corporations, stakeholders and sustainable development I: A theoretical exploration of business–society relations. *Journal of Business Ethics, 61*, 263–281.

Strand, R. (2014). Strategic leadership of corporate sustainability. *Journal of Business Ethics, 123*, 687–706.

Taylor, M. R., Rubin, E. S., & Hounshell, D. A. (2005). Control of SO2 emissions from power plants: A case of induced technological innovation in the U.S. *Technological Forecasting and Social Change, 72*, 697–718.

Theis, T., & Tomkin, J. (Ed.) (2012). *Sustainability: A comprehensive foundation*. Houston, TX: Rice University. Retrieved from: http://www.earth.illinois.edu/sustain/sustainability_text.html

Tichy, N. M., & Devanna, M. A. III. (1986). *The transformational leader*. New York: Wiley.

Tichy, N. M., & Ulrich, D. O. (1984). SMR forum: The leadership challenge–a call for the transformational leader. *Sloan Management Review, 26*, 59–68.

Tosey, P., Visser, M., & Saunders, M. N. K. (2012). The origins and conceptualizations of "triple-loop" learning: A critical review. *Management Learning, 43*, 291–307.

Tushman, M. L., & O'Reilly, C. A. III. (1996). Ambidextrous organizations: Managing evolutionary and revolutionary change. *California Management Review, 38*(4), 8–30.

UNEP. (2010). *Driving a Green Economy through public finance and fiscal policy reform*. Retrieved from: http://www.unep.org/greeneconomy/Portals/88/documents/ger/GER_Working_Paper_Public_Finance.pdf

Van de Ven, A. H., & Poole, M. S. (1995). Explaining development and change in organizations. *Academy of Management Review, 20*, 510–540.

Vera, D., & Crossan, M. (2004). Strategic leadership and organizational learning. *Academy of Management Review, 29*, 222–240.

VOX Global, Weinreb Group Sustainability Recruiting, and Net Impact, Berkeley. (2012). *Making the pitch: Selling sustainability from inside corporate America*. Retrieved from: http://voxglobal.com/wp-content/uploads/VOX-Global-2012-Sustainability-Leaders-Survey-Executive-Summary.pdf

Waddock, S., & Bodwell, C. (2007). *Total responsibility management: The manual.* Sheffield, UK: Greenleaf Publishing.

WCED. (1987). *Our Common Future.* Oxford: Oxford University Press.

Worley, C. G., Cummings, T. G., & Mobley, F. W. (2000). The dynamics of strategic change in hospitals: Managed care strategies, organization design, and performance. *Public Administration & Management: An Interactive Journal, 5*(1), 1–27.

Wu, M. (2011). Sustainability as stakeholder management. *Business and sustainability: Concepts, strategies and changes. Critical studies on corporate responsibility, governance and sustainability, 3,* 223–241.

Yukl, G. (1999). An evaluative essay on current conceptions of effective leadership. *European Journal of Work & Organizational Psychology, 8*(1), 33–48.

5   Decision Making as Sustainable Leadership

The Garbage Can Revisited

Dianne Bolton and Terry Landells

Introduction

This chapter explores decision making in volatile, uncertain, complex, and ambiguous—i.e. VUCA (Bennet & Lemoine, 2014)—environments against which corporate social responsibility (CSR) initiatives and sustainability agendas take shape. These agendas confront leadership and decision makers by embodying persistent dynamism and associated ambiguity through challenging rational decision-making processes and associated power relations, introducing multi-stakeholder interests in transient key decision-choices, and requiring relevant and emergent knowledge from stakeholder insights for more holistic decision making.

Decision making by leaders to progress CSR and sustainability agendas by its nature leverages stakeholder analysis, providing "a comprehensive and unifying framework for understanding the complex interactions between firms and their internal and external constituencies" (Doh & Quigley, 2014, p. 256). A stakeholder focus also helps identify shifting and often tension-ridden priorities for resource usage, in turn influencing decision making.

We highlight under-acknowledged aspects of responsible leadership concerning decision-making practices that engage stakeholders by focusing on institutional, organizational, and individual practice. The garbage can model (GCM) of decision making proposed by Cohen, March, and Olsen (1972) is revised and used as a lens to recognize temporal, or time-bound and emergent knowledge influenced by histories, processes, preferences, and agendas of decision makers, as well as power dynamics in the decision-making process.

Waldman in Waldman and Siegel (2008) suggested a key dimension of responsible leadership focused on long-term organizational sustainability through the involvement of multiple-stakeholder groups in decision making. We apply the GCM to explore this approach in three decision-making contexts, exemplifying domains of responsible leadership. At an *institutional level*, we critique decision-making processes before, during, and after the Copenhagen Climate Summit of 2009, challenging assumptions about leadership influence on emergent and diverse multi-stakeholder agendas in decision-making contexts. At an *organizational level*, we examine stakeholder interactions underpinning emergent knowledge and agreed action to progress organizational objectives. Finally, we focus on the impact of complex decision-making processes on *the individual*, identifying the psychological benefits of stakeholder collaboration in VUCA environments, again, with implications for leadership of CSR and sustainability agendas.

CSR Agendas: From Rational to Emergent and Integrative Thinking

Literature around CSR and sustainable business practice highlights how emergent understanding of business's broader responsibilities to society requires decision making based on ambiguous and shifting information, often challenging core business values and norms of diverse stakeholders. Yet many key CSR debates, such as those concerning the business case for CSR, can be perceived as dichotomous, searching for comprehensive, logical, and well-evidenced cases to support rational decision making by agents arguing for or against courses of action. For instance, although Kurucz, Colbert, and Wheeler (2008) highlight the diverse definitions of CSR, they nevertheless seek to establish a common rationale for its business case, seeking a formulaic alignment of complex agendas in dynamic and shifting temporal spaces.

More recently, such dichotomous and rationally based decision thinking has been challenged through exploring effective processes and skill sets underpinning collaborative and innovative stakeholder relationships that generate mutually acceptable outcomes over the long term (Freeman, 2010; Waldman & Balven, 2014). Thus it might be argued that discourse around CSR is evolving from the 'for or against' CSR, or the 'narrow versus broad' appreciation of the case for CSR, to greater interest in dynamic interdependencies between stakeholder interests (Freeman, 2010) at a global, organizational, and individual level. Waldman and Balven (2014) propose "a paradox management approach . . . a firm [being] able to simultaneously pursue multiple goals that would benefit a range of stakeholders" (p. 232). We argue that this more integrative and detailed appreciation of stakeholder interests can identify dynamics that help progress CSR and sustainability agendas.

Making decisions in multipolar, dynamic, and unpredictable local, national, and global environments has, in turn, stimulated discourse concerning shifts in the way leadership might conceptualize and support decision-making capability. Examples include the harnessing of emergent opportunities (Doh & Quigley, 2014); identifying and managing risk more holistically, including risk sharing between stakeholders (Bolton & Galloway, 2014; Chung, Hensher, & Rose, 2010); synergizing and critiquing dynamic information sources (Alvesson, 2011); recognizing process-based, decision-making models (Pearce, Wassenaar, & Manz, 2014); and leveraging knowledge generated through dynamic interactions with salient internal and external stakeholders (Griffin & Stacey, 2005; Maak & Pless, 2006; Western, 2013).

Further, the integrative approach to simultaneously achieving economic, social, political, and environmental goals, seen as defining more sustainable business practice (Benn & Bolton, 2011), embraces the potential for unresolvable uncertainty and tension in decision making, with implications for mindsets, skill sets, and power relations (Levy, Alvesson, & Willmott, 2003). Exploring power relations among stakeholders is intrinsic to understanding the contribution of collaborative decision making to organizational viability (Hart & Sharma, 2004). In addition, managerial and broader employee capability is challenged to cope with such extended and ambiguous agendas, such as being less determined and controlled by bureaucratic intelligence and accountability systems.

Thus not only is an integrative and emergent approach to collaborative decision making effective but also failure to leverage it can constitute a source of inefficiency. For instance, closed systems of innovation can dissipate resources and waste opportunities (Thompson, 1965). Degnbol and Mccay (2007) illustrated the unintended and perverse consequences of decision making in fisheries management when the interconnected nature of salient institutions and stakeholders were not fully comprehended. In this case, the biological modelling that informed national and international jurisdictions failed to consider the dynamic and wider institutional seascape of fisheries management.

Sustainable Outcomes: Interdisciplinary Discourse in Decision Making

Sustainable business practice has been defined as simultaneous achievement of integrated economic, social, and environmental goals in business, often referred to as the triple bottom line (TBL). Bendell and Kearins (2005) identified a fourth dimension of the TBL model—i.e. managing political and regulatory influences on otherwise voluntary business activity. We extend the 'political' dimension of TBL to include the effective management of the politics and psychology of stakeholder relations, embellishing complex, interdisciplinary understanding, and discourse in the process of decision making for sustainable outcomes.

Augier (2013), in discussing the evolution of Cyert and March's (1963) behavioural theory of the firm, identified its cross-disciplinary influence on the individual disciplines of economics, sociology, political science, and psychology, presenting the case for extending disciplinary depth with more integrative, interdisciplinary thinking in organization studies. Specifically, she notes "the great potential of the field of organizational studies to yield new insights into the relationships, nature and dynamics of individuals and the organizations they inhabit (and to help other disciplines understand these)" (2013, p. 648). Augier also supports March's (1998) argument for dialectical unity or balancing of opposites in the process of integration and disintegration of disciplinary perspectives. We suggest that decision making through stakeholder engagement reflects these critical processes. Responding to March's perspective on the dialectical process and the need for long perspectives on the past as a condition for developing long visions of the future, we draw on Cohen, March, and Olsen's (1972) original GCM of decision making and updated commentary, arguing its continuing relevance to understanding stakeholder engagement in decision making in three contexts: global initiatives to reduce greenhouse gases, organizational dynamics demonstrating managerial behaviours in developing emergent and integrated strategic initiatives, and, finally, to highlight challenges to the individual when dealing with ambiguity in emergent decision-making environments. These perspectives provide interdisciplinary and integrative insights into key challenges for organizational science through a focus on essential and emergent stakeholder-engaged decision making, thus reinforcing March's dialectical approach to complex organizational behaviour and Augier's call for unification and disintegration of disciplinary perspectives around emergent issues.

However, there are tensions for decision makers in unifying and disintegrating disciplinary traditions, especially those that raise questions around neoclassical premises in a world of more complex and divergent stakeholder interests. For example, Freeman (2010) challenges the economist's view of the world as being based on trade-offs "built into the utility functions of both consumers and producers" (p. 8). He argues that managers have to resolve multiple demands simultaneously, with stakeholder interests being tied together in the process of value creation. Thus rather than trading off, executives should try to reframe key challenges to maximize value for stakeholders. How decisions might be made in this environment is not well understood. Few conceptual frameworks provide insight into such situations. It is this lacuna that is of interest in this chapter.

The Garbage Can Model: A Lens for Interdisciplinary Thinking

The GCM of decision making is a starting point in recognizing key dimensions of complexity, dynamism, and uncertainty that impact decision-making processes. As we shall see, it allows for comparison and differentiation between decision-making processes that leverage dimensions of connectivity and interdependence in organizational ecosystems such as those involved in sustainability agendas.

Cohen, March, and Olsen (1972) describe complex decision making in an organization as "a collection of choices looking for problems, issues and feelings looking for decision-situations in which they might be aired, solutions looking for issues to which they might be the answer, and decision makers looking for work" (p. 2). They used the metaphor of the garbage can "playfully" to conceptualize a framework for decision making, *the container*, representing a potential "choice opportunity . . . into which various kinds of problems and solutions are dumped by participants as they are generated" (p. 2). The decision opportunity reflects both constraints and pressures on the organization to make a decision. The problems, solutions, participants, and choices represent streams or flows of activity acting somewhat independently, a decision-choice being made "only when the shifting combinations of problems, solutions and decision makers happen to make action possible" (1972, p. 16).

These decision-making contexts defy a more structured and orderly organizational decision-making process. Cohen, March, and Olsen (1972) described them as veering towards the "anarchic" because information, process, availability, and intent depended on timing of inputs that were not necessarily wholly related to the problem or decision, nor flowed in a logical linear manner. Implicitly, the impact of structure and hierarchy on decision making is also questioned. Positions of power cannot control the decision-making process through influencing participant perceptions, level of commitment, agendas, and outcomes. They identified three organizational features akin to "organizational anarchy":

- *Problematic preferences* of participants in the decision-making process were often inconsistent and ambiguous. Previous shared experiences, values, goals, and priorities differed based on the decision to be made.
- *Unclear technology* or an unpredictable organizational process was "not understood by its members [and] operate[d] on the basis of simple trial-and-error procedures, the residue of learning from the accidents of past experience, and pragmatic inventions of necessity" (1972, p. 1).
- *Fluid participation*—i.e. fluctuating levels of interest and commitment to "decision domains" (1972, p. 535) by decision makers—reflected competing priorities, different evaluations of decision-making importance, uneven investment in the process, and variations in continuity and quality of time allocated.

Cohen, March, and Olsen (1972) also identified that issues might be resolved tangentially as a component of other issues, with the tendency increasing as decisions multiplied. Decisions would not be finite; rather, they might morph or regenerate as new information became available or new interests arose. This reflects Etzioni's (2014) advocacy to revisit decisions as appropriate, thus recognizing that they have been made on partial information.

Power and Decision Making in Complexity

Cohen and March (1986) suggested that in more complex organizations, governance legitimated or overrode the decision-making process in practice, with involvement being determined more by status than by relevant contribution. By contrast, they suggested that 'substance' is more important than 'status' for effective decision making in complex environments—a finding increasingly recognized in the complex literature, as is the limitation on power and status in decision-making processes (Levy, Alvesson, & Willmot, 2003). Thus the GCM surfaces questions about the role of hierarchical power exercised in the decision-making process, thus identifying that decision makers using hierarchical power are restricted in their ability to define problems and impose preferences because problems and solutions are uncoupled.

As early as 1986, Cohen and March had identified that tensions that manifest in multiple projects potentially diluted control over strategic focus and resource usage. They warned against becoming overly committed to one project without consideration of new risks, opportunities, and knowledge emerging from integrative synergies. However, attempts by powerful actors to impose 'rationality' in response to complexity continue in contemporary environments (Cohen, March, & Olsen, 2012).

Supported by new forms of complexity modelling, the 'garbage can' paradigm can now be seen as highlighting transient spaces in which problems are constantly reconceptualized through technical input and stakeholder buy-in. It might be argued that it is in these spaces, and through the employment of appropriate skill sets, that more efficient decision making can be achieved through leveraging broader perspectives on opportunities for value generation and barriers to decision implementation. Conceptualizing dynamic decision-making processes in complex stakeholder environments through the GCM might support a better understanding of decision making centred on sustainability and CSR practices, with implications for responsible leadership.

Decision-Making Challenges for Stakeholders in Complex Contexts

Emergent Order

We noted earlier that the GCM probes the implications of dynamic, incomplete, and misaligned resources, information, and agendas impeding linear decision making. The theory of complex adaptive systems (CAS) adds important insight to the GCM by exploring how 'order' might be achieved in non-linear, random, and, apparently, anarchic contexts. It highlights self-generating, emergent order through the interaction of system and human agents (Burnes, 2005; Dooley, 1996; Olson & Eoyang, 2001). Importantly, Stacey (2003) suggested "[t]here is no possibility of standing outside human interaction to design a program . . . we are all participants in that interaction" (p. 309). Thus unilateral deterministic behaviour for the whole organization will not hold. The interactions of people and systems will alter the determinations of an empowered decision maker. For example, strategic planning decisions by leaders will not create order in business activity by themselves. However, strategic implementation involving organizational actors empowered to interpret strategic plans and to respond to dynamic, environmental conditions may succeed in creating 'emergent' order, at least temporarily. Mintzberg and McHugh (1985) foreshadowed this possibility, suggesting that only in hindsight can strategy be understood, when rational determinations have adapted to emergent responses in forming action towards achieving organizational goals.

Stacey (2003) embellished an understanding of emergence by suggesting it is the "aspects of *process* in complex adaptive system models that provide analogies for human interaction, not the *systemic* aspects of those models" (p. 310, italics added). In this vein, Cohen, Rioli, and Axelrod (2001) identified that social structures helped maintain cooperation among adaptive agents. Relevant to sustainability agendas, they proposed that in certain situations where collectively beneficial actions are costly to individuals in the short run, "structured interaction [can create] . . . a shadow of the *adaptive* future, allowing even a small set of co-operative strategies to grow into a co-operative regime" (p. 6). Thus the relationships between structure, system, process, and agency in decision making might be envisaged as time related and unpredictable, with their own form of rationality discovered by individual players, often through pattern recognition and intuition (Stacey, 2010). Accordingly, interactive processes between stakeholders may generate emergent solutions, but the ability to determine what is a relevant 'pattern' may still be subject to influence by structures and agents.

Implications for Leadership: Transparency and Emergence

The fluidity of information supporting emergent decision making reinforces the need for perceived transparency as an antidote to misunderstanding. Hood (2006) suggests that in complex decision making "the idea that sunlight is the best disinfectant has become a notion of quasi-religious significance" (p. 9). Etzioni (2010) has characterized 'up-front transparency' as a form of public good, legitimating public decision-making processes. Esaiasson, Gilljam, and Persson (2012) suggest also that individual involvement in transparent decision processes generates legitimacy beliefs, with these being more powerful than fairness of process or involvement in governance—an insight relevant to later discussion on individual coping with ambiguity in decision making. Transparency also supports more rational interactive involvement in decision making by reducing the ability of powerful stakeholders to determine the nature of problems and potential solutions.

Snowden and Boone (2007) maintain that most decisions in contemporary business contexts are 'complex', with there being no 'right' answers but many competing ideas and unknown unknowns. This calls for emergent decision making that is not based on "attempting to impose a course of action, [rather] . . . patiently allow[ing] the path forward to reveal itself" (2007, p. 74) through "creating an environment from which . . . desirable patterns can be sense-made by leaders".

Proponents of 'design-based' decision making (Brown, 2008; Jahnke, 2011; Koskinen, Zimmerman, Binder, Redström, & Wensveen, 2011) implicitly accept emergence in decision making. Jahnke (2011) indicates "design practice . . . is engaged in active interpretation of situations to manifest new meaning in designed objects (and services)" (p. 36), requiring stakeholders in decision processes to acknowledge the value of reflection and critique of perspectives generated. An additional observation relevant to a critique of the GCM is that the individual's bounded rationality (Simon, 1979) can be 'neutralized' to some extent through decision making embodied in learning by action, often through prototyping by stakeholders to shape problem definitions.

The GCM contributes to this discourse by highlighting the time-bound nature of decision making and the healthy tensions between rationality, structure, and emergence. Responsible leadership responding to ambiguous and shifting stakeholder interests may leverage this conceptual clarity.

Implications for Leadership: Structure, Power, and Decision Making

We noted earlier that the GCM might underplay the significance of political influence on decision making within complex environments. Other commentators have identified important benefits of the collaborative process as an antidote to overt political manipulation of the decision-making process. Snowden (2010) suggests effective leadership behaviour might include promoting open discussion whilst encouraging diversity and dissent. Eisenhardt & Sull (2001) see value in leaders setting loose boundaries and boundary rules, within which probes can identify appropriate action, thus supporting the sense-making of emergent patterns to facilitate shared stakeholder understanding. Scharmer (2007) attempted to give language to the social collaborative process of change highlighting the importance of co-initiating understanding, co-sensing shared interests, co-presencing as a form of reflection on collaborative efforts, co-creating through prototyping, and co-evolving innovation with other stakeholders. These approaches have been applied in knowledge management, IT design, and project management contexts (Snowden, 2010) focussing on structure and process. Yet it is not apparent whether such practices challenge power relations, or extend across other sectors. Martin (2010) warns against underappreciating the costs of execution associated with top-down managerial decision making that fails to recognize the complexity of stakeholder agendas, thus creating a false sense of control and efficiency. The GCM provides a lens for critiquing power relations in the decision-making process, especially the value of multi-stakeholder engagement and risks associated with closed systems.

Figure 5.1 demonstrates how the GCM's temporally ordered decision opportunity puts boundaries around discrete levels of problems and solutions embraced by a variety of decision makers with different levels of engagement, commitment, and goals.

Figure 5.2 embellishes that model by drawing from complexity theory to highlight how this environment is fertile ground for stakeholder interactions that can generate order, reduce ambiguity for individual and groups of stakeholders, and create order locally through instituting alternative, more transparent and transient power relations sensitive to individual stakeholder agendas. A key dimension of transient power relations is the capacity for stakeholders to create an agreed and shared understanding by holding both rational and emergent perspectives in tension as a basis for more emergent decision-making capability.

Next, we illustrate insights derived by applying this revised GCM model to review multi-stakeholder inputs in decision-making processes at global

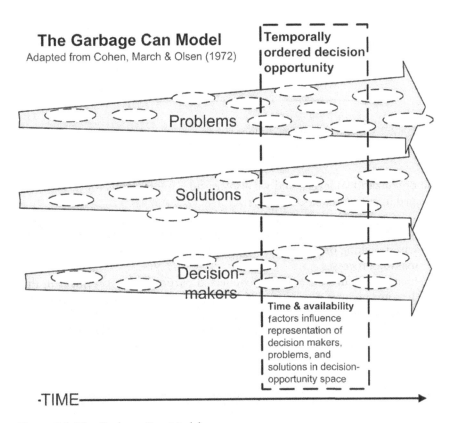

Figure 5.1 The Garbage Can Model

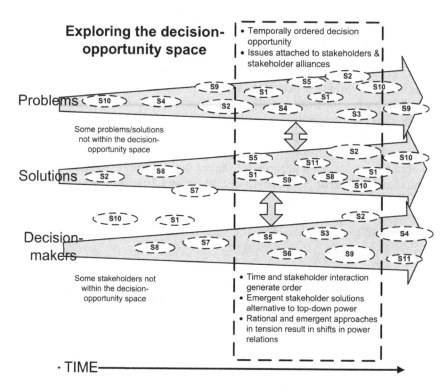

Figure 5.2 Exploring the Decision-Opportunity Space

and organizational levels, and we also consider implications for individuals engaged in environments characterized by

1. Increasing ambiguity of strategic goals (Carter, Clegg, & Wåhlin, 2011) whilst seeking order, rationality, control, and predictability in decision-making processes
2. Increasingly diverse and interconnected participant involvement in the decision-making process, reinforced by the transience of inclusion in any decision set
3. Decision boundaries often becoming subjective and political as attempts are made to restore rational order through controlling participant agendas

These features of the decision-making process highlight dynamic and transient interactions between problems, solutions, and decision makers within the decision-choice opportunity. Through this lens, the following examples explore issues seen as critical in CSR and sustainability discourse at the global institutional, organizational, and individual levels.

Global Decision Making: Emergence, Transparency, and Legitimacy

The negotiations over policy to constrain greenhouse gas emissions at Copenhagen's Climate Summit, comprising the fifteenth session of the Conference of the Parties (CoP) to the United Nations Framework Convention on Climate Change (UNFCCC) and the fifth meeting of the parties to the Kyoto Protocol, exemplify issues raised earlier concerning stakeholder-based decision making. These include attempts to impose rational decision-making frameworks on nation-states and alliances that ignore historical legacies influencing contemporary and tension-ridden perspectives on future economic, political, and social agendas and their alignment.

At CoP 13 in Bali in 2007, a post-Kyoto agreement was to be developed that detailed increased international efforts to address climate change. This was to be legally binding and agreed on in 2009 at Copenhagen. Commentators (see Black, 2009; Carter, Clegg, & Wåhlin, 2011; Saha & Talwar, 2010) have discussed the 'failure' of the Copenhagen Summit to "subscribe to a single course of action that might help halt man-made damage to the planet" (Carter, Clegg, & Wåhlin, 2011, p. 682). Drawing on characteristics of 'emergence' in the model described earlier, we question the label of 'failure'. This ambitious, strategic approach assumed that a rational, structured process would resolve multiple and conflicting philosophical, political, social, and economic perspectives on unequal development patterns and concomitant contributions to global warming of participant members. This agenda spawned multiple alignments, coalitions, and deals within and between the developed and the developing world. It might be asked why these complex dynamics emanating from different regional and state interests, clearly manifest since the Earth Summit of 1992, were ignored in setting this agenda.

Carter, Clegg, and Wåhlin (2011) highlight the difficulty of achieving firm agreement on a scientifically based agenda that had unknown consequences for economic and political futures and associated policy:

> The urgency of the scientific case as established by the IPCC demanded a time reckoning system . . . in advance of apparent political and public policy convergence around the issue. Action that was scientifically essential depended on political will; in most national cases that will had only apparently been forged, often on a rhetorically moral case . . . What was lacking in most national cases was the construction of what Giddens (2009) referred to as 'political convergence'; the degree to which policies on climate change overlapped with other areas of public policy.
> (2011, p. 684)

They likened the political process at this summit to the GCM, thus reinforcing the temporality of participant inclusion in any set of decisions:

> Problems, policies and politics sometimes converge but more often than not attach themselves randomly and independently of each other . . . . the

[Copenhagen] summit was the garbage can into which the concerns around the issues of global warming and climate change were poured, there to attach themselves to the various solutions that the main protagonists— radicals, mainstreamers and sceptics—promulgated.

(2011, p. 684)

Carter, Clegg, and Wåhlin (2011) also point out that no social structuring or ordering exists without being characterized by power relations. Imposing rational order from above was particularly difficult when attempted "inter-organizationally in a complex organizational field such as that of the international relations that attended the Copenhagen Summit" (p. 694). They also identified strategies for domination at the summit. Hidden agendas of the powerful to attain direct outcomes were exemplified by the leaking of the 'Danish Text' on day two of the summit. This text flagged a departure from the legally binding requirement for developed nations to shoulder greater costs than the developing world in reducing carbon emissions. Additionally, in the face of negotiation breakdown, a proposed meeting of 50 out of 192 countries would have excluded certain groups and agendas in the interests of surfacing 'safe' issues to further the agendas of the powerful. Lastly, and flying in the face of expectations of the conference, an 'accord' was eventually brokered by a restricted set of players, as a meaningful first step towards achieving the original agenda. As Black (2009) noted,

The end of the meeting saw leaders of the US and BASIC group of countries (Brazil, South Africa, India and China) hammering out a last minute deal in a back room as though the nine months of talks leading up to this summit and the Bali Action Plan to which they had all committed two years previously did not exist . . . The logical conclusion is that this is the arrangement that the big players now prefer—an informal setting where each country says what it is prepared to do—where nothing is negotiated and nothing is legally binding.

Thus the 'container' was essentially reconfigured at the Copenhagen Summit through emergent convergence of responses to rational solutions being imposed, resulting in a

clear political intent to constrain carbon and respond to climate change, in both the short and long term . . . limiting the maximum global average temperature increase to no more than 2 degrees Celsius above pre-industrial levels, subject to a review in 2015.

(UNFCCC, 2014a)

In recognition of the increased risk faced by developing countries, this review would consider limiting the temperature increase to below 1.5

degrees. This outcome might be seen as an essential and significant step forward towards Giddens's (2009) "political convergence" in the decision-option space.

Subsequently, the UNFCCC's CoP 16 in Cancun, Mexico, in 2010 formalized this agreement and established a Green Climate Fund to finance developing country initiatives. A strengthened reporting system facilitated emergent understanding of political positions of member nations through introducing mutual accountability for emission reductions and increased transparency of policy. For instance, national communications (NCs) detailing emission reduction targets and plans of developed nations were to be supplemented by biennial reviews (BRs) reporting progress against both commitments and provision of support to developing nations. The NCs and BRs became subject to an international assessment review (IAR) and a multilateral assessment of progress with participation of all parties (UNFCCC, 2014b). Developing nations could now question developed nations in a peer-review process and were subject to a less onerous review of NCs and a biennial update report (BUR) on progress. Technical experts collated all parties' responses and provided feedback on achievement of goals for reconsideration, given the agreed overall goal.

The transparent question-and-answer process helped reduce the potential for partial, obtuse, or politically oriented responses, consistent with Stahl, Pless, and Maak's (2013) suggestion that responsible global leadership responds to both global and local stakeholders. Specifically, fuller transparency-aided complex decision making resulted from surfacing a range of equally legitimate paradigms for determining actions that stakeholders could support in achieving the overall agreed goal. Thus from dynamic interactions within the 'garbage can' at Copenhagen there emerged new forms of transparency around nation-state positions as an antidote to 'rational decision making' introduced by the powerful at Copenhagen.

The Paris Climate Summit in 2015 updated and clarified the scale of global warming projections, and extended these transparent and dynamic processes. It might be argued that a more 'humble' approach to decision making (Etzioni, 2014) was created, thus allowing review and reconfiguration of responses to pollution control as a basis for emergent national and regional action.

The design of the decision-opportunity 'container' represented by the Paris conference also appeared sensitive to time constraints imposed by the conference—developing agile infrastructure for multiple and dynamic diplomatic actions to renegotiate and reshape global goals. Tension-ridden diplomatic outcomes agreed on in this manner included an EU back down on legally binding emission cuts, U.S. acceptance of clauses around 'loss and damage', and China's and India's agreement to an aspirational target of 1.5 degree warming. Transparency of process ensured that "none of the major countries wanted to be seen as wrecking a deal that had come so close . . . and all made compromises" (Harvey, 2015).

Shifting the Paradigm Towards Stakeholder Input at an Organizational Level

The GCM model in Figure 5.1 illustrates how problems, solutions, and decision makers come together in a time-constrained environment in which leaders attempt to deliver outcomes. Figure 5.2 modified this model to illustrate how time-bound, decision-choice opportunities engage dynamic and emergent mindsets and skill sets of stakeholders, with the decision-making process integrating both rational analysis and emergent contributions to define and take action on complex multi-stakeholder agendas.

Thus order is generated by conflation of time, dynamic interaction, and struggle. This dynamism can be conceptualized through the lens of process ontology (Langley, Smallman, Tsoukas, & Van de Ven, 2013, p. 5)

> in which the world itself is viewed fundamentally as made up of processes rather than things . . . entities (such as organizations and structures) are no more than temporary instantiations of ongoing processes, continually in a state of becoming . . . Changing . . . is not something that happens to things but . . . the way that reality is brought into being in every instant.

Examples of 'reality brought into being' through ongoing and dynamic decision-making processes are provided in findings of Landells's (2014) grounded theory study concerning the contribution of stakeholders to strategic decision making and implementation. He identifies at an organizational level the role and skills of managers in facilitating stakeholder contribution to both strategic and operational decision making in public- and private-sector organizations, thus illustrating the transience and fluidity of such processes.

Employing grounded theory as research methodology enabled the identification of emergence and dynamism, with the theory being developed from raw data (Glaser & Strauss, 1967) to allow a more nuanced understanding of behaviour in context. The research approach incorporates simultaneous processes of open coding, recording insights, comparing coded incidents and insights, sampling based on emergent themes, and theoretical coding to identify detailed properties of codes and their relationships to each other. As a result, a contextually bound theory is developed and validated (Glaser, 1978).

Landells's (2014) study found that managers co-created strategy with stakeholders through continual social interaction based on highly interdependent psychological and structural processes. These were categorized as shaping stakeholder cognitions to align agendas, creating a transient shared culture, reconceptualizing shared agendas through a stakeholder lens, and, as reflected in the GCM, forming transient or virtual structures with stakeholders to take relevant forms of strategic action.

For some respondents, forming transient structures to engage stakeholders in strategy making was intrinsic to business. As one private-sector manager noted,

> Feedback from other stakeholders will shape what we do at a local level. As an example of creating the transient space, partners, resellers, take our product, wrap their services around it and so doing provide integrated services to customers . . . How do we jointly plan for business next year? This is a dynamic process. It's an open process around strategy-making with our partners . . . we continually encourage our clients to review their strategy concerning new and emergent technologies and market opportunities.
>
> (Landells, 2014, p. 217)

Another respondent from the public sector described an initiative with stakeholders to create new cognitive and transient spaces outside the normal bureaucratic process. The objective was to fend off unanticipated and undesirable political consequences when stakeholders did not appear capable of complying with government policy. She described dynamics within such transient space:

> It's basically saying . . . "here's the problem we're in . . . join us in owning the problem and collectively fixing it because it's in our mutual interests". So you have an easier path for yourself than just basically inflicting decisions and imperatives on those who are going to be affected by them, and you might come up with a different solution by having their intelligence and their perspectives around the table.
>
> (2014, p. 110)

Continual activity with stakeholders included making strategic narratives credible by filling in gaps around emergent strategic intent to enable shared understanding and action. One manager noted this was an increasingly important skillset:

> We can't afford for people not to understand what's happening and therefore sabotage it. So what we're doing, and why we're doing it, and how we're going to do it, has got to be clearly visible, it's got to be credible and people have to be comfortable with what we're going to do.
>
> (2014, p. 175)

A critical, albeit transient social process was that of reshaping power relations in order to make strategic decisions that stakeholders considered acceptable and less risky against their often volatile agendas:

> I work across programs and pull [new options] together . . . I do regular trips to ask people about things. In a number of project teams we have

a number of management staff, team leaders, and a senior group of international staff members . . . interacting continuously and exchanging information . . . In my business we are all about risk taking and power relations. Often in the projects themselves, empowerment is the name of the game.

(2014, p. 196)

Another perspective emphasized risks associated with attempting to bring multiple stakeholders together and to accept shifting power relations to achieve outcomes and avoid perceptions of failure:

Sometimes there are so many relationships involved to get things done that it does go off target. Idealistically, you should not have to involve so many as it can direct you down a different path . . . it can get very complex when everybody puts their bit into it, however generally you have to find a way to get through it because nobody wants to admit that a project is a non-starter or a failure . . . we have to turn it into something else . . . [in the banking sector] they don't like bad news and there's a huge reluctance to call it a "failure".

(2014, p. 197)

As reflected in the GCM, stakeholders formed transient or virtual structures to generate strategic options and to take action in complex environments. From a private-sector perspective,

whenever I go to developing countries . . . my approach is, I am here to understand. I define the goals . . . but I tell them I have no idea of how we are going to get there. I say let's gather round the table and muster the best ideas we can put on the table so we can get to the goal. Along the way we can have other conversations about what we need to achieve—extra employment, benefit to the community . . . But I'm not there to prescribe how we are going to get there, just the ultimate outcome . . . in articulating goals we have to be much broader, and acknowledge, that in achieving them, we'll also achieve things that are important to us as a collective.

(2014, p. 222)

From a public-sector manager dealing with immigration programs, we offer the following:

You had to get . . . approval from the policy area. I had to try to do it within policy guidelines. The way I went about it had to bear scrutiny and to be palatable to the community, thus not have the propensity to negatively hit the headlines. I needed these numbers, but to get there I had to work with a whole range of stakeholders in a sensitive and strategic manner . . . boundaries are tough, but you can innovate in this area. I worked with stakeholders here to respect all the various stakeholder boundaries.

(2014, p. 224)

Where the boundaries were very tight, the subculture supporting prototyping as a form of generating options was weaker, requiring constant checking against the mainstream culture of key stakeholders.

Landells (2014) noted that these transient structures temporarily uniting stakeholder agendas

fostered a range of values, goals, approaches and behaviours to achieve a response or solution acceptable to those involved. The characteristics of these virtual structures appeared to be influenced by . . . the transparency of corporate agendas, the degree of control exerted over the implementation process and stakeholder compliance, the perceived appropriateness of central directions, the level of empowerment given by the centre in recognition of the complexity and unknown nature of possible local dynamics, and, the degree of acceptance of new forms of innovation and emergence in local solutions.

(2014, p. 223)

Landells's (2014) findings embellish the GCM model by illustrating the potential and unpredictable impact of subjective and political agendas on strategic and operational activities in complex multi-stakeholder environments. They also detail the perception of increasing ambiguity of strategic goals in the decision-making processes by stakeholders. This reflects studies concerned with understanding the emergent dynamics of strategy-as-practice (Vaara & Whittington, 2012) and Kaplan and Orlikowski's (2013) observations that stakeholders across hierarchies and functions moved forward in periods of uncertainty through a set of practices they conceptualize as "temporal work", which included reimagining the future, rethinking the past, and reconsidering present concerns, with the strategy being the result of complex synergies between different interpretations and interactions of organizational agents. This appears consistent with a critique of top-down structures articulating problem sets and identifying solutions rather than adopting shared leadership approaches (D'Innocenzo, Mathieu, & Kukenberger, 2014; Wang, Waldman, & Zhang, 2014).

Bird and Oddou (2013) suggest that there is little research connecting such new forms of knowledge sharing and creation with theories of responsible leadership. Nevertheless, Doh and Quigley (2014) purport, "Responsible leaders who communicate with and balance the needs of various stakeholders [will] likely model and (either intentionally or unintentionally) encourage knowledge sharing amongst organisational stakeholders themselves" (p. 263). They also note that through boundary spanning and engaging with peripheral and latent stakeholders, responsible leadership can create value through embedding emergent knowledge into organizational decision-making processes.

Landells (2014) found some organizational support for knowledge sharing, often driven by profit and growth imperatives. However, managers themselves often demonstrated responsible leadership practices through stakeholder involvement in knowledge creation as an essential dimension of decision making.

These multi-stakeholder, decision-making practices also have implications for learning and coping at an individual level in VUCA environments—an oft-neglected dimension of organizational sustainability. In the following section, we explore whether multi-stakeholder perspectives, open engagement, and perceptions of shared responsibility support individual well-being and effective functioning in ambiguous decision-making environments.

Temporality, Ambiguity, and Individual Coping

Snowden and Boone (2007) warn against reliance on rational processes to reduce complexity in contemporary and complex decision-making environments. Yet complex decision making can be stressful, requiring the integration of multiple and diverse information sources to produce stakeholder-relevant and socially mediated outcomes, generated far from centrally located decision-making structures (Mintzberg, 1973; Wood & Bandura, 1989).

Both the original and the revised GCM models in Figures 5.1 and 5.2 give context to contemporary challenges for individuals in decision-making environments by highlighting interactivity between environment and organizational actors, both structurally and psychologically. Relational definitions of stress recognize that the stimulus environment and individual responses are related (Lazarus & Folkman, 1984), taking into account employee perceptions, desires, and abilities in the broader context of organizational demands, thus providing insights into the process of adaptation in change environments (Edwards, 1992; White, 1959).

Zeffane and McLoughlin (2006) have demonstrated the importance of cooperation and communication effectiveness in the mitigation of workplace stress, also indicating a relational understanding of individuals in their environment. The partial and dynamic interactions in the decision-opportunity space identified in the GCM illustrates potential for stress because of ambiguity experienced by individuals in the decision-making process as well as opportunities for stress reduction. Landells's (2014) research found that by co-creating strategy through action with other stakeholders, managers often relieved ambiguity, tension, and frustration when implementing what they perceived as vague, tension-ridden, and inaccurate top-down agendas. Interviewees suggested that generating strategic options required relevant and tailored information, and when insights and information were derived through new forms of transparent interaction with stakeholders (Esaiasson, Gilljam & Persson, 2012), their sense of ambiguity was diminished by leveraging shared perspectives around problem sets and ways forward.

Similarly, Bridwell-Mitchell and Mezias (2012) highlight that gaining support of internal stakeholders for change aids the re-establishment of organizational legitimacy in heavy change environments and reduces ambiguity through improving role identity, sense of belonging, and purposiveness (Terry & Callan, 1998). As illustrated in the modified GCM, individuals face multiple conflicting agendas around problems, solutions, and decision-maker agendas, yet, though leveraging collaborative stakeholder practice, individual coping is enhanced.

Thus an extended GCM highlights issues of relevance to responsible leadership in developing cultures that can normalize "dynamism" and legitimate process-based decision making, thus helping employees sense-make their individual patterns of understanding and action. Doh and Quigley (2014), commenting on team leadership and conditions for trust building, note the potential psychological benefits associated with sharing leadership responsibilities with stakeholders, including aspects of decision making:

> A leader who can admit what he or she does and does not know and can confidently seek out those who are able to provide the necessary knowledge and perspectives on the issue is likely to be perceived by followers as more honest, trustworthy and effective.
>
> (2014, p. 262)

Leadership might, therefore, reflect on power structures that can create confidence and self-efficacy for individuals facing ambiguity through guidelines and governance to frame emergent and transient decisions (Etzioni, 2014). Decision making might be seen as a process rather than a finite outcome of a small group of decision makers. This approach is relevant to CSR and sustainability agendas that seek more integrative and innovative sustainable outcomes by challenging responsible leaders to adapt top-down cultures of decision making to include relevant collaborative process. Conditions for building self-efficacy of employees at every level to deal with dynamic environments might also pose threats to a leader's ego (Leary, Terry, Batts Allen, & Tate, 2009), thus requiring holistic and intelligent reflection and response.

Managing the Influence of Power on Multi-stakeholder Knowledge

Examples of decision making at institutional, organizational, and individual levels exhibit varying dimensions of the modified GCM (Figure 5.2), highlighting the importance of temporality as a key moderator of rational, static thinking in decision making in complexity. They also extend an understanding of the role and limitations of power seeking to influence the outcomes of dynamic processes where complex stakeholder interactions are key determinants of effective process and outcome. In this context, the role of the leader is to intelligently identify and shape stakeholder interests (Waldman, Siegel, & Javidan, 2006) towards achieving a shared and temporarily ordered understanding of goals (Maak & Pless, 2006). Responsible leadership needs to manage the influence of power to ensure stakeholder participation is optimized (Reave, 2005), both through greater transparency and through cultures that help sense-make emerging events (Maak & Pless, 2006; Plowman et al., 2007; Weick, 2009).

Conclusion

We have noted a tendency for decision making to rely on rational approaches purporting binary argument for or against ambiguous, emergent, and collaborative CSR and sustainability agendas. We built on Cohen, March, and Olsen's (1972) GCM to better identify forms of complexity, ambiguity, and emergence challenging 'rational models' of decision making in quasi-anarchic organizational environments. Three key areas of a GCM model were explored. These were the increasing ambiguity of strategic goals often in tension with cultures committed to order, rationality, control, and predictability; new and diverse forms of stakeholder involvement in the decision-making process, often transient and manifesting both focused and tangential interest in specific decision opportunities; and, lastly, the subjective and political impacts of attempting to restore or create order through influencing boundaries of the decision opportunity.

In 2012, Cohen, March, and Olsen (2012, p. 23) reminded us of the continuing relevance of the GCM, which is consistent with increasing tensions between rationality and emergence in decision making in organizations:

> Ideas about rational choice and problem solving that are relaxed in the garbage can model are firmly embedded in wider modern Western culture . . . in theories of free markets and democratic self-government and more generally in the ethos of the Enlightenment with its belief in human agency and the ability to solve problems, improve human conditions, and create progress through human purpose, understanding and control.

This mode of thinking, they suggested, supported a critique of formal organizations with

> defined missions, mandates, normative standards, goals, and demands for productivity, effectiveness and efficiency . . . Typically hierarchical relations are assumed, enabling superiors to tell subordinates what to do (within specified jurisdictions, pacts, and contracts) and to arrange and rearrange structural relations.

(p. 24)

Thus although the rational model is still broadly accepted, the global conditions for operationalizing such an approach are becoming more tenuous. We identified three different levels of decision making associated with CSR and sustainability agendas that illustrate this assertion.

The discussion of decision making centred on climate summits highlighted tensions in attempts to impose rational process over time across nations and between institutions. It demonstrated how emergent understanding of multiple-stakeholder interests and concerns (as manifestations of dynamic political, economic, and social developments) uncovered the difficulties of constraining them in a 'garbage can' decision opportunity dominated by developed nations.

At an organizational level, we highlighted how management is increasingly aware of its need to sense-make and facilitate complex multi-stakeholder agendas in the face of ambiguous corporate agendas that still exhibit rational strategic approaches manifesting limited perceptions of control and efficiency. We suggest that responsible leadership might shape culture that acknowledges the contribution of emergent knowledge and stakeholder-agreed action in decision making in VUCA environments, and organizational values and capability of leveraging dynamism rather than controlling it.

We also addressed the impact of these ambiguous and dynamic environments on individual behaviour, identifying the potential benefits of collaborative action for individual coping. This consideration is an important yet often neglected feature of sustainable business practice and management of human and social capital. Reflection on coping through stakeholder interactions contributes to twenty-first-century skill sets required for complex collaboration and negotiation in a globalized and interconnected world.

Thus increased transparency of options and agendas in increasingly dynamic environments, generated by an extended GCM, has the capacity to create greater clarity and understanding of decision making across complex multi-stakeholder agendas. As such, it is responsive to the World Business Council for Sustainable Development's (WBCSD) call for rethinking key definitions of business activities for a more sustainable future (WBCSD, 2010). We draw attention to the need to reconceptualize decision making as central to this agenda.

References

Alvesson, M. (2011). De-essentializing the knowledge intensive firm: Reflections on sceptical research going against the mainstream. *Journal of Management Studies*, 48(7), 1640–1661.

Augier, M. (2013). Behavioural theory of the firm: Hopes from the past; lessons from the future. *M@n@gement*, 16(5), 636–652.

Bendell, J., & Kearins, K. (2005). The political bottom line: The emerging dimension to corporate responsibility for sustainable development. *Business Strategy and the Environment*, 14, 372–383.

Benn, S., & Bolton, D. (2011). *Key concepts in corporate social responsibility.* London: Sage Publications Ltd.

Bennett, N., & Lemoine, G. J. (2014). What a difference a word makes: Understanding threats to performance in a VUCA world. *Business Horizons, 57,* 311–317.

Bird, A., & Oddou, G. R. (2013). Global leadership knowledge creation and transfer. In M. E. Mendenhall, J. S. Osland, G. R. Oddou, M. L. Maznevski, M. J. Stevens, & G. K. Stahl (Eds.), *Global leadership: Research, practice, and development* (pp. 162–182). New York: Routledge.

Black, R. (2009). Why did Copenhagen fail to deliver a climate deal? *BBC News.* Retrieved 14 June 2015 from: http://news.bbc.co.uk/2/hi/8426835.stm

Bolton, D., & Galloway, C. (2014). The holistic dilemma: Helping management students deal with risk. *The International Journal of Management Education, 12*(2), 55–67.

Bridwell-Mitchell, E. N., & Mezias, S. J. (2012). The quest for cognitive legitimacy: Organizational identity crafting and internal stakeholder support. *Journal of Change Management, 12*(2), 189–207.

Brown, T. (2008). Design thinking. *Harvard Business Review, 86*(6), 84–92.

Burnes, B. (2005). Complexity theories and organizational change. *International Journal of Management Reviews, 7*(2), 73–90.

Carter, C., Clegg, S., & Wåhlin, N. (2011). When science meets strategic realpolitik: The case of the Copenhagen UN climate change summit. *Critical Perspectives on Accounting, 22,* 682–697.

Chung, D., Hensher, D. A., & Rose, J. M. (2010). Toward the betterment of risk allocations: Investigating risk perceptions of stakeholder groups to public-private-partnership tollroad projects. *Research in Transportation Economics, 30*(1), 43–58.

Cohen, M. D., & March, J. G. (1986). *Leadership and Ambiguity.* Boston, MA: Harvard Business School Press.

Cohen, M. D., March, J. G., & Olsen, J. P. (1972). A garbage can model of organizational choice. *Administrative Science Quarterly, 17*(1), 1–25.

Cohen, M. D., March, J. G., & Olsen, J. P. (2012). 'A garbage can model' at forty: A solution that still attracts problems. *Research in the Sociology of Organizations, 36,* 19–30.

Cohen, M. D., Rioli, R. L., & Axelrod, R. (2001). The role of social structure in the maintenance of cooperative regimes. *Rationality and Society, 13*(1), 5–32.

Cyert, R. M., & March, J. G. (1963). *A behavioural theory of the firm.* Oxford: Blackwell Publishing.

Degnbol, P., & Mccay, B. J. (2007). Unintended and perverse consequences of ignoring linkages in fisheries systems. *ICES Journal of Marine Science, 64*(4), 793–797.

D'Innocenzo, L., Mathieu, J. E., & Kukenberger, M. R. (2014). A meta-analysis of different forms of shared leadership-team performance relations. *Journal of Management, 42*(7), 1964–1991.

Doh, J. P., & Quigley, N. R. (2014). Responsible leadership and stakeholder management: influence pathways and organisational outcomes. *The Academy of Management Perspectives, 28*(3), 255–274.

Dooley, K. (1996). A nominal definition of complex adaptive systems. *The Chaos Network, 8*(1), 2–3.

Edwards, J. R. (1992). A cybernetic theory of stress, coping and well-being in organizations. *Academy of Management Review, 17*(2), 238–274.

Eisenhardt, K. M., & Sull, D. N. (2001). Strategy as simple rules. *Harvard Business Review*, 79(1), 107–116.

Esaiasson, P., Gilljam, M., & Persson, M. (2012). Which decision-making arrangements generate the strongest legitimacy beliefs? Evidence from a randomised field experiment. *European Journal of Political Research*, 51, 785–808.

Etzioni, A. (2010). Is transparency the best disinfectant? *The Journal of Political Philosophy*, 18(4), 389–404.

Etzioni, A. (2014). Humble decision-making theory. *Public Management Review*, 16(5), 611–619.

Freeman, R. E. (2010). Managing for stakeholders: Trade-offs or Value Creation. *Journal of Business Ethics*, 96, 7–9.

Giddens, A. (2009). *The politics of climate change*. Cambridge, UK: Polity Press.

Glaser, B. G. (1978). *Theoretical Sensitivity: Advances in the methodology of grounded theory*. Mill Valley, CA: Sociology Press

Glaser, B. G., & Strauss, A.L. (1967). *The discovery of grounded theory: Strategies for qualitative research*. Mill Valley, CA: Sociology Press

Griffin, D., & Stacey, R. (2005). *Complexity and the experience of leading organizations*. London: Routledge.

Hart, S. L., & Sharma, S. (2004). Engaging fringe stakeholders for competitive imagination. *Academy of Management Executive*, 18(1), 7–18.

Harvey, F. (2015). Paris climate change agreement; the world's greatest diplomatic success. The Guardian, 14 December. Retrieved 17 November 2016 from: https://www.theguardian.com/environment/2015/dec/13/paris-climate-deal-cop-diplomacy-developing-united-nations

Hood, C. (2006). Transparency in historical perspective. In C. Hood, & D. Heald (Eds.), *Transparency: The key to better governance?* (pp. 3–23). Oxford, UK: Oxford University Press.

Jahnke, M. (2011). Revisiting design as a Hermeneutic practice: An investigation of Paul Ricoeur's critical Hermeneutics. *Design Issues*, 28(2), 30–40.

Kaplan, S., & Orlikowski, W. J. (2013). Temporal work in strategy making. *Organization Science*, 24(4), 965–995.

Koskinen, I., Zimmerman, J., Binder, T., Redström, J., & Wensveen, S. (2011). *Design research through practice: From the lab, field, and showroom*. Cambridge, MA: Elsevier.

Kurucz, E., Colbert, B., & Wheeler, D. (2008). The business case for corporate social responsibility. In A. Crane, A. McWilliams, D. Matten, J. Moon, & D. Seigel (Eds.), *The Oxford handbook of corporate social responsibility* (pp. 83–112). Oxford: Oxford University Press.

Landells, T. (2014). Co-creating strategy in action with stakeholders: A grounded theory explaining middle manager response to their concerns around progressing organisational strategic agendas in increasingly ambiguous environments. [PhD Thesis, Swinburne University of Technology]. Retrieved 9 August 2015 from: http://researchbank.swinburne.edu.au/vital/access/manager/Repository/swin:41251

Langley, A., Smallman, C., Tsoukas, H., & Van de Ven, A. H. (2013). Process studies of change in organization and management: Unveiling temporality, activity and flow. *Academy of Management Journal*, 56(1), 1–13.

Lazarus, R. S., & Folkman, S. (1984). *Stress, appraisal and coping*. New York: Springer.

Leary, M. R., Terry, M. L., Batts Allen, A., & Tate, E. B. (2009). The concept of ego threat in social and personality psychology: Is ego threat a viable scientific construct? *Personality and Social Psychology Review, 13*(3), 151–164.

Levy, D. L., Alvesson, M., & Willmott, H. (2003). Critical approaches to strategic management. In M. Alvesson, & H. Willmott (Eds.), *Studying Management Critically* (pp. 92–110). London, UK: Sage.

Maak, T., & Pless, N. (2006). Responsible leadership: A relational approach. In T. Maak, & N. Pless (Eds.), *Responsible leadership* (pp. 33–53). London: Routledge.

March, J. G. (1998). Research on organizations: Hopes for the past and lessons from the future. Paper delivered at the Scandinavian Consortium for Organizational Research, 'Samples of the Future', Stanford University, 20 September.

Martin, R. L. (2010). The execution trap. *Harvard Business Review, July/August,* 64–71.

Mintzberg, H. (1973). *The nature of managerial work.* New York: Harper & Row.

Mintzberg, H., & McHugh, A. (1985). Strategy formulation in adhocracy. *Administrative Science Quarterly, 30*(2), 160–197.

Olson, E. E., & Eoyang, G. H. (2001). *Facilitating organizational change: Lessons from complexity science.* San Francisco, CA: Jossey-Bass / Pfeffer.

Pearce, C. L., Wassenaar, C. L, & Manz, C. C. (2014). Is shared leadership the key to responsible leadership? *The Academy of Management Perspectives, 28*(3), 275–288.

Plowman, D. A., Solansky, S., Beck, T. E., Baker, L., Kulkarni, M., & Travis, D. V. (2007). The role of leadership in emergent, self-organization. *The Leadership Quarterly, 18*, 341–356.

Reave, L. (2005). Towards a paradigm of spiritual leadership. *Leadership Quarterly, 16*, 655–687.

Saha, A., & Talwar, K. (2010). India's response to climate change: The 2009 Copenhagen summit and Beyond. *NUJS Law Review, 159*, 159–190.

Scharmer C. O. (2007). *Theory U: Leading from the future as it emerges.* Cambridge, MA: The Society for Organizational Learning.

Simon, H. A. (1979). Rational decision making in business organizations. *The American Economic Review, 69*(4), 493–513.

Snowden, D. (2010). *The Cynefin framework.* Retrieved 23 April 2015 from: https://www.youtube.com/watch?v=N7oz366X0-8

Snowden, D., & Boone, M. (2007). A leader's framework for decision making. *Harvard Business Review, November,* 69–76.

Stacey, R. D. (2003). *Strategic management and organisational dynamics: The challenge of complexity.* Harlow, UK: Pearson.

Stacey, R. D. (2010). *Complexity and organizational reality.* Oxford, UK: Routledge.

Stahl, G. K., Pless, N. M., & Maak, T. (2013). Responsible global leadership. In M. E. Mendenhall, J. Osland, A. Bird, G. R. Oddou, M. L. Maznevski, & G. K. Stahl (Eds.), *Global leadership: Research, practice, and development* (pp. 240–259). New York: Routledge.

Terry, D. J., & Callan, V. J. (1998). In-group bias in response to organisational merger. *Group Dynamics: Theory, Research and Practice, 2*, 67–81.

Thompson, V. A. (1965). Bureaucracy and innovation. *Administrative Science Quarterly, 10*(1), 1–20.

United Nations Framework Convention on Climate Change (UNFCCC). (2014a). *Copenhagen Climate Change Conference—December 2009.* Retrieved 17 April 2016 from: http://unfccc.int/meetings/copenhagen_dec_2009/meeting/6295.php

United Nations Framework Convention on Climate Change (UNFCCC). (2014b). *The International Assessment and Review Process.* Retrieved 14 June 2015 from: http://unfccc.int/focus/mitigation/the_multilateral_assessment_process_under_the_iar/items/7549.php

Vaara, E., & Whittington, R. (2012). Strategy-as-practice: Taking social practices seriously. *The Academy of Management Annals, 6*(1), 285–336.

Waldman, D. A., & Balven, R. M. (2014). Responsible leadership: Theoretical issues and research directions. *The Academy of Management Perspectives, 28*(3), 224–234.

Waldman, D. A., & Siegel, D. S. (2008). Defining the socially responsible leader. *The Leadership Quarterly, 19*, 117–131.

Waldman, D. A., Siegel, D. S., & Javidan, M. (2006). Components of CEO transformational leadership and corporate social responsibility. *Journal of Management Studies, 43*(8), 1703–1725.

Wang, D., Waldman, D. A., & Zhang, Z. (2014). A metaanalysis of shared leadership and team effectiveness. *Journal of Applied Psychology, 99*(2), 181–198.

Weick, K. E. (2009). *Making sense of the organization: The impermanent organisation.* Chichester, UK: Wiley.

Western, S. (2013). *Leadership: A critical text.* London: Sage.

White, R. W. (1959). Motivation reconsidered: The concept of competence. *Psychological Review, 66*(5), 297–333.

Wood, R., & Bandura, A. (1989). Impact of conceptions of ability on self-regulatory mechanisms and complex decision making. *Journal of Personality and Social Psychology, 56*(3), 407–415.

World Business Council for Sustainable Development. (2010). *Vision 2050.* Retrieved 14 June 2015 from: http://www.wbcsd.org/vision2050.aspx

Zeffane, R., & McLoughlin, D. (2006). Cooperation and stress: Exploring the differential impact of job satisfaction, communication and culture. *Management Research News, 29*(10), 618–631.

6 Evaluating CSR, Sustainability, and Sourcing Within the UK Supermarket Industry

The Case of Waitrose/John Lewis Partnership

Ralph Tench and Martina Topić

Introduction

Whereas originally a voluntary concept according to which companies help society for philanthropic reasons, CSR has in recent years evolved to become much more than a charitable commitment to societies. Core aspects of CSR are protection of the environment and sustainability in growth, even though other aspects have grown in importance (e.g. relations with employees, environmental impact, paying a living wage, fair trade policies). However, the concepts of leadership and sustainability are intertwined with CSR because businesses are nowadays expected to have a sustainability policy, and business leaders clearly have an impact on setting the organizational goals.

Nowadays, all major supermarket chains also commit themselves to explicit policies seeking to minimize environmental impact. For example, the United Kingdom's premium-level food store, Marks and Spencer, leads the list of the most trusted corporations in the United Kingdom and has been recognized for its sustainability policies (Corporate-NGO Partnerships Barometer, 2010, 2011, 2012, 2013, 2014; Gill & Broderick, 2014). On the other hand, its closest competitor, Waitrose, prides itself on its sustainability policies and commitment to careful sourcing (Waitrose, 2015a). Recent new market-share winners, Lidl and Aldi (Kantar UK, 2014), also pay particular attention to the preservation of the environment and sustainability in sourcing and gaining profit (see e.g. Lidl, 2015).

In this chapter, we will examine policies that protect the environment and encourage sustainable business practice, and have helped with growth and profitability in one of the United Kingdom's top supermarkets, Waitrose—a company that is part of the John Lewis Partnership. The research question for the chapter is "to what extent do policies towards sustainability and growth depend on an organization's leadership model?"

In this chapter, we will look at the corporate website of Waitrose as well as policy documents of the John Lewis Partnership. The importance of this case lies in the fact that the John Lewis Partnership has been successful in increasing profit, even during periods when other companies in the United

Kingdom have faced a downturn in their sales. Furthermore, the company has achieved this business evolution and growth while at the same time having one of the most ethical business philosophies and a distinctive leadership model. For example, the highly critical non-governmental organization Ethical Consumer suggests that only a few UK companies are ethical, and the list includes the John Lewis Partnership (Ethical Consumer, 2015; 2014; 2013; 2013a). These commercial and contextual factors supported the choice of the John Lewis Partnership for this chapter's analysis, which demonstrates how a successful business model works and to what extent the company's success can be attributed to leadership. In other words, John Lewis's leadership model is centred on shared business responsibility, and participation of all partners in setting organizational goals has contributed towards sustainable growth and policies of environmental protection.

Corporate Social Responsibility, Environmental Protection, and Sustainability

Corporate social responsibility (CSR) has been a largely disputed concept; however, it has not lost importance because many companies enforce CSR policies to a certain degree. However, the major disagreement is centred on debates as to whether companies have responsibilities beyond caring for shareholders and generating profit. Expressing concern for shareholders only, while at the same time complying with laws, is at the centre of the classic understanding of business. The main proponent of this view was Milton Friedman (1962, 1970), who believed that the sole responsibility of companies is to generate profit while complying with laws. Everything else, according to Friedman, was an attempt at changing the economic regime and enforcing socialism only without overthrowing liberalism so openly. It involves standing against liberalism, which has protection of private ownership and economic freedom at the centre of its doctrine. This view of doing no harm has been predominant in the United States up to today, despite intense discussions in academia (see e.g. Albareda et al., 2007; Bowie, 2012; Hartman et al., 2007; Tschopp, 2005; Wood, 1991) and the fact that the stakeholder theory, as a main opponent to Friedman's views, emerged in the United States as well.

However, companies have realized that growing pressure from NGOs and social expectations cannot be ignored, and after the stakeholder theory emerged, corporations largely embraced this business model. The stakeholder theory argues that companies have responsibilities that go beyond caring only for the interests of shareholders and complying with existing laws. This means that companies should be socially responsible and make sure interests of all parties involved in business are satisfied, and that companies work for the betterment of societies and not just maximization of profit (see e.g. Crane et al., 2015; Freeman et al., 2010; Hörisch et al., 2014;

Pedersen, 2015). On the other hand, there are research studies that have different findings—e.g. research by Eweje (2006b) has revealed that

> the host communities blamed the companies when drawing the attention of governments to their plights. The host communities know that if they put pressure on the companies by involving the international community, the companies will in turn put pressure on the government to protect their image in developed countries where any unethical report can affect their market position.
>
> (p. 124)

However, even if different authors take different views on what constitutes CSR, all authors largely agree that companies should protect the environment and take care of stakeholders, be they suppliers, employees, or customers. For example, Bowie (2012, p. 8, our emphasis) stated,

> Corporate social responsibility includes profits for stockholders, high quality products for consumers, reasonable pay, benefits, and good working conditions for employees, a consistent market for suppliers who are paid promptly for their products, and investment in the local communities where the corporation operates.

Other authors have stated that CSR constitutes "animal rights, corporate governance, environmental management, corporate philanthropy, stakeholder management, labour rights and community development (. . .) corporate accountability, *socially responsible investment and sustainable development*, aimed variously at replacing, redefining or complementing the CSR concept" (Blowfield and Frynas, 2005, p. 501, our emphasis). Branco and Rodrigues (2007, p. 5, our emphasis) believe that elements of CSR are "*environmental protection, human resources management, health and safety at work*, relations with local communities, *relations with suppliers* and consumers" (ibid). Additionally, Simcic Bronn and Vrioni (2001, p. 210, our emphasis) offered a typology of CSR as corporate philanthropy, social disclosure, *company's environmental record, workforce diversity*, financial health and tendency to grow, and community involvement, whereas Freeman and Hasnaoui (2011, p. 419, our emphasis) included the terms "corporate responsibility, corporate citizenship, *sustainability*, and corporal social performance".

The view that companies must care for the society around them is present in the classic view through the notion of complying with laws and doing no harm to societies while it forms a constitutive part of the stakeholder theory, and nearly all companies nowadays enforce CSR policies. In other words, different authors emphasize different aspects of CSR as an unavoidable part of every CSR policy; however, environmental protection seems to be dominant in these definitions, as authors tend to agree companies should be cautious of the environment (see e.g. Falck & Heblich, 2007; Perrini, 2005).

The EU has also supported this view by incorporating environmental protection in its definition of CSR (Commission of the European Communities, 2001; European Multistakeholder Forum on CSR Report and Recommendations, 2004), and the EU in some ways does serve as a driver for CSR policies within the EU that some authors consider socialist (Bowie, 2012). Moreover, authors argue that there is a need for a fundamental change in the way corporations do business and understand environmental protection and sustainability (Ehrenfeld, 2000; Senge & Carstedt, 2001; Szekely & Knirsch, 2005) because of growing pressure on companies to introduce CSR policies that also include environmental policies, such as "assessing business products, eliminating waste and emissions, maximising efficiency and avoiding practices that damage the environment" (Eweje, 2006a, p. 28).

When it comes to sustainability, the term stands for

> building a society in which a proper balance is created between economic, social and ecological aims. For businesses, this involves sustaining and expanding economic growth, shareholder value, prestige, corporate reputation, customer relationships, and the quality of products and services. It also means adopting and pursuing ethical business practices, creating sustainable jobs, building values for all the company's stakeholders and attending to the needs of the underserved.
>
> (Szekely & Knirsch, 2005, p. 628)

Sustainability, however, also includes preservation of the environment, introduced in supply change management and defined

> as the management of SCs where all the three dimensions of sustainability, namely the economic, environmental, and social ones, are taken into account (. . .) When sustainable SCM principles are adopted, the companies adopting such principles hold themselves accountable for the social and environmental impacts arising along the SC, and are compelled to integrate ecological and social aspects into their decisions and actions along their SCs.
>
> (Ciliberti et al., 2008, p. 1580)

Much of the attention to sustainability has been generated because of corporate scandals, such as those concerning Royal Dutch Shell, Enron, WorldCom, Tyco, and other public liable companies that failed to grow sustainably and eventually engaged in dubious accountancy cover-ups that resulted in some filing for bankruptcy and leaving thousands unemployed and without pensions (Bowie, 2012; Moberg & Romar, 2003, 2006; Morsing & Schultz, 2006; Schouten & Remme, 2006; Silverstein, 2013; Tyco Fraud Centre, 2006; USA Today, 2005). After its corporate scandal, Shell redesigned its policies to become a responsible company that will grow sustainably, and its annual sustainability reports, as well as annual performance reports, are showing changes in the way they do business now (Ihlen, 2008). In other words, after corporate scandals, companies are generally pressured to introduce sustainable policies.

The reason continuous pressure on environmental protection is closely linked with sustainability is because sustainability is also seen as "a permanent concern of human kind" that "requires attention to environmental and social issues and for multi-dimensional cooperation, shared values and goals, participation and empowerment, and learning" (Tonn, 1990, cited from Eweje, 2007, p. 18). In addition, it is also widely known that the use of world energy is not sustainable because "eighty per cent of the world energy production relies on non-renewable fossil fuels" (Williams, 1994, cited from Korhonen, 2006, p. 200). Nevertheless, fuels are "emission intensive, and often on fuels imported to national and regional economies", and "production of chemicals and substances foreign to nature is risky even if there are no currently known negative impacts of certain substances" (ibid). Another widely known problem is an excessive harvest of renewable sources that is happening faster than resources can renew naturally, and this is a continuous problem in tropical areas (ibid). That is why it is crucial that companies implement sustainable and environment-friendly missions, visions, and values, and all this can help companies increase profit and enhance reputation in a long term (Szekely & Knirsch, 2005).

Moreover, companies now increasingly report on the environment in their non-financial reports, with which they are sharing

> the will to make CSR and sustainable development mutually compatible with one another, trying to communicate their ability to take into consideration needs expressed by the different stakeholders it deals with and the overall impact of its operation on the environment.
> (Perrini, 2005, p. 621, see also Szekely & Knirsch, 2005, Tench et al., 2014)

Clearly, an impact on environment and sustainability brings media attention that can be positive and negative, with negative attention having the potential to damage the reputation of a company at stake and trust in the business as a whole at issue. Indeed, media have increased their interest on business and CSR policies in the past decades (Buhr & Grafström, 2006; Grafström & Windell, 2011; Grayson, 2009; Ihlen, 2008; Tench et al., 2007). Even though the majority of coverage on CSR is negative (Tench et al., 2007), there are also examples when the media published positive articles and took a proactive role in boosting the reputation of a company. For example, *Fortune* published an article entitled "Walmart Saves the Planet" in 2006 that praised efforts of the company in the field of environmental protection (O'Connor et al., 2008).

When it comes to the link between sustainability and leadership, it can be argued that there is no sustainability without responsible management.

Corporate scandals explained earlier in this chapter clearly portrayed the need for responsible and moral management that will enforce sustainable policies (Szekely & Knirsch, 2005). Leadership would then mean

> securing the commitment of management (starting at the very top) and developing a system of incentives to reward leaders at all levels who develop and push for the adoption of sustainability practices. It also refers to the ability to respond flexibly to change and to engage in dialogue and partnerships with different members of society.
>
> (Szekely & Knirsch, 2005, p. 629)

This means that the key factors to achieve sustainability are leadership and vision, flexibility to change, and engagement with stakeholders (ibid).

The UK Supermarket Industry

Large multi-chains competing for market share dominate the UK supermarket industry. The four strongest supermarket chains in the United Kingdom are the so-called *Big 4*, or Tesco, Sainsbury's, ASDA, and Morrisons. However, in 2014, German discounters Lidl and Aldi increased their market share (Kantar UK, 2014; Kantar UK, 2015), which caused a fall in the share prices of the four largest supermarket chains (Ahmed, 2014). The UK supermarket industry has also been affected by the global recession, and this has had a direct impact on customer purchase behaviour; however, that stabilized in 2013 (Mintel, 2013a, 2013b). In 2014, the trend of recovery continued, as well as online shopping, which increased comparatively to purchases in stores (Mintel, 2014). Nevertheless, the profit of the largest UK supermarket is still falling (Craven, 2015; Prynn, 2015; Ruddick, 2015).

The supermarket industry in the United Kingdom has been affected by corporate scandals, such as the horse meat scandal in 2013 when it was discovered that meat sold by British supermarkets contained horse meat of unknown background and without declarations on food specifying that it was horse meat (for a detailed report see Lawrence, 2013). At first, the horse meat was discovered in meat sold by Tesco, Iceland, Aldi, and Lidl (Quinn, 2013), but later it was discovered that there were traces of horse DNA in meat sold also by Sainsbury's, ASDA, and the Co-Operative, albeit with a lower percentage of contamination. However, the meat has been removed from shelves as a precaution (Poulter et al., 2013). The John Lewis Partnership, including Waitrose, was not affected by the scandal, nor was Marks and Spencer, the closest competitor of Waitrose because of its premium position in the British market.

When it comes to market positioning, the so-called *Big 4* are positioned on the mass middle-class market, whereas upper-end supermarkets are traditionally Waitrose and Marks and Spencer. Lidl and Aldi are seen as bottom-end supermarkets (Armitage, 2015; Lowery, 2014; Neilan, 2014).

This profile can also be visualized at YouGov Profile (2015), which is a profiling page developed by the British government. For example, by entering the word "Waitrose" we get a detailed profile of their customers and their interests. The tool clearly reveals that Marks and Spencer's and Waitrose's customers belong to a wealthier part of the United Kingdom's population.

In 2013, Lidl launched its first TV campaign (*The Little Surprise Campaign*) (Mintel, 2013c) to combat the prejudice of being a lower-end supermarket and to challenge the image that shopping in Lidl presents a "social suicide" (Lowery, 2014, p. 3). In 2014, Lidl also launched a powerful Christmas campaign entitled *The Little Present Campaign*. This campaign featured guests going to a surprise Christmas party and guessing that the food was from Marks and Spencer or Waitrose and then expressing surprise after learning that the food was actually from Lidl (Lowery, 2014; Topić & Tench, 2015). The fact that Lidl used Waitrose and Marks and Spencer in their advertising also shows the reputation of Waitrose and Marks and Spencer when it comes to quality produce offers.

When it comes to Waitrose, they are famous for their charity work, often combined with promotional campaigns, which is not how other supermarket companies usually promote themselves. For example, in 2014, Waitrose launched a campaign called *Donate Your Voice*, which invited people to donate their voices for their Christmas advert by asking customers to record the soundtrack, and all profits from the adverts were donated to Great Ormond Street Hospital Children's Charity, Age UK, and the Trussell Trust (Farrell, 2014). Waitrose also tackled isolation during the Christmas period by calling for charities and NGOs to apply for funding to finance Christmas lunches for those in need through the campaign *Giving Back: Tackling Isolation at Christmas* (Waitrose, 2014). Other than the aforementioned, Waitrose has several other programmes to help local communities, such as, for example, the Community Matters programme and the Waitrose Foundation (Waitrose, 2015a, 2015b). The CSR element is particularly prominent within Waitrose's campaigns, as the company often emphasizes its ethical trade and fair treatment of employees (e.g. Boy and the Carrot campaign, 2014, and Waitrose with Heston Blumenthal's Lemon Tart advert, 2011). However, Waitrose also experienced a backlash when it tried to engage in a dialogue with customers by launching a Twitter campaign, #*Waitrose Reasons*, which asked customers to write why they love shopping at Waitrose. They ended up being mocked by some customers who tweeted, "I shop at Waitrose because it makes me feel important and I absolutely detest being surrounded by poor people", or "I shop at Waitrose but re-pack in Tesco bags so the rest of the estate doesn't know I won the Euromillions" (Clarke, 2015). This happened because of the general reputation of Waitrose as an overpriced supermarket chain (Dejevsky, 2014; Naylor, 2010), even though Waitrose has a price match policy with Tesco on branded products (Waitrose, 2015e).

On the other hand, Waitrose's main competitor, Marks and Spencer, has enjoyed the highest trust among the British public since the inception of the trust poll (Corporate-NGO Partnerships Barometer, 2010, 2011, 2012, 2013, 2014), and even though it is positioned as a premium supermarket, it does not have a problem with its high prices and reputation of being over-priced when it comes to food (Saner, 2013). Marks and Spencer also has successful campaigns that match its popularity among the British public. For example, the company's famous campaign is *Food Porn*, which was reused in 2014 because of its popularity (Ridley, 2014). The CSR element is less prominent within Marks and Spencer's advertising, albeit there is an attempt to position the organization as a company that cares for the well-being of the society. For example, the 2014 Christmas campaign #*Follow the Fairies*, which was a prime example of a successful integrated marketing campaign (Clarke, 2014) also made an attempt to influence social values while repositioning the company in line with its tradition—e.g. the adverts featured fairies shutting down the electricity, forcing children to stop using the electronics, and encouraging them to go out to play in the snow. Whereas Waitrose was ridiculed for its attempt to engage with stakeholders, the media and public did not engage in criticism of Marks and Spencer for its initiative to bring snow to schools but merely reported about it, stating that it was a surprise (see e.g. Clarke, 2014).

Method

In order to examine policies of the UK supermarket industry, we examined Waitrose's policies. We selected this supermarket due to its distinctive position in the UK—i.e. Waitrose is a part of the John Lewis Partnership, which is famous for its socially responsible policies and employee-owned business orientation (Ethical Consumer, 2015; John Lewis Partnership, 2015; Waitrose, 2015c). We analyzed the websites for Waitrose and the John Lewis Partnership, as well as policy documents, to examine what policies the Partnership has towards the environment and sustainable development, and how their leadership and employee management work.

The analysis of corporate websites is a common method when evaluating policies that constitute part(s) of CSR because it can show corporate vision, business philosophy, and CSR policies, including environmental and sustainability policies. Corporate websites became an important means of communicating CSR policies because companies have to ensure a good reputation due to pressure to do business in a socially responsible way, and this way of communicating CSR is particularly good because it works even in countries where people dislike CSR communication and/or CSR advertising (Capriotti & Moreno, 2007; Drumwright, 1996; Johansen & Nielsen, 2011; Perrini, 2005; Morsing et al., 2008; Nielsen & Thompsen, 2009; Vidaver-Cohen & Simcic Bronn, 2013).

We used a thematic analysis as a method of the analysis. Thematic analysis is a

> systematic approach to the analysis of qualitative data that involves identifying themes or patterns of cultural meaning (. . .) and classifying data, usually textual, according to themes; and interpreting the resulting thematic structures by seeking commonalities, relationships, overarching patterns, theoretical constructs, or explanatory principles.
>
> (Lapadat, 2013, p. 2)

The analytic approach of the thematic analysis focuses on coding, which means "inspecting text to look for recurrent themes, topics or relationships, and marking similar passages with a code or label to categorize them for later retrieval" (ibid, p. 3). However, thematic analysis does not seek to build a theory, such as, for example, grounded theory, and it can be essentialist or realist as well as constructionist. This means that "essentialist or realist (. . .) reports experiences, meanings and the reality of participants", whereas "a constructionist method (. . .) examines the ways in which events, realities, meanings, experiences, and so on are the effects of a range of discourses operating within society" (Braun & Clarke, 2006, p. 81). We used a constructionist thematic analysis in order to understand how the John Lewis Partnership constructs meaning in its corporate documents.

Thematic analysis was deemed appropriate for this research given the exploratory nature of the research and the fact that we had no intention to build a theory but to conduct an in-depth analysis of one case to build understanding and help direct future research and recommendations. Another possible method for a qualitative inquiry such as this one would be a discourse analysis; however, this method was deemed inappropriate given its focus on social justice and the interplay between power and dominance expressed in written materials (Fairclough, 2014; Van Dijk, 2007, 2009; Wodak, 1999, 2002). In other words, we wanted to discover whether there is a link between corporate conduct and the leadership model.

Finally, thematic analysis is a particularly convenient method for research guided by a research question that does not seek to establish a theory. Because we were guided by the research question "to what extent do policies towards sustainability and growth depend on an organization's leadership model?", this method was deemed appropriate because it enabled us to look at one aspect of John Lewis's communication to answer this question.

Findings

Waitrose is a part of the John Lewis Partnership, and it was founded in 1904 in London when Wallace Waite, Arthur Rose, and David Taylor opened the first Waitrose store, which was initially called Waite, Rose & Taylor. The

John Lewis Partnership acquired the store in 1937, and the first Waitrose supermarket was opened in 1955 (Waitrose, 2015d). During the course of our research, we identified several themes: business philosophy, employee's rights, sustainability and leadership (which are closely linked), and environmental protection.

However, because business philosophy, employee's rights, and sustainability and leadership are linked in the corporate strategy and embedded in the company's business orientation, we grouped these elements in one theme and analyzed them accordingly, whereas environmental protection formed another theme in the corporate strategy.

The first theme presents the extended business philosophy of the Partnership, whereas the other theme presents responsiveness in regard to current debates in British society as regards environmental protection and the impact business has on the environment.

The Business Philosophy, Employee's Rights, Sustainability, and Leadership

For Waitrose, business philosophy, employee's rights, sustainability, and leadership are closely linked and embedded in a coherent business philosophy, which goes in line with academic debates discussed at the beginning of the chapter that call for an embedded approach, where corporations will run sustainable businesses centred on building a proper balance between economic, social, and ecological aims of business (Szekely & Knirsch, 2005).

Therefore, Waitrose's business philosophy is summarized in four core values: *championing British, living well, treating people fairly*, and *treading lightly* (Waitrose, 2015a). All four values can be considered as constituting CSR for the company also, because each value expresses concerns for the society; however, in this particular case, these are the core values of the organizations as a whole and not part of a separate CSR policy. In other words, Waitrose/John Lewis Partnership embedded a stakeholder approach (Freeman et al., 2010) into their business before the approach earned wide appraisals and entered the mainstream. The company also went a step further and developed a model of business based on equality and joint leadership among all partners. Further, whereas scholars had to call for more responsibility of companies and insist on the need for fundamental change in the way corporations run and understand business because of corporate scandals (Bowie, 2012; Ehrenfeld, 2000; Eweje, 2007; Morsing & Schultz, 2008; Senge & Carstedt, 2001; Szekely & Knirsch, 2005), Waitrose had implemented this approach long before those debates had taken place.

Championing British, therefore, means that Waitrose is sourcing its products from British farms, including meat in Waitrose's ready meals (ibid), and these values are promoted in several adverts released by Waitrose such as "A Tour of Leckford, the Waitrose Farm—Interactive Video—Waitrose"

(2014) and "The Story Of the Farmer and the Precious Egg—Waitrose" (2013). In other words, the policy says,

> We build long-term relationships with our farmers and suppliers, working sustainably to deliver quality produce which helps our customers get the best possible products to help them to live more healthily—this is The Waitrose Way.
>
> (Waitrose, 2015a)

The living well value addresses social concerns about obesity (Fill, 2014) and promotes healthy living by emphasizing the following:

> We believe that eating well should be enjoyable. We have a wide range of healthy meals and snacks, low-fat recipes and calorie controlled eating plans to inspire you to eat more healthily.
>
> (Waitrose, 2015a; see also John Lewis Partnership, 2014, p. 31)

Treating people fairly promotes the fair treatment of employees and the promotion of fair trade products, whereas treading lightly refers to the protection of the environment, where Waitrose particularly emphasizes its policies:

> We believe in making the right choices for the environment by reducing packaging, waste, CO_2 emissions and responsibly sourcing our food. We stock more than 1600 organic products and our range is one of the widest selections in the UK. By choosing Waitrose organics you can be assured that the products not only taste fantastic but have been responsibly sourced.
>
> (Waitrose, 2015a; see also John Lewis Partnership, 2014)

> We believe in treating our customers, Partners, farmers and suppliers fairly, as well as supporting local charities through Community Matters.
>
> (ibid)

Nevertheless, the John Lewis Partnership (of which Waitrose is a part) places happiness of all partners and customers at the core of its business philosophy. For example, in the Partnership's Constitution, the fact that the partnership exists to ensure the happiness of its members is defined clearly:

> The Partnership's ultimate purpose is happiness of all its members, through their worthwhile and satisfying employment in a successful business. Because the Partnership is owned in trust for its members, they share the responsibilities of ownership as well as its rewards—profit, knowledge and power.
>
> (Constitution, Part 2, Principles, Purpose, clause 1, p. 7)

The organization is famous for its business model, in which all employees are partners and co-owners of the organization and share the profit at the end of the year. In other words,

> Our 93,800 employees, called Partners, are all owners of the business and share in its success. Our relationships with our Partners are based on mutual respect and courtesy. The Partnership's ultimate purpose is "the happiness of Partners through worthwhile and satisfying employment in a successful business".
>
> (John Lewis Partnership, 2015c)

In more detail, the John Lewis Partnership website emphasizes that employee-owned businesses form 2 per cent of businesses in the United Kingdom and that this business model presents the most successful business model (John Lewis Partnership, 2015d, 2015e). This claim is indeed supported by research carried out by the Employee Ownership Association (Employee Ownership Association, 2015). In addition, this business model is clearly in line with recommendations on effective leadership to achieve sustainable business growth where sustainable management is seen as a way of doing business by integrating all dimensions of sustainability (economic, environmental, and social) in a coherent business philosophy (Ciliberti et al., 2008). This indeed seems to be in line with the policies of the John Lewis Partnership that integrate all policies in an embedded business approach. Nevertheless, the organization's approach to employment is also famous and is explained in an organizational mission that heavily emphasizes the involvement of staff in the business:

> Partners are instrumental in all that we do. Our Partners own our business so have a vested interest in its success. They are at the heart of our service offering, embodying our values of trust, respect and fairness and they are the energy and passion that drives our work to be an evermore responsible and sustainable business. "The John Lewis Partnership faces similar challenges to other major retailers but in one respect our response is very different. That's the energy and passion of our Partners who, as co-owners of our business, drive our work to operate an evermore sustainable and responsible business".
>
> (John Lewis Partnership, 2015c).

In other words, the Partnership places emphasis on staff satisfaction, arguing that happy staff can ensure a sustainable and responsible business. This means that a crucial role in business sustainability is assigned to staff and their role in the business and not to leadership or management. The Partnership highlights this aspect in their advertising, especially when it comes to advertising for Waitrose. For example, in an advert "Boy and the Carrot", Waitrose particularly emphasized that "everyone at Waitrose owns

Waitrose", and thus "when you own something, you care a little more" (Boy and the Carrot campaign, 2014).

The way the Partnership functions is based on a model of shared interest and communication, or "aligning Partner interests", "communicating Partner interests", and "representing Partner interests". The Partnership's policy documents claim this is the most sustainable and the most successful way of doing business (John Lewis Partnership, 2014, p. 7), and this view is also supported with official data that shows an increase in profit for the John Lewis Partnership despite the crisis in the industry (Bold, 2014). The John Lewis Partnership was not affected by the crisis and created 6,300 new jobs in 2014 (John Lewis Partnership, 2014, p. 43). This model is also praised by academia, which argues that environmental protection and sustainability are linked in businesses that share these values and goals and where these values have an impact on the way the organization does business (for a more extensive debate on this matter, see Eweje, 2007).

In terms of the decision-making process, partners are represented in the Partnership Council, and there is a weekly Partnership magazine, the *Gazette*, that gives all the news on the decision-making process (John Lewis Partnership, 2014, p. 7). In other words,

> Partners are formally represented in two of the three governing authorities: the Partnership Board and the Partnership Council. This means all Partners can share their thoughts about our strengths, weaknesses, accomplishments and plans with everyone in the organisation—from the shop floor to the Board.
>
> (John Lewis Partnership, 2014, p. 7)

According to the Constitution of the Partnership, this model is a shared responsibility model:

> The Partnership Council represents Partners as a whole and reflects their opinion. In sharing responsibility for the Partnership's health with the Partnership Board and the Chairman, it holds the Chairman to the account. It discusses, influences and makes recommendations on the development of policy. It shares in making decisions about the governance of the Partnership. The Council may ask the Partnership Board or the Chairman anything it wishes, and they must answer unless doing so would in their opinion damage the Partnership's interests.
>
> (Constitution, Part 3, Rules, clause 7, p. 10)

If we link this model with academic debates, then the Waitrose/John Lewis Partnership clearly follows a model of good leadership centred on a dialogue between all employees/partners that also includes managers/leaders (Szekely & Knirsch, 2005). In 2014, this policy resulted in all partners sharing profits and bonuses that totalled GBP 203m (John Lewis Partnership, 2014, p. 11). This also means that when it comes to the leadership model, the Partnership operates on a principle of shared power among all partners who are represented by the Partnership Council, the Partnership Board, and the chairman. These bodies are also responsible for sustainable development because they must ensure prosperity of the Partnership, and all spending must be authorized by the board:

> The shared aim of the three governing authorities is to safeguard the Partnership's future, to enhance its prosperity and to ensure its integrity. They should encourage creativity and an entrepreneurial spirit but must not risk any loss of financial independence.
>
> (Constitution, Part 3, Rules, clause 4, p. 9)

> Commitments, either legal or moral, to spend Partnership funds may only be made upon written authority from the Partnership Board or from someone delegated to give authority on its behalf.
>
> (Constitution, Part 3, Rules, clause 5, p. 9)

The Partnership also seeks long-term growth, which is ensured through efficient expansion of the business. In other words,

> the Partnership needs a sufficiently wide commercial base to ensure its long-term vitality, and to achieve this it may engage in as wide a variety of enterprises as it can undertake efficiently.
>
> (Constitution, Part 3, Rules, clause 6, p. 10)

This long-term growth is closely linked with the founding principles of the Partnership that outline the purpose of the Partnership as well as the core components of business, or power, profit, members, customers, business relationships, and the community. In that, profit is closely linked with sustainability of the business and welfare of all partners who share profit, whereas the community concept is linked with the social role of the Partnership in the community in which it operates. In other words,

> the Partnership aims to make sufficient profit from its trading operations to sustain its commercial vitality, to finance its continued development, to distribute a share of those profits each year to its members, and to enable it to undertake other activities consistent with its ultimate purpose.
>
> (Constitution, Part 2, Principles, Profit, clause 3, p. 7)

> The Partnership aims to conduct all its business relationships with integrity and courtesy, and scrupulously to honour ever business agreement.
>
> (Constitution, Part 2, Principles, The Community, clause 7, p. 8)

What seems to be central to the business philosophy of the Partnership is the welfare of employees. Therefore, the Partnership is trying to achieve career satisfaction by "promoting Partners of suitable ability", "encouraging changes of responsibility", "providing knowledge and access to training to help them carry out their responsibilities better", and "encouraging their personal development and interests in fields not directly related to their work" (Constitution, Section 2—Partner's Rights and Responsibilities, Employment Conditions, clause 56). The system of awards works through the partner's annual bonuses, as explained earlier, and also through the philosophy of awarding partners who remain with the Partnership for longer than five years:

> Recognising that five years is a milestone for a Partner, this should be recognised in an appropriate way by the Partnership. A Partner with more than five years' membership will be encouraged, if his performance remains satisfactory, to develop his skills so that he may continue in the Partnership for all his working life.
> (Constitution, Section 2, Partners' Rights and Responsibilities, Security of Employment, clause 66, p. 21)

In other words, a whole business model is based on employees and their satisfaction rather than on the development of effective leadership, or educating staff to be more effective. The Partnership has educational programmes available to staff as well as permission to apply for leave to participate in volunteering; however, this seems to be more connected with staff satisfaction than their role in taking a lead in development of the Partnership as a whole.

The Environmental Protection

Waitrose and the John Lewis Partnership enforce various policies to protect the environment. In the "Sustainability Review" (John Lewis Partnership, 2014), the organization extensively reported on their environmental activities.

For example, they are working towards reducing carbon emissions from distribution, increasing gas dual-fuel trucks, reducing mileage when distributing merchandise to stores, and using environmentally friendly packaging. In Waitrose, in particular, the Partnership is working towards reducing waste and resourcing efficiently to minimize the impact on the environment. The only field in which the organization reports failure is in water management. In that, the organization reported a goal to manage water in a more efficient way to address the issue of water scarcity. However, the target of reducing water consumption "per square foot of trading floor area in our shops by 20% by the end of 2013/14, against a 2010/11 baseline" has not been entirely successful, and a new goal has been set for 2020/21 (John Lewis Partnership, 2014, p. 36).

These policies are strongly linked to the Partnership's four core values, or the one named 'treading lightly', where the Partnership emphasized reduced packaging, waste, and CO_2 emissions and responsible sourcing as one of the core values of the organization as explained earlier (John Lewis Partnership, 2014; Waitrose, 2015a). Nevertheless, these policies are in line with their perceived importance in the United Kingdom and the EU, where even the EU introduced environmental protection as part of corporate responsibility programmes of present business (European Multistakeholder Forum, 2004).

The organization is also supporting sourcing raw materials "from long-term sustainable supply chains" because these materials can have "a significant impact on people, environments and ecosystems, if not managed considerately" (ibid, p. 27). In addition, Waitrose only sources fish that is "responsibly caught", soya that only comes from sustainable sources, and palm oil that comes from reliable sources (ibid). When it comes to farm standards, Waitrose only uses British farms and awards farms for quality produce (ibid). Nevertheless, both Waitrose and the John Lewis Partnership have initiatives that celebrate and promote British products, such as Championing British (one of Waitrose's official values), and Made in UK (John Lewis Partnership's initiative) (John Lewis Partnership, 2014, p. 25).

These policies eventually resulted in consumer awards in 2013 and 2014 to both Waitrose and the John Lewis Partnership by the consumer association Which? This organization honoured Waitrose as the best supermarket, whereas John Lewis Partnership was recognized as the best retailer (Bachelor, 2014).

Conclusion

The John Lewis Partnership presents a successful model of sustainable business that achieved profit growth even during a time of crisis for the retail sector when many competitors were struggling to preserve their market position.

The John Lewis Partnership model seems to be a clear example of a textbook definition of a sustainable business. This model of business meets all elements of sustainable business as defined by Szekely and Knirsch (2005, p. 628)—i.e. the company has indeed contributed to "building a society in which a proper balance is created between economic, social and ecological aims".

As we have elaborated in the chapter, the John Lewis Partnership has created "sustaining and expanding economic growth, shareholder value, prestige, corporate reputation, customer relationships, and the quality of products and services", as well as a business philosophy that encompasses "ethical business practices, creating sustainable jobs, building values for all the company's stakeholders and attending to the needs of the underserved" (Szekely & Knirsch, 2005, p. 628).

The company has also answered recent social concerns on environmental protection by demonstrating that it has a proven concern for the society in which it operates. When it comes to leadership, this company presents a case of a very exceptional business model that is not based on a top-down approach but on a partnership and the inclusion of all employees in business management through active engagement and the inclusion of a system of profit share. In other words, John Lewis's leadership model is an example of an embedded model of leadership and employee management based on dialogue and communication.

Whereas corporate scandals discussed earlier in the chapter have demonstrated the need for changes in leadership because of corruption and malpractice that damage the interests of employees as well as companies and their reputations at large, the John Lewis Partnership has never been a part of any scandal. In this particular case, that is because there is a system of implementing decision making that includes all employees who can monitor policies being enforced from the top. It seems equally possible to apply some of the aspects of the John Lewis Partnership business model to other large companies who wish to ensure that their business policy is sustainable and ethical.

One possibility would be to implement a system of independent auditing that will ensure that no *manager(ment)* can act according to his or her (their) own personal beliefs without taking into consideration the interests of employees and the corporation at large. In other words, corporate scandals not only damage the prospects of employees but also of shareholders, and monitoring management and preventing individual decision-making processes could contribute to the well-being of both sides—i.e. employees and shareholders.

This approach could also serve as reconciliation between shareholders and the stakeholder view on CSR. It was Milton Friedman (1962, 1970) who argued that managers, when enforcing CSR, make decisions based on their private interests and beliefs, which is damaging for corporations, whereas the stakeholder camp looks at interests of stakeholders at large that can be negatively affected if the corporation is not pursuing ethical policies. No matter how we look at this, both sides can agree that irresponsible management can cause harm to the corporation, stakeholders, and societies at large. Whereas some could say that the John Lewis Partnership model is a 'socialist' model of doing business (Milton Friedman probably would), it is still, nevertheless, a business model that can serve as a foundation for improving business policies of other companies regardless of whether they will improve their profitability and profit share orientation or not.

References

Ahmed, K. (October 1, 2014). Tesco, Sainsbury's—the bad news just keeps coming. *BBC*. Retrieved from: http://www.bbc.co.uk/news/business-29444904 (27 March 2015)

Albareda, L., Lozano, J. M., & Ysa, T. (2007). Public policies on corporate social responsibility: The role of governments in Europe. *Journal of Business Ethics*, 74, 391–407.

Armitage, J. (2015). *Jim Armitage: Time for Sainsbury's to make a bolder move or lose investors.* Retrieved 21 April 2015 from: http://www.independent.co.uk/news/business/comment/jim-armitage-time-for-sainsburys-to-make-a-bolder-move-or-lose-investors-9964083.html

Bachelor, L. (2014). *Waitrose pips discounters to best supermarket title at which? Awards.* Retrieved 28 April 2015 from: http://www.theguardian.com/business/2014/jun/19/waitrose-best-supermarket-which-awards-john-lewis

Blowfield, M., & Frynas, J. G. (2005). Setting new agendas: critical perspectives on Corporate Social Responsibility in the developing world. *International Affairs, 81*(3), 499–513.

Bold, B. (2014). *John Lewis reports sales boost, although Waitrose profits hit.* Retrieved 27 April 2015 from: http://www.marketingmagazine.co.uk/article/1311 676/john-lewis-reports-sales-boost-although-waitrose-profits-hit

Bowie, N. E. (2012). *Corporate social responsibility in Business. A commissioned background paper about corporate social responsibility in Business as it relates to the creation of public value.* Retrieved 26 March 2015 from: http://www.leadership.umn.edu/documents/Bowie5–30.pdf

Boy and the Carrot campaign. (2014). Retrieved 21 April 2015 from: https://www.youtube.com/watch?v=1esFngx0vJs

Branco, M. C., & Rodrigues, L. L. (2007). Positioning Stakeholder Theory within the Debate on Corporate Social Responsibility. *EJBO: Electronic Journal of Business Ethics and Organization Studies, 12*(1), 5–15.

Braun, V., & Clarke, V. (2006). Using thematic analysis in psychology. *Qualitative Research in Psychology, 3*(2), 77–101.

Buhr, H., & Grafström, M. (2006). *The making in the media: The case of corporate social responsibility in the "Financial Times", 1988–2003.* Retrieved 26 March 2015 from: http://www.fek.uu.se/gems/publications/Buhr_Grafstrom_CSR_2006.pdf

Capriotti, P., & Moreno, A. (2007). Communicating corporate responsibility through corporate web sites in Spain. *Corporate Communications: An International Journal, 12*(3), 221–237.

Ciliberti, F., Pontrandolfo, P., & Scozzi, B. (2008). Investigating corporate social responsibility in supply chains: A SME perspective. *Journal of Cleaner Production, 16*, 1579–1588.

Clarke, J. (2014). *Surprise snow fall at Cornish school part of Marks & Spencer Christmas TV campaign.* Retrieved 21 April 2015 from: http://www.western morningnews.co.uk/Cornish-school-covered-snow-used-Marks-Spencer/story-24433242-detail/story.html

Clarke, S. (2015). *Did the #Waitrose reasons Twitter campaign backfire . . . or not?* Retrieved 27 March 2015 from: http://www.steveclarke.info/did-the-wait rose-reasons-twitter-campaign-backfire-or-not/

Commission of the European Communities. (2001). *GREEN PAPER: Promoting a European framework for corporate social responsibility, COM (2001) 366 final.* Retrieved 5 March 2015 from: http://www.csr-in-commerce.eu/data/files/resources/717/com_2001_0366_en.pdf

Corporate-NGO Partnerships Barometer. (2010). Retrieved 5 January 2015 from: http://www.candeadvisory.com/sites/default/files/C%26E%20Corporate-NGO%20Partnerships%20Barometer%202010%20Final%20Report_0.pdf

Corporate-NGO Partnerships Barometer. (2011). Retrieved 5 January 2015 from: http://www.candeadvisory.com/sites/default/files/Final_C%26E_Corporate_ NGO_Partnerships_Barometer_2011_.pdf

Corporate-NGO Partnerships Barometer. (2012). Retrieved 5 January 2015 from: http://www.candeadvisory.com/sites/default/files/C%26E_Corporate-NGO_ Partnerships_Barometer_2012_Final_0.pdf

Corporate-NGO Partnerships Barometer. (2013). Retrieved 5 January 2015 from: http://www.candeadvisory.com/sites/default/files/C&E_Corporate_NGO_Part nerships_Barometer_2013_FINAL.pdf

Corporate-NGO Partnerships Barometer. (2014). Retrieved 2 December 2014 from: http://www.candeadvisory.com/sites/default/files/Headline_Findings_Baro meter_2014.pdf

Crane, A., Matten, D., & Spence, L. J. (Eds.) (2015). *Corporate social responsibility: Readings and cases in a global context* (2nd edn.). London: Routledge.

Craven, N. (2015). *Combined profits at Tesco, Sainsbury's and Morrisons fall by £2.5bn—and is set to shrink further as shoppers cut back.* Retrieved 27 April 2015 from: http://www.thisismoney.co.uk/money/markets/article-3055443/ Combined-profit-Tesco-Sainsbury-s-Morrisons-fall-2-5bn-set-shrink-shoppers-cut-back.html

Dejevsky, M. (2014). *Everyone loves John Lewis, especially the government. But is its reputation justified?* Retrieved 21 April 2015 from: http://www.indepen dent.co.uk/voices/comment/PMFRAME=1&pubId=40991&siteId=40992&ad Id=80848&kadwidth=300&kadheight=600&SAVersion=2&js=1&kdntuid=1& pageURL=http://www.independent.co.uk/voices/comment/everyone-loves-john-lewis-especially-the-government-but-is-its-reputation-justified-9081028.html& inIframe=1&kadpageurl=http://www.independent.co.uk/&operId=3&klt stamp=2015-4-21%2012:56:27&timezone=1&screenResolution=1920x1080& ranreq=0.823759309176195&pmUniAdId=0

Drumwright, M. E. (1996). Company advertising with a social dimension: The role of noneconomic criteria. *Journal of Marketing*, 60, 71–87.

Ehrenfeld, J. R. (2000). Industrial ecology: Paradigm shift or normal science? *American Behavioral Scientist*, 44(2), 229–244.

Employee Ownership Association. (2015). *Reports and publications.* Retrieved 22 April 2015 from: http://employeeownership.co.uk/resources/reports/

Ethical Consumer. (2013a). *Ethical consumer markets report.* Retrieved 5 March 2015 from: http://www.ethicalconsumer.org/portals/0/downloads/ethical_consu mer_markets_report_2013.pdf

Ethical Consumer. (2013b). *Sector report on the food industry: Food, justice and corporate power.* Retrieved 5 March 2015 from: http://www.ethicalconsumer. org/ethicalreports/foodindustrysectorreport.aspx

Ethical Consumer. (2014). *Sector report on the fashion industry: Fashion victims.* Retrieved 5 March 2015 from: http://www.ethicalconsumer.org/ethicalreports/ fashionindustry.aspx

Ethical Consumer. (2015). *Top 5 high St shops.* Retrieved 15 May 2015 from: http:// www.ethicalconsumer.org/shoppingethically/topethicaltips/top5ethicalhigh streetshops.aspx

European Multistakeholder Forum on CSR Report and Recommendations. (2004). *European multistakeholder forum on CSR: Final results & recommendations.*

Retrieved 5 March 2015 from: http://www.corporatejustice.org/IMG/pdf/CSR_20Forum_20final_20report.pdf

Eweje, G. (2006a). Environmental costs and responsibilities resulting from oil exploitation in developing countries: The case of the Niger Delta of Nigeria. *Journal of Business Ethics, 69*, 27–56.

Eweje, G. (2006b). The role of MNEs in community development initiatives in developing countries: Corporate social responsibility at work in Nigeria and South Africa. *Business & Society, 45*(2), 93–129.

Eweje, G. (2007). Strategic partnerships between MNEs and civil society: The post-WSDD perspectives. *Sustainable Development, 15*, 15–27.

Fairclough, N. (2014). The discourse of new labour: Critical discourse analysis. In M. Wetherell, & S. Taylor (Eds.) *Discourse as data: A guide for analysis* (pp. 229–266). London: Sage.

Falck, O., & Heblich, S. (2007). Corporate social responsibility: Doing well by doing good. *Business Horizons, 50*, 247–254.

Farrell, C. (October 15, 2014). Waitrose invites public to sing on Christmas advert. *The Grocer*. Retrieved 27 March 2015 from: http://www.thegrocer.co.uk/channels/supermarkets/waitrose/waitrose-invites-public-to-sing-on-christmas-advert/372568.article

Fill, C. (2014). *Marketing communications* (3rd Ed.). London: Pearson.

Freeman, I., & Hasnaoui, A. (2011). The meaning of corporate social responsibility: The vision of four nations. *Journal of Business Ethics, 100*(3), 419–443.

Freeman, R. E., Harrison, J. S., Wicks, A. C., Parmar, B. L., & De Colle, S. (2010). *Stakeholder theory: The state of art*. Cambridge: Cambridge University Press.

Friedman, M. (1962). *Capitalism and freedom*. Chicago: University of Chicago Press.

Friedman, M. (1970). The social responsibility of business is to increase its profits. *The New York Times Magazine*, 13 September. Retrieved 12 December 2014 from: http://www.colorado.edu/studentgroups/libertarians/issues/friedman-soc-resp-business.html

Gill, D., & Broderick, A. (2014). Brand heritage and CSR credentials: A discourse analysis of M&S reports. In R. Tench, W. Sun & B. Jones (Eds.), *Communicating corporate social responsibility: Perspectives and practice* (pp. 179–201). Howard House: Emerald Books.

Grafström, M., & Windell, K. (2011). The role of infomediaries: CSR in the business press during 2000–2009. *Journal of Business Ethics, 103*, 221–237.

Grayson, D. (2009). *Corporate responsibility and the media*. Doughty Centre Corporate Responsibility. Retrieved 26 March 2015 from: http://www.som.cranfield.ac.uk/som/dinamic-content/research/doughty/crandthemediafinal.pdf

Hartman, L. P., Rubin, R. S., & Dhanda, K. K. (2007). The communication of corporate social responsibility: United States and European Union Multinational Corporations. *Journal of Business Ethics, 74*, 373–389.

Hörisch, J., Freeman, R. E., & Schaltegger, S. (2014). Applying stakeholder theory in sustainability management: Links, similarities, dissimilarities, and a conceptual framework. *Organization & Environment, 27*(4), 328–346. doi:10.1177/1086026614535786

Ihlen, Ø. (2008). Mapping the environment for corporate social responsibility. *Corporate Communications: An International Journal, 13*(2), 135–146.

Johansen, T. S., & Nielsen, A. E. (2011). Strategic stakeholder dialogues: A discursive perspective on relationship building. *Corporate Communications: An International Journal, 16*(3), 204–217.

John Lewis Partnership. (2014). *Sustainability review.* Retrieved 22 April 2015 from: http://www.johnlewispartnership.co.uk/content/dam/cws/pdfs/our%20 responsibilities/our%20progress%20and%20reports/review2014/John_Lewis_ Partnership_Sustainability_Review_2014.pdf

John Lewis Partnership. (2015a). *About us.* Retrieved 21 April 2015 from: http:// www.johnlewispartnership.co.uk/

John Lewis Partnership. (2015b). *The constitution.* Retrieved 27 March 2015 from: http://www.johnlewispartnership.co.uk/content/dam/cws/pdfs/about%20us/ our%20constitution/john-lewis-partnership.constitution.pdf

John Lewis Partnership. (2015c).*Our employees.* Retrieved 22 April 2015 from: http://www.johnlewispartnership.co.uk/csr/our-employees.html

John Lewis Partnership. (2015d). *Guide to employee ownership.* Retrieved 22 April 2015 from: http://www.johnlewispartnership.co.uk/content/dam/cws/pdfs/ our%20responsibilities/our%20employees/Guide_to_Employee_Ownership.pdf

John Lewis Partnership. (2015e). *Employee ownership.* Retrieved 22 April 2015 from: http://www.johnlewispartnership.co.uk/csr/our-employees/employee-own ership.html

Kantar UK. (2014). *UKs grocery market enters deflation.* Retrieved 28 October 2014 from: http://www.kantarworldpanel.com/global/News/UKs-grocery-market-enters-deflation

Kantar UK. (2015). *UK: Morrisons return to growth and Lidl reach new share high.* Retrieved 22 August 2015 from: http://www.kantarworldpanel.com/global/ News/UK-Morrisons-return-to-growth-and-Lidl-reach-new-share-high

Korhonen, J. (2006). On the paradox of corporate social responsibility: How can we use social science and natural science for a new vision? *Business Ethics, 15*(2), 200–214.

Lapadat, J. (2013). Thematic Analysis. In A. J. Mills, G. Durepos & E. Wiebe (Eds.), *Encyclopedia of Case Study Research.* London: SAGE. http://dx.doi. org/10.4135/9781412957397.n342

Lawrence, F. (2013). *Horsemeat scandal: Where did the 29% horse in your Tesco burger come from?* Retrieved 27 April 2015 from: http://www.theguardian.com/ uk-news/2013/oct/22/horsemeat-scandal-guardian-investigation-public-secrecy

Lidl. (2015). *Environment protection.* Retrieved 14 January 2015 from: http://www. lidl.co.uk/en/856.htm

Lowery, J. (2014). Lidl: Surprisingly high returns for a surprisingly low investment. *Warc UK* (pp. 2–20). Retrieved 27 March 2015 from: http://www.warc.com/Con tent/ContentViewer.aspx?MasterContentRef=59fcfbd2–8fe6–40b7–91fa-6a6630 f49d6b&CID=A102481&PUB=IPA

Mintel. (2013a). *Organic food and drink—UK—October 2013: Market size and forecast.* Retrieved 27 March 2015 from: http://academic.mintel.com/display/ 682986/

Mintel. (2013b). *Supermarkets: More than just food retailing—UK—November 2013.* Retrieved from: http://academic.mintel.com/display/687471/

Mintel. (2013c). *Supermarkets: More than just food retailing—UK—November 2013: Advertising and promotion.* Mintel Policy Report.

Mintel. (2014). *Online grocery retailing—UK—March 2014: The consumer—profiling online grocers' shoppers*. Retrieved 27 March 2015 from: http://academic.mintel.com/display/699222/

Moberg, D., & Romar, E. (2003). *WorldCom*. Retrieved 31 March 2015 from: http://www.scu.edu/ethics/dialogue/candc/cases/worldcom.html

Moberg, D., & Romar, E. (2006). *WorldCom case study update*. Retrieved 31 March 2015 from: http://www.scu.edu/ethics/dialogue/candc/cases/worldcom-update.html

Morsing, M., & Schultz, M. (2006). Corporate social responsibility communication: Stakeholder information, response and involvement strategies. *Business Ethics: A European Review*, 15(4), 323–338.

Morsing, M., Schultz, M., & Nielsen, U. (2008). The "Catch 22" of communicating CSR: Findings from a Danish study. *Journal of Marketing Communications*, 14(2), 97–111.

Naylor, T. (July 14, 2010). Should we all be shopping at Waitrose? *The Guardian*. Retrieved 21 April 2015 from: http://www.theguardian.com/lifeandstyle/wordofmouth/2010/jul/14/should-we-all-shop-waitrose

Neilan, C. (2014). *Are you a Waitrose Wendy or a Tesco Tracey: How do the UK's supermarket shoppers look?* Retrieved 21 April 2015 from: http://www.cityam.com/1416234688/are-you-waitrose-wendy-or-tesco-tracey-how-do-uks-supermarket-shoppers-look

Nielsen, A. E., & Thomsen, C. (2009). CSR communication in small and medium-sized enterprises. *Corporate Communications: An International Journal*, 14(2), 176–189.

O'Connor, A., Shumate, M., & Meister, M. (2008). Walk the line: Active Moms define corporate social responsibility. *Public Relations Review*, 34, 343–350.

Pedersen, E. R. G. (2015). *Corporate social responsibility*. Thousand Oaks: SAGE.

Perrini, F. (2005). Building a European portrait of corporate social responsibility reporting. *European Management Journal*, 23(6), 611–627.

Poulter, S., Brown, L., & Robinson, M. (2013). *Asda, Co-op and Sainsbury's withdraw burger ranges over horse meat fears as it's revealed tests found equine DNA in other supermarket products LAST NOVEMBER*. Retrieved 27 April 2015 from: http://www.dailymail.co.uk/news/article-2262961/Horse-meat-Tesco-burgers-Asda-Co-op-Sainsburys-withdraw-ranges-tests-equine-DNA.html

Prynn, J. (2015). *Tesco profits: Supermarket giant announces £6.4bn loss*. Retrieved 27 April 2015 from: http://www.standard.co.uk/news/uk/tesco-profits-plunge-by-637bn-supermarket-giant-announces-multibillion-pound-loss-10194010.html

Quinn, B. (2013). *Horsemeat discovered in burgers sold by four British supermarkets*. Retrieved 27 April 2015 from: http://www.theguardian.com/world/2013/jan/16/horsemeat-burgers-supermarkets

Ridley, L. (2014). *Marks and Spencer is bringing back its food porn adverts*. Retrieved 21 April 2015 from: http://www.huffingtonpost.co.uk/2014/09/02/marks-and-spencer-food-pudding-advert-this-is-not-just-any_n_5751628.html

Ruddick, G. (2015). *The market share of Tesco, Asda, Sainsbury's and Morrisons is the lowest for a decade*. Retrieved 27 April 2015 from: http://www.telegraph.co.uk/finance/newsbysector/retailandconsumer/11522968/Five-facts-that-show-the-dramatic-changes-in-the-supermarket-industry.html

Saner, E. (2013). Why did Marks and Spencer lose its edge, and how can it get it back? *The Guardian*, 19 April. Retrieved 21 April 2015 from: http://www.theguardian.com/business/2013/apr/19/why-marks-spencer-lose-edge

Schouten, E. M. J., & Remme, J. (2006). Making sense of corporate social responsibility in international business: Experiences from Shell. *Business Ethics*, *15*(4), 365–379.

Senge, P., & Carstedt, G. (2001). Innovating our way to the next industrial revolution. *Sloan Management Review*, *42*(2), 24–38.

Silverstein, K. (May 14, 2013). Enron, ethics and today's corporate values. *Forbes*. Retrieved 31 March 2015 from: http://www.forbes.com/sites/kensilverstein/2013/05/14/enron-ethics-and-todays-corporate-values/

Simcic Bronn, P., & Vrioni, A. B. (2001). Corporate social responsibility and cause-related marketing: an overview. *International Journal of Advertising*, *20*, 207–222.

The Story of the Farmer and the Precious Egg—Waitrose. (2013). Retrieved 22 April 2015 from: https://www.youtube.com/watch?v=z_epZ7EyE5U

Szekely, F., & Knirsch, M. (2005). Responsible leadership and corporate social responsibility: Metrics for sustainable performance. *European Management Journal*, *23*(6), 628–647.

Tench, R., Bowd, R., & Jones, B. (2007). Perceptions and perspectives: Corporate social responsibility and the media. *Journal of Communication Management*, *11*(4), 348–370.

Tench, R., Sun, W., & Jones, B. (2014). Introduction: CSR Communication as an emerging field of study. In R. Tench, W. Sun, & B. Jones (Eds.), *Communicating corporate social responsibility: Perspectives and practice* (pp. 3–25). Howard House: Emerald.

Topić, M., & Tench, R. (2015). Selling corporate social responsibility? An exploration of the use of CSR in Lidl's advertising & communication campaigns in Croatia and the UK. *Qualitative Report*, *21*(2), 352–376.

A Tour of Leckford, the Waitrose Farm—Interactive Video—Waitrose. (2014). Retrieved 22 April 2015 from: https://www.youtube.com/watch?v=aIOqlzJqFOU

Tschopp, D. J. (2005). Corporate social responsibility: A comparison between the United States and the European Union. *Corporate Social Responsibility and Environmental Management*, *12*, 55–59.

Tyco Fraud Centre. (2006). *Tyco Fraud Center*. Retrieved 31 March 2015 from: http://www.tycofraudinfocenter.com/information.php

USA Today. (June 17, 2005). Timeline of the Tyco International Scandal. *USA Today*. Retrieved 31 March 2015 from: http://usatoday30.usatoday.com/money/industries/manufacturing/2005–06–17-tyco-timeline_x.htm

Van Dijk, T. (2007). The study of discourse: An introduction. In T. Van Dijk (Ed.), Discourse studies, 5. vols. *Sage Benchmarks in Discourse Studies* (pp. xix–xlii). London: Sage.

Van Dijk, T. (2009). Critical discourse studies: A sociocognitive approach. In R. Wodak & M. Meyer (Eds.), *Methods of critical discourse analysis* (pp. 62–85). London: Sage.

Vidaver Cohen, D., & Simcic Bronn, P. (2013). Reputation, responsibility, and stakeholder support in scandinavian firms: A comparative analysis. *Journal of Business Ethics*, *127*, 49–64.

Waitrose. (2014). *Giving back: Tackling isolation at Christmas.* Retrieved 21 April 2015 from: http://www.waitrose.com/home/inspiration/community_matters/tackling_isolationatchristmas.html

Waitrose. (2015a). *About Waitrose.* Retrieved 14 January 2015 from: http://www.waitrose.com/home/inspiration/about_waitrose/the_waitrose_way.html.html

Waitrose. (2015b). *Community matters.* Retrieved 21 April 2015 from: http://www.waitrose.com/home/inspiration/community_matters/community_matterssupport.html

Waitrose. (2015c). *The Waitrose way.* Retrieved 21 April 2015 from: http://www.waitrose.com/home/inspiration/about_waitrose/the_waitrose_way.html.html

Waitrose. (2015d). *Company history.* Retrieved 22 April 2015 from: http://www.waitrose.com/home/about_waitrose/corporate_information/company_history.html

Waitrose. (2015e). *Brand price match.* Retrieved 27 April 2015 from: http://www.waitrose.com/content/waitrose/en/home/groceries/waitrose_brand_pricematch.html

Waitrose Heston Blumenthal's Lemon Tart advert. (2011). Retrieved 21 April 2015 from: https://www.youtube.com/watch?v=qAQ8hT4ZGMo

Wodak, R. (1999). *The Discursive Construction of National identity.* Edinburgh: Edinburgh University Press.

Wodak, R. (2002). Aspects of Critical Discourse Analysis, *Zfal, 36,* 5–31.

Wood, D. J. (1991). Toward Improving Corporate Social Performance. *Business Horizons, 34*(4), 66–73.

YouGov Profile. (2015). Retrieved 21 April 2015 from: https://yougov.co.uk/profiler#/

7 Corporate Social Responsibility and Leadership Style

Fatemeh Hakimian, Hadi Farid, and Mohd Nazari Ismail

Introduction

The idea behind corporate social responsibility (CSR) is a drive towards improving the community through business practices that make things better and through the use of the resources that a company has. CSR is not about being charitable towards the community; it is about a business strategy that helps in a natural way the environment in which that business is based (Bansal et al., 2015; Charkraborty, 2010). It is about how to strike a balance between running a business to make a profit and contributing in a natural and even way towards society. Research has already demonstrated that the best way to ensure CSR productivity is to start from the point of view of the leaders and managers within the organization (D'Amato et al., 2009). Regarding the importance of CSR, previous studies indicate that the policies and practices associated with CSR can improve firms' environmental management (Aguilera et al., 2007), corporate reputation (Turban & Greening, 1997), financial performance (McWilliams & Siegel, 2011), sustainable development (McWilliams et al., 2006), promote customer loyalty, and improve the relationship of stakeholders with organizations (Luo & Bhattacharya, 2006). This means that as part of leading a company, or managing an organization, every leader or manager should be involved in CSR measures. De Sousa et al. (2010) suggested that CSR should be placed within the framework of management, thus enabling the creation of meaningful and ethical relationships between all involved based on accountability and transparency. The rationale behind this placement is that it would allow the leaders to evaluate performance and enhance their understanding of effective improvement of management systems. Studies such as Waldman et al. (2006b) and Angus-Leppan et al. (2010) indicate the significance and importance of leadership on CSR; the findings of the aforementioned studies show that leaders play the main role as drivers to encourage and promote CSR. To clarify the essential role of leaders on promoting CSR, we will present some well-known examples. Three CEOs and founders of organizations who used CSR-driven strategies are Ben Cohen of Ben and Jerry's Ice Cream, Paul Newman of Newman's Own products, and Anita Roddick of The Body Shop (Waldman et al., 2006a). Ben Cohen and Paul Newman's strategies include the support of local businesses, the use of high-quality ingredients, and the donation of after-tax profits. Anita Roddick developed a new product category: cosmetics which use ingredients based on non-animal testing procedures. Therefore, the aforementioned examples show that characteristics, beliefs, and values of leaders can have an effect on business strategies, decisions, and actions associated with CSR.

Despite the influential role of leadership in the formation of strategies and practices within an organization, there is a significant absence of research on the interface between organizational leadership and CSR, which calls for attempts to fill the gap between CSR literature and leadership theories (Groves & LaRocca, 2011a; Waldman & Siegel, 2008). One approach is to widen the array of components and practice of leadership—for example, considering transformational and transactional leadership styles as drivers of CSR practices (Waldman et al., 2006a). Moreover, others have pointed to certain deficiencies in current leadership theories, especially in the interface between leadership and CSR (Maak & Pless, 2006b). By considering the stakeholders' perspective, the traditional leader-follower notion of leadership is altered to the leader-stakeholder relationship in responsible leadership theory. Maak and Pless (2006b) asserted that for leaders, building and cultivating such relations constitute one of their important responsibilities in an interconnected stakeholder society. The value of the stakeholders to an organization means that any CSR agenda should aim to satisfy them, and for that to happen, the role of leadership cannot be taken for granted. Firms are said to have become increasingly more alert to the importance of becoming a 'responsible player' for stakeholders who claim affiliation with the organization (Perrini & Minoja, 2008). Consequently, it becomes vital for leaders to take up the responsibility to comprehend, define, and convey their roles to eventually enhance satisfaction in the work environment. Mulki et al. (2009) suggested that determining a clear direction and fostering a supportive environment would be a practical way of achieving this goal, as organizational performance could be enhanced by the psychological well-being of a workforce highly impacted by the said factors. Furthermore, Usman (2010) pointed out the vital role of leadership in managing performance and ensuring good governance to achieve both internal and external satisfaction. What the leaders do would eventually reflect their ability to create and manage organizational culture. This chapter attempts to explore how leaders and managers influence CSR. Up to this point, this chapter has mainly sought to reveal the association of leadership and CSR. We will examine the association from two different perspectives. The first perspective refers to the theories about the leader as an individual including his/her personality, traits, abilities, skills, and charisma. The second perspective relates to the theories of a leader's behaviours and his/her interactions with followers. Hence the chapter will unfold as follows: initially, the definition of CSR will be presented to clarify what is meant by the term CSR. This will be followed by an overview of selected leadership theories. Then the chapter will use a leadership lens to examine CSR. In this regard, this chapter specifically focuses on leadership theories of transformational and transactional leadership, charismatic leadership, responsible leadership, and ethical leadership.

Corporate Social Responsibility

Corporate social responsibility (CSR) has been defined in various ways; a general definition of CSR can be a set of actions, mainly focused on social and environmental issues, that companies voluntarily take to benefit society; these are initiatives that go beyond compliance with laws, policies, and regulations (McWilliams et al., 2006; Rekker et al., 2014). During the last century, there has been a debate over "doing good and doing well", and to which the preference should be given (Wells, 2002). Kakabadse et al. (2005) highlight that the formalization of CSR theory goes back to the 1950s, although literature on this concept predates this. However, it is evident that since then the majority of research in this field has revolved around defining CSR as a term (Carroll, 1999; Lantos, 2001). Moreover, the critical absence of empirical evidence (Campbell, 2006; Sorsa, 2008) and numerous potential questions that are not being addressed by the existing definitions highlight their limitations. Hopkins (2003) stated that CSR focuses on ethical and socially responsible treatment of stakeholders of the firm—for instance, treating the corporation's stakeholders in a manner that is acceptable in a civilized society. In fact, social aspects include economic responsibility. A firm's stakeholders exist both inside and outside of the organization. The broader purpose of social responsibility is to create constant higher standards of living, while sustaining the profitability of the firm, for people inside and outside the corporation.

CSR, in general, includes certain actions of a firm aimed at promoting particular social benefits. These actions are beyond the requirement of law and regulations, and are not supposed to result in immediate profit for the corporation or the shareholders (Waldman et al., 2006a). Dahlsrud (2008) performed a content analysis on the available definitions of CSR in the literature and then developed five dimensions of this concept—namely, social, environmental, economic, stakeholder, and voluntariness. Each of these dimensions refers to a particular context. The social dimension of CSR embodies the society and business environment, whereas the environmental dimension covers the natural environment. The economic dimension of CSR refers to financial and socio-economic issues, such as defining this concept as a part of business operations. The stakeholder dimension concentrates on stakeholders, whether individuals or a group, and the voluntariness dimension focuses on actions that are not required by law.

Leadership Theories Overview

This section provides an overview of the existing studies about leadership concepts and issues and then examines the challenges and implications of various theoretical approaches, particularly in business ethics within the CSR context. Leaders, in today's business environment are facing new and growing challenges, including the amplification of social accountability. In fact, the growing demands requesting corporations to become more responsible about social issues have a direct impact on leaders' performance. Moreover, this has brought a new requirement to CEOs agendas to balance the two possibly divergent objectives of their firms' social responsibilities and profit maximization. The research on leadership has been conducted in many different fields; different leadership concepts and theories have led researchers to a variety of interpretations of findings and understandings. Generally, leadership is the "behavior of an individual when he is directing the activities of a group toward a shared goal", Hemphill and Coons, 1957, p. 7). Similarly, Janda (1960, p. 358) defined leadership as "a particular type of power relationship characterized by a group member's perception that another group member has the right to prescribe behavior patterns for the former regarding his activity as a group member". Moreover, Stogdill (1974) defined leadership as the process in which a leader influences a group of people based on meeting the targets. Leadership can be addressed as "the process of influencing the activities of an organized group toward goal achievement" (Rauch & Behling, 1984, p. 46). Lussier (1990) explained that leadership is "the process of influencing employees to work toward the achievement of objectives". It is "the ability to influence a group toward the achievement of goals" (Robbins, 1998). Leadership is also defined by Rowden (2000) as the leader's behaviour while he/she is leading and coordinating individual members towards achieving the group's objectives.

Having considered the aforementioned definitions of leadership, three common terms are notable—namely, "leader", "followers", and the "interactions" among them. Slocum et al. (2008) pointed out that some people think of a "leader" as someone famous who possesses power; however, not all the corporate leaders are as famous as CEOs of large companies. Indeed, it is important to realize that leaders might be found at all organizational levels. Yukl (2010) stated that in the previous literature, leadership was defined through various terms, such as individual traits and behaviours, interaction patterns, occupation of a position in the organizational chart, having influence over a group of individuals, role of relationships, and people's perception towards rightfulness of influence. Because leaders are usually the ones who represent the organization to subordinates, it was suggested that "in the working relationship between leaders and followers, leaders represent the personal actualization of the otherwise abstract, impersonal existence of the organization" (Wieseke et al. 2009, p. 126). Hence leaders' actions, qualities, and cognition have significant influence on followers' beliefs and behaviours associated with the organization and society, and there is no exception for CSR. Indeed, leaders are responsible for assigning the strategies as well as promoting the image of the organizations for the purpose of social responsibility practices.

Regarding the importance of leadership on CSR, which is the main focus of this chapter, the previous studies indicate that leaders play a vital role as drivers for the promotion of CSR (Angus-Leppan et al., 2010; Waldman et al., 2006a, b). Therefore, as mentioned before, this chapter aims to focus on those leadership theories associated with CSR from two perspectives: first, examining leadership theories and their definitions while considering the leader as an individual and, second, investigating the leader's role in CSR using the previously mentioned leadership styles. Initially, transformational theories are presented; it should be noted that the charismatic-transformational leadership theories emerged in the literature in the late 1970s and early 1980s (Bass, 1985; Burns, 1978; Conger & Kanungo, 1987; House, 1977). Because these theories include a number of elements, attributes, and traits of other leadership models, Yukl and Van Fleet (1992) called them 'hybrid theories'. Later, these theories were named 'neo-charismatic theories' in a social-scientific study (House & Aditya, 1997). Further in this section, more details are presented about charismatic, transactional, and transformational theories of leadership and their effects on CSR. Moreover, the other two types of leadership, responsible leadership and ethical leadership and their roles in CSR, are presented.

Charismatic Leadership

"Charisma" was first defined by Weber (1947), a German sociologist, as a personality characteristic in his famous book *The Theory of Social and Economic Organization*. As Weber explained, "Charismatic Leadership is defined more narrowly and refers to perception that a leader possesses a divinely inspired gift and is somehow unique and larger than life" (Yukl, 1989, p. 269). Max Weber was one of the scholars who discussed charismatic leadership, however, according to Yammarino et al. (2005), the contributions of House (1977), Conger and Kanungo (1987), and Shamir et al. (1993) have established the pillars of today's charismatic leadership theory. These researchers defined this concept from the perspective of the leader's effect on followers and their consequent relationships.

The charismatic leadership theory of House (1977) concerns the way leaders behave and the charismatic trait that is perceived by their subordinates. For instance, Northouse (2012) believed that followers trust actions of a leader whose characteristics portray the appropriate behaviours of a role model. There were some postulated key behaviours that were posited by Conger and Kanungo (1987) such as displaying unconventional behaviours at high personal risk, communicating a strategic vision, and engaging in realistic assessments of environmental resources and constraints. Additionally, Yammarino et al. (2005) took the discussion a step further and highlighted some other behaviours of leaders, including acting as a role model for subordinates, inspiring significant vision among them, exhibiting self-confidence and showing trust in followers, and expressing a sense of confidence in their competencies, which helps followers establish their individual identities. Eventually, these behaviours will improve the quality of the leader-follower mutual relationship. All the aforementioned characteristics of charismatic leadership make this type of leadership relevant to CSR, which we will discuss in further detail in this section.

The aforementioned studies indicate that charismatic leadership is rooted in moral and ethical values, where charismatic leaders reach higher moral development levels (Kanungo, 2001; Mendonca, 2001; Turner et al. 2002). Charismatic leadership is related to the notion of CSR by its very nature in that the leaders stress self-sacrifice for the good of the organization and/or the larger community. In this regard, researchers suggested,

> Charismatic leaders may be effective at forming a collective identity based on appealing values that go beyond the self-interests of individuals and even the greater organization. In line with CSR, such values may include an appeal to the greater needs of stakeholder groups and the good of society.
>
> (Waldman et al., 2006a, p. 1708)

The charismatic leader has a strong ethical and moral effect on followers, which may lead to the leader receiving help to face risks and to succeed in achieving the CSR goals; charismatic leaders express their values through a value-laden vision of the future (Sosik, 2005) and also express appropriate confidence that followers can accomplish their collective objectives (Wilderom et al., 2012) as well as foster inspirational motivation (Judge et al., 2005). Therefore, all these strong moral behaviours mean followers tend to develop a favourable perception of the leader (Waldman & Yammarino, 1999). Mendonca (2001) also mentioned that followers' fortitude creates courage for charismatic leaders to work at overcoming difficulties in the pursuit of CSR goals. By considering the effect of charismatic leadership on CSR, Shamir and his colleagues advanced a theory of charismatic leadership which particularly relates to the effect of CSR on the self-concept of the followers (Shamir et al., 1993). Their research was focused on leaders who communicate and symbolize messages of values and moral justifications. Thus the leaders have motivational effects on followers while expressing goals and visions in terms of values. Consequently, the followers' self-concept links to the presented values, which internalize a value on the part of the followers (Lord & Brown, 2001, 2004; Lord et al., 1999).

Transactional and Transformational Leadership

Transactional and transformational models of leadership were described by Burns (1978) after he analyzed the biographies of several political leaders. Later, Bass (1985) furthered Burn's idea about transformational leadership within the context of an organization's transformational processes. In contrast with Burn's approach, Bass did not perceive transactional and transformational leadership models as two opposite approaches; he instead believed that although the behaviours of leaders who apply these models are distinctive, they are valid and can be used in different situations (Bass, 1999; Yukl, 1989). Consequently, Bass postulated that both transactional and transformational leaders tend to the needs of their followers; however, transformational leaders are able to elevate the level of consciousness in everybody. Additionally, Lucas (2013) stated that the transformational leadership model is epistemologically based on the positivist/empiricist approach, where the traditional concepts of leadership were formulated.

In addition, previous studies indicate that leaders who demonstrated more transformational leadership behaviours were the most accepted leaders by followers (Bass, 1999). There are four dimensions of transformational leadership theory—namely, idealized influence, inspirational motivation, intellectual stimulation, and individualized consideration, which are also known as the '4Is'. The four dimensions of transformational theory are as follows: Idealized influence or charisma—followers' reactions can affect leaders' behaviours. Although these leaders, who have referent power, set high standards and determine challenging goals for their followers, they are deeply respected and admired by them. Inspirational motivation—this motivation varies based on how much subordinates desire to identify with the leader. Moreover, in order to raise awareness of shared and desired goals, the leader makes use of symbols and images. Intellectual stimulation—followers are encouraged to question their own beliefs, expectations, and values, as well as those of the leader and the organization itself. Individualized consideration—the leader treats followers equally yet uniquely. Bass and Avolio (1997) explained that the leader delegates particular tasks to followers to purposefully provide a learning opportunity for them and to train them in case they need it.

It should be noted that Bass (1999) believed "transformational leadership is universally applicable, and that a transformational leader inspires their follower to transcend their own self-interests for the good of the organization". Moreover, transformational leadership is a valid and generalizable theory in many study settings. Additionally, recent studies suggest a greater importance for transformational leadership in lower levels of management, refuting the previously held assumptions. Bennis and Thomas (2002) attempted to determine what makes a leader and concluded that the ability to learn from difficult circumstances leads to the necessary skills needed for extraordinary leadership. They claimed leadership behaviours are often the outcome of "unplanned experiences that had transformed them and had become the sources of their distinctive leadership abilities" (p. 40). These experiences were coined "crucibles of leadership" by the authors, which referred to a concept in the work of Kouzes and Posner (2003) that originated two decades earlier.

In considering the effect of leadership style on CSR, it should be noted that the behavioural theory of leadership may explain CSR behaviour which inspires others to pursue defined goals. Typical behaviours associated with the transformational style are influence by invoking ideals, inspirational motivation, intellectual stimulation, and individualized consideration— all of which can influence causes and behaviours related to environmental activism, social justice, other socially responsible outcomes, and CSR in general. Transformational leadership theory provides the foundation for emerging work on CSR and leadership, particularly for cases framing CSR along moral or altruistic terms. Transformational leadership demonstrates a strong relationship with follower beliefs in the stakeholder view of CSR. Therefore, the followers of such leaders are more likely to believe that socially responsible actions and the engagement of multiple-stakeholder groups are critical to organizational effectiveness. The influence processes employed by transformational and transactional leaders may be driven by divergent ethical values, which also appear to indirectly impact follower attitudes toward CSR. Transformational leadership was strongly associated with leader deontological values that drive impressive leadership outcomes in organizations. The leader's belief in selflessness, treating followers and teammates as ends rather than means, and viewing leadership practices as having ethical significance regardless of their consequences, facilitates an authentic demonstration of transformational behaviours that engender a belief in the stakeholder view of CSR.

Du et al. (2013) identified a number of reasons as the basis for expecting transformational, but not transactional leadership to more greatly encourage institutional implementation of CSR. First, unlike transactional leadership, which is associated with utilitarian ethics such as the use of power, rewards, and punishments, transformational leadership is essentially more reliant on altruistic ethics (Groves & LaRocca, 2011b). Bass and Steidlmeier (1999) argue that transformational leaders have great ethics and emphasize values. According to Kanungo and Mendonca (1996), one of the differences between transactional and transformational leaders is the higher level of moral development in the latter, thus enabling transformational leaders to verbalize a vision in a manner that is simultaneously just and in tune with the demands of stakeholders and consequently steering subordinates towards rising above self-interest to the benefit of the company's vision. This argument is supported by recent studies, both theoretical (Maak & Pless, 2006b) and qualitative (Angus-Leppan et al., 2010), that suggest there is a higher possibility of exhibiting responsible and ethical behaviours, such as pursuing and protecting the interests of secondary stakeholders, among transformational leaders.

The second reason given by Du et al. (2013) is that transformational leadership encourages intellectual growth and inspires followers to challenge archaic beliefs, enabling them to employ more innovative methods in dealing with complex situations (Bass, 1997). Similarly, Waldman et al. (2006a) claimed that transformational leaders, particularly those that stimulate intellectual abilities, acquire a comprehensive perspective of the environmental context and the way to serve various stakeholders. They found that intellectual stimulation of transformational leadership has a positive association with CSR practices. Consequently, there is a higher probability that transformational leaders comprehend the complicated interconnections of various stakeholders and come to the realization that the company is interdependent with its community and natural environment, not isolated from it and dependent on it (Du et al., 2013).

Responsible Leadership

Another type of leadership associated with CSR is responsible leadership: a moral and social phenomenon which draws from leadership ethics, developmental psychology, psychoanalysis, stakeholder theory, and systems theories (Pless, 2007). From a theoretical perspective, responsible leadership is defined as the art and ability of creating, developing, and sustaining a relationship of trust with all relevant stakeholders and achieving a shared meaningful corporate vision through coordinating responsible behaviour (Maak & Pless, 2006b). In other words, responsible leadership aims to understand the dynamic relationship between leaders and stakeholders that results in responsible actions for social change. For a better understanding of responsible leadership behaviours, a "roles model of responsible leadership" is presented here, which was recently developed by Maak and Pless (2006a, 2006b). They argue that business leaders in society are attached and embedded with stakeholders through direct reports, customers, suppliers, peers, family, community, etc. Because stakeholders have different backgrounds, values, cultures, and, sometimes, conflicting interests, in order for them to work together and to collaborate on a shared vision, leaders must practice certain roles. Therefore, the "roles model of responsible leadership" consists of nine roles which describe different characteristics of responsible leadership; the nine roles are distinguished as value-based and operational roles Maak and Pless (2006b). The value-based roles of responsible leadership see the leader as steward, as citizen, as servant, and as visionary, and the operational roles see the leader as coach, networker, storyteller, architect, and change agent. In this regard, the research by Waddock and Graves (1997) indicates better performance of CSR in companies with responsible leadership when compared with others that do not achieve the same social standards. In addition, Howell and Avolio (1992) argue that responsible leadership is a form of art through which leaders build and sustain relationships with all stakeholders involved, and this is only possible if they are socialized leaders, not personalized.

Waldman (2011) noted two differing approaches of responsible leadership with regard to its moral basis—namely, the normative stakeholder approach and the economic/strategic approach. According to the first approach, the normative stakeholder approach to responsible leadership is defined as being "in line with both integrative and ethical theories of CSR" (Waldman, 2011, p. 77). Indeed, the main task of a responsible leader is to "weave a web of inclusion, where the leader engages himself among equals" (Maak & Pless, 2006b, p. 104). Then socially responsible leaders should provide a balance between a broad set of stakeholders and act as a moral person with a focus on altruism.

The second approach, the economic/strategic approach to responsible leadership, refers to the leader's priority of productivity and the maximization of profits which is based on company law—firms have a responsibility to maximize dividends for shareholders. In this regard, Waldman and Siegel (2008) suggested responsible leaders make the strategic decisions associated with CSR investment and make sure of a financial return on the CSR activities. Wang et al. (2015, p. 438) noted, "Whether considering the normative stakeholder approach or the economic/strategic approach, both have benefits; however, for socially responsible leaders to advance, they need to combine both CSR and leadership".

Ethical Leadership

Ethical leadership is defined as "the demonstration of normatively appropriate conduct through personal actions and interpersonal relationships, and the promotion of such conduct to followers through two-way communication, reinforcement, and decision making" (Brown et al., 2005, p. 120). Mayer et al. (2012) mentioned that ethical leadership referred to moral identity by managing morality in an appropriate way. Therefore, ethical leaders possess traits such as honesty, fairness, and trustworthiness in taking responsibility for their own decisions and actions. Subsequently, ethical leaders practice appropriate rewards and punishments to hold followers responsible for their actions (Piccolo et al., 2010) as well as to encourage subordinates to express normatively appropriate behaviour in the workplace (Brown et al., 2005). Ethical leaders are considered from the stakeholders' perspective because of creating and developing the interactions/relationships which are based on a shared sense of purpose and meaning.

Previous studies indicate the effects of ethical leadership on CSR; initially, the study by Reed et al. (2007) showed moral identity as a predictor of prosocial behaviours, such as charity donation, and as a factor to prevent unethical behaviours such as cheating (Reynolds & Ceranic, 2007). Furthermore, studies show that organizations may have a positive influence on employees'

CSR perceptions via creating, developing, and enhancing a clear set of values and policies (Vitell et al., 2003; Vitell & Paolillo, 2004). Because a company's social responsibility needs to rely on the organizational culture associated with ethical values (Puffer & McCarthy, 2008; Schaubroeck et al., 2012), the leader is the main source of supporting and promoting a firm's ethical behaviour. An empirical study by Groves & LaRocca (2011b) indicates the effect of ethical leaders on their subordinates' perceptions regarding the CSR view of stakeholders. Ethical leadership has a positive impact on CSR while it is associated with the followers' perception and attitudes toward CSR in four different ways (Choi et al., 2015). First, since leadership styles have an effect on followers through a value system, ethical leadership promotes CSR by expressing the priority of social welfare and collective interest of the social unit. Thus the social learning perspective of ethical leadership has an impact on subordinates to express and perform their duties and tasks in an appropriate, ethical way. Second, followers of ethical leaders are inspired to look at social issues via an ethical point of view, which creates for them a positive sense of CSR (Kanungo, 2001). In this regard, the study conducted by Treviño and colleagues (2000) indicates that ethical leadership is able to direct followers' attention to the main issue of ethical messages within the organizational context. Third, ethical leadership influences followers' attitudes toward CSR because of its main characteristics such as honesty, fairness, caring, and trustworthiness. The aforementioned characteristics develop an open-minded organizational culture for sharing information and paying attention to collective social issues which may lead to CSR as well. Fourth, ethical leadership is associated with CSR based on the five key components of leader social responsibility, which were developed by Winter (1992)—namely, moral-legal standard of conduct, internal obligation, concern for others, concern about consequences, and self-judgment. The aforementioned social responsibility components make leaders role models for followers for promoting the perception and attitudes toward CSR.

Challenges of CSR From the Perspective of Leadership

Whereas implementing CSR companies often face challenges, usually related to political matters or organizational concerns which are culturally embedded, there are new demands posed on organizations as they operate in a global society. The literature shows that with the redefining of roles and responsibilities of government and the fading of the boundaries between government and business, leaders find themselves with overwhelming challenges ahead. Pless et al. (2012) highlighted the global economic crisis of 2008, which creates increasing pressure on leaders to have essential considerations for ethical practices and responsibility at the individual and systematic levels. In this regard, Wang et al. (2015, p. 436) mentioned,

> When social issues are addressed, not only is the rapport with stakeholders and the public maintained, but the company in turn contributes

to the sustainable development of their organizations; thus, in the interests of promoting these ends, practitioners and researchers alike have a significant motivation to explore the key drivers and outcomes of responsible leadership in the business world.

There is a new era of CSR in which a wide range of stakeholders, consumers, employees, domestic and international lawmakers, NGOs, watchdogs, and activist groups have to be satisfied (Hatcher, 2002). As a result, business leaders are held accountable for their relations and actions relating to the stakeholders as well as society (Pless & Maak, 2009). In addition, CSR has made organizational leaders focus on social issues and stakeholders' interests at the same time. Developing the type of leaders needed for a sustainable global society and figuring out how to cultivate the necessary abilities in individuals is the most challenging aspect of CSR implementation according to McGaw (2005); imagination must be encouraged and positive change actively promoted to achieve this task and overcome this challenge. To tackle the new challenge of developing leaders for the global society, a number of capabilities must be cultivated in leaders. They need to be able to relate in various ways to merge different visions into one, to listen sincerely and care for others, and to serve them. Therefore, to accomplish this task, global society and responsible leadership with ethics, diversity, and values must come together.

Conclusion

Corporate social responsibility is a thriving field in the current corporate environment. It is a self-regulating format that has merged into a business model. CSR policy is a mechanism through which a business regulates and monitors activities in order to ensure compliance with the law and ethical standards, as well as international norms. The global economy demands that organizations increasingly accept, demonstrate, and promote CSR. There are long-term sustainability needs, thus organizations have to alter their solely profit-making goals to focus on corporate citizenship. However, it is vital to remember that CSR is not the answer to all problems the world faces; it is a way for organizations to benefit while helping society benefit as well. Because this chapter aims to examine CSR through the lens of leadership, it should be noted that the study of leadership is fundamental to the study of human behaviour and predates the study of organizations and businesses. Historically, the dominant scholarly tradition (and typical lay practice) attributes credit to formal leaders for creating or endorsing competitive strategies and ultimately impacting organizations. This chapter clarifies the relationship between CSR and selected leadership styles, including transformational and transactional leadership, charismatic leadership, responsible leadership, and ethical leadership. Indeed, merging the leadership literature and CSR has several benefits; the combination of leadership and CSR may lead to providing an organizational framework based on leadership scholarship that invites inclusion of research from outside the leadership tradition. Looking to this range of scholarship invites CSR researchers to use validated measures and well-tested, individual-level constructs from many disciplines. Moreover, highlighting the relationship between emerging leadership theories and CSR activities contributes to organizations in a practical way. Other organizational scholars have already suggested that CSR actions happen and continue to happen even when increased firm profitability will not ensue. Therefore, only by combining emerging leadership scholarship with important new topics in CSR/strategy fields can both fields develop and move forward. The specific leader characteristics, traits, values, and attitudes positively relate to whether colleagues and followers enact CSR behaviours. Furthermore, merging leadership and CSR creates rich opportunities for theoretical advancement of both fields, particularly to jointly create work that explores the origins and outcomes of CSR.

According to Bernstein (2000), the public believes that business should be responsible to employees, communities, and any other stakeholders while making profits, even if the price they have to pay is the loss of some profits; and it may create increasing pressure on leaders. The good news is the impact of CSR is starting to become palpable in communities, from human and labour rights to health care and the environment, around the world. The more the importance of CSR is understood, the more the role of leadership gets accentuated. Leaders face daunting challenges in implementing CSR while maintaining profit and quality performance of organizations. Carly Fiorina, former CEO of HP stated,

> Leadership is not about hierarchy or title or status: It is about having influence and mastering change. Leadership is not about bragging rights or battles or even the accumulation of wealth; it's about connecting and engaging at multiple levels . . . Leaders can no longer view strategy and execution as abstract concepts, but must realize that both elements are ultimately about people.

Consequently, corporate responsibility or sustainability constitutes a prominent portion of literature on business and society, which explores topics of business ethics, global corporate citizenship, and stakeholder management. Management education can be an effective source to draw new ideas about shifting toward an integrated rather than a fractured knowledge economy, if the meaning and role of socially responsible leadership gets updated. The need for further research to establish better understanding of needs and requirements in both fields of leadership and leadership development associated with CSR is great, and they should be subjected to comprehensive scrutiny.

References

Aguilera, R. V., Rupp, D. E., Williams, C. A., & Ganapathi, J. (2007). Putting the S back in corporate social responsibility: A multi-level theory of social change in organizations. *Academy of Management Review, 32*(3), 836–863.

Angus-Leppan, T., Metcalf, L., & Benn, S. (2010). Leadership styles and CSR practice: An examination of sensemaking, institutional drivers and CSR leadership. *Journal of Business Ethics, 93*(2), 189–213.

Bansal, P., Guoliang, F. J., & Jae, C. J. (2015). Managing responsibly in tough economic times: Strategic and tactical CSR during the 2008–2009 global recession. *Long Range Planning, 48*(2), 69–79.

Bass, B. M. (1985). *Leadership and performance beyond expectations.* New York: Free Press.

Bass, B. M. (1997). Does the transactional-transformational leadership paradigm transcend organizational and national borders? *American Psychologist, 52*(2), 130–139.

Bass, B. M. (1999). Two decades of research and development in transformational leadership. *European Journal of Work and Organizational Psychology, 8*(1), 9–32.

Bass, B. M., & Avolio, B. J. (1997). *Full range leadership development: Manual for the multifactor leadership questionnaire.* San Francisco: Mind Garden.

Bass, B. M., & Steidlmeier, P. (1999). Ethics, character, and authentic transformational leadership behavior. *Leadership Quarterly, 10*(2), 181–217.

Bennis, W. G., & Thomas, R. J. (2002). Crucibles of leadership. *Harvard Business Review, 80*(9), 39–45.

Bernstein, A. (September 11, 2000). Too much corporate power: The twenty-first century corporation. *Business Week.* Retrieved from: http://www.businessweek.com/2000/00_37/b3698001.htm

Brown, M. E., Trevino, L. K., & Harrison, D. A. (2005). Ethical leadership: A social learning perspective for construct development and testing. *Organizational Behavior and Human Decision Processes, 97*(2), 117–134.

Burns, J. M. (1978). *Leadership.* New York, NY: Harper & Row.

Campbell, J. L. (2006). Institutional analysis and the paradox of corporate social responsibility. *American Behavioural Scientist, 49*(7), 925–938.

Carroll, A. B. (1999). Corporate social responsibility. *Business and Society, 38*(3), 268–295.

Chakraborty, S. (2010). Diffusion coefficients in olivine, wadsleyite and ringwoodite. *Reviews in Mineralogy and Geochemistry, 72*(1), 603–639.

Choi, S. B., Ullah, S. M., & Kwak, W. J. (2015). Ethical leadership and followers' attitudes toward corporate social responsibility: The role of perceived ethical work climate. *Social Behavior and Personality: An international journal, 43*(3), 353–365.

Conger, J. A., & Kanungo, R. N. (1987). Toward a behavioral theory of charismatic leadership in organizational settings. *Academy of Management Review, 12*(4), 637–647.

Dahlsrud, A. (2008). How corporate social responsibility is defined: An analysis of 37 definitions. *Corporate Social Responsibility and Environmental Management, 15*(1),1–13.

D'Amato, A., Henderson, S., & Florence, S. (2009). *Corporate social responsibility and sustainable business.* Greensboro, NC: Center for Creative Leadership.

De Sousa, F. J., Outtes Wanderley, L. S., Pasa Gomez, C., & Farache F. (2010). Strategic corporate social responsibility management for competitive advantage. *Brazilian Administration Review, 7*(3), 294–309.

Du, S., Swaen, V., Lindgreen, A., & Sen, S. (2013). The roles of leadership styles in corporate social responsibility. *Journal of Business Ethics, 114*(1), 155–169.

Groves, K. S., & LaRocca, M. A. (2011a). Responsible leadership outcomes via stakeholder CSR values: Testing a values-centered model of transformational leadership. *Journal of Business Ethics, 98*(Supplement 1), 37–55.

Groves, K. S., & LaRocca, M. A. (2011b). An empirical study of leader ethical values, transformational and transactional leadership, and follower attitudes toward corporate social responsibility. *Journal of Business Ethics, 103*(4), 511–528.

Hatcher, M. (2002). New corporate agendas. *Journal of Public Affairs, 3*(1), 32–38.

Hemphill, J. K., & Coons, A. E. (1957). Development of the leader behavior description questionnaire. In R. M. Stogdill, & A. E. Coons (Eds.), *Leader behavior: Its description and measurement* (pp. 6–38). Columbus, OH: Ohio State University Bureau of Business Research.

Hopkins, M. (2003). *The planetary bargain—CSR matters.* London: Earthscan.

House, R. J. (1977). A 1976 theory of charismatic leadership effectiveness. In J. G. Hunt, & L. L. Larson (Eds.), *Leadership: The cutting edge* (pp. 189–207). Carbondale: Feffer and Simons.

House, R. J., & Aditya, R. N. (1997). The social scientific study of leadership: Quo vadis? *Journal of Management, 23*(3), 409–473.

Howell, J. M., & Avolio, B. J. (1992). The ethics of charismatic leadership: Submission or liberation? *Academy of Management Executive, 6*(2), 43–54.

Janda, K. F. (1960). Towards the explication of the concept of leadership in terms of the concept of power. *Human Relations, 13*(2), 345–363.

Judge, T. A., Bono, J. E., Erez, A., & Locke, E. A. (2005). Core self-evaluations and job and life satisfaction: The role of self-concordance and goal attainment. *Journal of Applied Psychology, 90*(2), 257–286.

Kakabase, N., Rozuel, C., & Lee-Davies, L. (2005). Corporate social responsibility and stakeholder approach: A conceptual review. *International Journal of Business Governance and Ethics, 1*(4), 277–302.

Kanungo, R. N. (2001). Ethical values of transactional and transformational leaders. *Canadian Journal of Administrative Sciences/Revue Canadienne des Sciences de l'Administration, 18*(4), 257–265.

Kanungo, R. N., & Mendonca, M. (1996). *Ethical dimensions of leadership.* Thousand Oaks, CA: Sage Publications.

Kouzes, J. M., & Posner, B. Z. (2003). *The leadership challenge* (3rd Eds.). San Francisco: Jossey-Bass.

Lantos, G. P. (2001). The boundaries of strategic corporate social responsibility. *Journal of Consumer Marketing, 18*(7), 595–630.

Lord, R. G., & Brown, D. J. (2001). Leadership, values, and subordinates self-concepts. *The Leadership Quarterly, 12*(2), 133–152.

Lord, R. G., & Brown, D. J. (2004). *Leadership processes and follower self-identity.* Mahwah, NJ: Lawrence Erlbaum Associates.

Lord, R. G., Brown, D. J., & Freiberg, S. J. (1999). Understanding the dynamics of leadership: The role of follower self-concepts in the leader/follower relationship. *Organizational Behavior and Human Decision Processes, 78*(3), 167–239.

Lucas, M. (2013). Foundations of a neo-integral transformational leadership and organizational development. *Integral Leadership Review, 1*, 12–27.

Luo, X., & Bhattacharya, C. B. (2006). Corporate social responsibility, customer satisfaction, and market value. *Journal of Marketing, 70*(4), 1–18.

Lussier, R. N. (1990). *Human relations in organizations: A skill-building approach.* Boston: Irwin.

Maak, T., & Pless, N. M. (2006a). *Responsible leadership.* New York: Routledge.

Maak, T., & Pless, N. M. (2006b). Responsible leadership in a stakeholder society–a relational perspective. *Journal of Business Ethics, 66*(1), 99–115.

Mayer, D. M., Aquino, K., Greenbaum, R. L., & Kuenzi, M. (2012). Who displays ethical leadership and why does it matter? An examination of antecedents and consequences of ethical leadership. *Academy of Management Journal, 55*(1), 151–171.

McGaw, N. (2005). Developing leaders for a sustainable global society. *Strategic HR Review, 4*(6), 32–35.

McWilliams, A., & Siegel, D. S. (2011). Creating and capturing value: Strategic corporate social responsibility, resource-based theory, and sustainable competitive advantage. *Journal of Management, 37*(5), 1480–1495.

McWilliams, A., Siegel, D. S., & Wright, P. M. (2006). Corporate social responsibility: Strategic implications. *Journal of Management Studies, 43*(1), 1–18.

Mendonca, M. (2001). Preparing for ethical leadership in organizations. *Canadian Journal of Administrative Sciences, 18*(4), 266–276.

Mulki, J. P., Jaramillo, J. F., & Locander, W. B. (2009). Critical role of leadership on ethical climate and salesperson behaviors. *Journal of Business Ethics, 86*(2), 125–141.

Northouse, P. G. (2012). *Leadership: Theory and practice.* Thousand Oaks, CA: Sage.

Perrini, F., & Minoja, M. (2008). Strategizing corporate social responsibility: Evidence from an Italian medium-sized, family-owned company. *Business Ethics, 17*(1), 47–63.

Piccolo, R. F., Greenbaum, R., den Hartog, D. N., & Folger, R. (2010). The relationship between ethical leadership and core job characteristics. *Journal of Organizational Behavior, 31*(2–3), 259–278.

Pless, N. M. (2007). Understanding responsible leadership: Role identity and motivational drivers. *Journal of Business Ethics, 74*(4), 437–456.

Pless, N. M., & Maak, T. (2009). Responsible leaders as agents of world benefit: Learnings from "project ulysses". *Journal of Business Ethics, 85*(1), 59–71.

Pless, N. M., Maak, T., & Waldman, D. A. (2012). Different approaches toward doing the right thing: Mapping the responsibility orientations of leaders. *The Academy of Management Perspectives, 26*(4), 51–65.

Puffer, S. M., & McCarthy, D. J. (2008). Ethical turnarounds and transformational leadership: A global imperative for corporate social responsibility. *Thunderbird International Business Review, 50*(5), 303–314.

Rauch, C. F., & Behling, O. (1984). Functionalism: Basis for an alternate approach to the study of leadership. In J. G. Hunt, D. M. Hosking, C. A. Schriesheim, & R. Stewart (Eds.), *Leaders and managers: International perspectives on managerial behavior and leadership* (pp. 45–62). New York, NY: Pergamon Press.

Reed, A., Aquino, K., & Levy, E. (2007). Moral identity and judgments of charitable behaviors. *Journal of Marketing, 71*(1), 178–193.

Rekker, S. A. C., Benson, K. L., & Faff, R. W. (2014). Corporate social responsibility and CEO compensation revisited: Do disaggregation, market stress, gender matter? *Journal of Economics and Business, 72*, 84–103.

Reynolds, S. J., & Ceranic, T. L. (2007). The effects of moral judgment and moral identity on moral behavior: An empirical examination of the moral individual. *Journal of Applied Psychology, 92*(6), 1610–1624.

Robbins, S. (1998). *Organizational behavior: Concepts, controversies, applications* (8th Ed.). Upper Saddle River, NJ: Prentice Hall.

Rowden, R. W. (2000). The relationship between charismatic leadership behaviors and organizational commitment. *Leadership & Organization Development Journal, 21*(1), 30–35.

Schaubroeck, J., Hannah, S., Avolio, B., Kozlowski, S., Lord, R., Trevino, L., Dimotakis, N., & Peng, C. (2012). Embedding ethical leadership within and across organizational levels. *Academy of Management Journal, 55*(5), 1053–1078.

Shamir, B., House, R. J., & Arthur, M. B. (1993). The motivational effects of charismatic leadership: A self-concept based theory. *Organization Science, 4*(4), 577–594.

Slocum, J. W., Jackson, S. E., & Hellriegel, D. (2008). *Competency-based management.* South-Western: Thomson.

Sorsa, V. P. (2008). How to explain socially responsible corporate actions institutionally: Theoretical and methodological critique. *Electronic Journal of Business Ethics and Organization Studies, 13*(1), 32–41.

Sosik, J. J. (2005). The role of personal values in the charismatic leadership of corporate managers: A model and preliminary field study. *Leadership Quarterly, 16*(2), 221–244.

Stogdill, R. M. (1974). *Handbook of leadership: A survey of theory and research.* New York, NY: Free Press.

Trevino, L. K., Hartman, L. P., & Brown, M. (2000). Moral person and moral manager: How executives develop a reputation for ethical leadership. *California Management Review, 42*(4), 128–142.

Turban, D. B., & Greening, D. W. (1997). Corporate social performance and organizational attractiveness to prospective employees. *Academy of Management Journal, 40*(3), 658–672.

Turner, N., Barling, J., Epitropaki, O., Butcher, V., & Milner, C. (2002). Transformational leadership and moral reasoning. *Journal of Applied Psychology, 87*(2), 304–311.

Usman, I. (2010). The effect of leadership on performance management, good governance, internal and external satisfaction in study programs. *China-USA Business Review, 9*(5), 8–27.

Vitell, S. J., & Paolillo, J. G. P. (2004). Cultural study of the antecedents of the perceived role of ethics and social responsibility. *Business Ethics: A European Review, 13*(2/3), 185–200.

Vitell, S. J., Paolillo, J. G. P., & Thomas, J. L. (2003). The perceived role of ethics and social responsibility: A study of marketing professionals. *Business Ethics Quarterly, 13*(1), 63–86.

Waddock, S. A., & Graves, S. B. (1997). The corporate social performance-financial performance link. *Strategic Management Journal, 18*(4), 303–319.

Waldman, D. A. (2011). Moving forward with the concept of responsible leadership: Three caveats to guide theory and research. *Journal of Business Ethics, 98*(1), 75–83.

Waldman, D. A., de Luque, M. S., Washburn, N., House, R. J., Adetoun, B., Barrasa, A., & Debbarma, S. (2006b). Cultural and leadership predictors of corporate social responsibility values of top management: A globe study of fifteen countries. *Journal of International Business Studies, 37*(6), 823–837.

Waldman, D. A., & Siegel, D. S. (2008). Defining the socially responsible leader. *The Leadership Quarterly, 19*(1), 117–131.

Waldman, D. A., Siegel, D. S., & Javidan, M. (2006a). Components of CEO transformational leadership and corporate social responsibility. *Journal of Management Studies, 43*(8), 1703–1725.

Waldman, D. A., & Yammarino, F. J. (1999). CEO charismatic leadership: Levels-of-management and levels-of-analysis effects. *Academy of Management Review*, 24(2), 266–285.

Wang, S., Huang, W., Gao, Y., Ansett, S., & Xu, S. (2015). Can socially responsible leaders drive Chinese firm performance? *Leadership & Organization Development Journal*, 36(4), 435–450.

Weber, M. (1947). *The theory of social and economic organization, trans.* New York, NY: AM Henderson and Talcott Parsons.

Wells, C. A. H. (2002). The cycles of corporate social responsibility: An historical retrospective for the twenty-first century. *Kansas Law Review*, 51(1), 77–140.

Wieseke, J., Ahearne, M., Lam, S. K., & Dick, R. V. (2009). The role of leaders in internal marketing. *Journal of Marketing*, 73(2), 123–145.

Wilderom, C. P. M., van den Berg, P. T., & Wiersma, U. J. (2012). A longitudinal study of the effects of charismatic leadership and organizational culture on objective and perceived corporate performance. *The Leadership Quarterly*, 23(5), 835–848.

Winter, D. G. (1992). Responsibility. In C. P. Smith (Ed.), *Motivation and personality: Handbook of thematic content analysis* (pp. 500–505). Cambridge, UK: Cambridge University Press.

Yammarino, F. J., Dionne, S. D., Uk Chun, J., & Dansereau, F. (2005). Leadership and levels of analysis: A state-of-the-science review. *The Leadership Quarterly*, 16(6), 879–919.

Yukl, G. (1989). Managerial leadership: A review of theory and research. *Journal of Management*, 15(2), 251–289.

Yukl, G. A. (2010). *Leadership in organizations*. Thousand Oaks, CA: Prentice Hall.

Yukl, G. A., & Van Fleet, D. (1992). *Theory and research on leadership in organizations*. Palo Alto, CA: Consulting, Psychologists Press.

Section B

Global Challenges and Concerns

8 Practicing Corporate Social Responsibility

Loi Teck Hui

Introduction

The world and its natural laws interact with human societies to affect the well-being of all living things. An organization, be it public or private, is not detached from the society and the natural environment. Satisfying the diverse interests of its stakeholders is dependent on a complex balance of interconnected factors. Friedman (1970) argues that the primary social responsibility of a firm is to increase its profits without deceptions. There have been growing concerns in profit-seeking enterprises which are preoccupied with their profit-maximizing goals at the expense of the greater good (e.g. Chatterjee, 2003; Jackson, Wood, & Zboja, 2013). Tensions between maximizing profit for shareholders and optimizing returns for stakeholders persist (Crane, Palazzo, Spencer, & Matten, 2014). In addition, organizational leadership is also vital for generating combined insights capable of dealing with diverse and cognitively complex situations (Finkestein & Hambrick, 1996; Ireland & Hitt, 1999). With that said, whether practicing corporate social responsibility (CSR) can generate resilient socio-economic and environmental performances merits further academic investigation.

Management process essentially is a system of interdependency. The well-configured firms will thrive (Miller & Whitney, 1999). Pragmatic management upholds the output results, often justifying the inputs in terms of the results. By neglecting non-economic dimensions in both the input and output processes, the corporate sustainability of firms can be in jeopardy (Atkinson & Field, 1995, pp. 115–121; Hui, 2008). The existing empirical works, with narrowly defined CSR constructs, have been confined largely to specific projects and products rather than the entire firm (Crane, et al., 2014; Porter & Kramer, 2011). There have also been calls for more multilevel approaches and non-Western-tradition research on CSR (Aguinis & Glavas, 2012; Godfrey & Hatch, 2007). Against the research gaps identified, this chapter aims to examine the adoption of CSR in the strategic planning process of a major governmental agency in Malaysia: Bintulu Development Authority (BDA). The goal is to identify the strategic values of such adoptions which contribute to the said firm's positive triple-bottom-line performance, such as financial strengths, investment growth, industrialization, urbanization, core businesses with CSR added on, and environmental preservation, reflected in a subsequent section of this chapter, and the linkages of such values to the resource-based view (RBV) theory's assertions of a valuable asset. A well-encompassing CSR definition is adopted. People are essential to managerial thinking. Having appropriate leadership is necessary to organize a firm's strategic planning mechanisms to accomplish organizational goals and sustainability (Hamel & Prahalad, 1993; Quinn & Dalton, 2009). Along this line, the research also underlies the crucial roles top management plays in enabling the CSR adoptions which lead to better organizational performances.

This chapter has the following organization: first, we survey the related CSR and leadership theoretical foundations and adopt a well-encompassing CSR definition by the European Commission (2011); next, we present the data collection methods, data analyses, discussion on findings, and strategic implications of this research before making concluding remarks. In the data analysis and results discussion section, we examine the adoption of CSR, enabled by organizational leaderships, in the strategic planning process of BDA in four different components: (a) the strategic intent in engaging CSR practices, (b) the CSR planning that incorporates CSR strategies and programs into the organizational core businesses for implementation, (c) the control of CSR performance, and (d) the measurement of triple-bottom-line results, which addresses the tensions between the financial and the non-financial performances. The linkages between the CSR perspectives and the RBV theory are discussed in the section on implications. This exploratory study provides insight into the fact that by adhering to good citizen practices, commitments, especially from top management, to practice CSR can provide opportunities for firms to demonstrate value and to generate a form of sustainable competitive advantage or corporate sustainability supported by the larger society. There is relatively scant literature that pays attention on the adoption of CSR, with reference to leadership issues, in public-sector organizations. This research can make a positive contribution in this area.

Theoretical Framework

In this section, the adoption of CSR in the organizational strategic planning process is examined through the lens of the following CSR and related literatures.

CSR Definition

Several works have extensively reviewed the antecedents of CSR concepts and definition constructs covering the period between the 1950s and the 2010s. It seems that CSR is evolving into a highly heterogeneous literature (Carroll, 1999, 2008; Carroll & Shabana, 2010; Moura-Leite & Padgett,

2011). Carroll's (1979) definition of a four-part CSR—namely, economic, legal, ethical, and philanthropic—embedded in a conceptual model of corporate social performance perhaps was the earliest, more established, framework of CSR (Carroll, 1999). This CSR research adopts the European Commission's (2011, p. 6) definition of CSR:

> The responsibility of enterprises for their impacts on society . . . To fully meet their CSR, enterprises should have in place a process to integrate social, environmental, ethical, human rights, and consumer concerns into their business operations and core strategy in close collaboration with their stakeholders, with the aim of: maximizing the creation of shared value for their shareholders and stakeholders at large; and identifying, preventing, and mitigating their possible adverse impacts.

From the definition, a firm has an obligation to embed the elements of moral, social, environmental, legal, and stakeholder interests into its mainstream operations, while finding solutions to address its economic self-interests and stakeholder expectations. The definition corresponds with the holistic approach taken in this chapter—i.e. analyzing the adoption of CSR in a firm's strategic planning process and the associated triple-bottom-line results.

CSR and Strategic Intent

Managers are leaders who have specific roles to play within the management hierarchy. Having some forms of flexible hierarchical arrangements in an organization can assist it in fulfilling its obligations better (Denning, 2014; Mintzberg, 1975). Firms develop a clear set of goals within their organizational hierarchy of objectives, just as there is a hierarchy of managers to prevent drifting into an uncertain future. Resulting from an understanding of their internal organizations and external forces, they develop strategic intent and a strategic mission to form the basis of communication to their stakeholders (Hitt, Ireland, & Hoskisson, 2001). The vision and mission statements, externally focused, describe the central purpose of firms and guide the direction of their strategy formulation and implementation (Ireland & Hitt, 1992; Leuthesser & Kohli, 1997). If well crafted, the statements can also provide the impetus for influencing attitudes from the organizational leaders to the bottom of the organization and the powerful forces for organizational change (Mullane, 2002; Williams Jr., Morrell, & Mullane, 2014). Reconciling a firm's organizational ends to its means through strategic intent is necessary to achieve success. Strategic intent is the leveraging of firms' internal resource capabilities and core competences in relation to attaining their goals. It intimately ties firms' self-interests to their stakeholders', which reflects the unique ways firms can exploit competitive advantage (Hamel & Prahalad, 1989, Hamel & Prahalad, 1994; Sherman, 1995). It is also synonymous with the manner envisioned for making a vision a reality (Macmillan & Tampoe, 2001). Bartkus and Glassman (2008) argue that all stakeholders are interested in understanding how firms' CSR positions affect their well-being. They expect firms' actions are consistent with their publicized statements.

CSR and Strategic Planning

Strategic mission and strategic intent are not the end goals of CSR. For any CSR plans to be meaningful, firms will need to translate them into action, via their organizational strategic planning process, for value creation. In the case of BDA, two master development plans with structured development and action plans have guided the organization, since its formation, in drafting and implementing all of its business and CSR plans. A more detailed account of the subject matter will be discussed later in this chapter. A strategic planning process consists of three core components—namely, strategic analysis, strategic implementation, and strategic control. Forming strategic vision, setting objectives, conducting organizational strategic position analysis, and crafting a strategy for desired outcomes are the major agendas in the strategic analysis stage. The strategic implementation stage involves implementing and executing the chosen strategy effectively. On the other hand, evaluating performance and initiating corrective actions are the concerns of the strategic control stage (Hitt, et al., 2001; Thompson & Strickland, 1998). Crane, Matten, and Spence (2008, p. 417) indicate that some typical steps in integrating CSR into strategic planning would be a planning phase, an implementation phase, and an evaluation phase. In addition to these steps, leaders are also strong predictors of the degree to which organization members are guided by an established plan and the use of planning tools (Drago & Clements, 1999). Their commitment matters to organizational justice and social responsibility (Tatum & Eberlin, 2007). The financial return for major firms grows with sophistication in their strategic management (Miller & Cardinal, 1994; Pekar & Abraham, 1995). Hence a broad adoption of CSR plans would require the integration of such plans, with top management commitments, into firms' strategic planning process.

CSR Performance and Resource-Based View

In view of the limitations of financial return in measuring multifaceted aspects of firm performance, Elkington (1994, 1998, 2007) coined the notion of the triple-bottom-line concept, which considers the interdependencies of environmental, social, and economic aspects in achieving business sustainability and common good. The corporate social performance–relevant outcomes should include the following triple-bottom-line categories: economic, social, and natural environment impact (Wood, 1991; Wood, 2007). Appropriate leadership characteristics are necessary to positively affect these attributes

(Ashley & Patel, 2003; Ireland & Hitt, 1999). The triple-bottom-line principle has become an influential approach in major firms and countries (Elkington, 2007; The Global Reporting Initiative, 2002; Markus & Rob, 2013; Mintz, 2011).

By contrast, Carroll (1979, 1991) hints that fulfilling economic obligations is the primary concern of a business organization. The four-part CSR definition is presented as a CSR pyramid with economic responsibility depicted at the base of the pyramid and then built upward through legal, ethical, and philanthropic responsibilities. Existing research findings show a mixed result concerning the impact that CSR initiatives have on firms' financial performance. Positive results seem to be more dominant than mixed and negative results.[1] For firms to achieve the triple bottom line simultaneously, it is necessary that the three dimensions be reflected in their strategic planning process.

Maximizing returns for both shareholders and stakeholders represent huge challenges, requiring firms to develop unique resource capabilities in order to meet such challenges. The RBV relies heavily on assets that are specific, non-tradable, rare, non-substitutable, inimitable, and valuable. Firms may sustain their competitive advantage over a longer period of time if one, or any combination, of the following conditions exists: (a) they enjoy better expectations of future resource value, (b) the resource capabilities are path dependent or causally ambiguous, and (c) there is social complexity in which two or more different social and business systems combined to create excessive variations for a system to emulate accurately (Barney, 1986, 1995; Dierickx & Cool, 1989; Mahoney & Pandian, 1992; Peteraf, 1993).

CSR and Leadership

The attitude of top management toward CSR is one of the crucial factors in integrating CSR into strategy and culture. When the organizational leaders perceive CSR as an opportunity to maximize their firms' capabilities and to identify new competitive advantages, the adoption of CSR is likely. Their commitment to CSR is central to the effective institutionalization of CSR as a core organizational routine (Hilton & Gibbons, 2002; Mazutis & Zintel, 2015; Rake & Grayson, 2009; Werther & Chandler, 2011, pp. 119–143). Leadership with innovative vision was rated as one of the most important strategic capabilities of firms (Laczniak & Lusch, 1997; Simon et al., 2015, p. 17; Velsor, 2009). A distinctive mix of CSR leadership practices *inter alia* embodies knowledge, skills, vision, passion, action, and impact in order to confront the complex CSR dilemmas firms face (Courtice, 2007; D'Amato, Eckert, Ireland, Quinn, & Velsor, 2010). Kakabadse, Kakabadse, and Lee-Davies (2009) identify 10 leadership skills and capabilities needed to implement CSR in firms. The skills and capabilities—namely, clarity of CSR goals, integrity, CSR awareness, business case language, power of persuasion, ability to handle paradoxes, consistency of application, appropriate

CSR measurements, discipline to follow through, and will to act—form a portfolio for individual leaders to consider in their management of CSR. In summary, the executive's ownership of CSR initiatives, perceived to have positive organizational impacts, would be crucial for the adoption of CSR as part of the mainstream operations of firms.

Research Methodology and Context

To date, there is little theory and empirical research relating to the adoption of CSR in a complex, interactive, and multifaceted strategic planning process. Quantitative data can fail to capture the richness and complexity of firms' planning processes (Ramanujam, Ramanujam, & Camillus, 1986). It can be overly "thin", with a lack of consistency to describe the process (Boyd & Reuning-Elliott, 1998). Thus we adopt qualitative research in preference to a formal hypothesis testing to amplify what is not widely known in preference to a formal hypothesis testing (Bettis, Gambardella, Helfat, & Mitchell, 2015; Grant, 2003, pp. 495–496). By using both "deep data" and "thick description" approaches, the method investigates contemporary phenomena within real-life context and improves the validity of theories as it bridges the gap between abstract research and concrete practice (Eisenhardt, 1989; Yin, 1994). In the following, we discuss issues concerning qualitative data collection methods used, research context and sample selection, and data collection processes in this CSR research.

Research Methods

Semi-structured interviews with audio-tape recordings, observation, and secondary data analysis are the key data collection methods. The interview method can bring to the surface critical issues, solicit unbiased responses, and open up new inquiries that could answer any research question asked. Taped semi-structured interviews are transcribed to text. Multiple organizational internal and external records are analyzed to complement our understanding on the subject matters under investigation so as to reduce retrospective bias. We visit several key sites, for example, the venues for organizing the key social and CSR programs of BDA such as the Borneo International Kite Festival, regatta event, a welfare centre, and an orphanage complex.

Research Context and Sample Selection

Research Context

Malaysia has 13 states and three federal territories. The country was ranked among the top 20 most competitive economies of 2014–2015 by the World Economic Forum (World Economic Forum, 2014). Located in the state of

Sarawak, Malaysia, BDA was established following the discovery of huge reserves of natural gas and oil offshore in the Bintulu region. The development of these reserves warranted a central body that could not only coordinate the development projects but also plan and implement projects on its own. Hence BDA was set up on July 8, 1978, as a governmental development agency cum local authority (city council) under the BDA Ordinance 1978 to undertake these roles in Bintulu (The BDA Ordinance, 1978). The two roles form the core businesses of BDA. BDA also coordinates the development of Samalaju Industrial Park in Bintulu as part of the Sarawak Corridor of Renewal Energy (SCORE) project under the state government of Sarawak.

Bintulu is the home to some of the largest plants, infrastructure projects, and natural resource endowments in the state of Sarawak, the country, and the world. They include, for example, Petronas Liquefied Natural Gas Complex, Shell Middle Distillate Synthesis plant, Shell crude oil terminal, Bintulu deep water port, Samalaju port, Bakun hydroelectric dam, Samalaju Industrial Park, the Southeast Asia urea-ammonia plant, natural gas reserves, and palm oil refinery industrial cluster. It is a premier industrial city in Sarawak and Malaysia.

Sample Selection

BDA is the unit of analysis. It is a corporatized governmental entity governed by the BDA Ordinance 1978 with multifaceted governmental, societal, and business roles. Given its unique position, BDA's managerial decisions and corporate missions directly affect many aspects of the well-being of business communities and social and environmental infrastructures—stretching beyond national boundaries. Using richly restrictive governmental data sets, this research can generate insightful and valuable CSR data sets with high national impacts and global relevance.

Data Collection

We selected, in consultation with the management of BDA, out of about 800 BDA employees, 170 representative interviewees (Group A) and three interviewees (Group B) for interviews at the BDA premises—namely, at its headquarters and the municipal service centre. Group A consisted of senior managers and below. There were 8 senior managers, 26 managers, and 21 operational staff who completed the interviews. On the other hand, one assistant general manager, one assistant general manager cum deputy general manager, and one general manager were in Group B. There were two sets of interview questionnaires. Interview Questionnaire Set A was designed for Group A. It was more oriented towards the individual departmental focus and the operational aspects of CSR that had taken place in BDA. Interview Questionnaire Set B was for Group B interviewees who could speak with authority on the strategic aspects of CSR in BDA. The management of BDA reviewed and approved the distribution of the questionnaires. Over a period of approximately four months, stretching between December 2012 and May 2013, the semi-structured and tape-recorded interviews were completed. They were then transcribed into interview texts. One interview typically took 30–90 minutes to complete. For the set B questionnaire, it took about three hours per interview.[2]

To improve the methodological reliability of this research, we took the following measures: (a) prolonged the process of data gathering on sites to ensure findings accuracy, (b) conducted member checks by maintaining an active corroboration on the interpretation of data with those in BDA who provided the data, (c) collected referential materials by making use of extensive records data to support research findings, and (d) engaged in peer consultation—i.e. we consulted with colleagues, in company executives, and in external reviewers in order to establish validity through pooled judgments prior to composing the final draft of this chapter.

Most of the developed governmental agencies and city councils have a large pool of highly qualified personnel and the necessary research and development infrastructures. In order to produce high-quality public policies and competitive CSR agendas, policymakers are compelled to have strategic investments in the related premises and linkages. In reflecting on the rich opportunities for advancing the understanding of the vibrant CSR research and practices in public-sector organizations, the current single-case research can be expanded *inter alia* by conducting a complimentary qualitative study on how the major city councils acquire, develop, leverage, and maintain organizational resource capabilities and social capital to meet the demands of society and the challenges of the globalized competitive market. The replication study can make the underlying theory and practices used in the current study more mature and valid.

Data Analysis and Results Discussion

Strategic Intent on CSR

As BDA is the authority equipped with vast resource capabilities, it is quite natural for the general public and politicians to expect the company to do a lot of things. BDA has even incorporated social and environmental planning intents into its policymaking since its formation in 1978. Some salient social and environmental management oriented remarks[3] can even be extracted from the Bintulu Regional Centre Study (BRCS), the first Bintulu master plan that guided the orderly and integrated development of Bintulu during the period from 1979 to 1995. Lately, BDA, guided by its vision and mission, and approved by its board or top management in the early 2003, aimed to make Bintulu a more liveable industrial city with strong social and sustainability orientations. The vision is to develop "Bintulu into a friendly industrial city by 2020", and the mission "being a development agency and a city council, BDA is committed to manage the advancement of Bintulu, in partnership with its people, into a friendly and sustainable city through the provision of quality physical, social and economic development services". The vision and mission statements are embedded with strong CSR orientations; for instance, the elements of "friendly industrial city", "in partnership with its people", essentially the stakeholder engagement, "sustainable city", and "quality social services" along with the core businesses of BDA, such as "provision of quality physical and economic development services".

> We need targets set, not only for BDA and its staffs, but also for the people of Bintulu. The idea is to bring everybody together as a team to play their role whether as a government, an individual, or a private sector to achieve that vision. So in everything we do . . . we also have to take care of environment, making sure that the Environmental Impact Assessment is done, the minimum standards of the Environmental Acts are met . . . to make sure that we achieve the friendly industrial city by 2020.

In the early years of its establishment, BDA was preoccupied suitably with public infrastructural development activities. There were not many external requests for BDA to engage in community developments. In terms of development, the consultants from Australia, Pak-Poy & Associates Pty. Ltd., prepared for BDA the first structured master development plan for Bintulu, the BRCS, whereby land use was categorized into residential, commercial, industrial, green, and other usage (Australian Development Assistance Bureau, 1979). If one compares the shape of the structured plan with the satellite picture of Bintulu from the Tanjung Kidurong area to Kemena, one can see that they almost match each other. In that respect, what had been planned before in the early 1970s has actually been translated into the first 20 years of real development in Bintulu, which has grown from a population of 5,000 to more than 200,000.[4]

> On CSR programs, we have been doing these from year one, and now are about 35 years. We make donations and draw plans for communal buildings, community halls, places for worship, roads, drains, including landscaping, schools, and other commercial buildings.

The explosion of information and communication technology revolutionizes the channels that the societies use to interact with each other. This leads to the call for more transparent public policymaking and administration processes. The general public nowadays expects more effective public management, such as the authorities' responsiveness in addressing pressing problems in communities, ability to attract investments, creation of job opportunities, and intent to create liveable living environments.[5]

> As an officer of BDA, my role is to channel feedback from the public to the management of BDA. And what is justifiable and realistic, we

will implement to the satisfaction of the Bintulu people . . . nowadays, we have to practice what we call *"no-wrong door"* policy, whereby the public look on government, instead of BDA, Residence Office, Public Works Department and so on, as one government. We have been informed by the Sarawak State Secretary as well as the Chief Secretary of Government in Kuala Lumpur to adopt *"no-wrong door"* policy whereby if feedback from the public, even if not of our concern, we need to listen, record it down, and pass it on to the relevant people and departments for action. So, this is our official role that we are playing. Besides getting requests, we also implement what is budgeted on the CSR in an efficient way and to the satisfaction of the public.

The strategic intents of BDA to materialize its vision and mission are further evidenced in the formalization of its second master plan in 2004, the Bintulu Urban and Regional Study (BURS), building upon the success of the first one, the BRCS. Most of the proposed developments in the BRCS have been completed.[6] The BURS, which has much larger coverage than its predecessor, consists of three major components.

Strategic Development Plans

The plan provides a broad planning framework for the Bintulu and Samalaju Industrial Park area by taking into consideration the role of the Bakun hydroelectric dam that generates 2,400 megawatts of electric power for industrial developments. It covers the issues of land use, economic, infrastructure, social-economic, human resources, transport structure, and natural resources in the regional context.

Structure Plans/Local Plans

The plans address the issues of international accessibility of Bintulu, the establishment of adequate physical and social infrastructure and services, the need for environmentally sustainable development, and transforming Bintulu into a friendly industry city.

Action Plans

This section provides implementation schedules for the recommendations from (a) and (b).

In pursuing its vision through the implementation of the BUSR proposals up to 2020, BDA will develop Bintulu along the lines of a "healthy city" concept; the environment shall be clean with attractive townscape and adequate amenities to sustain healthy living for its residents, visitors, and investors. The BURS translates the vision and mission into all levels of development plans—human, economic, environment, social well-being, including the Central Business District.[7] Costing about RM2 billion, the current ongoing Central Business District development project will be the business, financial, and administrative hub of urbanized modern downtown of Bintulu. Apart from the aesthetic design, the Central Business District's development agenda takes into account major social and environmental issues to be addressed. Open spaces, green parks, flora gardens, commerce square, city hall, and convention centre will be built to compliment the downtown image of Bintulu as a premier liveable garden city.

> On CSR programs, we have been doing these from year one, and now are about 35 years. We make donations and draw plans for communal buildings, community halls, places for worship, roads, drains, including landscaping, schools, and other commercial buildings.

In summary, many social evils are associated with rapid urbanization, rural-urban migration, and rapidly rising incomes. BDA has provide accommodations not only for people to live a good life in Bintulu but also for the industries, whether they are heavy or light, to perform and make money in Bintulu. Its articulated vision and mission statements, with CSR embeddedness, are translated into real structured master development plans, with CSR added on to address its statutory obligations and stakeholder interests.

Planning for CSR Implementation

Well-articulated mission and strategic intent statements are not the end goals of CSR. A firm's CSR plans will only be meaningful when they are translated into action. Internal constraints can limit the formalization of CSR plans in a firm's core strategic planning process, especially when not everybody sees CSR as something of importance and finance is a concern.

> People know that BDA has very good source of income. But, our core businesses [priorities] are development and municipal services. CSR naturally is a joint product of the core businesses. It represents a good governance practice of the organization.
>   The following are several fundamental or CSR adoption enabling factors to the strategic planning process in BDA where CSR plans are also presented for evaluation, budget approval, and implementation.

Corporate Planning and Innovation Department

This department consists of two units: innovation management services and research and statistics units. The innovation management services unit is more involved in quality improvement efforts and managing ISO 9000 compliance when BDA was first certified by ISO in 1997. Occasionally, it organizes strategic retreats every one or two years to set the vision, mission, and revisit goals and objectives of BDA. The retreats provide inputs on BDA's vision and mission, core businesses, and CSR programs.

> The strategic retreat is an avenue for BDA staffs to discuss and put forward their ideas. BDA chooses a retreat probably because it has fewer disturbances. The strategic retreat is a strict and confined session with serious discussions and arguments for any programs and plans—for example, a 5-year program or 10-year program.

On the other hand, the research and statistics unit provides measurements of customer satisfaction on certain key projects—for instance, poverty alleviation programs and rural infrastructure development projects. The corporate planning and innovation department serves as the central coordinating unit for the BDA's annual strategic planning meeting. In BDA, the meeting is regarded as equivalent to the annual budget meeting.

Two Master Plans—The BRCS and the BURS

Although other plans are proposed during the annual budget meeting, these two master plans are the exclusive guides for BDA. As mentioned, the master plans embed social and environmental considerations in the drafting of all development plans.

Annual Budget Cycle

BDA needs to plan for the next year one year in advance. The annual budget meeting normally starts in March and is completed in July/August. The corporate planning and innovation department distributes the budget circulars. During the annual budget meeting, each department will submit bids for projects. After being screened by internal panels or during the strategic retreats, the endorsed plans are submitted to the BDA board for approval. What is approved with budget allocation will be implemented.

> We have our internal sources of revenue. We do our budget and then bring it to the board. Sometimes it comes from staff or management to ask and to present the budget for CSR.

Top Management's Role

Top management is the focus of the annual budget meeting, as they approve all the budgeted business and CSR plans. As they endorse CSR initiatives, they remind staff every now and then, in daily job routines as well as monthly management meeting, about the performance of the plans.

> I can say we work within our budget . . . It will be better by adding in some more budgets. Because now the places [to maintain in Bintulu]

become bigger and bigger . . . But within the budget limit, we try to perform the best we can. We have to optimize the usage of our manpower in order to get things going . . . Nowadays the management is very supportive.

Business Environments

Rapid changes in the business environment may reinforce the case not to go for formal strategic planning. BDA is very unique. It gets funding not only from the state and the federal governments but also from the bulk of income that actually comes from BDA itself through land-premium receipts as a result of massive industrial developments. As an economy heavily dependent on the performance of oil and gas, as well as resource-based industries with favourable market destinations, Bintulu has been immune from major external shocks, such as the Asian economic crisis of 1997/98 and the subprime crisis of 2008/09.

> The trend in the world has been toward democracy . . . As happened to Russia . . . and lately the Arab Spring. BDA cannot escape from this, as the education and income of people are getting better. People want a transparent government and BDA. We not only have to respond to the requests of the public, but also be proactive and to do survey to make sure that whatever we do is meeting the needs of the people.

Before the annual budget meeting, the corporate planning and innovation department distributes related circulars and directives to all concerned. Individual staff can offer ideas. In that respect, the strategic planning process in BDA is decentralized. Business and CSR plans come from the divisions themselves or from top management to the managers. The strategic planning process, as such, is a regular and formalized organizational routine that brings together these intertwining 'bottom-up' and 'top-down' organizing and strategizing initiatives.

> When we receive requests from the department(s) for a RM1 million budget, we will ask how many people will benefit from the budget, how much money will be generated from the project, and the direct and indirect impacts of the project. The linkages are there. For municipal services, we have put out the statistics, and we also have meetings twice a year. The Total Quality Management (TQM) Council will look at the statistics and complaints [regardless] whether it is landscaping, potholes, road maintenance or all other kinds of services. We have performance targets. If the complaints exceed the bottom line set, we ask the divisions to come out with measures not only to fix the problems but also on how to prevent it from happening again.

Responsible departments review regular or lead CSR and social programs along with newly proposed CSR programs for budget allocation approval during the annual budget meeting. Examples of lead CSR programs are the Borneo International Kite Festival, lantern and food festival, regatta cultural event, corporate donations, sports tournaments, enhanced staff welfare programs, low-cost housing projects, resettlement schemes, and friendly business policies. Top management can direct other ad hoc or facilitated CSR programs, either from BDA itself or the state and federal governments, to the department level for planning and execution. They are, for instance, poverty alleviation programs, a welfare centre, a state orphanage complex, and social programs in collaboration with private and public sectors.[8] Outcome-based and customer-first initiatives are the drivers that link the different units and departments, both development and municipal services, within BDA during the annual budget meeting.

The growing prominence of performance targets have reshaped the strategic planning mechanism within BDA from a corporate control system in the early years to the recent one that permits increased decentralized strategic decision making with greater adaptability and accountability to external expectations. BDA generates revenue through its two core businesses: development agency and municipal services. CSR budget figures, amounting to several million of Ringgit Malaysia (RM) yearly, are merged either under the budgeted expenditures of each of the core businesses—for example, enhanced staff welfare programs, landscaping beautification and resettlement schemes—or as a common expenditure of BDA, such as the Borneo International Kite Festival and regatta event.[9]

Performance Control on CSR

By virtue of the power conferred under its ordinances, BDA itself is an integrated business entity, governmental development agency, and city council. It has the roles of enhancing the reputation of the Malaysian government by attracting investments, improving the standard of living of the general public, and helping the government to achieve its vision to become a developed nation by year 2020.

> The services of BDA are actually the aspects of CSR . . . Nowadays the government projects are required to identify the public's needs first. This is geared toward CSR orientation as well. In projects initiation, CSR is very relevant before implementing infrastructure projects, as we need to get to know the needs of the people in order to assist us to design the projects in such a way that will benefit them directly. Although we do not use the phrase *"CSR"*, customer first, customer satisfaction, and impacts on the communities are CSR-equivalent terms with different names for us. All budgeted plans in BDA are outcome based—i.e. they must have good impacts on the public and the economy. Then, only the projects can be implemented . . . BDA has the responsibility to make sure that people coming from all over the place to Bintulu have a

sense of belonging. We promote rigorously inter-racial, social, and CSR activities, besides our core businesses, to promote social integration and harmony in Bintulu.

With that said, the annual budget meeting monitors the inputs into core organizational processes to ensure the desired project outcomes. The managers have to submit an estimate for the business or CSR plans they wish to carry out. Top management would then have to decide on the plans to allow them to be implemented without contriving budget restrictions.

When we approve the budgeted projects, they shall be completed within the prescribed time frame and goals set. If you can't finish, the projects will be withdrawn. Now, it becomes more critical to finish the project on time. We do have project management and monitoring meetings whereby we assign jobs for external and internal consultants to make sure that the projects are tendered out timely. The normal operational activities like yearly audit by the National Audit Department and the accounting statutory audit, whether internally or externally, are to make sure that the performance of BDA is in accordance with the relevant guidelines, the governmental rules regulations, etc. During the annual budget meeting, any business and CSR plans not consistent with the governmental treasury plans and, if possible, the best practices elsewhere will not be given consideration.

BDA has used the following organizational internal- and external-oriented control mechanisms to engage its stakeholders and measure its corporate performance: the board of management; the legal department; the committees in different areas, such as tender, recruitment, finance and investment, land, and audit; the public relation department; the innovation management services unit; the research and statistics unit; the monthly management meeting; the staff performance appraisal; the Total Quality Management council; the 5-star rating assessment exercise; the advisory council; the 24-hour customer hotline; the customers day; and the democracy means.[10]

When rewards are based on job-related performance results and not CSR compliance, the role of CSR can be of secondary importance when its execution is neither measured nor rewarded. In order for the staff to achieve excellent ratings in their formal job performance appraisals, BDA expects them to carry out two or more CSR or community service initiatives with positive impacts on the society and with international significance.

For staff, we have the guideline. In order to be excellent, we need to do something extra not just do the best in your work. For a staff to score 95% and above, he or she has to do something extra. Extra means if your duty is to carry out the project on schedule; that is still just good. In order to be excellent, you need to do two or three extra items, whether it is CSR in the social clubs or in the communities that will carry more points.

Triple-Bottom-Line Performance

A CSR initiative in a firm's profit-maximizing context is desirable when the benefits of such an initiative outweighs the costs of engaging it (Bagnoli & Watts, 2003; McWilliams & Siegel, 2000). CSR programs well received by those most affected by them could hint that there is success in matching the firm's plans with actions and results. In light of analyses done in the preceding sections, we will examine the corresponding salient triple-bottom-line performance of BDA.

Financial Performance

BDA has been able to generate enough revenue on its own to cover its operating expenditures. Compared to a mere RM3 million at the end of the first financial period in 1979, the net asset value of BDA as of December 31, 2012, was more than RM1 billion. This represents about a 10 per cent annual growth rate over a period of 34 years, an above-average return in relation to its peers in Malaysia, despite the occurrences of several external economic shocks over the past three decades.[11] It is the local authority with the largest combined municipal revenues and combined municipal expenses from 2010 to 2012 in the state of Sarawak (Department of Statistics Malaysia, 2013, p. 259). In 1981, the municipal services division recorded about RM0.96 million in revenue. As a result of the rapid growth in the number of rateable properties and collectible business licensing fees in Bintulu, the revenue soared to about RM46 million in 2012, equivalent to an average of 14.97 per cent growth per annum.[12]

> BDA is very unique. It gets funding not only from the state and federal governments but also the bulk of income actually from BDA itself to fund development expenditures. BDA's funding is depending very much on the economic activities in Bintulu. The more industrial estate set-ups, the more firms will buy land. And, the land premiums collected will go to BDA . . . The entitlement to the land premiums collected enables BDA to have its own lucrative source of income. So sourcing funds to cater for the needs of BDA's core businesses has not been a problem, a privilege envied by other departments because we have more revenue, and we can generate it on our own.

Core Businesses With CSR Added On

Governmental development agency and municipal services provider are two core businesses of BDA. Strategic CSR and our adopted CSR definition suggest that CSR elements must be embedded in the mainstream operations of a firm. We enlist the following material contributions (with year of completion and amount of a project) of BDA[13] from its core businesses with CSR added on:

Public infrastructure developments—Tanjung Kidurong road (1979, RM10 million), Tanjung Batu coastal protection works (1996, RM10 million), road construction and upgrading (ongoing, several hundred millions), and sewerage systems and treatment plants (ongoing, multimillions).

Industrial estate developments—Bintulu light industrial estate (1981, 13.89 hectares of land), Kidurong light industrial estate (1984, 86 hectares of land), Kemena industrial estate (1980s–1990s, 850 hectares of land), Jepak industrial estate (1997, 343 hectares of land), Kidurong industrial estate (1990s–2000s, 793 hectares of land), and palm oil industrial cluster (2014, 320 hectares of land).

Housing estate developments—Malaysian liquefied natural gas plant staff housing (1982, RM110 million), BDA staff quarters (1981, RM8.1 million), the ASEAN urea/ammonia plant staff housing (1987, RM120 million), Sun housing garden (1993), four-storey walk-up flats for BDA staff (1997, RM9.7 million), and BDA staff quarters at Tun Ahmad Zaidi road (2006, RM10 million).

Commercial centre developments—Kidurong town (1990s, 769 acres of land), BDA-Shahida commercial centre (1980s), Tanjung Batu commercial centre (1980s), Medan Jaya commercial centre (1995), Assyakirin commerce square (2010), Forego Jaya commerce square (2010), Bintulu town square (started in 2013, RM700 million), Columbia commercial centre (started in 2014, RM56.5 million), and Bintulu Sentral (started in 2012).

Public and recreational amenities—Bintulu civic center (1988, RM6 million), BDA sport hall (1986, RM1 million), 18-hole golf course (1996, RM11 million), zoo and botanical garden (1991, RM2.2 million), Bintulu central and wet markets (1990–1992, RM7 million), Red Crescent headquarters (1992, RM0.7 million), Olympic-size public swimming pool (1992, RM3 million), Bintulu outdoor stadium (1993, RM5.4 million), Bintulu indoor stadium (1996, RM7.4 million), Bintulu public library (1998, RM6.2 million), millennium park (2009, RM6 million), and Bintulu waterfront promenade (2007, RM70 million)

As an example, BDA awarded a contract worth RM719,988 in 1992 to construct the Red Crescent office in Bintulu. The contract amount was raised through public fund raisings and funding from BDA. BDA also helped to manage the design and the construction of the building, which was completed in 1993.

Investment Growth and Living Standard

Malaysia attracted the highest ever recorded foreign direct investments (FDIs) in 2011. Among the states, Sarawak attracted the most FDIs. More than 90 per cent of the FDIs in Sarawak went to Bintulu because of the initiation of the SCORE project with the Samalaju Industrial Park located in Bintulu as its major growth node. The park was launched in 2008 (Damodaran, 2012; Hillson, 2012). More or less, the same FDIs scenario was observed in 2012 and 2013. The FDIs concentration in Bintulu would mean the fellow citizens of Bintulu continue to enjoy relatively better quality of life or higher disposable income than their peers.

Industrialization and Strategic Diversification

In view of its core businesses that always have direct social impact, perhaps, as top management has said, the biggest success was when the state government entrusted BDA to manage the Samalaju Industrial Park. Since its inception in 2008, the park has attracted confirmed investments worth over RM30 billion (see Table 8.1), in spite of the lacklustre economic growth in major developed economies.

Table 8.1 Major Confirmed Projects at Samalaju Industrial Park

Company	Investment (RM)	Principal Activity
1. Press Metal Bhd	RM2 billion	Aluminium smelter plant
2. Tokuyama Corporation	RM7 billion	Poly-crystalline plant
3. Asia Mineral Ltd/Pertama Ferroalloy	RM790 million	Manganese ferroalloy smelting plant
4. OM Holding	RM1.8 billion	Ferro alloy smelting plant
5. Sakura Project (Sumitomo J/V Assmang and China Steel)	RM1.05 billion	Manganese smelting plant
6. Malaysian Phosphate Additive Sarawak Sdn Bhd	RM1.04 billion	Phosphorous plant
7. Dongbu Metal Co Ltd and Asian Cement Co Ltd	RM1.95 billion	Metalic silicon plant
8. Smelter Asia Sdn Bhd	RM4.5 billion	Aluminum smelter plant
9. Elkem A.S.	RM32.1 million	Electrode paste plant
10. Asia Advance Material Sdn Bhd	RM720 million	Metal silicon plant
11. Cosmos Petroleum and Mining Sdn Bhd	RM1.6 billion	Polysilicon plant
12. Press Metal Bhd Carbon	RM500 million	Carbon plant
13. Leader Universal Aluminum	RM2 billion	Aluminium smelter plant
14. Aimbest Steel	RM200 million	Alloy manganese plant
15. Ho Wah Genting Bhd	RM200 million	Alloy manganese plant

(*Continued*)

Company	Investment (RM)	Principal Activity
16. Makmoni Sdn Bhd	To be confirmed	Polymer-related plant
17. SIG Gase Bhd	RM5.2 million	Air separation unit
18. Samalaju Property Development	To be confirmed	Samalaju township development

Source: *The Renewable Corridor Development Authority and Bintulu Development Authority*

Petrochemical and palm oil industries together accounted for more than 90 per cent of the total export value of the state of Sarawak in 2012 (Department of Statistics Malaysia, 2013, pp. 152–152). The two industries are also reflective in the state of industrial development in Bintulu since the inception of BDA in 1978. The establishment of Samalaju Industrial Park provides a strategic diversification by creating an additional and reliable source of industrial revenue to the economy of Bintulu.

Environmental Preservation

Industrial developments are always related to pollution. The strategic thrust of BDA's vision is that as follows:

> We don't want the industries to pollute the environment. We have the Natural Resources and Environment Board of Sarawak and Department of Environment of Putrajaya, under the Ministry of Natural Resources and Environment to monitor the pollution to a level acceptable and within control. But besides taking care of air and water, we have to make Bintulu beautiful and good to see. BDA has assisted the two agencies looking after the environmental matters. We already have few big parks, reserved green areas at the Tanjung Batu coastal reserve where the BDA office and golf course are located. We have about 500 acres green area at the heart of the town, whereas you can hardly even see 100 acres elsewhere at the downtown centre.

In 2012, the air quality reading in Bintulu was acceptable despite it being the most industrialized town in Sarawak. The air quality was quite at par with Kuching with no undesirable air quality status recorded throughout the year (Department of Environment Malaysia, 2012, p. 18).[14]

Urbanization and Liveable City

BDA is preparing to move toward the friendly industrial city status. In June 2003, it commissioned consultants to carry out the Bintulu Central Business District Master Plan study for recommending proposals to be implemented between 2004 and 2020 (Konsortium Malaysia, 2005, p. 3).

"Liveable city" means the environment will be clean and the townscape attractive for both visitors and investors. Covering an area of about 328 hectares, the Central Business District is the new business, financial, and administrative hub of Bintulu. It needs to be friendly, attractive, vibrant, efficient, and adaptive to changes (Konsortium Malaysia, 2005, p. 2).

Population Growth

Population is an important factor for assessing the economic base and outlook for development of an urban area. Based on a census study in 2010, the Bintulu population reached 183,892 in 2010 compared to 86,132 in 1991. As a premier industrial centre in the state of Sarawak and Malaysia, it enjoys the highest population growth rate from 1991 to 2010, with an average of 4.06 per cent per annum in comparison to other major divisions such as Miri (3.19 per cent), Kuching (2.54 per cent), and Sibu (1.95 per cent) in Sarawak (Department of Statistics Malaysia, 2013, pp. 14).

Implications

The analyses of this case research conjure up the potential theoretical linkages between the RBV of the firm and the CSR perspectives, whereby the organizational leaderships are committed to adopt CSR in the strategic planning processes or the core routines of their firms. First, we purport that CSR is an organizational routine, which can be a valuable source of corporate sustainability. Organizational routines are repetitive and recognizable patterns of interdependent actions carried out by multiple actors. They have the power to coordinate and control complex organizational activities as they enable the consistent interactions of multiple actors. The organizational members remain capable of acting in situations pervasive with uncertainty as the routines fix organizational parameters (Becker, 2004; Feldman & Pentland, 2003). A CSR routine can be a valuable resource capability if a firm is can use it to create competitive advantages or shared values that further its corporate agendas. Firms vary in the routines they have developed to conduct their business. To survive in the long run, the least efficient and effective routines are either abandoned or changed (Nelson & Winter, 1982; Winter, 1987). As such, window dressing CSR actions, auxiliary social programs created in the absence of solid and legitimate organizational foundations, or CSR programs lacking top-management commitments, as a whole, will not be sustainable.

The discovery of huge oil and gas resources triggered the economic justification for the establishment of BDA (Friedman, 1970). There are ordinances, regulations, and institutional frameworks that govern the legitimate existence and operations of BDA. BDA has the legal responsibility to satisfactorily discharge its core roles as a development agency and municipal service provider in an ethical matter. The top management of BDA purports that CSR influences every aspect of its core businesses. As a public authority, everything it does causes it to interact with its stakeholders. CSR elements, as such, are tightly embedded in every organizational routine. In terms of performing financial stewardship, BDA generates responsible profits without monopolizing the markets through its unique position. Over the past 34 years, the net assets value growth on average has been about 10 per cent per annum. In the last 10 years, BDA has spent almost all of its income, such as rates and license fees generated from the general public, on the public through extensive township upgrading efforts to make the city more liveable, and it has promoted high-impact social causes (Caroll, 1979, 1991). The preceding section also presented other positive financial, social, and environmental performance results such as investment growth, core businesses with CSR added on, and urbanization initiatives. Although CSR involves the firm's strategic intents and daily routines, our analyses also show that BDA integrates regular CSR programs and CSR reward mechanisms, with top-management supports, in its strategic planning process and core businesses to create shared values. The CSR routines can be seen as a source of value to the organization.

Next, we argue that CSR routines can be a strategic asset with managerial value. The most efficient and effective routines generate competitive advantages for firms in the face of competition. The resource-based view of the firm argues that for the routines to be valuable, they may be inelastic in supply or rare—i.e. possessed by few (Barney, 1995; Dierickx & Cool, 1989) and regarded as a high-level collection of routines for producing significant outputs of a particular type (Winter, 2000; Winter, 2003). A stand-alone CSR program may be imitable and has limited social impact. A collection of complementary CSR programs embedded in core organizational routines, which develop over time, may be unique to a firm and a complex path-dependent asset for imitation. The leadership of BDA incorporates CSR perspectives in its strategic intents and strategic planning processes. Through its strategic mission and various stakeholder engagement mechanisms, BDA interacts with society to address issues of concern. As a corporatized public authority, every aspect of BDA's actions and policies has direct effect on the society and vice versa. As such, BDA is able to seek actively to benefit society as a consequence of the routines of its core businesses tightly embedded with CSR agendas and regular CSR programs, which represents an integrated bundle of plans that addresses the goals of maximizing both economic and social value.

Conclusion

Finding an idealized interpretation of a firm's CSR domains could be a subjective matter. Organizational leaders often encounter conflicting CSR stands when organizational internal systems and knowledge management are ambiguous. Relentlessly pursuing business profits to reach an organizational goal without conscience and failure of corporate governance is dangerous, as we have seen from many corporate mishaps. By fulfilling an obligation, especially from top management, to make core organizational decisions with CSR added on, our case analysis shows that a firm can demonstrate social responsibility values that benefit its stakeholders. This has tremendous spin-off effects. In the longer run, the organization benefits from more FDIs that strengthen its financial position. With the healthy financial position, the organization can better realize its social obligations by introducing more regular CSR programs, development projects, and public goods and services to promote social causes so as to benefit its stakeholders further. Essentially, the CSR perspective is embedded in the routines of the firm's core businesses. The strategic planning and decision-making processes that address the ethical components of strategies highlight what the firm values in fulfilling its statutory obligations, including the CSR agendas. As CSR becomes part of the organizational core resource capabilities, the firm's top-management level of decision making and external relationships reflect its continuous commitment to practice CSR as a way to achieve corporate sustainability.

Notes

1 Because of word limits, the fuller and extensive literature reviewed in the area is not presented.
2 Interview Questionnaire Sets A and B and detailed lists of BDA employees interviewed are enclosed in a separate document for review by reviewers.
3 Some examples of the remarks are, "Major concern will be the effects of emissions and effluent discharge from industries. Careful consideration is given to the types of effluent to be permitted and likely to be discharged and recommendations are made for waste disposal taking into consideration such factors as natural drainage systems, coastal longshore drift and marine and terrestrial flora and fauna", and, "From the consultants' population projections, it is possible to estimate future needs for social capital: housing, school places, municipal services, recreational and religion facilities, commercial facilities, transport facilities and utilities".
4 Our CSR interview and secondary sources on BDA and WAHBA Engineering Consultants and GHD Consultants (2006)—The Bintulu Urban and Regional Study Final Report: Land Use and Transport, vol. 1, part 3, p. 10–37.
5 Our CSR interview sources on BDA.
6 See WAHBA Engineering Consultants and GHD Consultants (2006).
7 See Konsortium Malaysia (2005). The Central Business District plan is a complementary study that forms part of the Bintulu Urban and Regional Study.
8 Due to space constraints, examples of lead and facilitated CSR and social programs are enclosed in a separate document for review by reviewers. Under the lead programs, BDA has full control over the organizing and implementation aspects of the CSR and social programs. For the facilitated programs, BDA joins other private- and/or public-sector firms in organizing and implementing CSR and social programs.
9 See BDA budget estimates handbook 2002–2004. BDA was the local authority in the state of Sarawak with the highest municipal revenues from 2010 to 2012 (Department of Statistics Malaysia, 2013, pp. 259).

10 Due to word limits, the fuller descriptions on the roles of the mechanisms were appended in an earlier version for review by reviewers.
11 See BDA annual report 1979–2012.
12 See BDA annual report 1980–2012.
13 See, for example, BDA annual report 1979–2012, BDA official newsletter 1979–2013, and secondary records from the related functional divisions of BDA.
14 The number of days considered "good" in Bintulu were 221 (Kuching, 243) and "moderate" 145 (Kuching, 123). Kuching is the administrative capital of the state of Sarawak.

References

Aguinis, H., & Glavas, A. (2012). What we know and don't know about corporate social responsibility: A review and research agenda. *Journal of Management, 38*(4), 932–968.

Ashley, A., & Patel, J. B. (2003). The impact of leadership characteristics on corporate performance. *International Journal of Value-Based Management, 16*(3), 211–222.

Atkinson, D. J., & Field, D. H. (Eds.) (1995). *New dictionary of Christian ethics and pastoral theology* (Economic Ethics, pp. 115–121). Leicester: Inter-Varsity Press.

Australian Development Assistance Bureau. (1979). Bintulu regional centre study (Vol. I–IV). Prepared by P.G. Pak-Poy & Associates Pty. Ltd and Associate Consultants on behalf of the Government of Australia.

Bagnoli, M., & Watts, S. (2003). Selling to socially responsible consumers: Competition and the private provision of public goods. *Journal of Economics and Management Strategy, 12*, 419–445.

Barney, J. B. (1986). Strategic factor markets: expectations, luck and business strategy. *Management Science, 32*, 1231–1241.

Barney, J. B. (1995). Looking inside for competitive advantage. *Academy of Management Executive, IX*(4), 49–61.

Bartkus, B. R., & Glassman, M. (2008). Do firms practice what they preach? The relationship between mission statements and stakeholder management. *Journal of Business Ethics, 83*, 207–216.

Becker, M. C. (2004). Organizational routines: A review of the literature. *Industrial and Corporate Change, 13*(14), 643–677.

Bintulu Development Authority. (1978). BDA: *Ordinance no. 1*. Malaysia

Bettis, R. A., Gambardella, A., Helfat, C., & Mitchell, W. (2015). Introduction: Multiple on-ramps to the qualitative review. *Strategic Management Journal, 36*(5), 637–639.

Boyd, B. K., & Reuning-Elliott, E. (1998). A measurement model of strategic planning. *Strategic Management Journal, 20*(10), 889–914.

Carroll, A. B. (1979). A three-dimensional conceptual model of corporate social performance. *Academy of Management Review, 4*, 497–505.

Carroll, A. B. (1991). The pyramid of corporate social responsibility: Toward the moral management of organizational stakeholders. *Business Horizons, 34*(4), 39–48.

Carroll, A. B. (1999). Corporate social responsibility: Evolution of a definitional construct. *Business & Society, 38*(3), 268–295.

Carroll, A. B. (2008). A history of corporate social responsibility: Concepts and practices. In A. Crane, D. Matten, A. McWilliams, J. Moon, & D. S. Siegel (Eds.),

The Oxford handbook of corporate social responsibility (pp. 19–45). Oxford, UK: Oxford University Press.

Carroll, A. B., & Shabana, K. M. (2010). The business case for corporate social responsibility: A review of concepts, research and practice. *International Journal of Management Reviews, 12*(1), 85–105.

Chatterjee, S. (2003). Enron's incremental descent into bankruptcy: A strategic and organizational analysis. *Long Range Planning, 36,* 133–149.

Courtice, P. (2007). Leadership. In W. Visser, D. Matten, M. Pohl, & N. Tolhurst (Eds.), *The A to Z corporate social responsibility* (pp. 306–308). Chichester: John Wiley & Sons.

Crane, A., Matten, D., & Spence, L. J. (Eds.) (2008). *Corporate social responsibility: Reading and cases in a global context.* Abingdon, Oxon: Routledge.

Crane, A., Palazzo, G., Spencer, L. J., & Matten, D. (2014). Contesting the value of "creating shared value". *California Management Review, 56*(2), 130–153.

D'Amato, A., Eckert, R., Ireland, J., Quinn, L., & Velsor, E. V. (2010). Leadership practices for corporate global responsibility. *Journal of Global Responsibility, 1*(2), 225–249.

Damodaran, R. (February 22, 2012). Highest ever FDI for Malaysia. *New Straits Times.* Retrieved from: http://www.nst.com.my/top-news/highest-ever-fdi-for-malaysia-1.50269

Denning, S. (April 18, 2014). No managers? No hierarchy? No Way! *Forbes.* Retrieved from: http://www.forbes.com/sites/stevedenning/2014/04/18/no-managers-no-hierarchy-no-way/#4620beea28f9

Department of Environment Malaysia. (2012). *Malaysia Environmental Quality Report 2012.* Putra Jaya: Ministry of Natural Resources and Environment.

Department of Statistics Malaysia. (2013). *Statistics Yearbook Sarawak 2013.* Kuching: Department of Statistics Malaysia.

Dierickx, I., & Cool, K. (1989). Asset stock accumulation and sustainability of competitive advantage. *Management Science, 35,* 1504–1511.

Drago, W. A., & Clements, C. (1999). Leadership characteristics and strategic planning. *Management Research News, 22*(1), 11–18.

Eisenhardt, K. M. (1989). Building theory from case study research. *Academy of Management Review, 14,* 532–550.

Elkington, J. (1994). Towards the sustainable corporation: Win-win-win business strategies for sustainable development. *California Management Review, 36*(2), 90–100.

Elkington, J. (1998). *Cannibals with forks: The triple bottom line of 21st century business.* Oxford: Capstone Publishing.

Elkington, J. (2007). Corporate sustainability. In W. Visser, D. Matten, M. Pohl, & N. Tolhurst (Eds.), *The A to Z corporate social responsibility* (pp. 132–139). Chichester: John Wiley & Sons.

European Commission. (2011). Communication from the Commission to the European Parliament, the Council, the European Economic and Social Committee and the Committee of the Regions—a renewed EU strategy 2011–14 for corporate social responsibility. Brussels.

Feldman, M. S., & Pentland, B. T. (2003). Reconceptualizing organizational routines as a source of flexibility and change. *Administrative Science Quarterly, 48*(1), 94–118.

Finkestein, S., & Hambrick, D. C. (1996). *Strategic leadership: Top executives and their effects on organization.* St. Paul: West Publishing.

Friedman, M. (September 13, 1970). The social responsibility of business is to increase its profits. *The New York Times Magazine.*

Godfrey, P. C., & Hatch, N. W. (2007). Researching corporate social responsibility: An agenda for the 21st century. *Journal of Business Ethics, 70,* 87–98.

The Global Reporting Initiative. (2002). *Sustainability Reporting Guidelines.* Boston, MA: Global Reporting Initiative. Retrieved from: https://www.globalreport ing.org/

Grant, R. M. (2003). Strategic planning in a turbulent environment: Evidence from the oil majors. *Strategic Management Journal, 24,* 491–517.

Hamel, G. H., & Prahalad, C. K. (1989). Strategic intent. *Harvard Business Review, May–June,* 63–76.

Hamel, G. H., & Prahalad, C. K. (1993). Strategy as stretch and leverage. *Harvard Business Review, 71*(2), 75–84.

Hamel, G., & Prahalad, C. K. (1994) *Competing for the future.* Boston, MA: Harvard Business School Press.

Hillson, Z. (September 12, 2012). Sarawak attracted highest FDI in 2011. *The Borneo Post.* Retrieved from: http://www.theborneopost.com/2012/09/12/swak-attracted-highest-fdi-in-2011/#ixzz2TMhfoLKs

Hilton, S., & Gibbons, G. (2002). *Good business: Your world needs you.* London: Textere.

Hitt, M. A., Ireland, R. D., & Hoskisson, R. E. (2001) *Strategic management: Competitiveness and globalization* (4th Ed.). Mason, OH: South-Western College Publishing.

Hui, L. T. (2008). Combining faith and CSR: A paradigm of corporate sustainability. *International Journal of Social Economics, 35*(6), 449–465.

Ireland, R. D., & Hitt, M. A. (1992). Mission statements: Importance, challenge, and recommendations for development. *Business Horizons, 35*(3), 34–42.

Ireland, R. D., & Hitt, M. A. (1999). Achieving and maintaining strategic competitiveness in the 21st century: The role of strategic leadership. *Academy of Management Executives, 12*(1), 43–57.

Jackson, R. W., Wood, C. M., & Zboja, J. J. (2013). The dissolution of ethical decision making in organizations: A comprehensive review and model. *Journal of Business Ethics, 116*(2), 233–250.

Kakabadse, N. K., Kakabadse, A. P., & Lee-Davies, L. (2009). CSR leaders roadmap. *Corporate Governance: The International Journal of Business in Society, 9*(1), 50–57.

Konsortium Malaysia. (2005). *Bintulu Central Business District Master Plan Study: Final Report, 1,* 21–50.

Laczniak, G. R., & Lusch, R. F. (1997). The flexible executive mindset: How top management should look at tomorrow's markets. *Journal of Consumer Marketing, 14*(1), 60–81.

Leuthesser, L., & Kohli, C. (1997). Corporate identity: The role of mission statements. *Business Horizons, 40*(3), 59–67.

MacMillan, H., & Tampoe, M. (2001). *Strategic management: Process content and implementation.* London: Oxford University Press.

Mahoney, J., & Pandian, J. R. (1992). The resource-based view within the conversation of strategic management. *Strategic Management Journal, 13*(5), 363–380.

Markus, M., & Rob, G. (2013). W(h)ither ecology? The triple bottom line, the global reporting initiative, and corporate sustainability reporting. *Journal of Business Ethics, 118*(1), 13–29.

Mazutis, D., & Zintel, C. (2015). Leadership and corporate responsibility: A review of the empirical evidence. *Annals in Social Responsibility, 1*(1), 76–107.

McWilliams, A., & Siegel, D. (2000). Corporate social responsibility and financial performance: Correlation or misspecification? *Strategic Management Journal, 21*(5), 603–609.

Miller, C. C., & Cardinal, L. B. (1994). Strategic planning and firm performance: A synthesis of more than two decades of research. *Academy of Management Journal, 37*(6), 1649–1665.

Miller, D., & Whitney, J. O. (1999). Beyond strategy: Configuration is a pillar of competitive advantage. *Business Horizon, 42*(3), 5–19.

Mintzberg, H. (1975). The manager's job: Folklore and fact. *Harvard Business Review, July–August*, 56–62.

Mintz, S. M. (2011). Triple bottom line reporting for CPAs. *The CPA Journal, December*, 26–33.

Moura-Leite, R. C., & Padgett, R. C. (2011). Historical background of corporate social responsibility. *Social Responsibility Journal, 7*(4), 528–539.

Mullane, J. V. (2002). The mission statement is a strategic tool: When used properly. *Management Decision, 40*(5), 448–455.

Nelson, R. R., & Winter, S. (1982). *An evolutionary theory of economic change.* Cambridge, MA: Harvard University Press.

Pekar, P., & Abraham, S. Jr. (1995). Is strategic management living up to its promise? *Long Range Planning, 28*(5), 52–44.

Peteraf, M. A. (1993). The cornerstones of competitive advantage: A resource-based view. *Strategic Management Journal, 14*(3), 179–191.

Porter, M. E., & Kramer, M. (2011). Creating shared value: Redefining capitalism and the role of the corporation in society. *Harvard Business Review, 89*(1/2), 62–77.

Quinn, L., & Dalton, M. (2009). Leading for sustainability: Implementing the tasks of leadership. *Corporate Governance: The International Journal of Business in Society, 9*(1), 21–38.

Rake, M., & Grayson, D. (2009). Embedding corporate responsibility and sustainability—everybody's business. *Corporate Governance: The International Journal of Business in Society, 9*(4), 395–399.

Ramanujam, V., Ramanujam, N., & Camillus, J. C. (1986). Multi-objective assessment of effectiveness of strategic planning: A discriminant analysis approach. *Academy of Management Journal, 29*(2), 347–472.

Sherman, S. (November 13, 1995). Stretch goals: The dark side of asking for miracles. *Fortune, 132*(10), 231–232.

Simon, A., Bartle, C., Stockport, G., Smith, B., Klobas, J. E., & Sohal, A. (2015). Business leaders' views on the importance of strategic and dynamic capabilities for successful financial and non-financial business performance. *International Journal of Productivity and Performance Management, 64*(7), 908–931. doi: http://dx.doi.org/10.1108/IJPPM-05-2014-0078

Tatum, B. C., & Eberlin, R. J. (2007). Leadership, ethics, and justice in strategic decision making. *Business Strategy Series, 8*(4), 303–310.

Thompson, A., & Strickland, A. J. (1998). *Strategic management: Concepts and cases* (10th ed.). Boston: McGraw-Hill.

Velsor, E. V. (2009). Introduction: Leadership and corporate social responsibility. *Corporate Governance: The International Journal of Business in Society, 9*(1), 3–6.

WAHBA Engineering Consultants and GHD Consultants. (2006). Bintulu urban and regional study: Final report. *Vol. 1*, Part 6, *Land Use and Transportation*, 10–37.

Werther, W. B., & Chandler, D. (2011). *Strategic corporate social responsibility* (2nd ed.). Thousand Oaks, CA: Sage.

William Jr., R. I., Morrell, D. L., & Mullane, J. V. (2014). Reinvigorating the mission statement through top management commitment. *Management Decision*, *52*(3), 446–459.

Winter, S. G. (1987). Knowledge and competence as strategic assets. In D. J. Teece, (Ed.), *The competitive challenge: Strategies for industrial innovation and renewal*. New York: Ballinger.

Winter, S. G. (2000). The satisficing principle in capability learning. *Strategic Management Journal*, *18*(7), 509–533.

Winter, S. G. (2003). Understanding dynamic capabilities. *Strategic Management Journal*, *24*, 991–996.

Wood, D. (2007). Corporate social performance. In W. Visser, D. Matten, M. Pohl, & N. Tolhurst (Eds.), *The A to Z corporate social responsibility* (pp. 120–122). Chichester: John Wiley & Sons.

Wood, D. J. (1991). Corporate social performance revisited. *Academy of Management Review*, *16*(4), 691–718.

World Economic Forum. (2014). *The global competitiveness report 2014–2015*. Geneva: World Economic Forum.

Yin, R. K. (1994). *Case study research: Design and methods* (2nd ed.). Thousand Oaks: Sage.

9 Environmental Social and Governance Reporting

A Case Study of the Australian Mining Sector

Kumudini Heenetigala, Anona Armstrong,
Chitra Desilva Lokuwaduge,
and Amali Ediriweera

Introduction

> CSR: a concept whereby companies integrate social and environmental concerns in their business operations and in their interaction with the stakeholders on a voluntary basis . . . every large corporation should be thought of as a social enterprise, that is an entity whose existence and decisions can be justified insofar as they serve public or social purposes.
>
> (Crowther & Capadi, 2008)

Fundamentally, concepts such as corporate social responsibility, corporate social performance, stakeholder management, corporate citizenship, business virtue, business ethics, or corporate sustainability all are manifestations of one and the same underlying position—namely, corporate decision makers should consider the moral consequences of their decisions (Freeman, 1994 quoted in Den Hond et al., 2007).

The moral argument is that corporations, because of the impact they have, should act socially responsible. Among other pragmatic reasons for attending to corporate social responsibility, not least are the impacts on companies and communities of the corporate excesses witnessed in recent years. At the time when Enron was founded, it was said to be complying with governance best practice structures, but the leadership of the company was rife with conflicts of interest, dubious manipulation of the energy markets, off-balance-sheet investments, a board that lacked independence, and an overbearing chairman. The chairman, chief financial officer, and directors subsequently lost the company and their reputations (Wearing, 2005). Enron was not the only company where ignoring governance and distain for social responsibility led to concerns about the sustainability of a business. The BP Oil spill in the Mexican Gulf was the result of indecision by leaders and their deliberate flaunting of safety measures.

In Australia, legitimacy for leaders of corporations to attend to corporate social responsibility emerged with the issue of corporate governance guidelines for listed companies by the Australian Securities Exchange. In its latest guidelines to Corporate Governance Principles and Recommendations for reporting requirements (ASX, 2014), Principle 3 requires companies to act ethically and responsibly. This means going beyond compliance with regulations and acting in a manner that is consistent with the expectation of investors and the broader community. The new recommendations attached to Principle 7 provide endorsement for socially responsible actions that mitigate risks (ASX, 2014, p.30):

> A listed entity should disclose whether it has any material exposure to economic, environmental and sustainability risks and if it does, how it manages or intends to manage those risks.

Company directors are also required to annually comply with applicable environmental regulation and product disclosure statements. They must disclose "the extent to which labour standards or environmental, social, or other considerations are taken into account in the election, retention or realisation of the investment" (Corporations Act, 2001 (Cth. Section 1013D (1)(1).

Among the most well-known of CSR measures to be developed included the Dow Jones Sustainability Index (DJSI), the UN Global Compact, the OECD Guidelines for Multinational Enterprises, and the Global Reporting Initiative (GRI). When the DJSI was established in 1999, its aims were to monitor the financial performance of sustainable companies. The role of leaders was specifically highlighted:

> Sustainability leaders are increasingly expected to show superior performance and favourable risk/return profiles. A growing number of investors is convinced that sustainability is a catalyst for enlightened and disciplined management, and thus, a crucial success factor.
>
> (DJSI 1999, quoted in Bader, 2005, p. 73)

The emergence of corporate social responsibility in a company is often foreshadowed by a 'conversion' in the leadership in a company from a sole focus on profit to the realization that the future of the company is tied to its sustainability and, with that, a commitment to its community and the wider society.

Leaders need to share their vision, not only with employees but also with other stakeholders—investors, shareholder, suppliers, customers, and the community in which they operate. Horrigan (2010) argues that a multinational corporation that does not take CSR or ESG seriously is increasingly unlikely to achieve enduring success under twenty-first-century global conditions for any of its stakeholders.

There are many ways in which companies may communicate their efforts; how they do so is in their annual reports. The perceived credibility of information in annual reports is related to the external auditing process that at least the financial parts of the annual report must undergo before it can be published. Annual reports help to shape the impressions that observers of a firm hold. They are intended to create confidence in the company and thus to gain external legitimacy for the firm.

External legitimacy for CSR is also enhanced by measurement, assurance, communication, and evaluation of CSR practices and performance. How firms write about issues of CSR in their annual reports provides insight into their positions via these issues. This study builds on a tradition within the management and accounting literatures of studying annual reports on CSR-related themes (Bakker et al., 2007).

This chapter explores the key dimensions of sustainability; environmental, social, and governance (ESG) performance; and its measurement and disclosure by the Australian mining industry. It reviews the meaning of sustainability, the benefits of sustainability disclosures, how it may be measured, and the difficulties in measuring it. It describes the results of a study that identifies the types of sustainability measures currently used in the mining industry in Australia and concludes with some recommendations for further research.

Sustainability

The term 'sustainability' has several different meanings depending on the context in which it is used. Business sustainability is often associated with managing the triple bottom line (TBL), a process by which companies manage their financial, social, and environmental risks (Armstrong et al., 2001; Armstrong and Sweeney, 2002). These three impacts are sometimes referred to as profits, people, and planet. By the early twenty-first century, the debate about the value of the TBL was flagging. However, interest was renewed when the BP Oil spill in the Mexican Gulf cost the company 54 billion U.S. dollars (Rushe, 2015). Investors were outraged. One response was the launch of the Principles for Responsible Investment (PRI) by the UN in 2006 at the New York Stock Exchange. This initiative put environmental, social, and governance disclosures firmly at the forefront of decision making by large pension funds. A recent UN publication (Jessop, 2015) goes further by advocating that it is a fiduciary duty for fund managers to take ESG matters into account in their investment decisions.

In the introduction to a review of 190 studies Clark et al. (2015, p. 8) stated,

> Sustainability is one of the most significant trends in financial markets for decades. Whether in the form of investors' desire for sustainable responsible investing (SRI), or corporate management's focus on corporate social responsibility (CSR), the content, focusing on sustainability and ESG (environmental, social and governance) issues, is the same.

The authors concluded that 88 per cent of the research shows that solid ESG practices result in better operational performance of firms and in 90 per cent of the studies on the cost of capital, sound sustainability standards lowered the cost of capital of companies.

ESG also creates value for companies through increased sales, decreased costs, or reduced risks, as well as creating financial value for companies (Bonini, Koller, & Mirivis, 2009). Cooper and Owen (2007) found that "there is a strong business case to implement sustainable management practices in relation to environmental social and governance issues", because firms can do well while doing good, which means that sustainability can increase profits and present opportunities for value creation and have an impact on a company's revenue. Case studies of environmental, social, and governance programs conducted by Bonini et al. (2009) also provided support for benefits accruing from growth, improved returns on capital, reduced risk, and improved quality of management. The findings were confirmed in a study by Peiris and Evans (2010), who reported a significant positive relationship between broader ESG factors and firm valuations and indicated that higher rated companies are associated with higher earnings multiples. By suggesting that ESG factors impact corporate financial performance, they concluded that they are, therefore, relevant for consideration by investment decision makers.

According to McKinsey Global Survey Results, "the most widely known way that environmental, social, and governance programs create value is by enhancing the reputation of companies and their stakeholders' attitudes about their tangible actions" (Bonini et al., 2009, p. 12). Bonini et al. also stated that financial objectives such as better regulatory settlements, price premiums, increased sales, reduced risk of boycott, and higher retention of talent partly depend on the reputation of the company. Horrigan (2010) asserted that the primary asset of multinational corporations is now their reputation, which can be lost in an instant with one globally communicated bad news story. In contrast, ESG programs that meet the needs of the community, and especially those that go beyond regulatory requirements and industry norms, enhance a company's reputation.

These studies support the contention that ESG offers many benefits to investors and the wider community. But what is the incentive for corporate leaders to take on responsibility for ESG disclosures?

Motivation for ESG Disclosure

Motivations for ESG disclosures can vary. Deegan (2002) refers to motivation for undertaking voluntarily reporting on social and environmental activities as a desire to comply with legal requirements, economic rationality consideration, a belief in an accountability or responsibility report, desire to comply with borrowing requirements, compliance with community expectations as a result of certain threats to the organization's legitimacy, management of particular stakeholder groups, attraction of investment funds, compliance with industry requirements or particular codes of conduct, forestalling efforts to introduce more onerous disclosure regulations, and winning particular reporting awards. However, he says it may be unrealistic to state that one motivation dominates the others, but many of these motivations may be interrelated.

Furthermore, a study conducted by the Chartered Accountants of Canada (2010) reported on five main reasons for use of ESG information by investors. They were to inform risk and return potential, evaluate management quality, engage with companies and inform proxy voting, develop customized investment products or portfolios, and assess asset managers. This study agreed with the February 2009 issue of the *McKinsey Quarterly*, which states 80 per cent of CFOs (more Europeans than North Americans) believe that ESG information serves as a proxy for the quality of a company's management. Accordingly, Corporate Knights (2010) reports that Goldman Sachs looks for managements' responses to ESG performance in five broad categories when assessing quality of management. These are corporate governance, leadership, employee recruitment and retention, stakeholder relationships, and environmental management.

What Is Environmental Social and Governance Performance?

ESG describes the environmental, social, and governance issues that are considered by investors to influence corporate behaviour in firms' investment decisions (IFAC, 2012). ESG is described as "a generic term used in capital markets to evaluate corporate behaviour and to determine the future financial performance of companies" (Theoran, 2012, p. 247). The concept of ESG is also described using different terminology in various context such as risk valuation, socially responsible investment, and corporate social responsibility (Galbreath, 2013). ESG is also seen as a key indicator of risk management, management competence, and non-financial performance (Galbreath, 2013 cited in Lundstrom & Svensson, 2014).

Measures of Environmental Performance

Measures of environmental performance are about the positive or negative impact of a company on the environment in relation to the natural resources consumed in delivering products and services. It covers issues such as carbon emissions, water use and pollution, climate change and energy (Galbreath, 2013), and conservation of natural resources and treatment of animals.

Measures of Social Performance

Social performance refers to corporations' responsibility to society. It is about how a company manages its various relationships in society with employees, suppliers, customers, and communities in which it operates. Thomson Reuters (2015) refers to social performance as a social pillar that measures a

> company's capacity to generate trust and loyalty with its workforce, customers and society, through its use of best management practices. It is a reflection of a company's reputation and the health of its license to operate, which are key factors in determining its ability to generate long-term shareholder value.

The social aspect of ESG is also related to the role that human capital plays in value creation. The importance of employees to the success of an organization has brought the attention to factors such as better working conditions, training, motivation, and rewards. Furthermore, human rights, labour rights, child labour, health and safety and discrimination, and harassment and bullying at the workplace are also important issues that have been given much attention (Bonime-Blanc, 2014). Other researchers such as Galbreath (2013) refer to additional social issues including human rights, gender equality, health and safety, fair trade principles, product safety, and minorities. Apart from the aforementioned, the impact an organization has on communities in which it operates is also important to the success of the organization.

Governance Performance

Sir Adrian Cadbury left us his influential definition of corporate governance:

> Corporate Governance is concerned with holding the balance between economic and social goals and between individual and communal goals. The corporate governance framework is there to encourage the efficient use of resources and equally to require accountability for the stewardship of those resources. The aim is to align as nearly as possible the interests of individuals, corporations and society.
> (Sir Adrian Cadbury in 'Global Corporate Governance Forum', World Bank, 2000)

As discussed earlier, corporate governance is essentially about the leadership of a company—that is, the role of a board of directors in directing and controlling a company (Cadbury, 1992). External governance mechanisms refer to those factors that impact a company, but are essentially beyond direct control of the board of directors—e.g. legislation and regulations, and actions of various stakeholders. Internal governance mechanisms are the structures and processes intended to ensure board independence and accountability through reporting and transparent disclosure, managing risk, and avoiding corruption and bribery. They include the structure of a board and its committees, their independence, and the systems of reporting and accountability to the board. Examples of governance issues include executive benefits and compensation, bribery and corruption, shareholder rights, business ethics, board diversity, board structure, independent directors, risk management, whistle-blowing schemes, stakeholder dialogue, lobbying, and disclosure. Therefore, directors in their role as leaders are required to act in a socially responsible manner, which is also referred to in ASX corporate governance principles (ASX, 2014) and the King report (Institute of Directors Southern Africa, 2009). The King report further states, "Boards should no longer make decisions based only on the needs of the present because this may compromise the ability of future generations to meet their own needs" (Institute of Directors Southern Africa, 2009, p. 11).

In regard to other stakeholders, directors have duties under the corporations law, first to the company and then to shareholders and other stakeholders. Whereas the law in regard to duties to other stakeholders is often debated, there is no doubt that if a company is listed on the ASX, directors are expected to comply with the ASX governance guidelines that make leaders of companies responsible not only for the social responsibilities described earlier but also for shareholder actions (including company meetings, mergers, minority shareholder actions, etc.), and the long-term (as opposed to short-term) interests of their company. In addition, they must ensure that their company complies with other laws regulating, for example, anti-discrimination, privacy, employment, and occupational health and safety.

A company's systems and processes should enable a board of directors and its executives to act in the best long-term interests of a company. Good governance facilitates robust decision-making and strategic planning, which contribute to performance. It also enables companies to ensure better compliance, accountability, and transparency. In this context, ESG disclosures and reporting have become an important responsibility of boards of directors.

Due to ongoing public discourse about pollution, climate change, human rights issues, and economic crises, there is an increased need for businesses to be responsible for society. This responsibility is evident in boards' focus on sustainability and the reporting of sustainability performance, as well as the groundswell of support and sophistication concerning ESG-related factors and their measurement.

Theories of ESG

As the focus of this chapter is on environmental, social, and governance reporting, theories that explain a company's motivation to disclose ESG information will be discussed in the following section. According to Jenkins (2006), there are many theories that relate to ESG. They relate to regulation and standards, legitimacy, and stakeholders. Therefore, in this study, we draw attention to social contract theory, legitimacy theory, and stakeholder theory. All the above, theories discuss the relationship between a company and its internal and external stakeholders.

Social Contract

Both social contract theory and legitimate theory see society as a series of contracts between members of society and society itself (Gray, Owen, & Adams, 1996). There is a school of thought which sees social responsibility as a contractual obligation the firm owes to society (Donaldson, 1983). If society is not satisfied with the way in which an organization operates, legitimacy theory suggests that the society will revoke the contract with the organization. This might be evidenced through reducing or eliminating consumer demand, withdrawal by suppliers of the supply of labour or financial capital to the business, or lobbying for increased taxes, fines, or laws to prohibit those actions that do not conform to the expectations of the community (Deegan, Rankin, & Tobin, 2002).

Legitimacy Theory

According to Suchman (1995, p. 574), "Legitimacy is a generalized perception or assumption that the actions of an entity are desirable, proper, or appropriate within some socially constructed system of norms, values, beliefs, and definitions". As Matthews (1993) notes,

> Organisations seek to establish congruence between the social values associated with or implied by their activities and the norms of acceptable behaviour in the larger social system in which they are a part. In so far as these two value systems are congruent, we can speak of organisational legitimacy.

However, an actual or potential disparity between the two value systems will result in a threat to organizational legitimacy. Accordingly, an organization has legitimacy when the entity's value system is congruent with the value system of the larger social system of which the entity is a part. As a result, if society feels that an entity has breached its side of the social contract, then the entity's legitimacy is under threat (Lindblom, 1994).

Legitimacy theory emphasizes that an organization must consider the rights of the public at large, not merely the rights of the investors. In most cases, these are regulated in laws and guidelines. Failure to comply with societal expectations may result in sanctions being imposed in the form of restrictions on firms' operations and resources, as well as demand for its products.

Social and environmental researchers particularly tend to utilize legitimacy theory to explain why corporate management undertakes certain actions such as disclosing particular items of social and environmental information. It does not provide a prescription for what management ought or should do; it is a positive theory which seeks to explain or predict particular managerial activities (Deegan, 2014).

Much empirical research has used legitimacy theory to study social and environmental reporting, and proposes a relationship between corporate disclosures and community expectations (Deegan, 2004). Tilling (2004) states legitimacy theory provides a powerful mechanism for understanding voluntary social and environmental disclosures made by corporations. According to Deegan (2002), because of the desire to legitimize an organization's operation, legitimacy theory has been used as the theoretical basis for environmental social disclosures. Furthermore, Lindblom (1994) and Patten (2005) have also suggested practice of environmental disclosures as a tool of legitimization. Therefore, in relation to legitimacy theory, a strategy used for legitimacy is disclosure.

Stakeholder Theory

A theory that provides similar insights to legitimacy theory is stakeholder theory (Gray, Kouhy, & Lavers, 1995; Jenkins, 2004). ESG disclosures made by the companies are regarded as issues important to a wide range of stakeholders.

A stakeholder is any group of individuals who can affect, or is affected by, the activities of the firm in achieving the objectives of the firm (Freeman, 1984). Apart from the shareholders, a company has a responsibility to suppliers, customers, and employees, as well as the government and the community, which means under the social responsibility model, they must be accountable to the other stakeholders (Thorne, Ferrell, & Ferrell, 2011). Accordingly, shareholder wealth maximization, as a way of thinking, is changing to stakeholder wealth maximization, where a company's value management system is based not only on economic profit maximization but also on ESG maximization.

According to Gray et al. (1996), efforts exerted in managing the stakeholder relationships depends on the importance of the stakeholder. They also refer to information as a major element that can be employed by the organization to manage (or manipulate) stakeholders in order to gain their support and approval, or to distract their opposition and disapproval. Accordingly, managers will have an incentive to disclose information on various programs and initiatives to those stakeholders who have a particular interest in the organization to indicate that they are conforming to stakeholder expectations (Deegan et al., 2002).

ESG maximization can be reached only if a stakeholder engagement process is implemented in the management system of the company (Martirosyan & Vashakmadze, 2013). This shows that in order to be successful, companies not only have to be responsible to shareholders but also rely on managing a variety of stakeholders who have a stake in the social and financial performance of the firm (Donaldson & Preston, 1995).

ESG Reporting

Pressure from stakeholders, such as governments, competitors, communities, suppliers, and consumers, has encouraged disclosure of ESG performance. The International Corporate Governance Network, United Nations Environmental Program Finance Initiatives, United Nations Principles for Responsible Investment, and the Organisation for Economic Co-operation Development Principles and Carbon Disclosure Project are some of the international organizations seeking improvement in various types of ESG disclosures. They are also signatories to initiatives to enhance ESG disclosures (Chartered Accountants of Canada, 2010).

ESG reporting has become possible with the growth in reporting frameworks such as the UN Global Compact, the United Nations Principles for Responsible Investment, the Carbon Disclosure Project, the Sustainability Accounting Standards Board, the American and European SRI markets and the Global Reporting Initiative.

International Guidelines for Selecting ESG Criteria

"Guidelines are sets of non-mandatory rules, principles or recommendations for procedures or practices in a particular field" (NHMRC, 2014). Currently, there are no uniform criteria that could be applied to measure ESG indicators. Several organizations have developed various indices such as Dow Jones Sustainability Index, KLD-Nasdaq Social Index, Domino 400 Social Index, FTSE4Good Index, and Global Reporting Initiative (GRI) have proposed various measures for CSR indicators.

In Australia, the Financial Services Council (FSC) and Australian Council of Superannuation Investors (ACSI) has published a *ESG Reporting Guide for Australian Companies* to identify and report their ESG risks (ACSI & FSC, 2011). The indicators developed by these organizations were commonly used as reference for stock market investments (Vintro & Comajuncosa, 2010).

The Global Reporting Initiative (GRI) is an international independent organization that helps businesses, governments, and other organizations understand and communicate the impact of business on critical sustainability issues such as climate change, human rights, corruption, and many other issues. GRI's Sustainability Reporting Standards are used in over 90 countries, and GRI claims that it provides the worlds' most widely used standards on sustainability reporting and disclosure, which enables businesses, governments, civil society, and citizens to make better decisions based on information that matters. They state that, 93 per cent of the world's largest 250 corporations report on their sustainability performance (GRI, 2015).

The GRI framework includes reporting guidelines and sets out the principles and indicators that could measure and report on economic, environmental, and social performance (Global Reporting Initiative, 2013b).

Even though GRI has been a useful tool in improving the standardization of reporting in many sectors, compliance differs between companies and also different interpretations of the tools are applied to the standards for their reporting (Hřebíček, Soukopová, Štencl, & Trenz, 2011).

With the updated version of the GRI guidelines, G4 Sustainability reporting guidelines and G4 Sector, the GRI framework can be applied to organizations in all sectors, sizes, and regions (Hřebíček et al., 2011). GRI has also developed specific standard disclosures for the mining and metal sector. Disclosures for mining-and-metal-sector companies were launched in 2013 (Global Reporting Initiative, 2013a).

Whereas these various frameworks identified many ESG sustainability indictors, their measurements pose different problems.

ESG Measures

Peter Drucker once said, "What you can't measure, you cannot manage. What you can't manage, you cannot change" (Blanc, Cozic, & Barochez, 2013). Unless you are able to measure it, you do not know if something is getting better or worse. You do not know if you are successful unless it is defined and tracked. Examples of studies which used different methods to measure ESG performance are described next.

A study conducted by Chartered Accountants of Canada (2010) reported the measures of indicators of human relations performance of companies. Examples of measures of labour and employee relations were the percentage of employee turnover, percentage of workforce unionized, ratio of lowest wage to minimum wage, and ratio of jobs offered to jobs accepted.

Bonini et al. (2009) state that even though executives and investors believe that the impacts of ESG programs are long term and indirect, measurement of ESG factors are impossible. However, their research suggests otherwise. They believe that companies can directly measure the financial effects of ESG programs. For example, the impact of environmental programs can be measured in the short term using traditional business metrics such as cost efficiency.

They also reported how environmental, social, and governance performance was measured using a social responsibility dashboard. The dashboard includes metrics for workplace engagement, ethics, and integrity; supplier diversity; environmental impact; employee-community involvement; stakeholders' perspectives on social responsibility; and community giving. These metrics track the company's progress in meeting its social mission and helping people live a healthier living. The dashboard is used by the board and the senior executives to measure the company's performance and as a guide for discussions on future priorities, programs, resources, and results. Bonini et al. (2009) also state that progress has been made by companies in relation to tracking operational metrics such as tons of carbon emitted, or social indicators, or example numbers of students enrolled in a program.

The Purpose of This Study

The previous research into ESG measurement discussed earlier indicates that whereas there is some research into the use of ESG measures, little research has been conducted in Australia and that, in particular, there is a lack of information about ESG reporting from specific sectors. The GRI guidelines appear to be widely respected as a measure of ESG, but the extent of their use is unknown.

The purpose of this research was to fill these gaps by investigating ESG reporting in the mining industry. The mining industry was selected for study because of its significance to the Australian economy. It is the major exporting industry in Australia, contributing more than 35 per cent of export receipts and nearly 6 per cent of GDP, 1.3 per cent to national employment, and represents 20 per cent of the Australian securities market capitalization (Galbreath, 2013).

The research questions were as follows:

- What kinds of ESG measures are being used in the mining industry?
- How many ESG reports are being issued? Are they separate or combined with annual reports? Are they integrated with financial information? Is the GRI framework popular in Australia?
- Are there differences in reporting between the 'top-tier' companies and other listed companies?

Relevance of ESG Measures for the Mining Sector

As stated in the previous section, the mining sector contribution to the Australian economy is relatively high. A mining boom has had a significant impact on the living standards of Australians. However, the negative impacts of mining operations have brought the attention of institutional investors to focus on ESG issues.

The mining industry is associated with many challenges related to economic, environmental, and social issues. Even though it has economic benefits related to employment and wealth creation, on the other hand, it has a variety of environmental impacts, including depletion of non-renewable resources, disturbance of the landscape, and above-average threats for health and safety of workers and citizens (Azapagic, 2004). Depletion of agricultural resources as a result of mining is a major concern for sustainability development.

Mining is regarded as one of the most environmentally and socially disruptive activities undertaken by business. According to Warhurst (2001), the majority of incidents related to environmental disasters and human rights are related to mining or petroleum industries. Maintaining a licence to operate is a constant challenge for mining-sector companies. For example, resistance by social organizations is associated with mining impacts on agriculture, pollution, health impacts, and lack of community engagement (Jenkins & Yakovleva, 2006).

Furthermore, Jenkins (2004) reports that CSR in the mining industry is about balancing the diverse demands of communities and protecting the environment whilst making a profit. Therefore, from the perspective of the mining sector, CSR is about responding to the shareholders as well as stakeholders including employees and customers, as well as affected communities and the general public, on issues such as human rights, employee welfare, and climate change (Hamann, R., 2003). Azapagic (2004) also identified many different stakeholders related to the mining sector such as industry stakeholders, employees, trade unions, contractors, suppliers, customers, shareholders, creditors, insurers, local communities, local authorities, governments, and NGOs.

GRI guidelines specifically refer to mining; as a result, the mining sector was selected as the focus of this study.

Methodology

Sample and Data Collection

To investigate the extent of disclosure of non-financial information, and the measures used for ESG indicators, a sample of 30 companies was selected from the top companies in the Australian Securities Exchange (ASX) for the diversified metal and mining sector. The companies selected were ranked based on their market capitalization. Market capitalization is the market value of a company's issued share capital. The sample was divided into two. The first 12 companies in the top tier of the market are called the 'top' sample. The remaining 18 companies were the 'second' sample. The purpose of dividing the companies into two samples was to explore whether the response to ESG measures differed depending on the size of a company.

Secondary data were collected from annual reports and/or sustainability reports for the year 2013. Annual reports were the source, because they are considered public and visible documents, they provide important social and environmental information, and they are produced regularly by companies (Neu, Warsame, & Pedwell, 1998; Tilt, 1994).

Results and Analysis of ESG Reporting and Indicators

The study compared the results from the top-12 companies based on their market capitalization with the second 18 companies. The results of the study confirmed the extent of ESG reporting by the mining companies in Australia and the measures used for indicators.

Demographics

First, the demographics of the sample were examined for both the top-12 companies and the second 18 companies. Table 9.1 reports the demographics of the study. A majority of the top-12 companies (33.3 per cent) had located

Table 9.1 Demographics of the Sample of Mining-Sector Companies in Australia

Demographics	Top 12	Second 18	Measures
Headquarters location	33% Melbourne	66.7% Perth	
Less than 10,000 employees	75%	22.2%	
Less than US$1,000 million net sales	50%	17%	
Reporting			
Separate sustainability report	83.3%	16.7%	
Integrated report	8.3%	72.2%	
GRI indicators	100%	11.1%	
Types of operations			
Extractive	91.7%	100%	
Recycling	8.3%	0%	
Size of the operational site	50%	5.6%	Square kilometres and hectares

their headquarters in Melbourne (Table 9.1). Sixteen per cent were in Perth, 16.6 per cent in Sydney, 8.3 per cent in Brisbane, and 25 per cent had their headquarters outside Australia. A majority of the second 18 companies (66.7 per cent) had their headquarters in Perth, 11.1 per cent in Melbourne, 16.7 per cent in NSW, and 5.6 per cent had their headquarters outside Australia. This implies that since the majority of large mining operations are conducted in Western Australia, headquarters in Perth were the preferred location.

The number of employees was compared for both samples. A majority (75 per cent) of the companies in the top-12 had less than 10,000 employees, and one company had more than 50,000 employees in the top-12 companies, whereas in the second 18 companies, 22.2 per cent of the companies had less than 10,000 employees, and 11.1 per cent employed between 10,000 and 50,000 employees. However, 50 per cent of the companies did not report on the total number of employees.

In the top-12 companies, 50 per cent had less than US$1,000 million net sales and 16.7 per cent had more than US$20,000 million net sales, whereas in the second 18 companies, 77.8 per cent had less than US$1,000 million net sales and 11.2 per cent had between US$1,000 million and US$20,000 million net sales.

Type of Sustainability Report

The investigation of the reporting practices of the top-12 companies showed 91.7 per cent had a separate sustainability report. However, only 16.7 per cent of the second 18 companies had a separate sustainability report.

This showed that the larger companies are more inclined to provide non-financial information in a separate sustainability report than the smaller companies are. Only 8.3 per cent of the companies in the top-12 had an integrated report, whereas 72.2 per cent produced an integrated report in the second 18 companies.

Use of GRI Framework

All the companies in the top 12 used GRI guidelines to report non-financial indicators. However, only 11.1 per cent in the second 18 companies used GRI guidelines to report non-financial indicators.

Types of Operations

The types of operations reported in the top-12 companies were extractive, 91.7 per cent (11), and recycling, 8.3 per cent (1). However, 100 per cent of the companies in the second 18 were operating in extractive. The size of the operational site was reported by 50 per cent of the companies in the top-12 companies and two reported the size of the operational site in square kilometres and four reported in hectares, whereas 5.6 per cent (1) reported the size of the operational site in the next 18 companies, and this was reported in square kilometres.

Environmental Indicators

Table 9.2 reports the extent of environmental reporting and measures used. Environmental indicators refer to disclosures relating to the impact of business interaction with the natural environment, environmental protection, and use of resources.

This study captured the use of renewable and non-renewable material. Renewable materials are those that are replenished in a relatively short term by the environment such as water, solar energy, wind, and bio fuels, whereas non-renewable energy is that which cannot be regenerated within a usable time frame, such as minerals.

In the top-12 companies, 16 per cent reported on renewable and 24.9 per cent reported on non-renewable material. However, none of the second 18 companies reported on renewable or non-renewable material. In both of the samples, measures reported varied from million tons, kilotons, and other measures. The value of the total material used was in either US$ or AU$.

All the companies in the top 12 reported on fuel consumption for renewable and non-renewable sources. None of the companies in the second 18 reported on fuel consumption for renewable sources; however, 5.6 per cent reported on non- renewable sources. The indicators used to measure the values were gigajoules, terajoules, and petajoules in both studies. Total fuel

Table 9.2 Extent of Environmental Reporting and Measures

Environmental Indicators	12	18	Measures
Renewable material	16% (2)	0%	Million tons, kilotons, other
Non-renewable material	24.9% (3)	0%)	As above
Fuel consumption—renewable	100%	0%	Gigajoules, terajoules, and petajoules
Fuel consumption—non-renewable	100%	5.6%	As above
Total fuel consumption	91.7%	50%	Gigajoules, petajoules
Volume of water withdrawn:			
Surface water	58.3%	22.2%	Kilolitres, megalitres, and gigalitres
Groundwater	66.6%	11.1%	As above
Rainwater	16.7%	0%	As above
Municipal water supplies	33.3%	5.6%	As above
Seawater	41.7%	0%	As above
Recycle and reused water	58.3%	5.6%	As above
Biodiversity value:			
Terrestrial	66.7%	88.9%	Numbers and hectares
Freshwater	8.3%	0%	
Both Terrestrial and Freshwater	16.7%	11.1%	
Direct GHG Emissions—Scope 1	100%	61.2%	Tons, kilotons, and megatons
Indirect GHG Emissions—Scope 2	75%	61.2%	Tons, megatons
Other Indirect GHG Emissions—Scope 3	41.7%	0%	Tons, megatons
Ozone-depleting substances	33.3%	0%	Kilograms and tons
Planned and unplanned water discharges	58.3%	5.6%	Kilolitres, megalitres, gigalitres
Hazardous non-hazardous waste	75%	11.2%	Tons, kilotons, million tons, and tons and litres
Spills	16.7%	5.6%	Litres

consumption reported by the top-12 companies was 91.7 per cent, whereas 50 per cent were reported in the second 18. Total fuel sold was reported in joules or megawatt hours in both studies. They also reported on volume of water withdrawn. The top-12 companies reported as follows: surface water 58.3 per cent, groundwater 66.6 per cent, rainwater 16.7 per cent, municipal water supplies 33.3 per cent, seawater 41.7 per cent, and recycled and reused water 58.3 per cent. The second 18 reported surface water

22.2 per cent, groundwater 11.1 per cent, rainwater 0 per cent, municipal water supplies 5.6 per cent, seawater 0 per cent, and recycled and reused water 5.6 per cent. Measures used varied from kilolitres, megalitres, and gigalitres.

According to the GRI guidelines (G4), reporting on GHG emissions was based on the reporting requirement of the World Resource Institute and the World Business Council for Sustainable Development (WBCSD). GHG Protocol Corporate Accounting and Reporting Standards (GHG Protocol) classifies GHG emissions into Scope 1, Scope 2, and Scope 3.

Scope 1 reports on direct GHG emissions and is related to operations that are owned and controlled by the organization. All the companies in the top 12 reported on direct GHG emissions. However, 50 per cent reported in tons, 8.3 per cent in kilotons and 41.7 per cent in megatons. In the second 18 companies, 61.2 per cent reported on direct GHG emissions and 55 per cent reported in tons and 5.6 per cent reported in megatons.

Scope 2 reports on indirect GHG emissions resulting from the generation of purchased or acquired electricity. Indirect GHG emissions were reported by 75 per cent of companies in the top 12 and 41.7 per cent reported in tons and 33.3 per cent reported in megatons. In the second 18 companies, indirect GHG emissions were reported by 61.2 per cent of companies. Fifty-two per cent reported in tons and 5.6 per cent reported in megatons.

Scope 3 reports emissions that are indirect and occur outside the organization including both upstream and downstream emissions. Scope 3 emissions were reported by 41.7 per cent of companies in the top 12. However, none of the second 18 companies reported on Scope 3 emissions. GHG emission reductions achieved as a direct result of initiatives to reduce emissions were reported as a quantity or as a percentage by 83.7 per cent in the top-12 companies, whereas only 5.6 per cent reported in the second 18 companies in quantity or as a percentage.

Ozone-depleting substances were reported by 33.3 per cent in the top-12 companies. This was reported in kilograms by 8.3 per cent and in tons by 25 per cent. However, none reported in the second 18 companies.

Total volume of planned and unplanned water discharges were reported by 58.3 per cent of the top-12 companies and 8.3 per cent reported in kilolitres, 41.7 per cent in megalitres, and 8.3 per cent in gigalitres. Total volume of planned and unplanned water discharges were reported by 5.6 per cent of the second 18 companies, and it was reported by 5.6 per cent in megalitres.

Total weight of hazardous and non-hazardous waste was reported by 75 per cent in the top-12 companies in tons, kilotons, million tons, and tons and litres, whereas only 5.6 per cent of the companies in the second 18 reported on hazardous and non-hazardous waste. They also reported in tons, kilotons, million tons, and tons and litres.

Only 16.7 per cent in the top-12 companies reported on spills and 5.6 per cent (3) of companies in the second 18 reported on spills. All the companies in both samples reported in litres.

Social Indicators

Social indicators focus on the wider responsibilities of business to the communities in which they operate, employees and to society in general (Azapagic & Perdan, 2000). Social issues reported by companies were mainly on employees, human rights, health and safety, and gender and employment of indigenous people. Table 9.3 reports the extent of social reporting and measures used.

Sixty-seven per cent of the companies in the top 12 reported on the total number of employees either as a percentage (16.7 per cent) or a number (25 per cent) or both (25 per cent). Thirty-three per cent reported by gender; 8 per cent reported by gender and age; 8 per cent reported by gender and region; 8 per cent reported by gender, region, and product; and 8 per cent reported by age, region, and product. Sixty-seven per cent of companies in the second 18 also reported on the total number of employees either as a percentage (61.1 per cent) or a number (5.6 per cent). However, they did not report by gender; gender and age; gender and region; gender, region, and product; and age, region, and product.

Table 9.3 Social Reporting and Measures

Social Indicators	12	18	Measures
Number of employees	67%	67%	Percentage, number
Gender	30%	66.7	
Gender and age	8%	0%	
Gender and region	8%	0%	
Gender, region, and product	8%	0%	
Age, region, and product	8%	0%	
Employee turnover	24.9%	0%	Region, gender, age
Health and Safety:			
Lost days and injury rate	83%	47.8%	Million hours, total hours, 200,000 hours
Fatalities	41.7%	11.1%	
Training for employees	16.6%	0%	No of hours per employees
Training on human rights policies	33.3%	0%	No of hours per employees
Employment of indigenous people	41.7%	5.6%	Percentage, numbers
Number of operations with implemented local community engagement	58.3%	16.7%	
Local community development programs	16.7% (2)	33.3%	

Employee turnover was reported by 24.9 per cent of the companies by region (8.3 per cent), gender and age (8.3 per cent), and gender, age, and region (8.3 per cent) in the top-12 companies. This was reported as a percentage and/or as a number. However, none of the companies in the second 18 reported on employee turnover.

Health and safety was reported in lost days and injury rate. Eighty-three per cent of companies in the top 12 reporting on lost days and injury rate used million hours (41.7 per cent), total hours (16.7 per cent), per 200,000 hours (16.7 per cent), and other (8.3 per cent). Forty-seven per cent of companies in the second 18 reported on injury rate and 22.2 per cent of the companies that reported on injury rate used million hours and 5.6 per cent reported in total hours.

Fatalities were reported by 41.7 per cent of companies in the top 12, but by only 11.1 per cent of companies in the second 18.

Training provided to employees in the top-12 companies was reported by 16.6 per cent of companies, whereas none were reported in the second 18 companies. Training on human rights policies was reported by 33.3 per cent of companies in the top 12 and none was reported in the second 18 companies. One company reported in number of hours used for training and three reported the number of employees participating in the training.

Employment of indigenous people was reported by 41.7 per cent of the top-12 companies, and 16.7 per cent reported as a percentage, whereas another 16.7 per cent reported as per numbers and 8.3 per cent reported in both. Employment of indigenous people in the second 18 was reported by 5.6 per cent. This was reported as a percentage.

The number of operations with implemented local community engagement was reported by 58.3 per cent of the top-12 companies, whereas only 16.7 per cent reported in the second 18 companies. Implementation of local community development programs were reported by 16.7 per cent of companies in the top 12, whereas 33.3 per cent of companies in the second 18 reported that they implemented local community development programs.

Governance Indicators Reported

Corporate governance in Australia is based on a principle-based framework. The recommendations are not mandatory. If a listed company considers a recommendation inappropriate to its particular circumstances, it has the flexibility not to adopt it—a flexibility tempered by the requirement to explain why it has not reported; it is an "if not, why not" approach.

This study investigated the governance practices of all the companies (Table 9.4). All the 30 companies reported on the structure of the boards relating to the number of executive directors, non-executives, independent directors, board committees, and females on the board. Eleven companies in the top 12 reported the tenure of the board, whereas 17 in the second 18 companies did so. The number of committees responsible for decision

Table 9.4 Governance Practices

Governance Indicator	Top 12 Companies	The Second 18 Companies
Board structure	12	18
Number of executive directors	12	18
Number of non-executive directors	12	18
Number of independent directors	12	18
Number of board committees	12	18
Number of companies with females on the board	12	18
Tenure on the board of directors	11	17
Number of committees responsible for decision making on economic, environmental and social impacts	12	16
Frequency of the director board's review of economic, environmental, and social impacts, risks and opportunities	12	17

making on economic, environmental, and social impacts was reported by all the companies in the top-12 companies, and 16 companies reported in the second 18 companies All the companies in the top-12 companies reported on the frequency of the director board's review of economic, environmental, and social impacts, risks and opportunities, whereas 17 reported in the second 18 companies.

Discussion on ESG Reporting

The main purpose of the measurement of indicators is to provide information for decision making regarding the sustainability of companies' actions. Indicators also help to identify whether the decision makers have addressed the needs of the multiple stakeholders for which companies are responsible. This study considered stakeholders to be shareholders, employees and contractors, communities, customers, suppliers, government and regulators, industry, NGOs, education and research, media, civil society, and investment community. Comparable indicators also help those stakeholders in their decision making, whether they share the same, different, or conflicting interests.

The companies in the study mainly reported on indicators that were regulated, confirming the relevance of legitimacy theory rather than stakeholder theory. Analysis showed that regulatory compliance was a motivation for environmental and social reporting. For example, 76 per cent of companies reported on direct greenhouse gas emissions and 66.7 per cent reported on indirect greenhouse gas emissions. The top-12 companies were more compliant with the ESG reporting when compared with the second 18 companies.

A significant issue for mining and mineral industries are the depletion of non-renewable resources, environmental impacts of air emissions, waste generation, and disturbance to natural habitats resulting in loss of biodiversity (Azapagic, 2004). This study also addressed the environmental reporting by mining companies related to non-renewable resources, GHG emissions, management of biodiversity, ozone-depleting substance, hazardous and non-hazardous waste, water usage, and spills. However, except for Scope 1, direct GHG emissions, and Scope 2, indirect GHG emissions, percentage of reporting was rather low.

All companies reported compliance with corporate governance best practices, mainly the result of compliance with ASX corporate governance principles. Because compliance with the corporate governance code was a requirement for all companies listed on the ASX, all companies reported on the board structure. Principle 3.1 of ASX corporate governance recognizes the legal and ethical obligations of a company. However, the companies in the study treated the recommended practices with minimal consideration. This poses the question of whether, in reporting disclosures, companies face difficulties related to measurement, cost benefit issues, etc. None of the companies reported on corruption, bribery, money laundering, or fraud. This makes it unclear to the stakeholders whether such activities occurred. Whether or not they were committed has not been reported.

Gender disparity is an issue for the mining industry, which is traditionally male dominated. This explains the limited disclosures on gender information in this study related to total number of employees, employee turnover, and females in senior management. However, all the companies reported on females on the director board because diversity is a requirement to comply with the corporate governance code for all companies listed on the ASX.

Azapagic (2004) considered social issues from both micro and macro perspectives. Micro referred to the perspective of employees and macro concerns society at large. Issues related to employees were the most reported in this study. Health and safety is an issue specific to the mining industry. Accidents in the mining industry, posing above-average risk to employees and resulting in high fatalities, were reported by over 80 per cent of the companies in the top 12 and over 47 per cent by the second 18 companies.

Mining employees were also exposed to health concerns related to a hostile working environment. However, companies did not report on such data. Therefore, it can be presumed that in relation to employees, too many companies follow an implicit rule of reporting the least, but required, information only. For instance, injury rates and employee number or percentage by gender were the most reported categories.

Training related to employee education and skills development is an important issue for many companies because of the need for attracting high-quality employees despite the negative image of employment in the mining industry. However, training-related information was only reported by 13 per cent of companies in the sample studied. Similarly, 13 per cent reported on human rights training policies. Although many companies mention that they implement such programs, details are scarce.

The results of the study showed that only 20 per cent reported on employment of indigenous people, even though indigenous employment is related to diversity policies of the federal and state legislation covering workplace diversity and equal opportunity in Australia.

Social issues related to society at large were reported mainly on health and safety. Mining activities posed health and safety risks for the local communities related to extraction activities or mineral products. Thirty-three per cent of the sample recorded explicitly a number or a percentage of operations they have implemented with local community engagements under the heading of society. However, some companies in the sample only declared whether they have such agreements or not.

Results reported measurements used for indicators. Measures used for environmental and social indicators is an issue, because the same indicator was measured differently by companies even in the same industry; for example, GHG emissions were reported in tons, kilotons, and megatons; value of renewable and non-renewable material was reported in AUD or USD; water withdrawn was reported in megalitres and gigalitres; training on human rights policies were reported in number of hours, percentages, or per employee. These findings show that comparability, even among the same sectors, is difficult for the purpose of decision making by investors and other stakeholders.

These findings suggest that the extent of reporting is either driven by regulators or to gain a reputation for social responsibility for capital markets and media. Therefore, it is questionable if all ESG information is being reported, especially related to negative impact.

This research shows that all the companies reported on non-financial indicators. However, the extent of reporting was different. The fact that a majority (93 per cent) had a sustainability report or an integrated report confirms non-financial reports are on the increase and ESG issues are becoming important among various stakeholders of companies. All the companies in the top 12 used GRI guidelines and 91 per cent issued sustainability reports. However, the majority of second 18 companies had an integrated report and only 11 per cent complied with GRI guidelines.

Conclusion

This study investigated the extent of ESG reporting and the nature and type of ESG indicators used to report ESG disclosures by Australian mining companies. Whilst the majority of companies at the top have a sustainability report, the trend for integrated reporting seems to be on the increase. Even though the extent of ESG reporting varied, those of a regulatory or compliance nature, as well as those influenced by other global institutions which promote good ESG practices and those that were investor driven, mostly reported ESG information. Examination of ESG information showed that information that might give a negative message to stakeholders was either not mentioned or mentioned with the purpose of providing an optimistic picture to the stakeholders.

To respond to challenges related to different sustainability issues and stakeholder concerns, it is important to be able to disclose information that can be comparable within different industries and sectors. Reporting of disclosure of information is not meaningful unless it is comparable. Findings of this study show that there is no uniformity in the types of measures used to report similar data. Even though the UN Global Compact and Global Reporting Initiative have developed frameworks for non-financial reporting that cover aspects of ESG reporting, these frameworks do not provide measures that are comparable between companies in the same or different sectors. Chvatalov´a et al. (2011, p. 246) reported,

> GRI served as an essential tool and a very useful means of improving the standardisation of company reporting. However, companies continue to have differing degrees of compliance with GRI and also may differ in their interpretation of the best means to apply the standards to their reporting.

The study confirms that the GRI guidelines are the most used, especially by the larger companies, in reporting ESG information in the mining industry.

Due to growing recognition that ESG measures can impact the value of a company, it is important for boards of directors to understand the ESG factors. ESG factors that are comparable help the boards of directors to formulate strategies that lead to better decision making. Finally, this study clearly shows the need for uniform measures for ESG indicators and for developing a framework that can be used to measure ESG indicators for mining-sector companies in Australia.

Most companies issue ESG reports, but there are differences between the top-tier companies and those in the second sample. The bigger the company the more information and the greater depth of information are provided.

The ESG reports have usually been issued separately from annual reports; there appears to be a move towards integrating the ESG information in the annual reports.

How useful is the ESG information to the leaders of companies, to investors, and to other stakeholders? This is a topic for further research. However, at the very least, changes in measures must surely provide a warning of imminent danger, and the more reliable the indicators and their measurement the more useful they can be.

References

ACSI & FSC. (2011). ESG reporting guide for Australian companies: Building the foundation for meaningful reporting, First Edition, June.

Armstrong, A., Mitchell, V., O'Donovan, G., & Sweeney, M. (June, 2001). Corporate social responsibility: Do Australian banks Toeing the Triple Bottom Line? *Banking and Financial Services Journal, 115*(3), 6, 8–10.

Armstrong, A., & Sweeney, M. (2002). Corporate governance disclosure: Demonstrating corporate social responsibility through social reporting. *New Academy Review, 1*(2), 33–51.

ASX Corporate Governance Council. (2014). *Corporate governance principles and recommendations* (3rd Edn.). Sydney, NSW: ASX Corporate Governance Council.

Azapagic, A. (2004). Developing a framework for sustainable development indicators for the mining and minerals industry. *Journal of Cleaner Production, 12*(6), 639–662.

Azapagic, A., & Perdan, S. (2000). Indicators of sustainable development for industry: A general framework. *Process Safety and Environmental Protection, 78*(4), 243–261.

Bader, E. E. (2005). Sustainable hotel business practices. *Journal of Retail and Leisure Property, 5*(1), 70–77.

Blanc, D., Cozic, A., & Barochez, D. (2013). *Choosing indicators to measure the ESG performance of investment*. Lille, Paris: Novethic Research.

Bonime-Blanc, A. (2014). Integrating "ESG" issues into global risk, compliance & integrity programmes. *Ethical Corporation*. Retrieved from: http://www.ethical corp.com/business-strategy/integrating-%E2%80%9Cesg%E2%80%9D-issues-global-risk-compliance-integrity-programmes

Bonini, S., Koller, T. M., & Mirivis, P. H. (2009). *Valuing social responsibility programs*. McKinsey on Finance, 32 (Summer). Retrieved from: https://www.research gate.net/publication/285737660_Valuing_Social_Responsibility_Programs

Cadbury, A. (1992). *Report on the committee on the financial aspects of corporate governance*. London: Gee.

Cadbury, A. (2000). *Global corporate governance forum*. New York: World Bank.

Capaldi, N., & Crowther, D. (2008). *The Ashgate research companion to corporate social responsibility*. Aldershot, England: Routledge.

Chartered Accountants of Canada. (2010). *Environmental, social and governance (ESG) issues in institutional investor decision making*. Ontario, Canada: Chartered Accountants of Canada.

Chvatalov́a, Z., Kocmanov́a, A., & Dočekalov́, M. (2011). Corporate sustainability reporting and measuring corporate performance. In J. Hřebíček, G. Schimak, & R. Denzer (Eds.), *Environmental software systems. Frameworks of environment* (pp. 245–254). Heidelberg, Germany: Springer.

Clarke, G. L., Feiner, A., & Viehs, M. (2015). *From the stockholder to the stakeholder: How sustainability can drive financial out performance*. Oxford, UK: University of Oxford Press.

Cooper, S., & Owen, D. (2007). Corporate social reporting and stakeholder accountability: The missing link accounting. *Organisations and Society, 32*, 649–667.

Corporate Knights. (2010). *Prioritizing GRI indicators by mainstream investors for mainstream investors*. Toronto, Canada: Corporate Knights.

de Bakker, F., Ohlsson, C., Den Hond, F., Tengblad, S., & Turcotte, M.-F. B. (2007). Tracing the evolution of corporate disclosures on corporate social responsibility: A longitudinal, lexicological study. In F. den Hond, F. de Bakker, & P. Neergaard (Eds.), *Managing corporate social responsibility in action: Talking, doing and measuring* (pp. 53–73). Hampshire, England: Ashgate Publishing Limited.

Deegan, C. (2002). Introduction: The legitimising effect of social and environmental disclosures—A theoretical foundation. *Accounting, Auditing & Accountability Journal, 15*(3), 282–311.

Deegan, C. (2004). *Financial accounting theory*, North Ryde, NSW: McGraw-Hill.

Deegan, C. (2014). An overview of legitimacy theory as applied within the social and environmental accounting literature. In J. Bebbington, J. Unerman, & B. O'Dwyer (Eds.), *Sustainability accounting and accountability* (2nd ed., pp. 248–272). New York, United States: Routledge.

Deegan, C., Rankin, M., & Tobin, J. (2002). An examination of the corporate social and environmental disclosures of BHP from 1983–1997. *Accounting, Auditing & Accountability Journal, 15*(3), 312–343.

Den Hond, F., de Bakker, F., & Neergaard, P. (2007). Introduction to managing corporate social responsibility in action: Talking, doing and measuring. In F. Den Hond, F. de Bakker, & P. Neergaard (Eds.), *Managing corporate social responsibility in action: Talking, doing and measuring* (p. 3). Hampshire, England: Ashgate Publishing Limited.

Donaldson, T. (1983). Constructing a social contract for business. In T. Donaldson, & P. Werhane (Eds.), *Ethical issues in business* (pp. 153–165). Englewood Cliffs, NJ: Prentice Hall.

Donaldson, T., & Preston, L. E. (1995). The stakeholder theory of the corporation: concepts, evidence and implications. *Academy of Management Review, 20*(1), 65–91.

Freeman, R. E. (1984). *Strategic management a stakeholder approach*. Boston, MA: Pitman.

Freeman, R. E. (1994). The politics of stakeholder theory. *Business Ethics Quarterly, 4*(4), 409–421

Galbreath, J. (2013). ESG in focus: The Australian evidence. *Journal of Business Ethics, 118*(3), 529–541.

Global Reporting Initiative. (2013a). *G4 sector disclosure: Mining and metal*. Amsterdam, Netherlands: Global Reporting Initiative.

Global Reporting Initiative. (2013b). *G4 sustainability reporting guidelines: Reporting principles and standard disclosures*. Amsterdam, Netherlands: Global Reporting Initiative.

Global Reporting Initiative. (2015). *What is GRI? Sustainability disclosure database*. Retrieved 30 October 2015 from: http://database.globalreporting.org/SDG-12-6/about-gri

Gray, R., Kouhy, R., & Lavers, S. (1995). Corporate social and environmental reporting: A review of the literature and a longitudinal study of UK disclosures. *Accounting, Auditing & Accountability Journal, 8*(2), 47–77.

Gray, R., Owen, D., & Adams, C. (1996). *Accounting and accountability: Changes and challenges in corporate social environmental reporting*. Harlow, England: Prentice—Hall.

Hamann, R. (2003). Mining companies' role in sustainable development: The "why" and "how" of corporate social responsibility from a business perspective. *Development South Africa, 20*(2), 237–254.

Horrigan, B. (2010). *Corporate social responsibility in the 21st century: Debates, models, and practices across government, law, and business*. Cheltenham, UK: Edward Elgar Publishing.

Hřebíček, J., Soukopová, J., Štencl, M., & Trenz, O. (2011). Integration of economic, environmental, social and corporate governance performance and reporting in enterprises. *Acta Universitatis Agriculturae Et Silviculturae Mendelianae Brunensis*, 15(7), 157–166.

IFAC. (2012). *Investor demand for environmental, social, and governance disclosures: Implications for professional accountants in business*. New York, NY: International Federation of Accountants.

Institute of Directors Southern Africa. (2009). *King Code of Governance for South Africa 2009*. South Africa: Institute of Directors South Africa.

Jenkins, H. M. (2004). Corporate social responsibility and the mining industry: Conflicts and constructs. *Corporate Social Responsibility and Environmental Management*, 11, 23–34.

Jenkins, H. M., & Yakovleva, N. (2006). Corporate social responsibility in the mining industry: Exploring trends in social and environmental disclosure. *Journal of Cleaner Production*, 14, 271–284.

Jessop, S. (September 7, 2015). Sustainable investing a fiduciary duty for fund managers says UN backed study. In M. Potter (Ed.), *Business*. New York: Reuters. Retrieved from: http://uk.reuters.com/article/uk-funds-investing-duty-idUKKCN0R610O20150906

Lindblom, C. K. (1994). The implications of organisational legitimacy for corporate social performance and disclosure. *Critical Perspectives on Accounting Conference*. New York, NY.

Lundstrom, E., & Svensson, C. (2014). Including ESG concerns in the portfolio selection process. (Degree Program in Industrial Engineering and Management), KTH Royal Institute of Technology, Stockholm, Sweden.

Martirosyan, E., & Vashakmadze, T. (2013). Introducing stakeholder-based frameworks for post-merger integration (PMI) success. *Journal of Modern Accounting and Auditing*, 9(10), 1376–1381.

Matthews, M. R. (1993). *Socially responsible accounting*. London, UK: Chapman & Hall.

Neu, D., Warsame, H., & Pedwell, K. (1998). Managing public impressions: Environmental disclosures in annual reports. *Accounting, Organizations and Society*, 23(3), 265–282.

NHMRC. (2014). *How NHMRC develops its guidelines*, Retrieved 8 May 2015 from: https://www.nhmrc.gov.au/guidelines-publications/how-nhmrc-develops-its-guidelines

Patten, D. M. (2005). The accuracy of financial report projections of future environmental capital expenditures: A research note, accounting. *Organizations and Society*, 30(5), 457–468.

Peiris, D., & Evans, J. (2010). The relationship between environmental social governance factors and U.S. stock performance. *Journal of Investing*, 19(3), 104–112.

Rushe, D. (July 2, 2015). BP set to pay largest environmental fine in US history for Gulf oil spill. *The Guardian*.

Suchman, M. (1995). Managing legitimacy: Strategic and institutional approaches. *Academy of Management Review*, 20(3), 571–610.

Theoran, C. (2012). Developments in environmental reporting and the rise of environmental and social governance: Why should law and business consider these issues? *Environmental Law and Management*, 24(5), 242–247.

Thomson Reuters. (2015). *Environmental, social and governance performance.* Retrieved 21 April 2015 from: http://thomsonreuters.com/en/about-us/corpo rate-responsibility/esg-performance.html

Thorne, D. M., Ferrell, O. C., & Ferrell, L. (2011). Business & society: Strategic approach to social responsibility and ethics (4th Edn.). Mason, USA: South-Western Cenagage Learning.

Tilling, M. V. (2004). Some thoughts on legitimacy theory in social and environmental accounting. *Social and Environmental Accountability Journal*, 24(2), 3–7.

Tilt, C. A. (1994). The influence of external pressure groups on corporate social disclosure. *Accounting, Auditing & Accountability Journal*, 7(4), 47–72.

Vintro, C., & Comajuncosa, J. (2010). Corporate social responsibility in the mining industry: Criteria and indicators. *Dyna*, 77(161), 31–41.

Warhurst, A. (2001). Corporate citizenship and corporate social investment: Drivers of tri-sector partnerships. *Journal of Corporate Citizenship*, 1(1), 57–73.

Wearing, R. (2005). *Cases in corporate governance.* Thousand Oaks, CA: Sage Publications.

10 A Study of Strategic CSR and BOP Business Practice

From the Perspective of Organizational Sustainability

Junichi Mizuo

Introduction

In developing countries in Asia and Africa, so-called bottom of the pyramid (BOP) businesses—companies that create new markets through meeting social needs by means such as prevention of infectious disease and improvement of medical care and foodstuffs—targeting the lower socio-economic layer (Prahalad & Stuart, 2002), where people live on no more than US$3,000 per year, are attracting attention.

According to *The Next 4 Billion* from the World Resources Institute and the International Finance Corporation (Hammond, Kramer, Tran, Katz, & Walker, 2007), approximately four billion people, roughly 72 per cent of the world's population, have annual incomes of no more than US$3,000 per year. While in 2008 the World Bank redefined the international poverty rate from the percentage with incomes of less than US$1 per day to the percentage with incomes of less than US$1.25 per day, the calculation here uses the figure of less than US$1 per day. This market totalling US$5 trillion, is equivalent to the real gross domestic product of Japanese global firms. Japanese firms are only just beginning to explore this field chiefly through public-private partnerships.

Because BOP businesses can lead not only to growth strategies aimed at a company's own sustainable growth but also to the practice of CSR to resolve the social needs of developing countries, they can be considered an important domain of strategic CSR. To the Japanese business community seeking to break free from sluggish economic conditions, they also constitute a promising market.

The leadership to BOP business leads to organizational innovation in creating new business opportunities. It can promise diverse innovation, product development, and technological development, improvements in competitiveness, and empowerment of human resources. Finally, the leadership to BOP business can lead to sustainable growth (Mizuo, 2009).

In this chapter, I will provide some implications on the significance of BOP businesses to global firms and future developments based on existing knowledge and case studies.

BOP Business Markets and Characteristics

BOP Business Markets

The term BOP was proposed by Prahalad and Hart in 2002 (Hart, 2007, pp. 112–113). According to Hart (2007), in 1997 Hart, and in 1998 Prahalad with K. Lieberthal, published papers with ideas based on this concept in the *Harvard Business Review* (July–Aug. 68–79), and then in 1998 this concept was developed together with Prahalad and announced in 2002 after four years of revision. They claimed that the BOP market will be as significant as the global impact of the BRIC community (Brazil, Russia, India, China).

It is estimated that approximately 72 per cent of the world has annual income of no more than US$3,000, making up the BOP layer, whereas the middle of the pyramid (MOP, middle-income earners) consists of 1.4 billion people, and the top of the pyramid (TOP, high-income earners) consists of only 175 million people (Nomura Research Institute, 2008).

The BOP layer is centred on the developing countries of Asia and Africa, which are seen to be promising as future growth markets.

Objectives of BOP Businesses

Many firms identify the objectives of BOP businesses as the Millennium Development Goals (MDGs), established by the UN to be achieved by 2015.

The MDGs combine the UN Millennium Declaration with international development goals adopted by international conferences and summits in the 1990s. The Millennium Declaration identifies a clear course for the UN's twenty-first-century role addressing peace and security, development and poverty, the environment, human rights and good governance, and the needs of Africa.

The leadership needed to help countries achieve the simultaneous eradication of poverty and significant reduction of inequalities and exclusion, and to promote human and sustainable development, requires a deep appreciation of the concepts of vulnerability and resilience.

Unless and until vulnerabilities are addressed effectively, and all people enjoy the opportunity to share in human development progress, development advances will be neither equitable nor sustainable.

There is a need for cooperation not only in international society but also among business enterprises, non-profit and non-governmental organizations, and numerous stakeholders to promote activities towards reducing vulnerability and building resilience.

In looking at the activities of business enterprises against this background, it is important to keep the following in mind.

BOP businesses are in agreement with the MDGs for helping resolve social needs. Specifically, they not only support the standard of living in the BOP layer but also contribute to progress in local economic development, from production through distribution, sales, consumption, and employment creation. To ensure that firms can continue these activities in a sustained manner, it is important that they secure revenues as main businesses, based on long-term sustainability, instead of being simple charity projects.

The Significance of Strategic CSR and BOP Businesses

When a company takes on BOP businesses, the final goal must be sustainable growth as a profit-making organization. Building on this, efforts must be based on strategic decision making, through selection and concentration of limited people, things, and money, in addition to resolution of social needs. BOP engagement results in employee empowerment, organizational innovation, and improvements in the company's reputation, ultimately leading to improvements in business performance.

Keeping this in mind, a pivotal point about the BOP project is that it leads to strategic CSR aimed at sustainable growth under competition through incorporating CSR into the company's main business and concentration of management resources. Therefore, a BOP project has the role of strategic CSR.

Western firms' efforts embody such a practice, and Japanese firms expect that they will be a new means of entering the market of four billion low-income people worldwide through meeting social needs based on strategic CSR and as part of corporate growth strategies.

For example, regarding the leadership of BOP, Volvic began the "1 L for 10 L" initiative to dig wells to secure a clean, safe supply of water in Africa and maintain it for 10 years. Each time a consumer buys one litre of Volvic water, the company donates enough to provide 10 litres of water to Africa through building wells in the Republic of Mali. According to the company's website, over the six-year period from 2007 through 2012, it provided aid equivalent to roughly 3.6 billion litres of clean, safe water.

These activities solve social issues in aid recipient regions and contribute to the promotion of sales by the companies providing aid.

Here I will discuss the significance of strategic CSR in greater detail. The CSR Initiative Committee in the Japan Society for Business Ethics Study formed in 2005; established CSR management philosophies, charters of conduct, and standards of conduct as CSR initiatives; and defined CSR (Mizuo, Tanaka, Ariu & Shimizu, 2005), and (Mizuo, Ariu & Shimizu 2007) as follows:

> CSR refers to the responsibility to perform systemic obligations and make active efforts together through multi-stakeholder engagement to prevent scandals and contribute proactively to the triple bottom line of the economy, the environment, and society, with the objective of promoting the sustainable growth of the company and society.

Here I would like to propose the following two CSR frameworks.

Subject Stakeholders Are Internal (Organizational) Vectors and External (Social) Vectors

First, the subject is internal (organizational) vectors and external (social) vectors. This refers to responding to stakeholders. For this reason, the subjects of BOP businesses are external stakeholders.

Subject Domains Are the Area of Defensive CSR and the Strategic Area of Proactive CSR

Second, the domains of CSR efforts can be prescribed from the two directions of defensive and proactive CSR. Next, I will describe the basic concepts of subjects and domains.

First, defensive CSR refers to protecting society and the firm from risks. These are preventive ethics activities to keep unethical behaviour from negatively impacting society or the company (Mizuo, 2000a; Mizuo, 2000b).

In 2000, I argued, in *Marketing Ethics*, for the importance of decreasing external and internal diseconomies based on the concept of "preventive ethics"(Mizuo, 2000a; Mizuo, 2000b). When viewed from the macro perspectives of humanity, society, and environment, external diseconomies such as air pollution, water pollution, and traffic congestion ultimately have a negative impact on consumers. Accordingly, it is important that enterprises reduce the factors that cause such external diseconomies. At the same time, internal diseconomies are an area that leads directly to customer dissatisfaction through activities such as misleading advertising, collusion, and alteration of expiration dates.

In preventive ethics, it is important that members of the organization recognize correct actions and best behaviour daily, through means such as standards and charters of conduct. Also important are internal systems and maintenance organizations, training, and drills. Leadership has to achieve employees' satisfaction through employees' understanding of CSR activities along with their active involvement in this process. Employees' eyes are essential for CSR and BOP.

Second, proactive CSR in the strategic area refers to proactive ethics activities contributing to society based on strategic thinking (Mizuo, 2000a; Mizuo, 2000b).

The proactive domain in CSR includes activities that support stakeholders proactively to achieve the "objective of promoting the sustainable growth of the company and society" (Mizuo, 2000a; Mizuo, 2000b). This refers to promoting social welfare and sustainable development.

For example, Aderans, a leading global company focused on total hair-related solutions, was early in concentrating on social issues, by providing wigs and scalp-care science to the medical field (Sato, 2014, pp. 18–19). Its Ai no Charity (Charity with Love) campaign, in which it gives wigs as presents to children in elementary and middle school concerned about their hair for reasons such as illness or injury, is a good example of social needs and welfare. This Christmas-season campaign has continued for more than 37 years since its start in 1978.

Proactive CSR demands compatibility with the environment, giving back to the community, contributing to society at large, or corporate support of the arts and culture. BOP businesses are included in this domain because they involve proactive contributions towards meeting social needs.

The Four Responsibilities of CSR

Figure 10.1 depicts the concept of strategic CSR based on aforementioned frameworks.[1]

(i) Legal Responsibility

The first responsibility of CSR is legal. This is the minimal level of responsibility of a company as a presence in society. For example, one meaning for a company is found in compliance with laws and regulations, as well as compliance with social rules on subjects such as consumer safety and the environment in the local community. This also includes responsibilities such as those of fair transactions in dealing with business partners.

It is companies' responsibility to protect the lives and safety of the public and to prevent legal violations or unfair transactions.

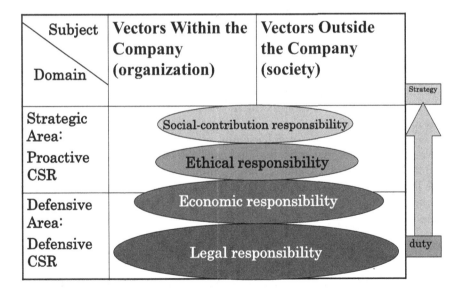

Figure 10.1 Strategic CSR

(ii) Economic Responsibility

When it has performed its legal responsibility, the company needs to fulfill its economic responsibility. This refers to dividends, wages, and taxes. Economic responsibility to stakeholders also refers to responsibilities such as paying appropriate prices to business partners.

(iii) Ethical Responsibility

Companies must also fulfill ethical responsibilities. Ethical responsibility can include voluntary ethical standards and rules of the industry, or the company itself, above and beyond legal restraints. Ethical responsibility consists of human rights and the working environment, dealing with consumers, and environmental protection.

Whereas legal responsibility is the minimum level that should be complied with, ethical responsibility is a target set by the industry or a company individually. It will be an important element of corporate strategy from now on.

(iv) Social-Contribution Responsibility

Social-contribution responsibility includes protection of benefits to consumers, social-contribution and cultural-aid activities, environmental protection, and proactive contributions.

Internally, this refers to systems to support social contributions or employee-focused programs such as volunteer leave or childcare leave and day-care centres for working women, as well as an environment that makes it easier for employees to work. There is a need to address such areas through strategic thinking, as means of addressing costs to society. The domain of BOP businesses mainly is found here in the social area.

Decisions need to be made from a strategic perspective, judging matters such as MDGs the company can help resolve through putting its people, things, and money, as well as its capabilities, to effective use while maintaining its main businesses.

From the perspectives of defense and offense, once a company has performed its legal responsibility and practiced defensive CSR, strategic CSR to deploy proactive CSR to succeed amid competition is the next step. Because the level of responsibilities build up from bottom to top, a firm cannot perform its social-contribution responsibility if it neglects its lower-level legal responsibility.

The Meaning of Strategy

In strategic CSR, social contribution is important as a strategic element. CSR efforts must not be a charity project such as a non-profit or similar organization. They are not the efforts of non-profits. CSR must truly be strategic, in combination with the company's main businesses, as part of profit-making activities.

If CSR is not a social and strategic investment, then it cannot be sustainable amid limited management resources. CSR is strategic once incorporated into the core of management based on strategic thinking instead of being confined to a single CSR section. BOP businesses are the best example. In order to integrate all of these necessary activities, leaders are required to discuss them with employees. Leaders must gain understanding and sympathy from employees.

Porter and Kramer (2002) have pointed out the following regarding competitive advantage and strategic philanthropy: "This refers to focusing on strategic context to benefit both the company and society, through addressing social and economic goals simultaneously and providing the firm's own assets and specialized capabilities" (Porter & Kramer, 2002). Here philanthropy is similar to the kind of social contribution that underpins the discussion in this chapter. Strategic CSR points out the importance of aiming to combine social needs and the company's main business.

Later, Porter and Kramer (2006) pointed out the importance of "strategic CSR" above and beyond "responsive CSR", thus organically linking business activities to CSR (pp. 78–92). A BOP business can also be judged on whether it will be a "strategic BOP business" linked with the main business. Because BOP business leads to organizational innovation in creating new business opportunities, it can promise diverse innovation, product and technological development, improvements in competitiveness, and empowerment of human resources.

In 2011, Porter and Kramer introduced the concept of "creating shared value" to build win-win relationships in which both companies and developing countries enjoy creating value (pp. 62–77).

From the perspective of strategy, Barney and Clark (2007) advocated for the importance of "resource-based strategy" (pp. 49–72) that seeks the possibilities of CSR through analysis of strengths and weaknesses from the company's own resources and capabilities based on social adaptability, pointing out that strategic CSR should be conducted through the company's main business purpose.

As a result, for the first firm to link it to market development, a BOP business not only leads to sustainable growth through new 'blue ocean' markets (Kim & Mauborgne, 2005, pp. 4–5) but also is evaluated highly by society as CSR. To a later entrant to a 'red ocean' existing competitive market, competitive strategy utilizing its strengths is important, but this is true of business in general, not just BOP businesses.

Either case leads to resolution of social needs in developing countries, such as securing employment from production through distribution and sales, support for living, and improvements in medical care and food. If

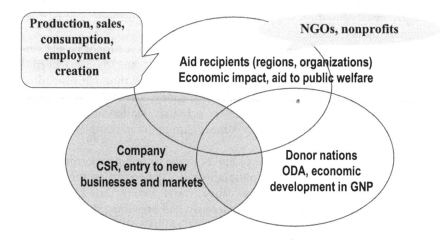

Figure 10.2 The BOP Business Is a New Business Model Based on a Win-Win-Win Relationship

Japanese firms can advance such efforts with government aid agencies, NGOs, and non-profits, they will be highly regarded as official development assistance (ODA) as well.

As shown in Figure 10.2, the BOP business can be said to represent a new business model based on a win-win-win relationship in which the company, its country, and the developing country all benefit.

Learning From Companies That Have Succeeded in BOP Businesses

In what follows, I propose issues that leaders might consider when entering the BOP arena.

Starting With High Aspirations and a Mission to Contribute to Public Welfare

A BOP business must be linked to resolution of social needs. At the planning stage, there is a need for consistency with management philosophy. Just as Kōnosuke Matsushita, the founder of Panasonic Corporation, set forth management policies based on his saying, "First of all, what must be considered the fundamental is the fact that a business is a public instrument of society. That is, it is considered not personal property but the property of society". (Matsushita, 1974), a BOP business needs to advance with high aspirations and a mission to contribute to public welfare. A company can press forward to a shared objective in agreement with its management philosophy.

According to the minister of economy, trade, and industry (METI), Nippon Poly-Glu Co., Ltd. in Osaka has started a BOP business, setting forth this point clearly (METI, ed. 2010, pp. 241–244). Founded in 2002, the company has capital of just 100 million yen (US $1 million). Even so, it is putting into practice its lofty mission of ensuring "that the World Community can drink raw water without fear".

Chairman Kanetoshi Oda says he had this mission in mind at all times. One day, he noticed polyglutamic acid, which makes fermented soybeans sticky. Polyglutamic acid long had been used as a raw material in cosmetics because of its water retention. Nippon Poly-Glu decided it could use this property in water purification. This is a traditional product-development strategy of putting an ingredient to new use.

Ultimately, Oda's business started with the development of the PGα21 series of water purifiers that cause no harm to the environment or the human body, and they are made by using polyglutamic acid.

A small quantity of PGα21 can purify a large volume of water, and it has high purification capabilities when used together with aluminium flocculating agents.

Cyclone Sidr in Bangladesh in 2007 led to the use of this equipment in social-contribution activities. Nippon Poly-Glu's aid activities, centred on water, began in February 2008.

The company continued its activities in Bangladesh, training 'Poly-Glu Ladies' locally to deploy businesses to resolve social needs.

Oda says in the water field "our intention is to build the Poly-Glu brand, and already we have earned a certain reputation. In the water business, the Poly-Glu name is the best-selling one among the public". It has already received numerous invitations for joint projects. The company states that the first discussions towards a partnership with Grameen Bank took place in February 2010.

BOP business ability does not depend on company size. If a company has a unique ability, strong purpose of mind and foresight, and a strong sense of mission, it can take part in BOP businesses.

Getting to Know the Market Through Feasibility Studies

In Japan, a company can start gathering information from the Japan International Cooperation Agency (JICA), Japan External Trade Organization (JETRO) and the United Nations Development Programme (UNDP). Then it can visit to learn about actual conditions in the field. The company must not simply leave everything to local agents. It is important to go to the field and check things with one's own eyes. This refers to seeking out needs through the *sangen shugi* ('three reals': real place, real things, and real facts) approach. Top management also needs to participate in final decision making.

Once the actual conditions are clear, a feasibility study must be conducted in the field to seek out local needs and to identify local systems and laws, government agencies and private organizations, and cooperation partners and NGOs to make the blueprint real. Assistance for this may be available from JICA or the Ministry of Economy, Trade, and Industry (METI, ed. 2010). If no expertise is available through local partnerships, another means is partnership with local subsidiaries, such as Dentsu India, which is advancing a condom program with the Indian government.

Discerning Social Needs

There is a need to discern social needs in the local BOP zone through gathering information, fact-finding, and feasibility studies to seek out the aid needed by the BOP layer. Whereas taking local culture, religion, and customs into consideration and keeping the company's businesses in mind, the MDGs serve as important milestones. For example, more than one billion people in the world lack access to safe drinking water. To improve this situation, efforts are targeting the water business. Swiss-based Vestergaard Frandsen has developed and supplies a portable water filter called the LifeStraw, approaching it as a new business towards resolution of social needs.

Working Towards Compatibility With the Company's Own Core Competencies

A BOP business is not a non-profit project. It requires strategic efforts. Porter and Krammer (2002, pp. 57–68) argued for strategic philanthropy or strategic CSR, pointing out the importance of CSR activities that generate revenues through the company's main business.

To seek out the green shoots of growth of a BOP business, strategic decision making through the company's main business, as proactive CSR, is needed. Barney and Clark (2007, pp. 49–72) argued that strategic CSR should be conducted through the company's main business, insisting on the need to discern 'resources' and 'capabilities' in light of social adaptability. In this regard, it is important to screen new businesses through proactive CSR, adding to these the company's own 'strengths'.

BOP businesses with high levels of social impact are in fields that can be entered using the management resources of human beings, products, and money while choosing adaptable technologies and businesses from the company's own strengths and differentiating core competencies (Prahalad & Hamel, 1990, pp. 81–84) from strategic perspectives, while discerning where social needs are high. Figure 10.3 illustrates these points.

Olyset Net from Sumitomo Chemical is an early example reflecting these strategic perspectives. This effort began with participation in the Roll Back Malaria Partnership begun in 1998 with the UNDP playing a central role and with support from other organizations including the World Health Organization (WHO).

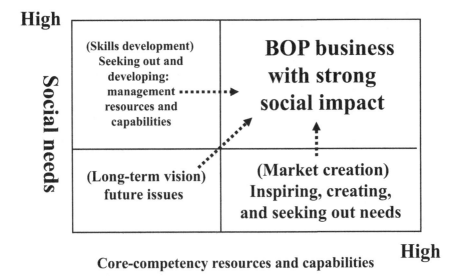

High

Social needs

(Skills development)
Seeking out and
developing:
management
resources and
capabilities

**BOP business
with strong
social impact**

(Long-term vision)
future issues

**(Market creation)
Inspiring, creating,
and seeking out needs**

Core-competency resources and capabilities **High**

Figure 10.3 Strategic Decision Making Using the BOP Business Matrix (prepared
by the author)

As part of this activity, Sumitomo Chemical developed the Olyset Net,
which in 2001 was the first to be recommended by the WHO as a long-
lasting insecticidal net.

A to Z Textile Mills in Tanzania manufactures and sells these nets using
technology provided by Sumitomo Chemical. The company produced
29 million nets and created 7,000 jobs in 2010.

As one of its core competencies, Sumitomo Chemical developed window
screens with long-lasting insect-repellent effects. A staff member came up
with the idea for mosquito nets to prevent malaria. This represents a BOP
business in a sector where the need to prevent malaria matched up with
Sumitomo Chemical's core competencies.

There is a need for strategic decision making on BOP businesses through
screening core competencies in terms of resources, capabilities, and strengths.
The Olyset Net, too, was an idea from research in the field—adapting pesti-
cide development to insect-repellent window screens and linking it to a new
business domain.

Resolution of Social Needs in Addition to Business Perspectives

Hindustan Unilever began selling low-priced detergents and shampoos in
small volumes after identifying prevention of infectious diseases in rural
areas as its goal for resolution of social needs (METI, ed. 2010, pp. 95–97).

This program has received financial support from USAID, World Bank, and UNICEF as a public-private partnership to promote washing hands with soap. According to data from the McKinsey Global Institute, in 2025, India's BOP layer will be 710 million people (vs. 950 million in 2005), shrinking to about 50.7 per cent of the total population. The MOP layer is projected to increase rapidly to 470 million people (vs. 60 million in 2005). Already Western firms are competing to enter this market.

The sales strategy of Hindustan Unilever involves networks of women, with members of an NGO called Shakti playing a central role. This company has raised awareness of hygiene and carried out sales by throwing human resources at the challenge nationwide. They have developed a business outline of achieving mass consumption through selling each pouch at a low price of one rupee to large numbers of buyers purchasing a little at a time and using the products every day.

When viewed from the perspective of combining resolution of social needs with a BOP business, this is an attractive market with great potential.

Thinking About Deployment of a BOP Business Using a Matrix of Product, Expertise, and the Market

A BOP business represents a new entry to the low-income market, and it constitutes development of a new market. One can consider such a business based on the product/market strategy (Figure 10.4) of Ansoff (1965,

Product \ Market	Present expertise, products	New expertise, products
Present markets	**Market penetration**	**Product development**
New BOP markets	**Market development** · Ajinomoto · Hindustan Unilever (detergent, shampoo) · Grameen Danone	**Diversification** · Olyset Net · Shea butter · Nippon Poly-Glu

Figure 10.4 Perspectives From Ansoff's Product/Market Matrix Strategy

(Source: Prepared by the author based on Ansoff (1965) *Corporate Strategy*, McGraw-Hill, Inc.)

p. 109), with the first opportunity being development of a new market using an existing product. Ansoff depicts a matrix of products and markets categorized into four groups: existing product; new market, existing product; existing market, new product; new market; and new product, existing market. The business of selling products in small sizes, one model of a BOP business, can be categorized as an existing product—new market business model.

Many cases of selling products in small individual quantities such as that of Hindustan Unilever employ the same approach used as the initial business model in Japan. They represent development of new markets using existing products (expertise). The case of Ajinomoto can be analyzed from a similar perspective (Ajinomoto, 2011).

Ajinomoto's core product brand and its corporate brand are central to its global strategy. The BOP business targeting low-income consumers in developing markets is experiencing marked growth.

For example, considering improvements in nutrition in developing countries to be one of its important missions, Ajinomoto's activities include the Ajinomoto International Cooperation Network for Nutrition and Health Program (Ajinomoto CSR Div. materials). The project, which began with the University of Ghana and the International Nutrition Foundation to develop and promote foods to realize improvements in nutrition for children in the weaning period in Ghana, is being advanced to develop a sustainable business model towards resolution of malnutrition in developing countries.

Each of these involves selling a single meal's worth of the product in small polyethylene pouches at prices representing a single coin in each country. For example, in India a 2.5-gram pouch sells for one rupee (approx. US¢1.5), whereas in Nigeria, a 9-gram pouch sells for five naira (approx. US¢2.5). Today, Ajinomoto produces the product by employing local workers and utilizing its expertise in pouch products to target the BOP layer.

However, dealing with differences in religion and living customs was an issue. In Indonesia, eating pork is prohibited under Islamic practice, and on one occasion, Ajinomoto was forced to cease production because it switched to an ingredient derived from pork. This was rectified when the company retained halal certification. In fiscal 2009, sales of its business in Indonesia had grown by more than 10 per cent from the previous year to 26 billion yen (US $260 million) as consumption grew together with a rising standard of living. Looking to grow sales in rapidly growing Asian markets, in 2011, the company added a plant for the Ajinomoto seasoning in Karawang.

Figure 10.4 depicts the positioning of the products addressed in this chapter.

Advancing Thorough Localization Policies Throughout the Entire Supply Chain

Because BOP businesses both help resolve social issues and lead to local economic development, the businesses are accepted by local society. There is a need to advance thorough localization by looking at the entire supply chain.

A good example is that of Danone, which partnered with Grameen Bank in Bangladesh to help improve children's health through yogurt (Yunus & Weber, 2007, pp. 149–162; Yunus & Weber, 2010, pp. 33–56).

One of Danone's beliefs calls for "deployment of social-contribution activities under the philosophy that there can be no business growth without growth in society, in all processes from product development through management" (Danone Group website).

Grameen Bank is a bank established in Bangladesh by its president, Muhammad Yunus. It has grown to number 2,400 branches serving seven million individual customers. Yunus won the Nobel Peace Prize in 2006 for promoting micro-credit services. Danone and Grameen signed an agreement on a joint venture. Yunus described this partnership between Danone and Grameen as a social business in March 2006. This concept of social business is a new business model developed by Yunus, with profit reinvested to grow the business or returned to the local community.

It is essential that a BOP business localize all processes from procurement of raw materials through sales. This is where it differs substantially from the traditional business model of exporting yogurt produced in France. Localization needs to take place throughout the entire supply chain. This leads to resolution of social needs through improving child nutrition and improvements in the local standard of living.

All raw materials are purchased from local farmers. Because dairy farmers borrow funds from Grameen Bank to raise dairy cattle locally, the supply of the raw material of milk is stable. Yogurt produced in the local plant is sold under the name Shoktidoi (a Bengali word meaning 'energy'), with one cup of yogurt providing 30 per cent of a child's necessary daily nutrition intake. A container of 80 grams of yogurt sells for about five taka (approx. US ¢ 10). In addition, women called 'Grameen Ladies' distribute the yogurt produced in the local plant to individual households.

Grameen has established a micro-credit fund to fund the project, and the Grameen Ladies also invest in this fund. Local participation through participatory development, instead of just a top-down, blueprint-like method, leads to motivation.

Efforts From a Long-Term Perspective

A BOP business needs to be nurtured as a business over the long term. In recent years, the number of Western multinationals identifying long-term investment in the community as a basis of corporate strategy has begun to increase. For example, Vodafone of the United Kingdom has assigned a unique position to BOP businesses (Tsuchiya, 2009, p. 260).

Until the business gets on track, there is a need for management policies that give more importance to future market growth than the profitability of the business from a long-term perspective. It also is possible that official development assistance (ODA) or aid from METI or the Japan Bank for International Cooperation could be employed as well.

One goal is for business income from a new business to turn positive in about the third year after the start of the business, with cumulative losses being covered by about the fifth year. However, because a BOP business involves various obstacles such as language and local customs, it also takes some time to succeed. It should be possible to create models with income turning positive in the fifth year and cumulative losses covered in the seventh, or in the seventh and tenth years, respectively.

Towards Spreading and Raising Awareness of the BOP Business

Co-creation of Mutual Value in the BOP Business Is Unrelated to Business Size

Tree of Life, an herb and aroma firm, has capital of only 10 million yen (US $0.1 million). Since 2005, it has taken part in a BOP business manufacturing shea butter soap in Ghana (the JETRO website). According to Ryouichi Udagawa, senior managing director of Tree of Life and chairperson of the Aroma Environment Association of Japan, whereas shea butter itself is a profitable business, it has little added value, and its price gets beaten down, but processing it into soap increases added value (Aroma Environment Association of Japan website). As a result, the women producers can earn more.

At the Center for Sustainable Global Enterprise of Cornell University's Johnson Graduate School of Management, Simanis and Hart et al. (2008) have issued the BOP protocol, guidelines for companies' efforts in BOP businesses. These include the concept of co-creating mutual value (Simanis & Hart et al., 2008, pp. 8–9). Tree of Life's project in Ghana truly represents co-creation of mutual value from shea butter.

Whereas companies in the Western natural-cosmetics industry already sold shea body butter, this was the first Japanese firm to enter the industry. Udagawa took part in the development project in Ghana by visiting the field and providing on-site guidance.

The first task was to develop a soap-production workshop. After much hard work, the workshop was completed. Later, a total of six people, including five members of the local women's group, Sagnarigu, were instructed in soap manufacturing.

The fully manual processes to manufacture the soap and then cut and package it faced considerable difficulties in Ghana. Still, JETRO, the NGO, and Tree of Life worked as a team to achieve a successful example of a BOP business. Local government cooperated too.

BOP businesses do not depend on a company's size. They are businesses that can be realized with just high ambitions and the ability to act, backed by corporate philosophy.

Innovation and Reputation Lead to Enlightened Self-Interest

As seen from the preceding cases, a BOP business leads to organizational innovation in creating new business opportunities. The business can promise diverse innovation, product and technological development, improvements in competitiveness, and empowerment of human resources. As Milstein argued, a BOP business can lead to sustainable growth (Cornell University Johnson School, Center for Sustainable Global Enterprise website).

These results are linked to the corporation's reputation, both internally and externally. Decisions should be made that include not only current profits but also corporate reputation for future profits. Such concern for corporate reputation represents enlightened self-interest and is linked to a company's sustainable growth (Mizuo, 2003, p. 1). Management giving importance to stakeholders increases consumers' trust in the company, thus improving its reputation and loyalty, and, ultimately, its business performance, which will make it a new source of new corporate value.

Ansoff (1965) argued for the clear necessity of enlightened self-interest, arguing that it improved the welfare of society and provided individual companies with economic benefits in long-term growth (pp. 32–38).

Meiji Co., Ltd. implements environmental-conservation and community-contribution activities in the regions of South America that produce cocoa beans. It has been argued that this represents BOP business activities by the company (Aramori, 2011, pp. 78–81). Meiji's cocoa sustainability project in the Republic of Ghana also can be seen as constituting a BOP business effort, which makes corporate value so-called enlightened self-interest.

Building Distribution Networks Through Personal Selling in Areas Such as Partnerships With NGOs

A BOP business must also employ NGOs in the field and obtain the participation of the public in funding. In a developed country, where a distribution market, including ordinary retailers and convenience stores exists, there are considerable possibilities for businesses through building up a sales network. However, this is not the case in Bangladesh. In rural areas, there are few retailers at all, and they tend to be far away, which leads to the need for the use of the Grameen Ladies NGO.

The sales strategy of Hindustan Unilever also built a women's network around members of the NGO Shakti.

Conclusions

Amid the tough business conditions, in future growth strategies, Asia should be seen as a domestic market with Japan. Increasing income in Asia through infrastructure improvements can power growth of Japanese firms as well. This truly describes the BOP business itself. The keywords are 'sustainability' and 'profit', or prosperity for local people and continuation over the long term.

Fast Retailing (Uniqlo) and Grameen Bank established an apparel joint venture in 2010, which represented the start of a BOP business in Bangladesh. Japanese firms need to follow the lead of Sumitomo Chemical, Fast Retailing, and others in linking BOP businesses to growth strategies.

Finally, I would like to propose that the key to BOP business success is cooperation with non-profits and NGOs. Regarding its cooperation, the Japan Inclusive Business Support Center started operations in 2010, carrying out activities in which industry, government, and academia, along with NGOs and non-profits, work together, with METI playing a central role. Whereas these also constitute an important domain, they are a subject for future research.

※This work was supported by the Ministry of Education, Culture, Sports, Science, and Technology, Grant-in-Aid for Scientific Research (23530492, 26380471).

Note

1 The aforementioned is a partially revised version of a matrix framework and four responsibilities proposed by Mizuo and Tanaka (2004). The four responsibilities were revised from Carroll (1979).

References

Ansoff, H. I. (1965). *Corporate strategy: An analytic approach to business policy for growth and expansion.* New York, NY: McGraw-Hill.
Barney, J. B., & Clark, D. N. (2007). *Resource based theory: Creating and sustaining competitive advantage.* Oxford, UK: Oxford University Press.
Carroll, A. B. (1979) *Business & society: Ethics and stakeholder management* (1st ed). Mason, OH: Thomson.
Hammond, A., Kramer, W. J., Tran, J., Katz, R., & Walker, C. (2007). *The next 4 billion: Market size and business strategy at the base of the pyramid.* Retrieved from Washington DC: http://www.wri.org/sites/default/files/pdf/n4b_fulltext_hi.pdf
Hart, S. L. (2007). *Capitalism at the crossroads.* Upper Saddle River, NJ: Prentice Hall.
Kim, W. C., & Mauborgne, R. (2005). *Blue ocean strategy.* Boston, MA: Harvard Business School Press.
Porter, M. E., & Kramer, M. R. (2002). The competitive advantage of corporate philanthropy. *Harvard Business Review*, Dec. 57–68.
Porter, M. E., & Kramer, M. R. (2006).Strategy & society: The link between competitive advantage and corporate social responsibility. *Harvard Business Review*, Dec. 78–92.
Porter, M. E., & Kramer, M. R. (2011). Creating shared value: How to reinvent capitalism-and unleash a wave of innovation and growth. *Harvard Business Review*, Jan–Feb. 62–77.
Prahalad, C. K., & Hamel, G. (1990).The core competence of the corporation. *Harvard Business Review*, May–June. 81–84

Prahalad, C. K., & Hart, S. L. (2002). The fortune at the bottom of the pyramid. *Strategy+Business*, (26), *Jan.* 54–67.
Prahalad, C. K., & Lieberthal, K. (1998). The end of corporate imperialism. *Harvard Business Review, July–Aug.* 68–79.
Simanis, E., & Hart, S. L. et al. (2008). *The base of the pyramid protocol: Toward next generation BOP strategy.* Retrieved from: http://www.johnson.cornell.edu/sge/docs/BOP_Protocol_2nd_ed.pdf
Yunus, M., & Weber, K. (2007). *Creating a world without poverty.* New York: Public Affairs.
Yunus, M., & Weber, K. (2010). *Building social business.* New York: Public Affairs.

Japanese Books

Ajinomoto (2011) CSR Report.
Aramori, I. (2011) Contributing to society through a core business, reviving the Amazon through chocolate, *Nikkei Business*, November 17, 2011.
Matsushita, K. (1974) What is a company's social responsibility? PHP Inc.
Mizuo, J. (2000a) A corporation's social responsibility and marketing ethics. *Japan Society for Information and Management*, 20(3), 15–21.
Mizuo, J. (2000b) Marketing ethics. Chuokeizai-sha.
Mizuo, J. (2003) Management ethics of self-governance. Chikura Pub.
Mizuo, J. (2009) Nikkei economics lesson Business in developing countries: A pressing need for realization, *Japan Economics Newspaper*, December 22.
Mizuo, J., Ariu, T., & Shimizu, M. eds. (2007) *Easy CSR initiatives.* Japanese Standards Association.
Mizuo, J., & Tanaka, H. eds. (2004) *CSR management.* Seisansei Pub.
Mizuo, J., Tanaka, H., Ariu, T., & Shimizu, M. eds. (2005) *CSR initiatives-recommended models of CSR management philosophies, charters of conduct, and standards of conduct. (Japanese/English).* Japanese Standards Association.
Nomura Research Institute (2008) Management strategies for social innovation.
Sato, A. (2014) Aderans Plus, Vol 2. Retrieved from http://www.aderans.co.jp/corporate/rd/pdf/aderans-plus02.pdf
Trade Finance and Economic Cooperation Division, Trade and Economic Cooperation Bureau, METI, eds. (2010) Frontiers in BOP business. Research Institute of Economy, Trade and Industry.
Tsuchiya, S. (2009) A study of new-generation businesses as seen in BOP market strategies. *Business & Economic Review*, JRI Europe, Dec. 2009.

Websites

Aroma Environment Association of Japan website http://www.aromakankyo.or.jp/magazine/ghana03_02.html
BBC News website http://news.bbc.co.uk/1/hi/business/8100183.stm
Cabinet Office of Japan nonprofits website http://www.npo-homepage.go.jp/data/pref.html
Cornell University Johnson School, Center for Sustainable Global Enterprise website http://www.johnson.cornell.edu/sge/
Danone Group website http://www.danone.co.jp/group/activity/mission/

Hayami, Yutaka *Beikoku no bijinesu enjeru ni tsuite* ("U.S. business angels"), in JETRO bayspo.com website http://www.bayspo.com/weekly/jetro/jetro1010.html

Japan Inclusive Business Support Center website <https://www.bop.go.jp/>JETRO website http://www.jetro.go.jp/jfile/report/05000912/05000912_002_BUP_0.pdf

Ministry of Foreign Affairs of Japan website http://www.mofa.go.jp/mofaj/gaiko/oda/doukou/mdgs.html

Nippon Poly-Glu websitehttp://www.poly-glu.com/index.html

11 Constructive Consumption

Corporate Leadership in Bridging Livelihoods and Conservation in Democratic Societies

Saleem Ali and Mirza Sadaqat Huda

Introduction

Consumerism inflicts a tyranny of small decisions which could incrementally undermine the life support systems of the planet. Contemporary environmentalism has of late been at odds with consumption and the dominant paradigm of economic growth that encourages consumption. Population and consumption are no doubt both integral parts of the sustainability conundrum. However, the guilt which environmentalism had to contend with in criticizing poor developing countries for their population growth has been assuaged by focusing on consumption as the primary concern. Rather than berating a developing country for its population growth, many environmentalists have shifted their ire to consumerism in affluent societies, which they see as a more cogent and plausible policy target. No doubt, consumerism is indeed linked closely to environmental degradation, quite often in developing countries. Yet compelling as the appeal of anti-consumerism rhetoric may be, one is still left with a lingering question of how best to address global poverty and growing inequality?

In this chapter, we argue that consumption needs to be considered with greater nuance, particularly by corporate leaders at the individual and organizational levels. We ask questions such as what are the means by which a collaborative form of leadership between private and public interests might allow for wealth transfer to occur to reduce human suffering beyond the simplistic recommendation of reverting back to subsistence lifestyles or lavishing foreign aid, which skews performance incentives? Furthermore, how do we also reconcile pluralism of human tastes for goods and services with the imperative to reduce consumption?

Providing more efficient means of procuring and producing goods and services might be a win-win situation, but researchers like Peter Dauvergne (2008) dismiss that prospect since it may still spur latent demand. The idea of constructive consumption is based on the notion that the impact of an increase in efficiency has broader implications beyond lowering costs in the developed world. Efficiency measures that increase the purchasing power of consumers in the West can have a significant impact on the demand of products that sustain millions of livelihoods in developing countries. A case in point is the export-oriented garments industry, where employment in the manufacturing sector is 77, 90, and 89 per cent (Keane & Velde, 2008) in the least-developed countries of Bangladesh, Cambodia, and Lesotho, respectively. This rate is also high for low-income countries such as Pakistan (44.3 per cent) and El Salvador (50.2 per cent) (Keane & Velde, 2008). The consumption of commodities, electronics, and services in the developed world has not only sustained livelihoods in poorer countries, but it has also had far reaching implications on women's empowerment through cottage industry demand. In measuring issues such as efficiency and consumption, we must not be in denial of the global, interconnected implications of our decisions on poverty alleviation.

Although it has been suggested that a move towards the service economy can reduce environmental harm, this notion is simplistic as it does not take into consideration the manufacturing base of global supply chains. As eloquently stated by Henriques and Kander (2010) "any transition to a service economy by the developed world may be due to a new division of labour on a global scale, accompanied by developing countries producing energy-intensive exports for the developed world" (p. 271). Whereas the West should recognize that great environmental harm is created in developing and emerging economies from the production of export-oriented goods, this should not result in abstinence from consumption. Rather a more holistic understanding of the global division of labour, the borderless nature of climate change, and links between consumption and livelihoods should stimulate policymakers in the West to encourage sustainable and efficient production of goods in the developing world. However, this complex task cannot be left to the policymakers alone and must see proactive efforts by the private sector. Transnational companies with their global outreach and economies of scale can play a unique role in linking environmental goals and development outcomes to the consumption of their products.

Theoretical Framework: Leadership

If corporations are to play a role in constructive consumption, the particular brand of leadership that will drive such change will need to be examined. This creates an obvious dilemma: Leadership has traditionally been conceptualized at an individualistic level and the conventional theories of leadership are less than adequate when applied to corporations. Badshah (2012) has undertaken a historical analysis of leadership theories while accounting for the complexity and overlaps in conceptualizations. The author's detailed explanations of 'trait', 'behavioural', 'charismatic' and other theories of leadership highlight the prominence of the individual in these concepts.

Wang, Van Wart and Lebredo (2014) have relayed the inadequacy of the 'charismatic' and other theories in framing sustainability leadership and have stated that the ideal perspective for this purpose is 'the social change leadership' theory, which stresses collective actions rather than individual goals. Wang et al. (2014) have explained social change leadership as

> an awareness of the need for adaptation of a multitude of minor societal practices to achieve a larger goal. No single actor can create a successful outcome for a complex policy problem; it requires collective action, although different actors may have distinctly different contributing roles.
>
> (p. 342)

An important corollary to this is provided by Raelin (2015) who stresses a renewed vision of leadership in the corporate world that puts emphasis on collective action of people who work together, rather than on the leaders themselves. He argues that because of the availability of communication technology and a complex operating environment, a top-down approach should be replaced by a collective form of leadership that encourages communication and self-assessment. The conceptualization of leadership by Raelin (2015) and Wang et al. (2014) is more systemic rather than based on individual traits, and this whole-of-business approach may be more suitable for accessing the leadership role played by corporations in spearheading sustainability. It is important in this light to highlight how corporations themselves articulate their goals of becoming sustainability leaders.

There have been several explicit and implicit indications of corporations acting as leaders in implementing sustainable practices. Anisa Kamadoli Costa, the chief sustainability officer at Tiffany and Co., has stated in an article in the *Stanford Social Innovation Review* "we aspire to be a leader among jewelry companies in promoting responsible practices in the mining industry" (Costa, 2015, p. 55). In 3M's 2014 sustainability report, the company envisions itself as a

> leader in setting and achieving visionary goals to improve our energy efficiency and make a positive impact on the environment through early reduction of greenhouse gas emissions. When others were talking about making reductions, the Company took leadership actions to achieve those reductions in real life.
>
> (3M, 2014)

Sustainability leadership has also been expressed in the goals of global companies such as Coca-Cola and Walmart with the explicit aim of reaching out to stakeholders and suppliers.

In regard to the leadership of corporations, Lubin and Etsy (2010) have conceptualized sustainability as a 'megatrend' similar in relevance and transformative quality to the spread of digital technology in the 1980s and 1990s. They have suggested that the leadership capabilities that have enabled a smooth adjustment to historical megatrends can provide some important clues on creating a strategy to integrate sustainability and commercial goals. In particular, they highlighted five key areas to integrate key execution capabilities: leadership, assessment, strategy development, management integration, and reporting and communication.

Leadership by corporations in enhancing sustainability in their respective industries should thus ideally be conceptualized as a collective, integrated, whole-of-system approach, where varied responsibilities are directed towards a common goal. Within this context, it is important to examine how corporations can act as drivers for constructive consumption.

Corporations as Leadership Drivers for Constructive Consumption

Envisioning consumption within a broader framework of sustainable livelihoods and efficiency is of greater salience than the well-meaning calls to reduce consumer expenditure. Consequently, the implementation of sustainable practices in supply chains becomes even more important than choices made by the consumer. Transnational companies can play an important role in this regard, as they are not only a significant constituent of economies around the globe but also potent architects of social, political, environmental, and cultural developments. In 2011, foreign affiliates of transnational companies employed an estimated 69 million workers, who generated US$28 trillion in sales and $7 trillion in value added, some 9 per cent up from 2010 (UNCTAD, 2012). Due to their size and influence, transnational companies have come under increasing pressure to act responsibly and many well-known corporations have been accused of being complicit in human rights violations, sourcing goods from unsustainable sources, condoning the exploitation of workers, and causing irreversible harm to the environment. Several cases of malpractice have been reported to the Compliance Advisor Ombudsman, and details of such incidents are available on their website. At present, transnational companies are starting to recognize the need to extend their responsibility from the shareholder to the well-being of the community in which they operate—an approach that is widely understood as 'corporate citizenship'. A few transnational companies have pioneered a holistic approach towards sustainability by not confining it to the ethical sourcing of raw materials and efficiency in production, but also addressing key social and environmental goals through the design and marketing of their products.

Unilever's Sustainable Living Plan (Unilever, 2014) includes social, environmental, and economic goals that aim to reduce deforestation, enhance sustainable agriculture, and increase access to safe drinking water, sanitation, and hygiene. Innovations that deserve mention include detergents that use less water and projects that encourage consumers to buy products that will help them reduce their greenhouse gas emissions while washing and showering. Another transnational company that has garnered attention for the championing of sustainable practices is the Body Shop. The company pioneered fair trade in the beauty industry through the "Community Fair Trade" program, which created trading partnerships directly with marginalized communities, such as smallholder farmers living on the edges of the rainforest in Campeche State in the far southeast of Mexico. The Body Shop also refrains from testing products on animals, supports human rights issues, initiates projects that counter negative body image, and undertakes efforts to protect the environment in which it operates (The Body Shop, 2016). Although the economies of scale enjoyed by transnational companies greatly enhance the impact of their policies on sustainability, social businesses such as Who Gives a Crap (2016) have demonstrated that smaller companies that link consumption to development can have an important role in reducing human suffering. An online business that sells recycled toilet paper, Who Gives a Crap donates 50 per cent of its profits to build toilets in the developing world. The company has estimated that every toilet roll they sell goes towards providing toilet access to a person in need for a week (Who Gives a Crap, 2016).

Corporations have a major role to play in ensuring that growth does not undermine the environment or result in the oppression or exploitation of human beings. Although many companies have solely pursued and continue to pursue profits at the cost of human rights and environmental degradation, several businesses have shown great leadership skills in integrating their businesses with economic, social, and environmental priorities. Although there is scope for improvement, the aforementioned examples demonstrate that with a more collaborative calibre of leadership, corporations can be important partners in moving society towards more sustainable consumption patterns while contributing to economic development through their products and services. In addition to the role of corporations, the consumption habits of the future will be greatly influenced by the rise of 'the shared economy', which has been debated as a viable alternative to traditional practices of ownership.

Sharing Resources

Goodwin (2015) sums up the phenomenon of the shared economy by stating "Uber, the world's largest taxi company, owns no vehicles; Facebook, the world's most popular media owner, creates no content; Alibaba, the most valuable retailer, has no inventory; And Airbnb, the world's largest accommodation provider, owns no real estate" (p. 1). As explained by Sacks (2011), the basic characteristic of 'collaborative consumption' is that access to goods and skills is more important than ownership of them. The shared economy can be divided into three broad categories: product-service systems that facilitate the sharing or renting of products such as a car, redistribution markets that enable re-ownership of a product such as Craigslist and the sharing of assets and skills, such as workspace. Price Waterhouse Coopers has estimated that the five main sharing economy sectors generate $15 billion in global revenues at present but may account for $335 billion in 2025 (PWC, 2014).

Theoretically, collaborative consumption has several advantages: Owners make use of unused assets, consumers pay less, and the environment benefits because of a reduction in ownership of assets such as cars (Allen and Berg, 2014). Despite the unprecedented rise of the shared economy, according to an entrepreneur of a sharing website, it is generally limited to products that share three key characteristics: They cost more than $100 but less than $500, can be easily transportable, and are infrequently used (Sacks, 2011). A study by the European Commission has accounted for the competition faced by hotels from Airbnb but has also contended that the lack of trust and unfamiliarity with web-based, peer-to-peer platforms act as significant constraints to greater market penetration (Dervojeda, Verzijl, Nagtegaal, Lengton & Rouwmaat, 2013). The study found that the locations of the products and the age of the clients are contextual issues that determine the acceptability of shared economies. Although collaborative consumption is an extremely significant phenomenon in regard to certain products that cater to specific demographics in particular locations, we believe that ownership of assets will continue to be the dominant trend in consumption on a global scale in the near future. Whether the savings made via the sharing of certain assets such as cars are then used to consume a greater number of other commodities such as electronics is another question that should be raised. Overall, although not a viable alternative to hyperconsumption at present, collaborative consumption can reduce wastage and increase competition and efficiency. Therefore, despite the rise of the shared economy, material usage may still occur and impact human beings as well as the environment.

Issues around consumption, however, cannot be fully understood without an insight into human behaviour and the policies undertaken by governments to exploit or constrain the basic human impulse to consume. The rather discomforting aspect of the findings from research on human behaviour is that our consumption decisions may well be made with less direction, purpose, or forethought than would be expected. In such circumstances, the role of institutions of authority becomes all the more salient. How might government or other controlling forces respond to these traits in human societies? Much can be gleaned from considering world politics in the twentieth century.

Operation Abundance

United States of America President Woodrow Wilson (1913–1921) acknowledged the power of consumption as a means of hegemony most explicitly in one of his landmark speeches in 1916 to the World Salesmanship Congress. Much of Europe was embroiled in World War I, and Wilson was quite concerned about conflict resolution and global governance, but with an American edge. He stated to the congress that "America's democracy of business" would prevail in "the struggle for the peaceful conquest of the world". His business focus at the time was on palpable consumer products that could "force the tastes of the manufacturing country on the country in which the markets were being sought". As a scholar as well as a policymaker, Wilson also pontificated on the larger ramifications of using the psychology of "tastes" more constructively by stating "that the great barriers in this world is not the barrier of principles but the barrier of taste". By homogenizing tastes, Wilson implied that we could somehow rid the world of at least one prime contributor to our conflict with foreigners and "convert them to the principles of America". This same line of reasoning has prevailed to this day with Thomas Friedman's "Golden Arches Theory of Conflict Prevention", where he somewhat simplistically proposed that countries with McDonald's restaurants are less likely to go to war with each other because of a homogenization of cultural proclivities through fast food (Friedman, 2000).

The rhetoric of consumption for a greater good resonated most alarmingly with our species, which already had a treasure impulse. Consumption thus came to be perceived as a societal positive and made us all far more vested and dependent on the system. In *Irresistible Empire*, Victoria de Grazia's (2006) comments that President Wilson was "the first leader to recognize that statecraft could find leverage in the physical needs, psychic discomforts and situations of social unease being unleashed by the new material civilization of mass consumption" (de Grazia, 2006, p. 10).

Three decades following Wilson's presidency, after yet another world war, we were confronted with a further push towards activist consumption. This time it was to show how modes and strategies of consuming materials could ideologically differentiate the left and right wings of the political spectrum. Having fought collectively against a common enemy, the Soviet Union and the United States soon discovered that they had less in common and the world consequently endured five decades of 'Cold War'. Frigid as the war might have seemed to the military realists, the metal smelters and factory furnaces were as hot as they had ever been in human history. Not only were countries producing weapons at an unprecedented pace, but they were also manufacturing consumer goods under the pretext that sheer production of palpable products (often at the expense of services) would give them an edge over competing economies. The Soviets were consuming materials for governmental trophy projects whereas the United States was consuming them to promote contrasting lifestyles of affluence. Both sides were getting hooked on their consumption of materials, but the American arsenal of abundant consumerism was to prevail globally. Our ability to creatively market our products was clearly a competitive edge.

Appealing to the senses and to human acquisitive desires is the United States of America's forte. Capital markets are well suited to nurture such creativity, and with the help of mass media and advertising, we were able to entrance the world with our products. Nobel Laureate economist Gary Becker was among the first to consider that addictive behaviour was possible in the context of consumption, even in the absence of a pathological condition that might inhibit regulatory hormones. In his essay with economist Kevin Murphy titled the "Theory of Rational Addiction", Becker built on his earlier work on behavioural economics to suggest that even a gradual implementation of a consumption plan with full information about addiction potential "rationally" leads people to addictive behaviour because of the way people discount their utility (reduce the value) for a product over time (Becker & Murphy, 1988). Although much of the research in this regard focused on drug addiction, consumerism and material exchanges are also captured by this provocative insight. By one estimate, 5 per cent of the American public is clinically addicted to shopping and around 0.7 per cent is addicted to gambling (Lemonick & Park, 2007). However, if we were to consider the larger issue of conspicuous consumption and its impact on fashion trends, and a domino effect of influence, the addictive definition becomes much broader and encompasses a far greater demographic. Even between enemies, the common human impulses for acquisition and the propensity for addiction in various contexts remains salient. Additionally, behavioural economists are discovering that human beings often do not learn from their mistakes and tend to repeat certain kinds of irrational behaviour patterns because of some visceral impulses that we may not fully understand (Ariely, 2008; Harford, 2008). For example, what started off as a move towards conscious consumerism about water pollution has transformed into an obsession with drinking bottled water. Sociologist Andrew Szasz refers to this phenomenon as "inverted quarantine", where individually cautious behaviour is becoming a societal scourge instead of being a means of following the fabled "precautionary principle" of ecological protection (Szasz, 2007).

The sheer scale of current mass consumption is hard to fathom without some visual images, captured with phenomenal artistic flair by photographic artist Chris Jordan. His works include an entire replica of Georges Seurat's famous painting, *Sunday Afternoon on the Island of La Grande Jatte*, made with a chromatic assortment of 106,000 aluminium cans—the amount used in the United States every 30 seconds. Another portrait comprises 32,000 cyclically arranged Barbie dolls in the form of a shady image of a woman's breasts—the number of dolls signifying the average number of aesthetic silicone implant surgeries performed in the United States in 2006. Such artistic expression, therefore, provides an unconventional medium of grasping the enormous impact of consumerism on modern society.

Sociologist David Riesman observed the Cold War of materialism as early as 1951, when he wrote a satirical essay titled "The Nylon Wars". The narrative concerns a U.S. army effort titled "Operation Abundance", in which 200,000 pairs of nylon socks, 4 million packs of cigarettes, 35,000 Toni permanent-wave kits, 20,000 yo-yos, 10,000 wristwatches, and an assemblage of other excess consumer items are rained down from the air on Soviet population centres (Castillo, 2005; Reisman, 1961). The goal of this onslaught was to make the deprived Soviet population crave the material goods and rebel against their communist masters. The plot thickens when the Soviets respond with their own air raids of caviar, fur coats, and collections of Stalin's speeches. The Americans are able to claim victory ultimately because of a timely drop of two-way radios that empower the Soviet population to order consumer goods as if from a store catalogue. With an onslaught of electronic products, the electricity grid in the Soviet Union collapses and the capitalist model prevails. Yet the breakdown of the electric grid remains a loose end in the narrative, which perhaps unwittingly reflected the darker side of mass consumption with an environmental twist. The rise of polymeric materials such as nylon also occurred as a result of fossil fuel consumption being taken for granted during much of that period in history. The Cold War period was a time of great introspection for human civilization. Scholars such as Reisman considered the paradox of progress which left them perplexed. How might we balance goals of development through sustenance of human livelihoods with the security imperative that ideological differences had thrust upon the world? Perhaps a better understanding of the links between consumption, human behaviour, and happiness can provide clues to answering this Cold War–era dilemma, which policymakers of today have struggled to resolve.

Does Consumption Lead to Happiness?

In his acclaimed dialogue essay, "The Critic as Artist", Oscar Wilde (1891) stated that humanity likes to "rage against materialism, as they call it, forgetting that there has been no material improvement that has not spiritualized the world". Wilde's insight on the dichotomous attitude of society that benefits from materialism yet reviles its impact has also been picked up by many revisionist scholars of consumerism and material culture who ask us to reflect upon the social ties created by gift giving and the livelihoods created by the products which are produced as a result of conspicuous consumption. In his provocatively titled book *Lead Us Into Temptation*, James Twitchell (1999) tries to make the case primarily through observational analysis that consumer fashions and branding lead to bonding in an age of individualism. Renegade environmentalists such as Jesse Lemisch have also been irritated by many green activists, such as Ralph Nader, whom they feel have "turned their backs on people's reasonable and deeply human longings for abundance, joy, cornucopia, variety and mobility, substituting instead a puritanical asceticism that romanticized hardship, scarcity, localism and underdevelopment" (Horowitz 2005, p. 255). British sociologist Daniel Miller (2001) believes that we can "feel sympathetic to the dreadful plight of cosmopolitans who feel they have too many pairs of shoes . . . and they bought their child a present instead of spending quality time with them" (p. 227). However, he considers it "not acceptable that the study of consumption, and any potential moral stance to it, be reduced to an expression of such peoples' guilt and anxieties" (p. 227).

To respond to these criticisms, let us turn to Nobel Laureate Bertrand Russell's very simple assertion that "good" conduct, which could suggest behavioural attributes such as being industrious, studious, morally proper, might not necessarily make you happy. In his seminal work *The Conquest of Happiness*, Russell (1930) conceded that such attributes may lead to wealth if our system worked well. You work hard and you play hard—the mantra of many Wall Street treasure seekers. The wealth in turn from working hard may allow for consumer spending, which the aforementioned revisionists would contend makes us happier. It is thus worth considering how far this line of reasoning is valid, especially because Russell urged us to also consider the reverse—if we are happy, we are more likely to do well for society. The data on this latter assertion is fairly well established. If people are happy individually (but not to the point of selfish complacence, that can be a temperamental trait in some subjects), they are more likely to perform better in their work, be more productive family members, and active philanthropists in their societal contributions. There is also circularity to this premise as the research shows that philanthropy itself makes people happier (Dunn, Aknin & Norton, 2008). Thus the wealthy hoarder has been shown to be less 'happy' in contemporary research than the benevolent one.

Although Adam Smith is better known for his treatise on *The Wealth of Nations*, which posits a rather self-centred acquisitive view of human impulses, he also wrote another notable book, subsequently, *The Theory of Moral Sentiments*, in which he writes,

> How selfish so ever man may be supposed, there are evidently some principles in his nature, which interest him in the fortunes of others, and render their happiness necessary to him, though he derives nothing from it, except the pleasure of seeing it.
>
> (Gintis, Bowles, Boyd & Fehr, 2005, p. 3)

This view has been picked up by some economists who work with psychologists, ethnologists, and neuroscientists to understand the chemical triggers of human behaviour, particularly in understanding cooperative behaviour within societies and the possible role of material gifts as a mark of reciprocity to reinforce such cooperation (Hauser, 2006; Shermer, 2007; Zak, 2008).

As far as issues of wealth, acquisitive impulses, and happiness are concerned, the data are far more complex and deserve some careful consideration as we ponder material desires. The term 'feeling good' can have a number of connotations. Researchers tend to use terms such as 'quality of life', 'well-being', 'life satisfaction', and simply 'happiness' to define that visceral positive emotion that has physical connotations related to non-mental health as well as psychological aspects such as a state of mind and consciousness (which may ultimately have some physical connections as well). The research in this arena is effusive with popular books by psychologists, economists, and medical doctors claiming to provide resolution to that elusive quest for perennial smiles.

Before considering the ways in which material acquisition, wealth, and other factors can lead to joy, we have to be clear about what control individuals may have on their abilities in this regard. According to social psychologist Sonja Lyubomirsky, the acclaimed author of *The How of Happiness*, there is a happiness "set point" that accounts for about 50 per cent of happiness that is determined by temperamental factors (genetically determined). An additional 10 per cent is determined by social circumstances and perhaps around 40 per cent is within our control in terms of behavioural choices. Consumption behaviour would fall within this 40 per cent of behavioural attributes that could potentially give us a higher sense of well-being (Lyubomirsky, 2007).

So the questions still remain: Where we do have control? What makes us happy? Could wealth and material consumption make us happier? Psychologists have struggled to understand human 'needs' versus 'wants' and their impact on motivation and a potentially consequent sense of well-being. Much of this line of study can be traced to a hierarchy of 'needs' developed in the 1940s by the American psychologist Abraham Maslow. This hierarchy of needs now graces most introductory psychology courses and is often presented as a pyramid with physiological needs at the base, followed by safety, love, esteem, and self-actualization (at the apex). Maslow had suggested that the higher needs only become focused when the lower needs have been met and the individual has overcome the baser necessities. In this mode, a certain quantum of material well-being is essential before other aspects are realized. Whereas the delineation provided by Maslow is useful, there is now general consensus among psychologists that material well-being is also inextricably linked to other factors in the hierarchy and that in comparison across populations, self-actualization may be higher among individuals whose physiological needs are comparably lower.

Clayton Alderfer subsequently developed a non-linear version of Maslow's view in 1969 which was termed "An Empirical Test of a New Theory of Human Need". The key attributes of this model were existence, relatedness, and growth (ERG), which may be particularly useful in our attempts to understand both the positive and negative dimensions of our treasure impulse. Even though Alderfer developed this model in the context of organizations, the applicability is much broader. The elegance of this simple model is that it shows how connections between material needs and more intangible aspects of well-being can be positive as well as negative, given the motivational direction. There are some kinds of acquisitive impulses and material usage beyond basic needs which could have a positive impact on satisfaction, whereas there are many others that might not have that positive impact. Much depends on what the motivation and causal mechanism are for the consuming act and what meaning is derived from it.

In general, a certain amount of material wealth is important for individuals to be happy, but wealth is not a sufficient condition for happiness. Researchers are quite sensitive to differentiating 'income' from 'wealth'. The former category is an economic indicator of monetary flow in households and the economy at large, whereas the latter is an indicator of more lasting financial security. For our purposes of understanding material consumption, wealth is a better indicator because it includes material assets and may account for factors such as debt and long-term financial security (and hence less worry). However, for research purposes, it is easier to get data on income, and so most studies tend to focus on income which can lead to what has been termed "focusing illusions" by Nobel Laureate Daniel Kahneman, who opined that people exaggerate the contribution of income to happiness because they focus, in part, on conventional achievements when evaluating their life or the lives of others (Kahneman, Krueger, Schkade, Schwarz, & Stone, 2006). We are thus better served at understanding the complexities of human interactions with material acquisition to understand well-being.

The mere act of seeking wealth can potentially increase well-being if we have a clear goal in mind, but it can be self-defeating if we do not have clear markers of achievement. One of the most important insights from psychological research on human well-being has been that the process of attainment is even more significant than the substantive goal itself. Human beings tend to settle very quickly into a state of pleasure and then become 'bored' with their situation—a phenomenon called 'hedonic adaptation'. To remain satisfied, we thus need to be experiencing change, whether through motivational flow of creative behaviour or through a positive quest. Remaining satisfied with life was thus likened by psychologists Brickman and Campbell (1971) as a "hedonic treadmill" (p. 287–302). As the analogy implies, the individual on the treadmill doesn't move forward, but to stay in a stable position, he or she has to continuously strive—the connotation is thus rather pessimistic in the psychologists' description of the phenomenon:

> The nature of [adaptation] condemns men to live on a hedonic treadmill, to seek new levels of stimulation merely to maintain old levels of subjective pleasure, to never achieve any kind of permanent happiness or satisfaction.
>
> (Brickman & Campbell, 1971, p. 289)

The negativity implied in this assertion has been widely refuted in the literature since their article was published in 1971. So far in this chapter on constructive consumption, we saw how biochemical pathways definitely lead to feelings of joy and the ability of some individuals to feel measurably 'happy'. Surveys of happiness, despite their many methodological problems, have been found to show that individuals are definitely happier in some circumstances and geographies more so than others (Brereton, Clinch, & Ferreira, 2008). However, despite the various dissenting views, what has emerged is that positive pursuit is indeed an essential ingredient in well-being.

In addition, it is essential to blend subjective well-being with objective criteria of human prosperity such as health, which usually figures as the most significant factor in well-being according to most surveys. Furthermore, given the transient state of human happiness at a given point in time, it is highly consequential to consider long-term impacts of consumption at other levels. The interface between consumption, the environment, and human well-being is now a subject of increasing academic inquiry. Scholars such as Thomas Princen have been asking us to consider the trade-offs between efficiency of large-scale, production-focused economies on the one hand and the "logic of sufficiency" on the other. If we consider longer time scales in our decision-making frames, it is more likely that we would act with what Princen terms "ecological rationality" (Princen, 2005, p. 25). He argues that by welcoming and not resisting limits to ever-increasing material throughput, human beings can recognize the importance of "living well by living within our means" Princen (2010, p. viii).

We might begin to consider individual consumption decisions such as shopping choices with greater care. Just as nutrition labels made shoppers savvier with health-conscious shopping, perhaps longer-term consumption impacts may also lead to greater product differentiation by consumers.

Even with responsible shopping, some ardent environmental critics of consumerism such as Juliet Schor would suggest that Americans are over-shopping (Schor 1999). If all the little additional trinkets and consumer goods that we buy are not definitively improving our quality of life, then why do we have to go on spending? Part of the answer may be that we have had greater access to credit, often to our detriment in terms of long-term planning, as exemplified by the financial crisis of 2008. With huge credit availability, we have been able to view opportunity for immense wealth as far more reachable than in prior generations. Schor argues that material acquisition may provide the illusion of bridging financial inequality. However, the larger question remains to be addressed regarding what impact shopping has on the economy as a whole and on livelihoods of those who produce the goods as a trade-off against environmental impact. In this regard, innovative ways of integrating human activities with the natural environment have recently received considerable interest.

Environment and Society: Can the Two Coexist in Harmony?

Although the actions of human societies have often been attributed to environmental degradation, it is just as impossible to expect modern civilization to return to subsistence lifestyles as it is to pursue unbridled materialism at the risk of ecosystem collapse. An approach that aims to harmonize societies with nature, such as the Satoyama Initiative, can provide a more realistic pathway towards balancing consumption with conservation. A joint project by the Ministry of the Environment of Japan and the United Nations

University Institute for the Advanced Study of Sustainability, the core vision of the Satoyama Initiative is to realize landscapes where the maintenance and development of socio-economic activities align with natural processes (The International Partnership for the Satoyama Initiative, 2010). These 'socio-ecological production landscapes and seascapes' (SEPLS) are defined as "dynamic mosaics of habitats and land uses where the harmonious interaction between people and nature maintains biodiversity while providing humans with the goods and services needed for their livelihoods, survival and well-being in a sustainable manner". What is interesting about SEPLS is that they have a global presence. In Japan, such landscapes are known as "satoyama", in Spain they are called *dehesa*, and in Hawaii *ahupua'a*. Unique forms of land use and natural resource management are also identified by various names around the world, such as *mauelsoop* in Korea, *muyong* in the Philippines, and *kebun* in Indonesia and Malaysia. With 167 member organizations, from countries as diverse as Peru, Ghana, and Cambodia, the International Partnership for the Satoyama Initiative gives a truly global interface to the promotion of SEPLS, which led to its recognition by the tenth meeting of the Conference of the Parties to the Convention on Biological Diversity.

By consolidating knowledge on diverse ecosystems, integrating traditional knowledge with modern science, and creating a new co-management system, the Satoyama Initiative recognizes the importance of livelihoods derived from nature while advocating sustainable practices. Such an approach does not demonize consumption or human interaction with nature, but recognizes the potential harms posed by rapid industrialization and urbanization. In relation to our concept of constructive consumption, the Satoyama Initiative demonstrates that the consumption of agricultural products that employ an overwhelming number of poor rural people in the developing world can be utilized to invest in farming areas modelled on SEPLS landscapes. This will ensure environmental protection while also sustaining much-needed livelihoods. A renewed look at protectionist trade policies that have resulted in a dramatic decline in agricultural exports from the developing to the developed world may also need to be undertaken as a means of elevating rural poverty, which stands at 40 per cent in South Asia and 51 per cent in Sub-Saharan Africa.

Despite the potential of initiatives such as the Satoyama, the reality is that the production of commodities and manufactured goods has greatly harmed the environment. If mass consumerism is to be blamed for this, as per the claim of many environmentalists, the question arises as to whether governments are willing or even able to control what and how much people buy.

Liberal Democracy Necessitates an Acceptance of Suboptimal Decision Making

Even if regulation is liberally applied in matters of environmental security, there are still certain fundamental individual liberties that we have now come to accept as beyond the reach of regulation. Regulating birth decisions, for example, would have been the single most potent regulatory mechanism for the ardent neo-Malthusian in mitigating resource depletion and environmental harm, but is no longer plausible as a policy choice. China regulated population through denial of any services to families with more than one child, but this too has drawn rebuke from human rights activists. Gone are the days when scholars such as Garrett Hardin (1974) were proposing "Life Boat Ethics", that advocated apathy towards the poor and the elderly or condoned a demise of populations to sustain "spaceship earth". Environmentalism has been more universally humanized, but it has also led to a conundrum of how best to address our fundamental resource constraints. Even ardent proponents of population control have mellowed their conversations on the matter considering the enormous ethical implications of such rash rhetoric. In addition to ethical considerations, harsh regulatory restrictions can have a negative impact on societal harmony.

The economist and philosopher Amartya Sen recognized the challenge of reconciling efficiency and 'optimal' societal behaviour with liberalism several decades ago in his famous essay "The Impossibility of a Paretian Liberal" (Sen, 1970). Sen was concerned with human propensity for conflict when certain inalienable values collide within a liberal system that may also be trying to achieve 'Pareto' optimality. Named after the nineteenth-century Italian economist Vilfredo Pareto, this move towards optimality could be theoretically achieved when a movement from one allocation to another can make at least one individual better off without making any other individual worse off. Sen showed that when we define certain unrestricted domains of human behaviour, such as decisions on having children or what we wear or eat, then we cannot aspire towards having an optimal society. Kenneth Arrow (1950) arrived at a similar insight with regard to voting behaviour in his famous 'impossibility theorem', that suggested that voting systems are not capable of converting the ranked preferences of individuals into a community-wide ranking of societal preferences. Our approach to consumption and the environment must grapple with this fundamental challenge and thus a multifaceted approach with incentive-driven regulations, technological innovation, and literacy-based behavioural change is essential, which calls for exceptional levels of leadership.

Leadership by corporations to implement sustainable practices in the production of goods and services can be an effective way of balancing consumption with ecological protection. As mentioned previously, the type of leadership required here is not individualistic, but dispersed throughout the economic ecosystem. Leadership in this collective sense would require a systems approach and the collaboration between public and private sectors. Innovation, efficiency, and development of human resources can form the operational aspects of leadership that strives to balance economic growth with environmental responsibility.

Conclusion

The treasure impulse that has been at the heart of human development for centuries should no longer be limited to a base desire to plunder the earth's resources. Rather a more responsible channelling of this impulse can encourage extraction practices of minerals that minimize environmental harm, reduce wastage, and facilitate green sources of energy generation. Innovation is the key that leads to the conceptualization of marketable goods and services and the creation of new livelihood opportunities.

The evidence gathered in this chapter shows that while environmentalists started from much more uncompromising positions on societal norms, they are moving towards pragmatic partnerships that recognize the value of 'constructive consumption'. They have perhaps come to the realization that societal choice and the yearning for some measure of material well-being cannot be stifled. Furthermore, incentive-driven development paths necessitate some measure of consumerism around luxury goods in developed countries. We can educate and regulate but must always be cautious about totalitarianism, for that may stifle our ultimate salvation out of the environmental crisis—the capacity to innovate. Collaborative corporate leadership from the private sector can find common ground with the public sector in moving society towards a more constructive and nuanced view of consumerism and consumption. As a locus of analysis, consumption of myriad products and services provides an essential link between economic development and environmental impact. Yet a polarized view that considers consumption as only a problem of ecological decadence needs to be avoided. Instead, leadership that considers responsible consumption of goods and services as a mechanism by which we can balance the development needs of the indigent, consumer choice, and corporate innovation. There are two aspects of this leadership trajectory. First, corporate leaders need to consider their own internal supply chains and how consumption of goods and services impacts their sustainability performance. This arena has already been covered through existing procurement policy reform across industries. However, more consequentially for society at large, business leaders need to consider the external dimension of how their products impact consumption patterns in the general public. In both of these trajectories, a common metric of success can be the human development outcomes of leadership decisions, which can be encompassed by the new United Nations Sustainable Development Goals (UNSDG Secretariat, 2015). Thus leadership in the current nexus of corporate engagement necessitates internal and external engagement from the corporate developers as well as lateral engagement from the development enterprise. Corporations cannot be development agencies, but they are inevitably agents of development (or lack thereof). Collective responsibility between the public and private sector on furthering such a leadership agenda is likely to be most fruitful in achieving longer-term goals of CSR and its ultimate sustainability targets.

References

2014 sustainability report. 3M. Retrieved from: http://multimedia.3m.com/mws/media/1029600O/3m-2014-sustainability-report.pdf

Alderfer, C. (1969). An empirical test of a new theory of human needs. *Organizational Behavior and Human Performance, 4*(2), 142–175.

Allen, D., & Berg, C. (2014). *The sharing economy: How over-regulation can destroy an economic revolution.* The Institute of Public Affairs. Retrieved from: https://ipa.org.au/portal/uploads/Sharing_Economy_December_2014.pdf

Ariely, D. (2008). *Predictably irrational: The hidden forces that shape our decisions.* New York, NY: HarperCollins.

Arrow, K. (1950). A difficulty in the concept of social welfare. *Journal of Political Economy, 58*(4), 328–346.

Badshah, S. (2012). Historical study of leadership theories. *Journal of Strategic Human Resource Management, 1*(1), 49–59.

Becker, G., & Murphy, K. (1988). A theory of rational addiction. *Journal of Political Economy, 96*(4), 675–700.

Brereton, F., Clinch, F., & Ferreira, S. (2008). Happiness, geography and the environment. *Ecological Economics, 65*(2), 386–396.

Brickman, P., & Campbell, D. (1971). Hedonic relativism and planning the good society. In M. H. Appley (Ed.), *Adaptation-level theory: A Symposium* (pp. 287–302). New York, NY: Academic Press.

Castillo, G. (2005). Domesticating the cold war: Household consumption as propaganda in Marshall plan Germany. *Journal of Contemporary History, 40*(2), 261–288.

Community Trade. (2016). *The body shop.* Retrieved from: http://www.thebodyshop.com.au/our-commitment.aspx#.Vud_xXrLJA4

Costa, A. K. (Summer 2015). Alignment is not a luxury. *Stanford Social Innovation Review, 13,* 55–56.

Dauvergne, P. (2008). *The shadows of consumption.* Cambridge, MA: MIT Press.

De Grazia, V. (2006). *Irresistible empire, America's advance through twentieth-century Europe.* Cambridge, MA: The Belknap Press of Harvard University Press.

Dervojeda, K., Verzijl, D., Nagtegaal, F., Lengton, M., Rouwmaat, E., Monfardini, E., & Frideres, L. (2013). *The sharing economy: Accessibility based business models for peer-to-peer markets.* Business Innovation Observatory, European Commission, Case Study 12. Retrieved from: http://ec.europa.eu/DocsRoom/documents/13413/attachments/2/translations/en/renditions/native

Dunn, E., Aknin, L., & Norton, M. (2008). Spending money on others promotes happiness. *Science, 319*(5870), 1687–1688.

Friedman, T. (2000). *The Lexus and the olive tree.* New York, NY: Picador.

Gintis, H., Bowles, S., Boyd, R., & Fehr, E. (Eds.) (2005). *Moral sentiments and material interests: The foundations of cooperation in economic life.* Cambridge, MA: MIT Press.

Goodwin, T. (2015). The battle is for consumer interface. *Techcrunch.* Retrieved from: http://techcrunch.com/2015/03/03/in-the-age-of-disintermediation-the-battle-is-all-for-the-customer-interface/

Hardin, G. (1974). Lifeboat ethics: The case against helping the poor. *Psychology Today.* Retrieved from: http://www.garretthardinsociety.org/articles/art_lifeboat_ethics_case_against_helping_poor.html

Harford, T. (2008). *The logic of life: The rational economics of an irrational world.* New York, NY: Random House.

Hauser, M. (2006). *Moral minds: How nature designed our universal sense of right and wrong.* New York, NY: Ecco.

Henriques, S., & Kander, A. (2010). The modest environmental relief resulting from the transition to a service economy. *Ecological Economics, 70*(2), 271–282.

Horowitz, D. (2005). *Anxieties of affluence: Critiques of American consumer culture, 1939–1979.* Boston, MA: University of Massachusetts Press.

Kahneman, D., Krueger, A., Schkade, D., Schwarz, N., & Stone, A. (2006). Would you be happier if you were richer? A focusing illusion. *Science, 312*(5782), 1908–1910.

Keane, J., & Willem te Velde, D. (2008). *The role of textile and clothing industries in growth and development strategies.* Investment and Growth Programme, Overseas Development Institute. Retrieved from: https://www.odi.org/sites/odi.org.uk/files/odi-assets/publications-opinion-files/3361.pdf

Lemonick, M., & Park, A. (2007). The science of addiction. *Time, 170*(3), 42–43.

Lubin, D., & Esty, D. (2010). The sustainability imperative. *Harvard Business Review, 88*(2), 42–50.

Lyubomirsky, S. (2007). *The how of happiness: A new approach to getting the life you want.* New York, NY: Penguin Press.

Miller, D. (2001). The poverty of morality. *Journal of Consumer Culture, 1*(2), 255–243.

Princen, T. (2005). *The logic of sufficiency.* Cambridge, MA: MIT Press.

Princen, T. (2010). *Treading softly: Paths to ecological order.* Cambridge, MA: MIT Press.

Raelin, J. (2015). Rethinking leadership. *MIT Sloan Management Review, 56*(4), 95–96.

Riesman, D. (1961). *Abundance for what? And other essays.* New York, NY: Doubleday.

Russell, B. (1930). *The conquest of happiness.* London, UK: Allen & Unwin.

Sacks, D. (2011). *The sharing economy.* FastCompany. Retrieved from: http://www.fastcompany.com/1747551/sharing-economy

Satoyama Initiative. (2010). *The international partnership for the Satoyama Initiative.* Retrieved from: http://satoyama-initiative.org/wp/wp-content/uploads/2011/09/satoyama_leaflet_web_en_final.pdf

Sen, A. (1970). The impossibility of a Paretian Liberal. *Journal of Political Economy, 78*(1), 152–157.

Schor, J. (1999). *The overspent American: Why we want what we don't need.* New York, NY: Harper Perennial.

PricewaterhouseCoopers. (2014). *The sharing economy—sizing the revenue opportunity.* Retrieved from: http://www.pwc.co.uk/issues/megatrends/collisions/sharingeconomy/the-sharing-economy-sizing-the-revenue-opportunity.html

Shermer, M. (2007). *The mind of the market: Compassionate apes, competitive humans, and other tales from evolutionary economics.* New York, NY: Holt Paperbacks.

Szasz, A. (2007). *Shopping our way to safety: How we changed from protecting the environment to protecting ourselves.* Minneapolis, MN: University of Minnesota Press.

Twitchell, J. (1999). *Lead us into temptation: The triumph of American materialism.* New York, NY: Columbia University Press.

Unilever. (2014). *Unilever sustainable living plan.* Retrieved from: https://www.unilever.com/sustainable-living/

United Nations Sustainable Development Goals. (2015). Retrieved from: https://sustainabledevelopment.un.org/

Wang, X., Van Wart, M., & Lebredo, N. (2014). Sustainability leadership in a local government context. *Public Performance & Management Review, 37*(3), 339–364.

Who Gives a Crap. (January 2016). Impact Update. Retrieved from: http://au.whogivesacrap.org/pages/2016-impact-update

Wilde, O. (1891). *Intentions.* London, UK: James R. Osgood, McIlvaine & Co.

United Nations Conference on Trade and Development (UNCTAD). (2012).World Investment Report Retrieved from: http://unctad.org/en/PublicationsLibrary/wir2012_embargoed_en.pdf

Zak, P. (Ed.) (2008). *Moral markets: The critical role of values in the economy.* Princeton, NY: Princeton University Press.

12 The Louis Vuitton Foundation

The Gift of a CSR Leader and Art Lover to the World

Elen Riot

Introduction

In the wake of the opening of the Louis Vuitton Foundation, on October 26, 2014, Jean-Paul Claverie, one of the curators, declared this was "the triumph of utopia" and "talent, skills and innovation" (Press Kit, October 17, 2014), echoing Bernard Arnault, CEO of the LVMH group, who declared the Parisian foundation to be the realization of "the dream of an art collector". Frank Gehry, the star architect, hoped this would do for Paris what his Guggenheim had done for Bilbao. He also insisted on the transformative nature of the project: He firmly believed the place would be the origin of a new era for all kinds of creations in relation to both nature and high modernity. Yet inside the foundation, the first exhibition showed art pieces that shared the same spleen and apocalyptic inspiration.

In the official communication of LVMH, the foundation was presented as a corporate social responsibility (CSR) gesture and an act of philanthropy in favour of both the artists and contemporary art lovers. The media, for the most part, were much more interested in socialites' and celebrities' display of lavish taste and fashion. Despite this silence, questions may be raised as to the intention behind this public display. Was the foundation a gift from a business leader or a communication strategy by a global fashion group? Was it a major step in the direction of a more sustainable dimension of luxury items or just a fashionable event where CSR held only a marginal dimension—a green shade as a defense against voices that may oppose an extravagantly lavish showcase?

More specifically, it is worth questioning the meaning of the foundation and the values of the LVMH group—one constituted as a personal empire by Bernard Arnault. The luxury tycoon made his fame as a skilled financial raider, building a portfolio of brands in the luxury business. Having built a reputation in the luxury business and then as an art collector, now he seemed to be intent to build yet a new reputation in committing to CSR values and principles. This spectacular transformation led to people taking positions for or against the foundation in relation to their opinions on the luxury business, LVMH as a luxury empire, and Bernard Arnault as a person. Little was said about the potential for transformation offered by CSR and art, and the new vision presented at this occasion, as a strategic and political stand.

Accordingly, in this chapter, I focus on this last question. I describe and interpret the inauguration of the Louis Vuitton Foundation as the project of Bernard Arnault, whose ambition is to act as a CSR leader setting principles for the future, now that he is in a position of power. I begin by examining what a CSR leader stands for today and by looking at the role of CSR in such specific industries as the fashion and luxury business. I insist on the central role of art to bridge the gap between realms of values that may have been quite separate in the past. Art is related to creation and invention; therefore, it opens new horizons with no pre-existing norms and standards, whereas CSR might be, on the contrary, referred to as standards in relation to moral values that might not naturally alloy with the norms in the luxury and fashion world.

I argue that, whatever the position one adopts regarding the Louis Vuitton Foundation, its inauguration offers a highly visible situation where one figure of the contemporary CSR leader is presented. I use critical discourse analysis to categorize the various positions as to the legitimacy of this figure and, in complement to the media image, I provide direct information gathered via participant observation during a visit to the Louis Vuitton Foundation.

Based on this material and analyses, I conclude that the role of contemporary art to create a common ground between luxury and fashion activities and CSR is quite ambivalent. Looking at the foundation, the art collection, and the inauguration as major displays of power by a business elite, there is no knowing whether Bernard Arnault, as a business leader, is fulfilling his life mission or if this is all perfunctory—just for show. This is what my final interpretation of what I saw in the foundation, in complement to the media, would like to come to terms with, because I believe this ambivalence reflects on the audience of the Louis Vuitton Foundation, whereas it could be empowering us by providing new representations based on a deep understanding of our present challenge when dealing with the future of the planet.

Part I. Can You Be a Leader in Luxury, Art, and CSR? The Debate Behind the Louis Vuitton Foundation

The opening of the Louis Vuitton Foundation brings into sharp relief a combination of ideas, values, and images. To date, the luxury business and CSR may have seemed worlds apart, because of their different realms of values: one of hedonism and one of thrift and scarcity. I am therefore prompted to examine why a leader in the luxury business would want to become representative of the CSR movement and why, as Bernard Arnault, he would chose an art foundation to do so.

I first describe the tradition of leaders gaining legitimacy by exposing their taste posing as 'arbiter elegantiae', using both luxury and art as assets for one's public image. I then describe an alternative tradition—one that corresponds to CSR and may be traced back to antique virtues such as frugality. Finally, I identify why, in our age, an influential leader would want to be transformative and explore common ground between these two traditions, using culture and education as an alternative to mass consumption and using art as a way to invent new representations.

Leaders, Art, and Luxury

The aristocratic tradition of powerful patrons of arts and crafts is still vivid in a post-industrial age where many famous leaders and large businesses sponsor art, especially via art foundations. In doing so, they do more than just launch a new venture; they explicitly act as founders in a long-term vision.

It may be helpful to understand how the positive transformation of a leader's image via artists' talent operates by referring to past occurrences. Leaders in power traditionally like to associate their vision with that of leading creators and artists (Haskell, 1980; Wyszonirski & Clubb, 1989). Often, artists would associate their picture and that of their family to ancient gods, heroes, or allegories of virtue. It also involved emblems (heraldic or symbolic) as easily recognizable images of a dynasty or an empire. For instance, Baxandall (1985) describes merchants' expectations as patrons of the arts when, in the Quattrocento, they also became sponsors of the art such as religious orders and royal courts. Their culture and tastes were reflected in new forms of art, different from traditional religious commands (Bertrand-Dorléac, 1992). Just as the influence of patrons can be felt on the nature of art, in the dominant representations of a period of time, an artistic culture is a source of transformation for powerful elites, and it also involves science and techniques. For instance, rich merchants liked paintings with a perspective because they pictured proportions and measurements they used in their everyday deals. Both Leonardo and Machiavelli (Boucheron, 2012) devised new plans and changed dominant representations of power in Europe. They were dealing with representations of the world involving nature (now the environment) and power (now polity and society).

In the industrial age, according to DiMaggio (1988), reformists views (such as John Dewey's in the 1900s) progressed when major industrialists such as Guggenheim and Carnegie sponsored major institutions such as the New York Public Library, the Metropolitan Museum of Art, or the Museum of Modern Art in an effort to make public education and major art more accessible to all members of society. Although Arian (1988) believes this promise failed for lack of public and private commitment to make art part of every man's culture, it seems that at least in the elite world, the alliance between art and luxury proved influential to this day.

In this chapter, the focus is on the relationship between art, CSR, and a specific kind of business leader: one who rules over luxury and fashion, the kind of luxury and fashion corresponding to the upscale part of mass consumption—for instance, branded accessories such as handbags, perfume, and clothes (Clifton & Simmons, 2012).

CEOs (such as Bernard Arnault or François Pinault) coming to power after decades of family business transmission corresponded to a change in the scale of the luxury world. For about 40 years now, its global expansion and its democratization (Kapferer & Bastien, 2009a) was supported by massive financial investments and churned by high returns. To achieve its performance targets, so far, the luxury business recipe has been balancing the industrialization needed for mass production to meet the demand and a great deal of communication expenses to convey the idea of an 'abundant rarity' (Kapferer & Bastien, 2009b). Despite its major hits and the appeal of star brands, such projects were always risky and adventurous because of the versatility of the fashion world (Auguste & Gusatz, 2013; Cavender & Kincade, 2014; Chatriot, 2007). Not strictly business oriented, but also rooted in traditions and cultural identity (Hartner, 2001), the global success of major European fashion brands was often based on designers' long-term collaborations with famous artists such as the American Stephen Sprouse and the Japanese Takashi Murakami (Riot, Chamarret, & Rigaud, 2013). According to some, the collaboration of major fashion designers and contemporary artists was no longer the privilege of the elite, but a key component of the globalization and democratization of luxury fashion (Joy, Wang, Chan, Sherry, & Cui, 2014). It is present indifferently in boutiques, concepts stores, museums, palaces, and places of interest; every place where being visible is a source of influence.

Although the luxury market has been growing considerably in the past 30 years, its popularity does not necessarily make it legitimate in such areas as CSR. More specifically, many customers may combine different consumption patterns and dissociate sustainability (everyday habits) and pleasure (luxury and fashion). When luxury was associated with small businesses and craftsmen, it was associated with quality, and CSR standards were not so central. Now that publicly traded conglomerates managing global value chains dominate the luxury world, CSR norms are much more important. Not only are all corporations and multinationals compelled to abide by CSR standards but (Bendell, 2004; Corey & Kearins, 2002; Fombrun, 1996) also some prominent actors such as Vivienne Westwood have popularized the association of luxury fashion and ecology. By educating customers, such actors have transformed the world of fashion and luxury.

Frugality as the Virtue of a CSR Leader

Recently, authors associated luxury with a form of hedonism in relation to egotism (Lipovetsky & Serroy, 2013) or a form of nihilist destructivity; one author pioneered the figure of the romantic artist (Bataille, 1962, 1985).[1] They argue that the importance of luxury and the appeal of excessive consumption is the sign of what was called, in history, decadent times. However, contrary to Bataille's provocative praise of decadence, such accusations often involve a moral stand and a desire for reform. Just as members of the business elite supported CSR, reformatory positions also emerged in society as pioneered by dominant actors, who also enjoyed luxury and art. This may be yet another way to differentiate from the average amateur of luxury, who is content with the good feelings. Yet this may also reflect the ambivalence of social feelings towards rules on proper consumption and excess. In any case, this shows the weight of implicit rules and norms for both luxury and CSR.

For instance, in Ancient Rome, Petronius, arbiter elegantiae and a close friend of Nero's,[2] opposed the lavish spending of the 'nouveau riche', and old patrons restrained offerings in his satires, *Satyricon*. It is interesting to observe that although Tacitus despises Petronius as a figure of decadence, as an author, he is a good analyst of the complex limit between the good and the bad rich and between the proper and the improper gift. The picture of the man, by Tacitus, illustrates the evolution of a political regime and its elite where being an expert in sophisticated pleasures (the emperor's advisor) becomes a much better source of influence than exerting a traditional form of power (in that case, just being a provincial governor).

Tacitus describes his contemporaries in reference to Republican figures such as Cato and values such as the ones exposed in Aristotle's *Nicomachean Ethics* (Barnes, 1984), frugality and a form of austerity are presented as an ideal of morality and good taste—a sum of values that should be revived against the decadence of the empire. This advice seemed to have been quite popular among reformist elites, and we can find a clear analogy with leaders presently advocating for CSR.

Leaders of large multinationals have a considerable influence on the future of the planet, and as such, many of them support CSR norms and standards (Waddock, 2008). Their commitment to CSR may be directly related to the core activities of their businesses and therefore an essential component of their strategies, or it may be more marginal.

Companies that have been representative of CSR have been proactive in this field by creating profitable business ventures. For example, Patagonia (Dickson & Chang, 2015; Husted & Allen, 2007), Ben & Jerry's, and the Body Shop (Mack & Pless, 2006) proved successful ventures. In an age where business transparency had become a concern for many customers (Appadurai, 1988; Douglas and Isherwood, 1979), they offered customers specific information on the sourcing of their products and the industrial value chain (Gartner, 2010). The role of a leader, often the entrepreneur at the origin of the venture, was important in impersonating these choices (Maak & Pless, 2006; Pless, Maak, & Waldman, 2012) and defining a sustainable way with a passionate voice (Quinn & Dalton, 2009). One of the essential dimensions of CSR is its educational capacity. Art may be a way to communicate about CSR (Hodgkinson, 1991) because of a "catch 22 of CSR" (Morsing, Schultz, & Nielsen, 2008), especially in the luxury business (Janssen, Vanhamme, Lindgreen, & Lefebvre, 2014). Despite its legitimacy, CSR is lacking in popularity among customers. First, CSR standards depend on specificities of each value chain (Sweeney & Coughland, 2008). Second, various stakeholders may value different CSR priorities (Morsing, 2006). Most customers may be shocked by scandals related to unsustainable practices, but they seem to be taking for granted firms' commitment to CSR. It seems quite necessary that people take charge and find representations that make it easier to understand CSR inside customer culture; otherwise, it may remain a dead letter. This represents an interesting challenge for a transformative leadership.

A Leader and His Vision: Art Bringing Luxury and CSR Together

Quite different from businesses concerned with CSR in their core business (mass-market products, energy, transport, and waste), luxury and fashion industries may be more identified with pleasure and hedonism, sometimes involving lavish spending and waste. This is precisely why they are so popular and prestigious. What CSR may lack in popularity, luxury may lack in legitimacy on strategic issues about climate change or social inequalities. Yet because the luxury and fashion industry now has a global reach (Kapferer & Bastien, 2009a), its leaders inevitably come into direct contact with CSR pioneers—a confrontation that may turn out to be challenging if their goods are perceived unethical and immoral. This may have to do more with image than with actual modes of production. It seems the traditional luxury business has been responsive and has adapted its offer to CSR norms and standards. However, controlling the chains of production and complying with technical standards and social regulation may not be enough. For instance, it may put forward crafts and traditions, as some were concerned that image was promoted at the expense of production. In France, the Comité Colbert is a cooperative supported by the ministry of industry and large luxury groups to deal with such issues. Nevertheless, luxury leaders may be expected to take a more personal stand in terms of values.

If, consistent with the position of many business groups and NGOs, the people at the head of large corporations acknowledge a public responsibility, they are required to take a stand in terms of values. Art may not be involved if the values and representations are clearly set. Such is the case in the mission of public managers in the 1960s: "The executive becomes a statesman as he makes the transition from administrative management to institutional leadership" (Selznick, 1957, p. 39) by being "an expert in the promotion and protection of values" (Ibidem, 42). This posture is easy to assume if performance and values are in alignment (Goleman, Boyatzis, &

McKee, 2002; Nahavandi, 2009). For instance, in the commodity industry, CSR may lower risks of exposure for the company by introducing a more inclusive stakeholder approach (Angus-Leppan, Metcalf, & Benn, 2010).

Yet this position can be weaker if the business environment is unstable, as is often the case in our age, and if the core business of the firm is not related to commodities but to fashion. In that case, there might be a discrepancy between the role of the manager and his or her stand as responsible leader. For instance, CSR may lower financial profits. If it deflates the expected returns on capital, investors will look for compensation. They will at least want an explanation, a narrative (Cooren & Fairhust, 2003; Gartner, 2010). In that case, combining distinct commitments may involve a form of transformative leadership, so as to be able to involve various stakeholders (Bryman, 2011; De Pree, 2011; Gardner, 1993). In that case, adopting an artist-leader position (Adler, 2006; Bolman & Deal, 2011; Hatch, Kostera, & Kosminski, 2009; Woodward & Funk, 2010) may prove to be transformative.

For lack of a pre-existing doctrine about how luxury and CSR worlds could find a common ground, art may act as a force of transformation (Bathurst, Williams, & Rodda, 2007) for both the luxury industry and its leaders. New representations may open everyone's mind and avoid the capture of the issue by opportunistic apostles. The luxury and fashion business is influential in terms of shared representations, and, therefore, its appropriation of CSR is significant and representative of our age. In particular, if leaders can find a new form of legitimacy and a new approach to leadership, it may be transformative. Working with grassroots associations and artists involves a new way of doing business. It means taking risks in allowing major experimentations (Bathurst, Jackson, & Statler, 2010).

In that regard, because an aesthetic approach to the world introduces a new perspective to business and organization, art may favour a transformative approach to leadership (Bathurst, 2007). It brings new dimensions to pre-existing images, possibly more presence, and closer contact to everyday practices (Bathurst & Monin, 2010), as well as possibly a common ground for a more collective approach to leadership (Monin & Bathurst, 2008). For major leaders, especially those at the head of a family empire who have been in the public eye for a generation, it may be a source of rejuvenation and sustainable influence. It may represent a more lasting contribution than year-on-year profit margins for shareholders (Ladkin & Taylor, 2010). Their image may contribute to the prestige of the group and even legitimate bold choices and strategic turns.

When working with designers and artists, as well as with managers and engineers, different visions may emerge and new forms of leadership can be experimented because major artists also have the reputation of being capable of dealing with creative tensions (Csikszentmihalyi, 2004). That would provide an answer to those who believe no self-respecting artist should agree to collaborate with business leaders as stewards and decorators of their new green standing. They may also have an interest in committing with major business groups to introduce stakeholder governance with CSR views. It can be said that they are entrepreneurs in the field of art. Inspired by Bourdieu's analysis of strategic actors, Grenfell and Hardy (2007) describe the art world as a strategic action field where artists can make alliances with dominant actors in other fields to become leaders in the art; they can trade their reputational capital as owners of social and financial capital may want to invest in art to strengthen their positions. One famous case is the collaboration of artists, members of the Young British Artists, with Charles Saatchi, a media mogul (Grenfell & Hardy, 2003). Damian Hirst, Jeff Koons, Takashi Murakami, and other popular artists claimed they were able to trade up their own ideas and talent via branding. With this relation with their audience being central in their creation, as part of a 'relational aesthetics' they could achieve a direct reach with their audience (Bourriaud, 2009). Because Robert Smithson, Giuseppe Penone, and Joseph Beuys imagined alternative views of society and nature (via land art, for instance) (Tufnell, 2006), artists have been publicly dealing with similar issues as CSR. So the opening of the Louis Vuitton Foundation offers an occasion to see how luxury, CSR, and art can help come up with strategic ideas and meaningful representations to understand the world and to take proper action.

Part II. Methodology and Data

The methodology followed to investigate the role of a CSR leader, patron of the arts, is that of a single case study (Burawoy, 1998). It allows us to test the three different views of such a figure in the present state of society and to take a stand as to its contribution as it is, in line with "engaged scholarship" (Flyvbjerg, 2001). My case study does not consist of just covering a key event in terms of leaderships, CSR, and arts; I selected the opening ceremony of the Louis Vuitton Foundation because I believe it is presented in the media as a symbol of power in the present age.

Accordingly, I investigate this case by confronting direct and indirect sources of information. I use critical discourse analysis (CDA) to investigate the dominant representations in a field of power (Fairclough, 2001), where CSR and arts are an object of knowledge and discourse (Fairclough, 2003).

My data comes from three sources of information, two are direct, the other indirect. My first data is a press review of the Louis Vuitton opening day, on October 20, 2014, following two distinct codings: one related to the Louis Vuitton Foundation and the other Bernard Arnault.

The opening of the Louis Vuitton Foundation was an important media event.

Foundation Vuitton, 257 papers
(October 17, 2014 to December 17, 2015)

The importance of the media coverage of this event was tested by conducting two other data collections in relation to the Louis Vuitton Foundation and Bernard Arnault. One sample in the previous year when the foundation was still in construction shows the project was gathering little attention because the LVMH communication team did not promote it:

Foundation Louis Vuitton, 36 papers
(November 20, 2013 to November 20, 2014)

Another sample about Bernard Arnault, as a leader, five years in succession, reveals that he is the target of considerable media attention and that the foundation seems to be closely associated with him:

Bernard Arnault, 13 157 papers
(November 20, 2009 to November 20, 2014)

However, during the previous period, the peaks of media attention were related to the evolution of the stock price of his company and his personal fortune in the international rankings, as well as with a series of controversies. In particular, Bernard Arnault was accused of making financial choices that were at the limit of legality (dissimulated acquisition of stocks in luxury companies and attempts at tax evasion). Therefore, the media attention about the opening of the Louis Vuitton Foundation, predominantly laudatory, stands, in my view, in sharp contrast with the previous reports. This points to an increase in the reputational capital of the leader of the LVMH group, Bernard Arnault.

The data was coded according to the three issues investigated: the role of the leader, CSR, and art. This data once coded was compared with the other source of indirect information: the external communication of the Louis Vuitton Foundation as well as that of the LVMH group (27 documents in total). Although the CSR theme corresponds to very few occurrences in the media, in the official communication of the LVMH group, it is much more important. This second discrepancy is quite relevant, but it tells very little about the actual importance of CSR in the Louis Vuitton Foundation. As we have seen, CSR is not necessarily easy to popularize, whereas the celebrity culture is under the spotlight of the media.

This is why this archival data was later triangulated with a direct source of information: in this case, my main data consists of field notes taken during a participant observation that the author conducted, when visiting the Louis Vuitton Foundation on February 20, 2015. A half day was spent waiting in line outside the building and then visiting the foundation taking notes on the setting and the interactions on site.

This visit was undertaken as a test of the previously collected data. As pointed out by Fairclough (2013), media groups can be both allies and adversaries in the quest for the acquisition of power and among large multinational companies. In the French context, the business fields interfere, so conglomerates also own dominant players in the media, with LVMH being one of them with major publications such as *Les Echos*, *Le Parisien* and *l'Opinion*.[3] Additionally, key players have shared vested interests in other companies as shareholders and board members (Mayer & Whittington, 1999). Consequently, I felt it was necessary to complement indirect information (the data collected in the media about the opening of the foundation) by a direct experience of the place and its project in the Louis Vuitton Foundation. In that attempt based on perceptions and feelings (Riot & Bazin, 2013), methods such as semiotics (Pink, 2003; Rose, 2012) proved essential, so as to go beyond discourses and dominant opinions and interpret the role of the Louis Vuitton Foundation as a symbol of leadership based on personal impressions and direct experience.

Part III. Context of the Louis Vuitton Foundation

The Louis Vuitton Foundation is Bernard Arnault's project as the CEO of LVMH, a luxury empire he built in 40 years. It is interesting to show how this man became legitimate in the luxury world and then in the art world to understand what the foundation represents. Finally, it is enlightening to know that LVMH has been proactive in introducing CSR policies in all its activities.

Bernard Arnault as an Influential CEO in the Luxury World

One may say that if the Louis Vuitton Foundation is so much under the media spotlight, it is because it is a project that only a very influential man could orchestrate. The luxury market is a very dynamic one. It was on target to reach €223 billion in 2014. According to Euromonitor International (2014), the luxury market has gone up 20 per cent since 2008 and should grow 34 per cent by 2018. As a leader in the field, LVMH (Moët Hennessy Louis Vuitton) is the world's top luxury products group, with recorded revenue of €30.6 billion in 2014—an increase of 6 per cent over the previous year. Organic revenue growth was 5 per cent in that period.

The LVMH group owns a portfolio of more than 50 brands, 60 subsidiaries, 83,000 employees, and 17,000 stores.

Louis Vuitton is the star brand of the group. It is the world's most valuable brand in the luxury category in "BrandZ Top 10 Luxury Brands" ranking. In 2014, Louis Vuitton had a brand value of $25.873 billion, a 14 per cent growth from 2013. 'Louis Vuitton', nicknamed the "McDonald's of the luxury industry", has an average profit of about 40 to 45 per cent; sales were up 16 per cent in the first quarter of 2015.

Bernard Arnault is an important figure in the business world. In 2007, he was listed among *Time* magazine's "100 Most Influential People in the

World". *Forbes* ranked him fourth in global fortune in 2011. His personal salary in 2013 passed 35 million euros (it had reached more than 50 in the previous years), and his personal fortune is 21 billion dollars. In the elite world where Bernard Arnault operates, it is not uncommon to own private art collections and to build foundations.

Bernard Arnault as a Major Patron of the Arts

Bernard Arnault has shown great strategic skills in building his empire, and he has always avoided being in the media eye. This may explain why he chose to name the art foundation he decided to build 'Louis Vuitton', in the name of the star brand of his firm.

Louis Vuitton was an entrepreneur, from wrapping to cloth bags, with the logo to avoid counterfeiting (made gold for his canvas bags) (Bonvicini, 2004; Léonforté, 2010; Pasols, 2005), on cars (Bellu, 2007), in ships (Chevalier & Troublé, 2008), and in architecture Castets et al., 2009). Following the hiring of Marc Jacobs in 1997 (Giblin, 2012), as Loïc Prigent's (2007) video documentary illustrates, the company also became very fond of contemporary art. Marc Jacobs contributed to changing the image of Louis Vuitton as a brand by using contemporary art (Gasparina, 2006, 2009) in relation to major public art institutions such as le Louvre, Orsay, Versailles (Castets, Igarashi, Gasparina, & Hermange, 2009; Dagen & Gasparina, 2010), and many places of interest in the world (Mendes and Rees-Roberts, 2015).

Following fruitful collaborations in the 1980s with artists such as Sol LeWitt, César, and Olivier Debré (Mendes & de la Haye, 1999), Louis Vuitton initiated a stimulating dialogue between the visual arts and the brand's own creativity (White & Griffith, 2000). Bob Wilson, Olafur Eliasson, and Ugo Rondinone decorated Christmas display windows, whereas Marc Jacobs asked Stephen Sprouse, Takashi Murakami, Richard Prince, and Yayoi Kusama to work directly on creations for Louis Vuitton (Golbin, 2012). The result was a fresh and vibrant new vision of Louis Vuitton. (*Website Louis Vuitton Foundation*, retrieved July 20, 2016). Another reason why Bernard Arnault would want to promote his brand, Louis Vuitton, is to defend it against a commoditization threat, because it is the most popular brand in the world. A few artists mocked this brand as the emblem of fashionistas, celebrity culture, and bad taste. Such art critiques by Alberto Sorbelli (in the 2007 Venice Biennale), Tom Sachs, Dodie Rosenkrans, Kidult (against Steven Sprouse), and the Darfurnica initiative (Riot et al., 2013) may have nothing to do with CSR, and socio-art is much less popular than famous creations by popular artists. Besides, for years, Bernard Arnault had been commissioning the most famous curators and art dealers to constitute a contemporary art collection. As a collector, he favours works by Pablo Picasso, Alberto Giacometti, Andy Warhol, and Yves Klein. At one point, his rivalry with the head of Kering (ex-PPR), François Pinault, in the art market, attracted a great deal of interest in the media because it was a side of their business feud involving winning bids to complement their brand portfolios. As a major collector of famous artists, Arnault is an important sponsor of blockbuster art shows in major art institutions as well as an important buyer of living artists in major art shows. He was the first non-American collector to receive the David Rockefeller prize at the MoMa in New York on March 2015—a tribute to a major patron of the arts. The strength of this reputational capital in the field of contemporary art makes it possible to envision a bright future for the Louis Vuitton Foundation. More important may be that it makes it difficult to accuse him of using art just for business. However, because Bernard Arnault is above all a manager and relies on a team of experts to constitute his collection, he may not be in a position to come up with a new perspective for business in society, including art and CSR.

LVMH: A Proactive Multinational in Terms of CSR

Because of the increasing control of the group over all of its subsidiaries' value chains, LVMH is in a position to comply with the CSR audit standards. Yet in the meantime, luxury conglomerates face more and more challenges as they control more and more activities. This explains why Bernard Arnault, as a leader, is in the process of building reputational capital as a sponsor of CSR values.

CSR is perceived by customers in stores, where they have direct access to the products and where they can find specific information about the process of production if they wish to. LVMH controls its distribution channels. Bernard Arnault applied a method of vertical integration (control over production, distribution and marketing, done in-house), which led to an increase in sales and profits (Marchand, 2001). The revenues of its leading subsidiaries allowed it to grow, especially by building a strong network of retail stores. One of its major assets in this regard is the integration of Sephora (a chain of stores selling beauty and health products) and one of the two major companies of duty-free shops, present in ports and airports.

Despite this control over distribution, distinct issues remain related to the core business of the group: luxury and fashion. LVMH brands depend on global trade, import, export, and tourism. All these activities may be accused of causing climate change. Reports by the Clean Clothes Network NGO mention worsening work conditions in Italy, where they are increasingly aligned with that of Eastern Europe and Asia for suppliers working for LVMH, Chanel, and Kering. LVMH bought Singapore-based Hong Long, one of the world's top-five suppliers and tanneries of crocodile leather, which is an activity perceived as problematic for many NGOs protecting animal rights. Finally, Spar (2006) mentions the problem of the value chain in the international diamond market (an oligopoly with regulation imposed by major groups).

The success of the LVMH group made it a key player in the luxury wars because its growth was based on external growth and the acquisition of famous companies. Bernard Arnault claims his intention is to build a long-lasting business (Arnault, 2000) and to create a luxury empire for a dynasty (Kelan, 2010). His road to success involved controversial methods, however. Some describe him as a cold-blooded, predatory leader using finance to take over the industry (Forestier & Ravai, 1990; Pinçon & Pinçon Charlot, 2010; Ravai, 1997; Routier, 2003; Villette, 2003; Vincent & Monnin, 1990). His nickname, 'the death angel', possibly came at the occasion of the legal case of Gucci against LVMH after Arnault's failed hostile takeover. It was recurrently used during the Hermès and LVMH battle (2010–2014) (Kapferer & Tabatoni, 2011), which was another failed takeover attempt by the family company. In 2012, the media echoed an attempted exile in Belgium to avoid paying taxes on his very significant income. Finally, at the time when Arnault was communicating on his CSR policy in luxury subsidiaries, his shareholder style in dealing with his participation in supermarket chain Carrefour (via its Blue Capital subsidiary) was clearly directed towards pushing for higher financial performance. Consequently, Bernard Arnault's leadership can be described as traditional; his move towards CSR and art is in alignment with a business strategy focused on profitability.

According to its website (retrieved on July 20, 2016) LVMH signed the UN Global Compact in 1999 and then again in 2003; it fills CSR reports annually and communicates on its increasing efforts directed towards sustainability along the value chain of the more than 60 subsidiaries of the group. It is proactive in following the sustainability reporting guidelines (for instance, in shipment and wrapping). It conducts audits on its suppliers. It involves sustainability in its most innovative lines: The bikini line by Dior uses the skills of ethnobotanists in Burkina Faso.

Finally, all luxury corporations such as LVMH, Kering, and Richemont are engaged in a competition to promote their image in a form of impression management. All major luxury groups sponsor specific causes and NGOs, and this is very present in their corporate communication. LVMH focus includes childhood, public health, humanitarian causes (children in Afghanistan), research programs in AIDS, aging and cancer, and the Claude Pompidou Foundation (Alzheimer's). Kering (ex-PPR) supports the UNICEF schools for Africa and via Yves Saint Laurent it sponsors the Metropolitan Opera in an effort to make it accessible to everyone in New York City. Because of the size of the investment and the large media contingent, the opening of the Louis Vuitton Foundation was significant and influential. Its goal was to change the image of the luxury business, LVMH, Louis Vuitton, and Bernard Arnault. According to CSR standards, there might be problematic choices and practices to be transformed, and this appeared to be the promise and the intention contained in all dimensions of the Louis Vuitton project from the day of its construction.

The Louis Vuitton Foundation stands as an official commitment to art, CSR, the city of Paris, and the Louis Vuitton brand on the part of Bernard Arnault and LVMH, according to the communication of the group. It is emblematic of the leadership of both a man and a luxury empire. At this point, it seems important to provide a more detailed description of the foundation.

Part IV. Description: The Opening of the Louis Vuitton Foundation by Bernard Arnault

With a more complete view of Bernard Arnault's figure as a major leader, of his commitment as a patron of the arts, and as a CSR proponent, understanding the project of the Louis Vuitton Foundation becomes easier. This foundation is, as might be expected, an emblem of the power of the LVMH group and a symbol of the success of what Bernard Arnault expects to become a dynastic empire of fashion. The conception of the foundation, the constitution of the art collection, and the organization of the inauguration have been the object of considerable efforts. They are interesting to describe in detail in reference to both artistic prestige and CSR standards.

The Louis Vuitton Foundation

The total cost of the foundation may seem very important (it is reported to have cost much more than the initial €100 million dedicated to the project), yet it should be seen in the context of the size of the luxury industry and the size of the LVMH group. On many occasions, concept stores and headquarters have reached such sums because they are part of a communication strategy.

Looking at the Louis Vuitton Foundation is like looking at the equivalent of a large glass ensemble, with wings or sails spread out. It defies the laws of gravity and has more to do with a Brancusi sculpture than with a building whose function is to shelter social activities. To define the ambition of the building, Bernard Arnault chose to put forward his architect, the American Frank Gehry. He claims they co-conceived the foundation as the symbol of a new vision for the future of Paris and the world.

Gehry is remarkable for his trajectory; just like Bernard Arnault, he claims to be a self-made man with a vision. In the public eye, he stands as a creative leader (Arnell, 1987; Bennis, 2003; Bennis and Bennis, 2009). He first designed his own house in Santa Monica (Los Angeles periphery) using cheap material such as chain link fencing. Then he redesigned industrial wastelands and drew shopping malls in the suburbs. This proved a major hit and led to many prestigious building projects for the architect. Prominent figures in the United States commissioned him to build their private homes or business offices. In the 1990s, Gehry also received public commissions; he specialized in city centres in decay (Bilbao and Brooklyn Atlantic Yards). As part of the Rouse Company in charge of city planning and communities, he worked with realtors and creators to make 'experiments in architecture' (Friedman, 1999; Gehry, 2004). Later, as illustrated in the Louis Vuitton Foundation, his team pioneered 3D technologies.

Gehry presents himself as a humanist, he frequently quotes the Talmud and Michelangelo to describe his buildings as sculptures, and he favours the company of famous artists and thinkers. Today, Frank Gehry is an 86-year-old 'starchitect' who seems to have little patience for his profession and the media in general. This was recently expressed at the occasion of a prize he received when a journalist alluded to his omnipresence:

> For once, Gehry was too tired to be polite. He extended his middle finger. (. . .) "In the world we live in, 98 percent of the buildings built are pure shit", he said. "There's no sense of design, or respect for humanity or for anything. Once in a while, however, a group of people do something special. Very few, but for God's sake, just leave us alone. We are dedicated to our work . . . I work with clients who respect the art of architecture. Therefore, please don't ask questions as stupid as that one.
> (Vanity Fair, September 15, 2014, p. 36, retrieved July 20, 2016)

Happening right before the opening of the Louis Vuitton Foundation, this event caused a stir; it was neither in line with the humanist image Gehry had composed along the years, nor acceptable in a strictly business approach, not to speak of CSR standards about corporate and ethical commitments. However, the message was consistent with many previous declarations made by Gehry regarding the influence of his clients on his work. To him, any project is really shaped by the client, and his relation with them explains why he is more or less inspired and the building more or less original. His inspiration comes from the way in which clients and constraints, as well as his knowledge and his intuition, come together. "On a building, I don't know where I'm going when I start", he said. "If I knew where I was going, I wouldn't go there, that's for sure" (Goldberger, 2015, p. 264). Improvisation is part of the project, as is going beyond the basic norms and standards. It also includes some kind of risk taking and negotiable commitment in the sense that to get what you want, you need to really want it. In the case of the Louis Vuitton Foundation, it is significant that no one (to my knowledge) pointed out how similar the building was to Frank Gehry's past works, although large shows about his work, in the foundation and in the Centre Pompidou-Beaubourg, made that quite obvious. They were all very similar; their common feature being that they were shaped like sculptures of birds and vessels. From what I saw, the building of the foundation was similar to other buildings, except it was located in a Parisian park—a green environment. A glass bird looking like a sculpture was a challenge for builders to create, and a book was dedicated to that construction, paying a tribute to the excellence of Dassault System and Vinci, two French multinationals Bernard Arnault has been involved with for years. On paper, this building corresponds to the fashion prevailing in the global elite world, and its technical skills and engineering relate more to the tight links of major French firms and their CEOs than CSR concerns.

This impression is confirmed by a personal experience of the venue and the facility. The building seems quite far from the ideal set by the CFM (Center for the Future of Museums) in 2016, which set trends for the public experience of art places quite consistent with CSR norms and standards. When referring to these new ideas in terms of innovation, co-working spaces, and openness to community building, the Louis Vuitton Foundation, isolated in the most elegant Parisian park, facing the skyscrapers of La Défense, feels more like entering a very large glass totem—just for looking, no touching.

Although CSR norms have been taken into account, if many environmental problems were solved, it seems they were mostly a consequence of the major challenges set by the shape of the building itself and the glass material chosen for purely aesthetic reasons. It may be pointed out that this is an interesting challenge for architects and engineers to design. Whereas it is, an impressive view to contemplate at a distance, it is not a comfortable place to be in. A whole team of at least 30 attendees was busy inside the building keeping visitors from trespassing or falling from the stairs and the balconies, and keeping the place pristine (marble and white walls are fragile). The unexpected turns, the steep and narrow stairs, the high volumes of balconies with little space to move make circulation difficult; the contrast between dark corners and overexposed rooms make the visit a voyage companions comment on along the way. In my view, as a symbol of the CSR commitment of the head of LVMH, sponsor of the Louis Vuitton Foundation, the Frank Gehry building sends a contradictory message with CSR norms and standards. A good analogy of this inner contradiction at the heart of the Louis Vuitton Foundation would be the use of a corset in fashion today: It is a constraint that designers reintroduce and they insist it can be both fancy and comfortable, spending considerable efforts on its ergonomics. Still, it is by essence an unpractical, superfluous object and an unnecessary artifice.

Often compared with a diamond, a jewel, and a gem, the foundation seems more in line with the luxury and fashion world standards. This general impression is in line with what the art collection represents.

Consistent with CSR, complementary dimensions of the foundation project have been presented as actions supporting a sustainable approach according to its four pillars (Carroll, 1999):

> From the construction site to using the building, the Foundation has worked in a constant high environmental quality approach. The Foundation Louis Vuitton project has adopted an exemplary environmental approach and was chosen as a pilot project for drawing up new HQE® guidelines dedicated to cultural buildings. Since the project's launch, the concern to have a site with a low environmental impact has been placed

at the heart of the approach. Carrying out a number of prior detailed studies on fauna, flora, ground water, noise pollution and accessibility has made it possible to determine, take into account". More specifically, it includes "all of the environmental parameters at each stage of the project: design, construction and use" such as effective waste traceability and reduced energy consumption via HQE® innovation in the choice of materials with a reduced environmental impact and the implementation of a carbon assessment. In the long run, the building will use geothermal energy and filtered rainwater.

(Louis Vuitton Foundation website, retrieved on July 20, 2016)

In parallel to the inauguration, many opportunities were offered to the public to discover the details of the plans. These included multiple shows in the foundation and in Paris museums (Centre Pompidou). They were the occasion to present in detail the choices made by the architect and his client in relation to eco-conception systems and innovativeness in the use of material. As we shall see, artists' works were also part of the whole project with original commands complementing the building and Bernard Arnault's art collection. This was also exposed in the official presentation of the foundation. This attention gave the impression that a great deal of attention had been paid to all the details of the project. The same is true about the inauguration.

The Inauguration of the Foundation

The event took place on October 20, 2014. It received a great deal of attention, especially in the French national press. As an echo to the many pictures and videos displayed in the media, the focus of the media interest is well captured by the catchphrase of a long paper in *Le Figaro*—one of the most popular dailies in France: "The president of France inaugurated Gehry's building last evening with the head of LVMH, Bernard Arnault, in the jardin d'Acclimatation. From Anna Wintour to Sophia Coppola and the gastronomic menu, discover the backstage of the evening of the year" (Le Figaro, October 21, 2014, p. 3)[4].

On average, what captures the attention in the media is first the building, then the power show of Bernard Arnault and his family, and, finally, the presence of celebrities: major political figures, major businessmen, and movie stars and famous artists.

Most of the artists, such as Olafsur Eliasson, Christian Boltanski, Daniel Buren, Bertrand Lavier, Ellsworth Kelly, Taryn Simon, and Sarah Morris, had been commissioned to work for the foundation. Political and business leaders present that evening had been part of the foundation project. Finally, the most famous figures of the fashion world had proven good allies as promoters or ambassadors of the brand. In that regard, the inauguration was a tribute to the success of Bernard Arnault in both the luxury and the art market, making him a leading figure in the French economic, social, and political spheres and a member of the global elite.

In regard to that legacy, if the foundation was leaning towards a sustainable future, offering enlightening views of the past and the present, it would be more through its content then by the people present at the opening of the foundation. The project was devised as a concession by the French state for 55 years to the LVMH group to provide a space for contemporary art open to the public.

The Collection: Three Emblematic Art Pieces

After its opening night, the Louis Vuitton Foundation was open to the public. After the wave of papers on the highly fashionable event, many people were eager to discover the place and make their own opinion, and this curiosity was echoed by a new wave of media coverage. There was still very little attention paid to the CSR dimensions of the project, although they were detailed on the website, the official data for the press and visitors, and the exhibitions about the project. In the following description, I more or less follow the classic depiction of the foundation as a token of the experience of any visitor. Visiting the foundation is an experience that involves three dimensions: the general impression given by the building as a showcase for artworks, the impression given by the collection as a token of the personality of the art collector, and some emblematic pieces of the art collection.

The Aesthetics of the Sublime: The White Cube Inside the Glass Bird

The Louis Vuitton Foundation is a fashionable art place. It does not disparage the brand; it reinforces its prestige by identifying it with the aesthetic of the sublime: a crystal vessel filled with treasures. Yet the service paid to the purposes of the corporation (LVMH) leaves little room for personal implication. Bernard Arnault made no real effort to explain why he had decided to call his art foundation by the name of Louis Vuitton.

Bernard Arnault declared,

> For the opening exhibition, the Foundation Louis Vuitton invites visitors on a "voyage of creativity" through a discovery of the architecture and emblematic works from the permanent collection, including creations by Frank Gehry to Gerhard Richter via Thomas Schütte, Pierre Huyghe, Christian Boltanski, Ellsworth Kelly, Olafur Eliasson, Sarah Morris, Adrián Villar Rojas, Bertrand Lavier, Taryn Simon, and many others. Each of them has contributed to the dynamics of our approach. I could never fully express our gratitude for their help in realizing the artistic endeavor led by Suzanne Pagé, with her widely-recognized experience and inventiveness, supported by the engagement of her entire team.
>
> (Louis Vuitton Foundation website, retrieved July 20, 2016)

This declaration acknowledges the absence of Bernard Arnault personally as a collector relying on his team of curators who work with a strictly business orientation (Horowitz, 2014; Salzman & Appleyard, 2012; Zorloni, 2013). Far from being a transformation in his leadership, Bernard Arnault's commitment to CSR and contemporary art might be yet another bet on risk and profit balance in building his art portfolio in parallel to his corporate brand portfolio.

The French press mostly presents the art foundation as a token of Arnault's (so far) mysterious personality. The media coverage in the international press contrasts with the French media in revealing the leader's tastes, which are quite different from what can be seen in the foundation:

> Whereas Arnault says he only buys artworks for his personal collection that he likes and "can live with for a long time", buying for the Foundation Louis Vuitton is different: Not only does he have to like it, but foundation curator Suzanne Page Pagé has to consider it something worth showing. " 'I mean, I don't think she would like to have my Monet,' the chairman quips. The foundation focuses on the connection between contemporary artists and the second part of the last century. 'So you see the evolution,' " he tells the FT.
>
> (Artnet, September 18, 2014, retrieved July 20, 2016)

As such, the art collection by Bernard Arnault is consistent with what major curators in the art world consider valuable. It is in line with savvy company investments—a field that has adopted financial valuation, although it is still plagued with a lack of transparency because of regular speculative deals in an illiquid and narrow market. The opening of the show, gathering celebrities from all over the world, and the minimalist setting (white wall, glass, and marble) transform the Franck Gehry bird into the White Cube. It is very much in line with the standards of the contemporary art world, including those who claim to be 'alternatives' and those who prefer 'pop philosophy'. This is still what Damian O'Doherty (1986) described as "an ideology" of contemporary art galleries—that of an elitist, conceptual art based on provocation. Dominant since the 1970s, this aesthetic world has built an ambivalent relationship with the world of business and politics—a combination of easy deals and bitter irony. CSR and its principles, just as luxury and fashion, prove an easy target.

"Can Art Save the World?": An Art Sample From the Louis Vuitton Foundation

Artists who were in the spotlight at the occasion of the show, committed and curated for the opening, were more than three, but the small sample presented here can be an emblem—a general picture of Bernard Arnault's vision of his values and commitment for his group because they occupied the major spots in the foundation. I see this choice as a clear determination to have the visitors of the first show in the Louis Vuitton Foundation reflect deeply on our natural environment and the fate of the earth. This is why I selected a sample of three art pieces that I found representative of the show. They all explore elements of the sublime—an aesthetic that combines terrible nature, pure beauty, and tragic fate.

The first work is more of an experience in the basement of the building. The idea is that of a corridor of light. It felt like walking in a hospital corridor under neon spots, with no door at the end. The artist, Olafur Eliasson, declared he had the idea of "creating the kaleidoscopic illusion that one is walking on the skyline" when invited by curator Suzanne Pagé and Bernard Arnault himself to open the foundation, even before it was built (Les Echos, November 17, 2014). The work does not give any kind of hope as to what we may expect in the near future, and this impression is confirmed by the artist's vision.

Olafur Eliasson is famous for his work on time and space, his interest in scientific and social phenomena, and working in a studio with architects and designers. He has a political stance and a social view similar to NGOs working with prestigious art galleries and multinational enterprises such as Volkswagen and LVMH. He believes climate change and the world inequalities are problems multinationals are good partners to work on.

Commissioned by Louis Vuitton in 2006, lamps titled *Eye See You* were installed in the Christmas windows of Louis Vuitton stores; a lamp titled *You See Me* went on permanent display at Louis Vuitton Fifth Avenue, New York. Each of the 400 deliberately low-tech apparatus is composed of a mono-frequency light source and a parabolic mirror. All fees from the project were donated to Ethiopia.org, a charitable foundation initially established by Olafur and his wife to renovate an orphanage (*New York Times Magazine*, p. 12, December 9, 2007, retrieved July 20, 2016).

Accordingly, he declared at a show at the Serpentine Galleries in London entitled *Your Engagement Has Consequences*,

> We should avoid what we might call a Disneyfication of experience in order to leave room for individual evaluation, feelings and thoughts. When preserving the freedom of each person to experience something that may differ from the experiences of others, art will be able to have a significant impact on both the individual and on society.
>
> (Eliasson, 2009, p. 23)

Yet his work for the Louis Vuitton Foundation seems to deal with the impossibility of seeing any form of future from that place, which is an idea he tactfully hinted at in an interview at the time of the opening of the show (Le Figaro, December 17, 2014, p 5, retrieved July 20, 2016) and at an on-site conference on January 15, 2015, From Representation to Presence. Obviously, the artist thinks little of a world where representation only consists of impression management by the elite. Yet he attended the inauguration of the show. His art is shown in a Gehry building, and he praised it as if Gehry's work for Walt Disney (Hench et al., 2003) and this foundation were worlds apart from a "Disneyfication of experience". Contrary to Claudio Parmiggiani, a more radical artist who identifies the "Guggenheim effect" of art foundations to the "Disneyfication of experience" (Didi-Huberman, 2001, p. 23), Olafur Eliasson opposes the two as if one provided a ready-made experience (Disney World) and the other an authentic emotion (global art tourism). In the same way, he takes a stand that seems to beg for a much more radical change than multinational enterprises abiding by CSR standards, but his art is a perfect fit the Louis Vuitton brand identity, one of the most profitable brands in the world, and it does little to change the system.

The other artwork is one floor up, entirely occupying one of the galleries. Tacita Dean finds her inspiration in the dark romantic tradition, where darkness, death, and minerality refer to the sublime and a form of infinity alluding to human disappearance (Dean & Groenenboom, 2001). As such, her work correspond to a long tradition, and in the foundation, it echoes Alberto Giacometti's *Capsizing Man* in the next gallery.

One may gain an idea about Tacita Dean's creation by reading the catalogue of the show. Entitled *Cloud Paintings*, the piece is made up of four translucent paintings in the middle of which has been placed a four-billion-year-old meteorite, symbolizing the cosmic nature of the whole. In the same ensemble, the monumental photographs by Tacita Dean, *Majesty (Portrait)* and *Hünengrab*, and a series of drawings on 'alabaster and paper', evoke the traces of immutable time. In a sense, this inspiration is not so different from the minimalist provocation of Coco Chanel's "little black dress" (Riot, 2013) in the world of fashion.

In a video inside the show, she describes ideas very much in line with previous essays about her vision. In the essay, a critic wrote,

> Dean's camera, affixed to a tripod, gazes impassively at its subjects—decaying buildings; boats, lighthouses, and seascapes; and, lately, artists, among them Claes Oldenburg and Cy Twombly—for minutes on end. She is an anatomist of passing time. Like her medium, the objects and the people in Dean's films tend to be outmoded or aging, and her work has an elegiac tone. "All the things I am attracted to are just about to disappear", she likes to say.
>
> (Dean, 2011, p. 75)

Although this elegiac tone is presented as an inspiration to act rather than contemplate (Dean & Miller, 2005), as I stood in front of the large stone in its spectacular ovoid white room, the only useful actions to be undertaken seemed to be individual attempts at securing minimal means for survival. In that universe, CSR actions seem outdated: fate will not be overturned.

Adrián Villar Rojas's work is located outside, on the balcony, because it needs to be in direct contact with the elements and, more specifically, affected by climatic change. According to the catalogue,

> The title of (his) sculpture, Where the Slaves Live, refers to the Latin root of the word "vernacular" ("verna" meaning "slave")". The caption also tells us about what the art piece looks like: "This mysterious object evokes a water tank, a popular architectural form and a recurring motif in the work of Adrián Villar Rojas. Displaying a timeless strangeness, this work is conceived as "a small planet" that has landed on the terrace, a subtle hybrid of archaeology and science fiction.
> (Louis Vuitton Foundation website retrieved on July 20, 2016)

Because, even after a period of contemplating the work, the ingredients may not be easy to identify, a list is provided to that effect: "Composed of multiple layers of organic and inorganic materials sourced from all over the world (such as earth, pigments, plants, vegetables, stone, coal, cement, grasses, fossils, coral, bread, fruit, clothing and shoes . . .) ".

Finally, the catalogue describes the artist's idea in building this work:

> Where the Slaves Live is designed to be a "living sculpture" that transforms continuously with the passing of time. The presence of human beings in this ecosystem is suggested by the insertion of the artist's personal effects into the body of the sculpture. Humans become protagonists in nature and its evolution, undergoing, like nature, the effects of constant change.[5]

Looking at the artwork, the viewer is left with many questions as to the message of the artist regarding CSR. Namely, what we see, and the name of the piece, is not entirely optimistic, but it may pave a way for a more responsible, self-conscious, sustainable future. Considering the rest of the show and documenting the artist's views at the occasion of other events, however, the pessimistic interpretation takes precedence.

According to the artist, there is at present little hope of survival and barely enough strength to document the disappearance of life on Earth. A critique of a similar show of the artist in London noted,

> The mummified corpse of Kurt Cobain is cracking apart even as some plastic bottles, propped up by metal frames, pour life-giving water into it. Can Adrián Villar Rojas bring his musical hero back to life? Or will this dry, grey effigy of the rock 'n' roll suicide crumble into dust?
> Or, to put it another way, can art save the world? In another aisle of his east London workshop, the Argentinean artist is examining potato plants growing out of the gutted flank of a fish. "This whole project is about trying to force life to appear", he says, eyeing the green shoots

rising from the bulbous potatoes swaddled in rich, black soil. "We will fail. No matter what we do, they will die".

(*Guardian*, September 19, 2013, p 22, retrieved on July 20, 2016)

This vision also illustrated in the Louis Vuitton art piece, located outside on the balcony facing La Défense and its skyscrapers (France's city or Wall Street), make CSR efforts seem a little naive for the purpose of saving us all (slaves), even if we have made it so far through the dark glass corridor and the fall of the meteorite. Our collective attempts to save the world may only be a temporary solution is the message I get from that art, in a perfect echo of that of Eliasson and Dean. An expert in the field described this posture as characteristic of contemporary artists:

The question: "what can art?" precisely, is not well put, since contemporary creation is proud to display its powerlessness; it refuses to be capable of anything: this refusal of power is, let us be clear, assumed, vocal and militant.

(Ardenne, 1997, p. 384)

This author believes it is a form of convention for artists to be elegiac, just as it was more or less compulsory to be engaged in the 1960s. In the context of a corporate art foundation associated with considerable business power and influence, this posture may be interpreted in two ways: a dismissal of issues not related to art for art's sake or as a sign of anxiety, begging for collective action.

Part V. Not One Conclusion: Three Possible Interpretations of the Meaning of the Louis Vuitton Foundation

My initial question was about the meaning of the Louis Vuitton Foundation. I argued it could be just a symbol of power, a move to promote CSR, or an effort to come up with a truly meaningful vision of the future in relation to climate change and inequalities. Combining the media account of the inauguration of the Louis Vuitton Foundation, the official discourse of the LVMH group and its CEO, and my own field investigation inside the foundation, provided a richer view but it did not give me a clue as to the initial question. The mass of data, however, conveys a discordant impression. As a result, it only makes it more complex to interpret because the different views do not lead to the same conclusion. In the media accounts, the inauguration matters more, with the presence of celebrities from the world of luxury and fashion and members of the elite in arts and politics. Yet in the official communication of the group, the foundation matters as a philanthropic gesture by Bernard Arnault in line with CSR values. Finally, when one focuses on what could be seen as emblematic pieces of the art collection, the dangers of climate change seem an overwhelming burden for the future. This makes it difficult to decide what meaning to retain as a visitor and, more importantly, as a recipient of this gift to the public. In short, all of my three initial hypotheses could be true, yet I find weaknesses in all of them.

Going back to those initial views of the role of a leader in relation to art, luxury, and CSR, I provide three possible interpretations of the Louis Vuitton Foundation, all of them assembling the discrepant pictures associated with it. The first interpretation identifies the foundation as the legacy of the traditional patron of the arts with artists leading the way towards CSR in a more or less open resistance to the dominant representation of our age. The second interpretation sees the Louis Vuitton Foundation as a place where the LVMH group intends to promote various causes, among them CSR, by officially commissioning artists, thinkers, and creators. The third interpretation identifies the foundation with a pioneering platform for creative and innovative works on the representations and the realities of the contemporary world, the gift of the CSR CEO, and a pioneering leader with a transformative vision. All of the interpretations pave the way to future research, because each of them exposes a great deal of contradictions in the elite world and in the CSR representations it pioneers.

A Traditional Art Patron and Artists as CSR Leaders

This first interpretation of the vision contained in the Louis Vuitton Foundation for the arts is that it is a rather traditional art foundation but is open to experiments by artists in relation to the ongoing transformations of our world, in particular climate change. Possibly both Frank Gehry, the architect, and the artists whose works were shown in the foundation were pioneering CSR in a form of resistance against the dominant order of things, where fashion and luxury, icons of mass consumerism, are more popular (Florida, 2004) today. I may have discovered artists who paved new ways for CSR by using both innovation and creation, leaving the business purpose of the foundation and its lavish inauguration for the traditional (conservative) media to focus on.

In that radical approach, as suggested by Boltanski and Chiapello (2005), the new spirit of capitalism would never be really be in a position to appropriate the critique by artists and by environmentalists who would join forces against that dominant order. CSR and contemporary art would then act as temporary compromises to a more authentic vision, laboratories, and incubators before launching new successful ventures. Just as artists worked for the pope, princes, and rich merchants in the Quattrocento (Baxandall & Chester, 1988), today many famous artists successfully use public and private institutions (such as private foundations and wealthy patrons) to launch their vision of business and society in a transformative way (Guillet de Monthoux, 2004). For instance, artists such as Pistoletto, in Cita dell'Arte, are quite independent from all forms of external influences, although their creations involve a great deal of cooperation with business institutions.

Yet in the face of all existing studies discussing the relationship between art and ideas, the influence of ideologies and power on artists (Ades, 1995), I find it very difficult to determine the specific engagement of art for or against CSR in that case. Even when artists put forward their engagement in their art, it can be interpreted in many ways, and it remains subject to interpretations. For instance, Bourdieu and Haacke (1995) criticize the Cartier foundation as the symbol of foul art in the age of capitalism. Yet Paul Ardenne (2002) shows that Haacke has been very ambivalent in his commitments for or against capitalist foundations. He also shows that avant-garde artists such as Daniel Buren, who stood as a virulent critique of the influence of the market on art and society, later worked for Hermès, and he had a major show in the Louis Vuitton Foundation in the spring of 2016. Christian Boltanski, who was in the same avant-garde group in the 1970s, publicly exposed why he felt free to work for rich patrons of the arts and corporations. His work was shown in the Louis Vuitton Foundation, and he attended the inauguration as a guest of honour. In the face of such complex trajectories, possibly characteristic of infinite varieties in "the politics of aesthetics" (Rancière, 2013) it seems quite adventurous to leave the fate of CSR to artistic individual resistance to the capitalist order.

LVMH Leadership in Promoting CSR

In another interpretation, one could argue that artists might not necessarily be in a confrontation with Bernard Arnault to promote new ideas, but rather follow his group's influence and help him stand as a visionary leader in promoting alternative ideas and views (Scheff & Kotler, 1996). In this more reformist view, going back to DiMaggio's (1988) analysis of the Guggenheim and Rockefeller foundations, Bernard Arnault would be pioneering an artistic avant-garde just as he was able to build a global fame for French brands in decline before.

Yet I find little support for such a pioneering vision in Bernard Arnault's project, mostly because too many interests intersect in the project of the foundation. It is too well adapted to the present strategic order of control of the elite field to be disruptive. First, all the conditions are met to make the foundation good for LVMH business. The land in the Bois de Boulogne was a concession to Marcel Boussac that would soon expire if not taken advantage of. The concession involves a long-term strategy because it is to last 55 years. As such, it complements the opening of a concept store in La Samaritaine, near le Louvre museum, and other boutiques in the Golden Triangle of Paris. LVMH uses Paris as a showcase of French luxury, and the foundation proves that he has an official mandate by public authorities to do so. The building was in fact financed not by Bernard Arnault himself but by funds coming from all the business units of the group. Also, a legal agreement was signed with the mayor of Paris, and in parallel, the Ministry of Finance seemingly dropped its investigations about tax evasion. The foundation is also the perfect showcase to help sustain the value and reputation of his personal art collection in a highly speculative art market. This point to a good sense for business opportunities—one that Bernard Arnault has made a name from. This is quite contradictory with genuine commitment to an original vision.

Another sign of that possible lack of sincere commitment to a new vision on the part of Bernard Arnault as a leader is (by his own admission) his lack of interest in contemporary art. This is why Suzanne Pagé and Jean-Paul Claverie acted as curators. As a result, despite their legitimacy and the funds they were endowed with, the three famous artists I mentioned, and other artists as well, do not seem to have been especially committed to the project of the foundation. In the case of Olafur Eliasson, his work was also shown in the MoMa, in the Tate Gallery, and in major fairs and festival. The next year, it became a key element of the Paris Climate Submit, and it was also shown in the Versailles Palace after Jeff Koons and Anish Kapoor. Other major luxury brands committed to art foundation, and in the case of the Prada art foundation, the disturbing work of Louise Bourgeois also comes in sharp contrast with the pop art used as an inspiration for the fashion collections. Finally, even Frank Gehry's declarations about his passion for Paris and Bernard Arnault's project may be questioned in the face of the various displays of his art as an architect. The Louis Vuitton Foundation, a glass bird facing La Défense, is not his most original piece; indeed, it is quite similar to a series of recent buildings streamlined by his agency.

Aesthetically, the foundation had ambitions to be an open platform for creators and the public to meet and discover new visions, yet from what I experienced, it rather corresponds to a pre-existing frame—that of modern art museums and corporate foundations. Next, the foundation is focusing on a contemplative nature—mostly picturesque wild landscapes—rather than on social dimensions of CSR. Besides, a characteristic sample of three artworks from the collection represents a dark, post-romantic picture of a world in ruins, making it difficult to believe in any possibility of action to change the fate of the world. This should lead to further examination of what a CSR leader stands for and what this one leader proposes doing about the current situation.

CSR Informs a Pioneering Vision in the Louis Vuitton Foundation

In that second interpretation of the leading vision in opening his foundation, one must picture Anault as a transformative leader (Bathurst, Jackson, & Statler, 2010) with a good understanding of the influence of aesthetics. His goal would be to promote CSR via creation. After building reputational capital in the luxury world as an engineer with a background in construction, this CEO built an art collection, which is a sign that he became aware of the influence of art on all forms of representations. Possibly he became aware of the driving force of creation and of the attraction of art and decided to use this "Kunstwollen" (Panofsky, 1915) by allying with creators to strengthen the leadership of his group. So the choice of promoting CSR via art in his foundation would be a deliberate one endowed with considerable means. In that case, his gesture in favour of CSR is not striking; it may be caused by a lack of support from his leading partners, artists, architects, and NGOs who prove incapable of coming up with a transformative leadership capable of finding new representations for radical action.

It is also quite possible that this strategic intention was not so original, but that the ambition of promoting CSR via art proves very challenging. Bernard Arnault may have moved in a more adaptive than pioneering mood: Many other shows in major art institutions had been focusing on the environment—for instance, la Documenta and, more recently, shows and biennales displayed Olafur Eliasson, Shepard Fairey, and Tomas Saraceno, with the sponsorship of Leonardo di Caprio. Eliasson installed public ice from Greenland in the centre of Paris during the Paris Climate Submit, and his work was shown in the Versailles Palace and gardens a few months later. After meeting with such official success, it seems difficult to imagine that such an emblematic artist would (in fact) resist the art market system when he is warning about climate change. Yet there are many reasons why promoting CSR may turn out to be a very long-term commitment.

One reason is that Bernard Arnault, who always was very discreet in expressing his views, chose art precisely because this was a way to commit to CSR in an indirect way and dodge public controversies. Betting on indirect cues may prove safer. CSR is not a simple cause to defend and requires sustaining the same actions in the very long term. It may also involve having a pristine reputation so as to withstand public scrutiny. For instance, on June 2016, the CEO of Danone took a radical stand in favour of CSR. Although his speech was a hit in the audience of HEC Paris students who stood up for him, both the man and the speech were immediately under scrutiny, and it was easy to demonstrate that there were contradictions between that speech and the choices a man makes when he is to become the CEO of a multinational.

The other reason why heralding CSR is difficult is that CSR norms and standards, once adopted by major companies and world leaders, must provide a guideline for a set of actions applied universally. This is a difficult ideal to reach up to, and the inner contradictions of the CSR doctrine may prove an obstacle to the most determined transformative leadership. In its efforts to find good representations for CSR, the Louis Vuitton Foundation might be confronted by its many stakeholders' divergent views. CSR can be challenged politically and many of its choices were hotly debated at the occasion of the Paris Climate Summit (2015). For instance, despite prominent figures and major steps forward, questions can still be raised as to what CSR represents (Prieto-Carron, Lund-Thomsen, Chan, Muro, & Bushan, 2006)—namely, the different cultures it possibly downplays in different parts of the world (Visser & Tolhurst, 2010) and the limits to multinationals' concern for social and environmental causes (Tench, Sun & Jones, 2012), such as the "irresponsibility" CSR allows them to legally maintain by imposing standards they have set. Going beyond that criticism, Banerjee (2008) even claims that CSR is a distortion of genuine concerns for the environment and social inequalities and that it may in fact prompt the dominant actors to accumulate and spend more while they can. However, that last stand involves a very clear picture of what a good alternative to that fake CSR would be—one that many authors (Kurutz, Colbert, & Wheeler, 2008; Wagner, Lutz, & Weitz, 2009) believe quite difficult to determine once and for all. If some aspects of CSR seem related to a form of hypocrisy because boards tend to use it to avoid external rules and regulations, debates in boardrooms on the issue of CSR (Bendell, 2009) also prove that it genuinely involves taking into account various stakeholders' interests and financial investments. Compromises had to be made to solve open conflicts.

To some (Rehn, 2009), the so-called creative economy may suffer from the same ambiguity CSR does. Instead of being responsive to major causes such as climate change and social inequalities, dominant actors in the creative industry might be holding different stakes. They would do so by selecting low standards of artistic creation compatible with the mass media and entertainment standards (Thornton, 2012). They would thereby support a speculative field of star authors (Thompson, 2009) and fetish art pieces (Heinich, 2012) with more public visibility than meaning. However, such vision in the contemporary art world (a symbol of the decadence of our civilization) in the tradition of the Frankfurt School would also involve a clear set of standards and hierarchy that I find are hardly ever unanimously accepted.

A Transformative Leadership With a New Picture of the World

The third interpretation of the Louis Vuitton Foundation defines it as a product of a truly transformative leadership. Only it may be more strategic than altruistic in the sense that it serves the interest of the founder and the other prominent figures involved in the project before that of the recipients of their gift (the general audience).

In the face of very controversial fields, CSR and contemporary art, when committed to the cause of promoting new representations, one finds the best position for a powerful leader is to invest and not take position and for leading artists to rely on strong impressions that speak for themselves—for instance, an apocalypse. Doing otherwise might be putting one's leadership in jeopardy.

If, according to this last remark, I analyze the foundation, the art collection, and the inauguration as a single tactical choice made by a collective leadership of a patron of the arts and a team of artists and curators, rather than as individual expressive choices, the sample of artworks becomes significant. It no longer lacks consistency, and because it is emblematic of the entire collection and of the spirit of the foundation, their intention becomes clear. By their participation, as major figures of the art world receiving a command by the Louis Vuitton Foundation, the artists play a key role in it in relation to Bernard Arnault. This alliance matters more for their public image than any specific message they could try to send to the audience through the media. Besides, all three artists, Eliasson, Dean, and Villar Rojas seem to be in alignment in terms of aesthetics and rhetoric, and for that reason, their work had been selected in the most prominent art galleries, and they were chosen to be exposed together by the most select curators. They are highly legitimate, and they convey a bleak vision of the future: a Cassandra role that neither business leaders nor public officials like to play. Besides, contrary to the pop art that seduces most clients of luxury goods and accessories in their everyday life, darkness and austerity departs from the ordinary to reach the realm of religiosity and sacredness.

The dramatic scene of the glass bird of the Louis Vuitton Foundation is then in the tradition of a neo-baroque vision of the world, related to nature and the world via death, and above all, ambivalent about power, truth, and virtue (Marin, 1981). It is in line with the most prestigious art exhibitions and art foundations in the world today. As such, it is both abstract and metaphysical, yet rooted in the materiality of what exists. And there is not much left to contemplate in that dreary universe: vanity, all is vanity. As a political representation and social inspiration, that vision is one of doubt, disharmony, and turmoil. In the past, it led to frugality and selflessness just as it authorized such behaviours as predation and a ruthless accumulation of resources in the struggle for survival. So the success of these artists and their dreary representations could possibly express the philosophy of action of global elite groups. For instance, Boltanski and Esquerre (2014) envision new concern for the environment and CSR as part of the post-industrial "economy of enrichment" where value narratives focus on tradition, genealogies, identities, and pedigrees to define enclosures. To them, the fame of contemporary artists contributes to make more visible and impose that new logic of appropriation and valuation to a vast audience. This would explain the return of the trend in favour of foundations and famous leaders' desire to stand as founders for a dynasty. Boltanski and Esquerre may be right, but then if such were the case, in my view, then there would be nothing new under the sun. The only transformation involved in that kind of leadership would be the appropriation of patrimonial goods by a new clique: the global elite. Yet, per se, the appropriation of nature and the heritage by 'the nouveaux riches' is hardly a new form of investment, even if its legitimization by CSR may be. For the others, as a gift, the Louis Vuitton Foundation, as unappealing as it may be, proves a blessing in disguise because, in terms of representations, it mirrors the contradictions inherent to society.

Notes

1 For instance, Georges Bataille analyzed the transgressive nature of luxury consumption in relation to social violence and excess: "Transgression piled upon transgression will never abolish the taboo, just as though the taboo were never anything but the means of cursing gloriously whatever it forbids. (. . .) 'There is

nothing, writes de Sade, that can set bounds to licentiousness . . . The best way of enlarging and multiplying one's desires it to try to limit them.' Nothing can set bounds to licentiousness . . . or rather, generally speaking, there is nothing that can conquer violence". (Bataille, 1962, p. 47). This view may be read as a form of dark romanticism, a dandy sacrilege in the face of death (Bataille, 1985) standing as a challenge to any moral order.

2 Tacitus gives this account of Petronius in his historical work the *Annals* (XVI.18): "He spent his days in sleep, his nights in attending to his official duties or in amusement, that by his dissolute life he had become as famous as other men by a life of energy, and that he was regarded as no ordinary profligate, but as an accomplished voluptuary. His reckless freedom of speech, being regarded as frankness, procured him popularity. Yet during his provincial government, and later when he held the office of consul, he had shown vigour and capacity for affairs. Afterwards returning to his life of vicious indulgence, he became one of the chosen circle of Nero's intimates, and was looked upon as an absolute authority on questions of taste (*elegantiae arbiter*, note the pun on Petronius' cognomen) in connection with the science of luxurious living".

3 Among major French business people, it has always been a tradition to invest in the media. Serge Dassault owns Le Figaro, Xavier Niel (Iliade/Free)-Pigasse (Banque Lazare)-Bergé owns *L'Obs*, *Télérama*, *Courrier International*, *La Vie* Le Monde and Le Nouvel Observateur, François Pinault (Kering) owns Le Point, Arnault Lagardère (Matra) owns le Journal du Dimanche and Paris Match, Patrick Draho owns Libération and l'Express The Amaury family owns le Parisien and L'Equipe and Vincent Bolloré owns communication groups Havas and Vivendi.

4 http://www.lefigaro.fr/arts-expositions/2014/10/20/03015-20141020ARTFIG 00176-fondation-louis-vuitton-un-vaisseau-de-verre-dedie-a-l-art.php (retrieved November 18, 2016).

5 http://www.fondationlouisvuitton.fr/content/flvinternet/en/la-collection/la-collec tion-vilar-rojas.html This link is no longer active.

References

Ades, D. (1995). *Art and power: Europe under the dictators 1930–45* (Vol. 23.). Brussels: Hayward Gallery.

Adler, N. J. (2006). The arts & leadership: Now that we can do anything, what will we do? *Academy of Management Learning & Education*, 5(4), 486–499.

Angus-Leppan, T., Metcalf, L., & Benn, S. (2010). Leadership styles and CSR practice: An examination of sensemaking, institutional drivers and CSR leadership. *Journal of Business Ethics*, 93(2), 189–213.

Appadurai, A. (Ed.) (1988). *The social life of things: Commodities in cultural perspective*. Cambridge, UK: Cambridge University Press.

Ardenne, P. (1997). *ART, l'âge contemporain. Une histoire des arts plastiques à la fin du XXème siècle*. Paris: Editions du Regard.

Ardenne, P. (2002). *Un art contextuel: création artistique en milieu urbain, en situation, d'intervention, de participation*. Paris: Editions Flammarion.

Arnault, B. (2000). *La Passion créative, entretiens avec Yves Messarovitch*. Paris: Editions Plon.

Arnell, P. (Ed.) (1987). *Frank Gehry: Buildings and projects*. Milano: Rizzoli.

Auguste, G., & Gutsatz, M. (2013). *Luxury talent management: Leading and managing a luxury brand*. London, UK: Palgrave Macmillan.

Banerjee, S. B. (2008). Corporate social responsibility: The good, the bad and the ugly. *Critical sociology, 34*(1), 51–79.

Barnes, J. (Ed.) (1984). *The complete works of Aristotle, Volumes I and II.* Princeton, NJ: Princeton University Press.

Bataille, G. (1962). *Death and sensuality: A study of eroticism and the taboo.* New York, NY: New York Press.

Bataille, G. (1985). *Visions of excess: Selected writings 1927–1939* (Vol. 14.). Manchester, UK: Manchester University Press.

Bathurst, R. (2007). Leadership the Kiwi way: An artistic investigation. *Organization, Identity, Locality, III,* 2.

Bathurst, R., Jackson, B., & Statler, M. (2010). Leading aesthetically in uncertain times. *Leadership, 6*(3), 311–330.

Bathurst, R., & Monin, N. (2010). Shaping leadership for today: Mary Parker Follett's aesthetic. *Leadership, 6*(2), 115–131.

Bathurst, R., Williams, L., & Rodda, A. (2007). Letting go of the reins: Paradoxes and puzzles in leading an artistic enterprise. *International Journal of Arts Management, 9*(2), 29–38.

Baxandall, M. (1985). *Patterns of intention: On the historical explanation of pictures.* Yale: Yale University Press.

Baxandall, M., & Chester, W. (1988). *Painting and experience in fifteenth century Italy: A primer in the social history of pictorial style.* Oxford, UK: Oxford University Press.

Bellu, S. (2007). *Louis Vuitton et l'élégance automobile.* Paris: Editions La Martinière.

Bendell, J. (2004). *Barricades and boardrooms: A contemporary history of the corporate accountability movement.* Geneva: United Nations Research Institute for Social Development.

Bennis, W. (2003). Frank Gehry artist, leader, and neotenic. *Journal of Management Inquiry, 12*(1), 81–103.

Bennis, W., & Bennis, W. G. (2009). *On becoming a leader.* London. UK: Basic Books.

Bertrand-Dorléac, L. (1992), *Le commerce de l'art de la Renaissance à nos jours.* Paris: éditions de la Manufacture.

Bolman, L. G., & Deal, T. E. (2011). *Reframing organizations: Artistry, choice and leadership.* London, UK: John Wiley.

Boltanski, L., & Chiapello, E. (2005). *Le Nouvel Esprit du Capitalisme.* Paris: Gallimard.

Boltanski, L., & Esquerre, A. (2014). La collection, une forme neuve du capitalisme la mise en valeur économique du passé et ses effets. *Les temps modernes, 679*(3), 5–72.

Bonvicini, S. (2004). *Louis Vuitton: une saga française.* Paris: Fayard.

Boucheron, P. (2012). *Léonard et Machiavel.* Paris: Editions Verdier.

Bourdieu, P., & Haacke, H. (1995). *Free exchange.* Cambridge, UK: Polity Press.

Bourriaud, N. (Ed.) (2009). *Altermodern: Tate Triennial.* London, UK: Tate Publications.

Bryman, A. (Ed.) (2011). *The Sage handbook of leadership.* Thousand Oaks, CA: Sage Publications.

Burawoy, M. (1998). The extended case method. *Sociological Theory, 16*(1), 4–33.

Carroll, A. B. (1999). Corporate social responsibility evolution of a definitional construct. *Business & Society, 38*(3), 268–295.

Castets, S., Igarashi T., Gasparina J., & Hermange, E. (2009). *Louis Vuitton: Art, Mode et Architecture*. Paris: Editions La Martinière.

Cavender, R., & Kincade, D. H. (2014). Leveraging designer creativity for impact in luxury brand management: An in-depth case study of designers in the Louis Vuitton Moët Hennessy (LVMH) brand portfolio. *Global Fashion Brands: Style, Luxury & History, 1*(1), 199–214.

Chatriot, A. (2007). La construction récente des groupes de luxe français: mythes, discours et pratiques. *Entreprises et histoire, 46*(1), 143–156.

Chevalier, F., & Troublé, B. (2008). *Histoire de la Louis Vuitton Cup: 25 ans de régates pour conquérir l'America's Cup*. Paris: Editions La Martinière.

Clifton, R., & Simmons, J. (Eds.) (2012). *Brands and Branding*. Princeton, NJ: Bloomberg Press.

Cooren, F., & Fairhurst, G. T. (2003). The leader as a practical narrator: Leadership as the art of translating. In Holman, D., & Thorpe, R. (Ed.), *Management and language: The manager as a practical author* (pp. 85–103). Thousand Oaks, CA: Sage.

Corey, S. M., & Kearins, K. (2002). Transparent and caring corporations? A study of sustainability reports by The Body Shop and Royal Dutch/Shell. *Organization & Environment, 15*(3), 233–258.

Csikszentmihalyi, M. (2004). *Good business: Leadership, flow, and the making of meaning*. London, UK: Penguin Books.

Dagen, P., Gasparina, J., Établissement public du musée et du domaine de Versailles, & de Versailles-Spectacles, C. (2010). *Murakami Versailles*. X. Editions du Musée de Versailles, Versailles: Barral.

Dean, T. (2011). Save celluloid, for art's sake. *The Guardian, 22*.

Dean, T., & Groenenboom, R. (2001). *Tacita Dean*. London, UK: Tate Gallery.

Dean, T., & Millar, J. (2005). *Art works: Place*. New York, NY: Thames & Hudson.

DePree, M. (2011). *Leadership is an art*. London, UK: Crown Business.

Dickson, M. A., & Chang, R. K. (2015). Apparel manufacturers and the business case for social sustainability: World class CSR and business model innovation. *Journal of Corporate Citizenship*, (57), 55–72.

Didi-Huberman, G. (2001). *Génie du non-lieu. Air, pousddsière, empreinte, hantise*. Paris: Editions de Minuit.

DiMaggio, P. (1988). Progressivism and the arts. *Society, 25*(5), 70–75.

Douglas, M., & Isherwood, C. (1979). *The world of goods*. New York, NY: Basic Books.

Eliasson, O. (2009). Your engagement has consequences. *Experiment Marathon: London, Serpentine Gallery*, 18–21.

Fairclough, N. (2001). *Language and power*. London, UK: Pearson Education.

Fairclough, N. (2003). *Analysing discourse: Textual analysis for social research*. New York, NY: Routledge.

Fairclough, N. (2013). *Critical discourse analysis: The critical study of language*. New York, NY: Routledge.

Florida, R. (2004). *The rise of the creative class*. New York, NY: Basic Books.

Flyvbjerg, B. (2001). *Making social science matter: Why social inquiry fails and how it can succeed again*. Cambridge, UK: Cambridge University Press.

Fombrun, C. J. (1996). *Reputation: Realizing value from the corporate image*. Cambridge, MA: Harvard Business School Press.

Forestier, N., & Ravai, N. (1990). *Bernard Arnault ou le goût du pouvoir*. Paris: Olivier Orban.

Friedman, M. S. (1999). *Gehry talks: Architecture+ process.* Milano: Rizzoli.

Gardner, J. (1993). *On leadership.* London: Simon and Schuster.

Gartner, W. B. (2010). *ENTER: Entrepreneurial Narrative Theory Ethnomethodology and Reflexivity: An issue about The Republic of Tea.* Clemson, SC: Clemson University Digital Press.

Gasparina, J. (2006). *L'art contemporain et la mode: I love fashion.* Paris: Cercle d'art.

Gasparina, J. (2009). *Louis Vuitton: Art, fashion and architecture.* Rome: Rizzoli International Publications.

Gehry, F. O. (2004). Reflections on designing and architectural practice. In R. J. Boland & F. Collopy (Eds.), *Managing as designing* (pp. 19–35). Stanford, CA: Stanford University Press.

Golbin, P. (2012). *Louis Vuitton / Marc Jacobs, Rizzoli, coll.* Paris: coédition BNF.

Goldberger, P. (2015). *Building art: The life and work of Frank Gehry.* London, UK: Alfred A. Knopf.

Goleman, D., Boyatzis, R. E., & McKee, A. (2002). *The new leaders: Transforming the art of leadership into the science of results.* London, UK: Little, Brown.

Grenfell, M., & Hardy, C. (2003). Field manoeuvres Bourdieu and the young British artists. *Space and Culture, 6*(1), 19–34.

Grenfell, M., & Hardy, C. (2007). *Art rules: Pierre Bourdieu and the visual arts.* London, UK: Berg.

Guillet de Monthoux, P. G. (2004). *The art firm: Aesthetic management and metaphysical marketing.* Stanford, CA: Stanford University Press.

Hartner, N. (2001). Luxury, waste, excess and squander. *Philosophy of Management, 1*(2), 75–86.

Haskell, F. (Ed.) (1980). *Patrons and painters: A study in the relations between Italian art and society in the age of the Baroque.* Yale: Yale University Press.

Hatch, M. J., Kostera, M., & Kozminski, A. K. (2009). *The three faces of leadership: Manager, artist, priest.* London, UK: John Wiley.

Heinich, N. (2012). *De la visibilité: excellence et singularité en régime médiatique.* Paris: Editions du Seuil.

Hench, J., Van Pelt, P., & Gehry, F. (2003). *Designing Disney: Imagineering and the art of the show.* New York, NY: Disney Editions.

Hodgkinson, C. (1991). *Educational leadership: The moral art.* New York, NY: Suny Press.

Horowitz, N. (2014). *Art of the deal: Contemporary art in a global financial market.* Princeton: Princeton University Press.

Husted, B. W., & Allen, D. B. (2007). Strategic corporate social responsibility and value creation among large firms: Lessons from the Spanish experience. *Long Range Planning, 40*(6), 594–610.

Janssen, C., Vanhamme, J., Lindgreen, A., & Lefebvre, C. (2014). The catch-22 of responsible luxury: Effects of luxury product characteristics on consumers' perception of fit with corporate social responsibility. *Journal of Business Ethics, 119*(1), 45–57.

Joy, A., Wang, J. J., Chan, T. S., Sherry, J. F., & Cui, G. (2014). M (Art) worlds: Consumer perceptions of how luxury brand stores become art institutions. *Journal of Retailing, 90*(3), 347–364.

Kapferer, J. N., & Bastien, V. (2009a). The specificity of luxury management: Turning marketing upside down. *Journal of Brand Management, 16*(5), 311–322.

Kapferer, J. N., & Bastien, V. (2009b). *The luxury strategy*. Paris: Editora.

Kapferer, J. N., & Tabatoni, O. (2011). LVMH-HERMES: Le dilemme des entreprises familiales du luxe. *Analyse Financiere*, (38), 7.

Kerlau, Y. (2010). *Les dynasties du luxe*. Paris: Perrin.

Kurucz, E. C., Colbert, B. A., & Wheeler, D. (2008). The business case for corporate social responsibility. In A. Crane (Eds.), *The Oxford handbook of corporate social responsibility*. Oxford, UK: Oxford University Press.

Kurucz, E. C., Colbert, B. A., & Wheeler, D. (2008). The business case for corporate social responsibility. In A. Crane, D. Matten, A. McWilliams, J. Moon, & D. S. Siegel (Eds.), *Oxford handbook of corporate social responsibility* (pp. 83–112). Oxford, UK: Oxford University Press.

Ladkin, D., & Taylor, S. S. (2010). Leadership as art: Variations on a theme. *Leadership*, 6(3), 235–241.

Léonforté, P. (2010). *Louis Vuitton. 100 malles de legends*. Paris: Editions La Martinière.

Lipovetsky, G., & Serroy, J. (2013). *L'esthétisation du monde. Vivre à l'âge du capitalisme artiste*. Paris: Editions Gallimard.

Louis Vuitton Foundation Press Kit (https://www.lvmh.fr/actualites-documents/documentation/?doc_type=release, retrieved November 18, 2016)

Maak, T., & Pless, N. M. (2006). Responsible leadership in a stakeholder society–a relational perspective. *Journal of Business Ethics*, 66(1), 99–115.

Marchand, S. (2001). *Les guerres du luxe*. Paris: Editions Fayard.

Marin, L. (1981). *Le Portrait du Roi*. Paris: Editions de Minuit.

Mayer, M. C., & Whittington, R. (1999). Strategy, Structure and Systemness': National Institutions and Corporate Change in France, Germany and the UK, 1950-1993. *Organization Studies*, 20(6), 933–959.

Mendes, S., & Rees-Roberts, N. (2015). New French luxury: Art, fashion and the re-invention of a national brand. *Luxury*, 2(2), 53–69.

Mendes, V., & de la Haye, A. (1999). *20th century fashion*. London, UK: Thames and Hudson.

Monin, N., & Bathurst, R. (January 2008). Mary Follett's nowhere man: The leadership of Everyman. *Conference of Practical Criticism in the Managerial Social Sciences. Journal of Politics, Culture, and Society*, 18(3–4), 161–188.

Morsing, M. (2006). Corporate social responsibility as strategic auto-communication: On the role of external stakeholders for member identification. *Business Ethics: A European Review*, 15(2), 171–182.

Morsing, M., Schultz, M., & Nielsen, K. U. (2008). The "Catch 22" of communicating CSR: Findings from a Danish study. *Journal of Marketing Communications*, 14(2), 97–111.

Moulin, R. (1994). *L'artiste, l'institution et le marché*. Paris: Editions Flammarion.

Nahavandi, A. (2009). *The art and science of leadership*. London, UK: Pearson Prentice Hall.

O'Doherty, B. (1986). *Inside the white cube: The ideology of the gallery space*. Santa Monica, CA: The Lapis Press.

Panofsky, E. (1991). *Perspective as symbolic form* (C. S. Wood, Trans.). New York, NY: Zone Books.

Pasols, P.-G. (2005), *Louis Vuitton: La naissance du luxe modern*. Paris: Editions La Martinière.

Pinçon, M., & Pinçon-Charlot, M. (2010). *Sociologie de la bourgeoisie*. Paris, La découverte.

Pink, S. (2003). Interdisciplinary agendas in visual research: Re-situating visual anthropology. *Visual studies*, 18(2), 179–192.

Pless, N., Maak, T., & Waldman, D. (2012). Different approaches toward doing the right thing: Mapping the responsibility orientations of leaders. *The Academy of Management Perspectivces*, 26(4), 51–65.

Prieto-Carrón, M., Lund-Thomsen, P., Chan, A., Muro, A. N. A., & Bhushan, C. (2006). Critical perspectives on CSR and development: What we know, what we don't know, and what we need to know. *International Affairs*, 82(5), 977–987.

Prigent, L. (2007). *Marc Jacobs & Louis Vuitton*. Paris: ARTE France [société productrice].

Quinn, L., & Dalton, M. (2009). Leading for sustainability: Implementing the tasks of leadership. *Corporate Governance: The International Journal of Business in Society*, 9(1), 21–38.

Rancière, J. (2013). *The politics of aesthetics*. London, UK: A&C. Black.

Ravai, N. (1997). *La République des vanités*. Paris: Editions Grasset.

Rehn, A. (Ed.) (2009). *Creativity and the contemporary economy*. Copenhagen: Copenhagen Business School Press.

Riot, E. (2013). Woman in love, fashion artist or entrepreneur? The edifying, mystifying life of Coco Chanel. *Society and Business Review*, 8(3), 7–7.

Riot, E., & Bazin Y. (2013). Imperceptible or insensible? The aesthetics of gestures, choices and moves at work. *Society and Business Review*, 8(3), 3–10.

Riot, E., Chamaret, C., & Rigaud, E. (2013). Murakami on the bag: Louis Vuitton's decommoditization strategy. *International Journal of Retail & Distribution Management*, 41(11/12), 8–8.

Rose, G. (2012). *Visual methodologies: An introduction to researching with visual materials*. London, UK: Sage.

Routier, A. (2003). *L'Ange exterminateur*. Paris: Editions Albin Michel.

Salzmann, M. J., & Appleyard, M. C. (2012). *Corporate art collections: A handbook to corporate buying*. Farnham: Ashgate Publishing, Ltd.

Scheff, J., & Kotler, P. (1996). How the arts can prosper through strategic collaborations. *Harvard Business Review*, 74(1), 52.

Selznick, P. (1957). *Leadership in administration: A sociological interpretation*. Berkeley: Berkeley University Press.

Spar, D. L. (2006). Markets: Continuity and change in the international diamond market. In *The Global Diamond Industry* (pp. 11–26). UK: Palgrave Macmillan.

Sweeney, L., & Coughlan, J. (2008). Do different industries report corporate social responsibility differently? An investigation through the lens of stakeholder theory. *Journal of Marketing Communications*, 14(2), 113–124.

Tench, R., Sun, W., & Jones, B. (Eds.) (2012). *Corporate social irresponsibility: A challenging concept* (Vol. 4.). London, UK: Emerald Group Publishing.

Thompson, D. (2009). *The $12 million stuffed shark: The curious economics of contemporary art*. Montreal: Anchor Canada.

Thornton, S. (2012). *Seven days in the art world*. London, UK: Granta Books.

Tufnell, B. (2006). *Land art*. London: Tate.

Villette, M. (2003). L'accès à la puissance économique de Bernard Arnault, (1974–1989). *Gérer et Comprendre*, June(76), 60–69.

Vincent, C., & Monnin, P. (1990). *Guerre du luxe: l'affaire LVMH*. Paris: F. Bourin.

Visser, W., & Tolhurst, N. (Eds.) (2010). *The world guide to CSR: A country-by-country analysis of corporate sustainability and responsibility*. London, UK: Greenleaf Publishing.

Waddock, S. (2008). *The difference makers: How social and institutional entrepreneurs created the corporate responsibility movement*. London, UK: Greenleaf Publishing.

Wagner, T., Lutz, R. J., & Weitz, B. A. (2009). Corporate hypocrisy: Overcoming the threat of inconsistent corporate social responsibility perceptions. *Journal of Marketing*, 73(6), 77–91.

White, N., & Griffiths, I. (Eds.) (2000). *The fashion business: Theory, practice, image*. Oxford, UK: Berg.

Woodward, J. B., & Funk, C. (2010). Developing the artist-leader. *Leadership*, 6(3), 295.

Wyszomirski, M. J., & Clubb, P. (Eds.) (1989). *The cost of culture: Patterns and prospects of private arts patronage* (Vol. 6.). New York, NY: Americans for the Arts Books.

Zorloni, A. (2013). *The economics of contemporary art*. Berlin: Springer.

13 Conclusion

Leading Responsibly and Sustainably

Ralph J. Bathurst and Gabriel Eweje

Introduction

It is pertinent to posit that the introduction of CSR and sustainability to the business paradigm has shifted the narrow economic responsibility to a more comprehensive approach that embraces economic objectives with environmental and social responsibilities. This prompts the question, how can leaders in corporations bring these elements together into a productive whole? The contributors in this book have explored this question in depth, establishing and providing arguments to support the notion that leadership, CSR, and sustainability are inextricably linked and that the role of leadership is fundamental to a sustainable business. As suggested by Epstein and Buhovac (2014, p. 48), "a primary goal of leadership for sustainability is setting principles and practices that will help institutionalise the concept of sustainability in the organisation". They further argue that a leader needs to demonstrate a combination of humility and ambition towards achieving social, environmental, and economic goals. Marshall, Coleman, and Reason (2011) went further to suggest that we need leadership for sustainability going beyond conventional notions, and we need to step outside and challenge current formulations of society and business because sufficiently robust change means questioning the ground we stand on. If this is the case, and these notions are taken seriously, why then do companies such as Toshiba in 2015 and Volkswagen in 2016 still persist in corrupt practices that impact globally? These two large corporations have previously proclaimed CSR and sustainability are paramount to their business operations. These assertions resonate with Newman-Storen's (2014) theory that strong and resilient leadership requires thinking differently in order to deal with 'wicked problems' associated with social responsibility and sustainability. The argument further states, "sustainability requires change, and change requires leadership" (p. 5957).

In Chapter 2, McGhee and Grant offer some practical steps on how best to encourage proper sustainability leadership within business. They state that we need a different way of thinking about how we do business, and we need business leaders who can progressively shift our focus towards a *telos* that reflects what is best for humanity and the world in which we live. Conversely, Jamali, Mohanna, and Panossian in Chapter 3 suggest some implications in relation to the construct of responsible leadership both in theory and in application. They establish that leaders play a significant role as architects of sustainable change that successfully strikes a balance between economic, environmental, and social bottom lines.

The key messages in this book have been essentially the same. The contributors have explored different arguments to reach a conclusion that leadership needs to be more engaged and collaborative in their various organizations to achieve sustainable business practices. As Bolton and Landells (Chapter 5) succinctly argue, "Interactive processes between stakeholders may generate emergent solutions, but the ability to determine what is a relevant 'pattern' may still be subject to influence by structures and agents" (see also Chapter 4 for a similar thesis). Thus it is imperative that leaders integrate social and environmental concerns into economic functions and engage their stakeholders to create organizations with sustainability values.

Theoretical Arguments and Future Research Imperatives

The contributors to this book have highlighted that issues exist in terms of the way leaders inculcate productive and sustainable practices into their organizations. Currently, significant shortcomings have been costly and at times lead to reputational crisis. In addition, the contributors to this book have also strongly argued that the call on corporations to integrate social, environmental, and economic dimensions is not an empty rhetoric; it is crucial to a firm's long-term success and survival. In Chapter 4, Wu and Ma, drawing on the literature on sustainability, leadership, organizational learning, and change, propose a framework linking the styles of leadership with strategic change towards corporate sustainability. In a similar vein, Tench and Topić (Chapter 6), using examples from their case study, attribute sustainability success to a leadership model centred on shared business responsibility, and participation of all partners in setting organizational goals has contributed towards sustainable growth and policies of environmental protection. Ali and Huda (Chapter 11) further reiterate that leadership in the current nexus of corporate engagement necessitates internal and external engagement from the corporate developers, as well as lateral engagement in developmental processes. They emphasize that collaborative corporate leadership from the private sector can find common ground with the public sector in moving society towards a more constructive and nuanced view of consumerism and consumption.

To this end, in this book, we proposed that employee engagement and collaborative efforts should be encouraged and that employees should be allowed to have a significant influence on the way CSR and sustainability initiatives are prioritized and implemented. This approach, we believe, will embed CSR and sustainability as fundamental to an organization and enhance the sustainability values leaders intend to entrench within them. Hargett and Williams (2009) have vehemently argued that engaging and aligning employees with a company's sustainability efforts will lead to shared values and a successful implementation of a corporation's CSR and sustainability vision. As this occurs, engaged staff will feel associated with their company's sustainability achievements and help drive the leadership vision (see Chapter 7 by Hakimian et al. for more on this view).

This book has modestly reviewed most of the extant literature on CSR, sustainability, and leadership. Accordingly, Hui (Chapter 8) posits that a distinctive mix of CSR leadership practices, *inter alia*, embody knowledge, skill, vision, passion, action, and impact in order to confront the complex CSR dilemmas corporations face. The argument further stated that having appropriate leadership is necessary to organize a company's strategic planning mechanisms to accomplish organizational goals and sustainability. And that sustainability can increase profits and present opportunities for value creation and have an impact on a company's revenue (Chapter 9, Heenetigala et al.)

The emergent future research on the topics covered in this book is manifold. However, what we have identified as the most pressing for future studies is how leadership in the head office influences the CSR and sustainability practices in their various global locations and how such leaders engage their employees, in particular, at global locations where CSR and sustainability are not prominent in the political discussion. Yet the need for leadership in bringing all elements together is not just the responsibility of major corporations. As Mizuo argues in Chapter 10, enterprises oriented towards the bottom of the pyramid sector also play a significant role.

The outcome will inform us on different understandings and values attached to CSR and sustainability in different regions by various companies. It will also shed more light on what motivates CSR and sustainability and the impact of stakeholder pressures on CSR and sustainability in different global locations.

Conclusion

This concluding chapter has demonstrated that whereas CSR, sustainability, and leadership discourses are important, significant work in terms of new studies have to be done to form a complete picture. This will necessarily also focus on the leisure industries, for as Riot argues in Chapter 12, the arts sector is profoundly implicated in the discussions.

As we indicated in our opening chapter, global sporting fixtures are opportunities to raise consciousness of the key issues that are at stake among the global citizenry. We wonder, then, how organizations such as the Fédération Internationale de Football Association (FIFA) will enact its responsibilities to promote and achieve socially responsible leadership. That it has been dogged by accusations of corruption at the highest level in this sporting body mirrors those of the business sector and is further evidence of the urgent need for leaders to understand that their seniority is not cause for personal gain but a warrant for responsible decision making.

References

Epstein, M. J., & Buhovac, A. R. (2014).*Making sustainability work: Best practices in managing, and measuring corporate social, environmental, and economic impacts*. Sheffield, UK: Greenleaf Publishing.

Hargett, T. R., & Williams, M. F. (2009). Wilhelmsen shipping company: Moving from CSR tradition to CSR leadership. *Corporate Governance*, 9(1), 73–82.

Marshall, J., Coleman, G., & Reason, P. (2011). Taking up the challenge. In K. Marshall, G. Coleman, & P. Reasons (Ed.), *Leadership for sustainability: An approach research approach* (pp. 1–12). Sheffield, UK: Greenleaf Publishing.

Newman-Storen, R. (2014). Leadership in sustainability: Creating an interface between creativity and leadership theory in dealing with "wicked problems". *Sustainability*, 6, 5955–5967.

Index

Printed in the United States
by Baker & Taylor Publisher Services